The Roads to Congress 2008

The Roads to Congress 2008

Edited by
Robert P. Watson
with assistance from Robert Dewhirst

LEXINGTON BOOKS
A division of
ROWMAN & LITTLEFIELD PUBLISHERS, INC.
Lanham • Boulder • New York • Toronto • Plymouth, UK

Published by Lexington Books
A division of Rowman & Littlefield Publishers, Inc.
A wholly owned subsidiary of The Rowman & Littlefield Publishing Group, Inc.
4501 Forbes Boulevard, Suite 200, Lanham, Maryland 20706
http://www.lexingtonbooks.com

Estover Road, Plymouth PL6 7PY, United Kingdom

Copyright © 2010 by Lexington Books

All rights reserved. No part of this book may be reproduced in any form or by any electronic or mechanical means, including information storage and retrieval systems, without written permission from the publisher, except by a reviewer who may quote passages in a review.

British Library Cataloguing in Publication Information Available

Library of Congress Cataloging-in-Publication Data

The roads to Congress 2008 / edited by Robert P. Watson, with assistance from Robert Dewhirst.
    p. cm.
 ISBN 978-0-7391-4209-7 (cloth : alk. paper) — ISBN 978-0-7391-4211-0 (electronic)
 1. United States. Congress—Elections, 2008. 2. Elections—United States.
3. United States—Politics and government—2001-2009. I. Watson, Robert P., 1962- II. Dewhirst, Robert E.
 JK19682008 .R63 2010
 324.973′0931—dc22
                                                                            2010000300

∞™ The paper used in this publication meets the minimum requirements of American National Standard for Information Sciences—Permanence of Paper for Printed Library Materials, ANSI/NISO Z39.48-1992.
Printed in the United States of America

Contents

Foreword ix
    Congressman Ken Hechler

Preface xv
    Robert P. Watson and Robert Dewhirst

Part I: Introduction

1 The 2008 Congressional Elections: The "Other" Democratic Victory of 2008 3
    Robert P. Watson

Part II: House Elections

2 Mississippi District 1 Race (Childers v. Davis): Three Elections and a Stunning Upset 17
    Tom Lansford

3 Missouri District 6 Race (Barns v. Graves): "Change" Comes Up Short against a Negative "Values" Campaign in a Rural District 33
    Daniel E. Smith

4 Illinois District 14 Race (Foster v. Oberweis): A National Proxy Fight for a Special Election and a Former Speaker's Seat 53
    Jeffrey Ashley and Justin Sinner

5 New York District 13 Race (McMahon v. Straniere): A Congressman's Fall from Grace Turns a Red Seat Blue 73
    Jeffrey Kraus

6 Texas District 23 Race (Rodriguez v. Larson): A Vulnerable Candidate in a High-Profile Race . . . Proves to Be Neither   95
John David Rausch Jr.

7 California District 26 Race (Warner v. Dreier): Anti-Republican Sentiment Proved No Match for Money and Incumbency   111
Marcia Godwin and Richard Gelm

8 Ohio District 16 Race (Boccieri v. Schuring): One of the Nation's Most Competitive Open Seats   127
William Binning and Sunil Ahuja

9 Florida District 21 Race (Martinez v. L. Diaz-Balart) and Florida District 25 Race (Garcia v. M. Diaz-Balart): The Change in "Little Havana" That Did Not Happen   147
Sean Foreman

10 Florida District 13 Race (Jennings v. Buchanan): Rematch—a Clash of Politics and Personalities   169
Peter Bergerson and Margaret E. Banyan

Part III: Senate Elections

11 Louisiana Senate Race (Landrieu v. Kennedy): History and Incumbency Benefit a Vulnerable Candidate   185
Joshua Stockley

12 Virginia Senate Race (Warner v. Gilmore): A Presidential Campaign and a New Kind of Democrat Turn the Old Dominion Blue   205
Bob N. Roberts

13 Alaska Senate Race (Begich v. Stevens): Scandal, Upset, and the End of an Era   227
Gerald McBeath and Amy Lauren Lovecraft

14 Colorado Senate Race (Udall v. Schaffer): A Campaign of Ideological Differences and a Changed Political Landscape   245
Robert J. Duffy, Kyle L. Saunders, and Andrew Kear

Part IV: Conclusion

15 The Legacy of Election 2008   271
Robert Dewhirst

Appendix A: Constitutional Requirements for Congress   281

Appendix B: Party Control of Congress   283

Appendix C: Length of Service in Congress   285

Appendix D: Reelection Rates in Congress   287

Appendix E: Margins of Victory in Congressional Elections   289

Appendix F: Voting Turnout in Congressional Elections   291

Index   293

Contributors   301

Foreword

*Congressman Ken Hechler, Democrat
(West Virginia, 1959–1977)*

My first campaign for Congress was in 1958. Quite frankly, it was a long shot at best. I was running against a popular Republican incumbent named Will Neal, if I even made it past two strong opponents in the Democratic primary. The favorite in the Democratic primary was a longtime resident of the main city in the district and had been endorsed by most of the region's political establishment. The district was conservative and rural, and distrustful of liberal newcomers like me. Readers should note that I had only moved to West Virginia in 1957, and from *New York* of all places. Moreover, as *Pageant* magazine noted at the time, I "was a plain-looking, bespectacled bachelor . . . with no pretty wife or adoring children to parade before the television screens." Both friends and opponents dismissed my chances.

In 1956 I was working as director of research for Adlai Stevenson's presidential campaign. After Stevenson lost for a second time to Ike, I needed a break from politics. I worked previously as a professor but that career had been three times interrupted—the first time when I was drafted into the Second World War in 1942, the second time when I was recruited to join Harry Truman's White House staff, and again in 1953 when I became the associate director of the American Political Science Association. You don't turn down any of these offers! But I was eager to get back into the classroom and took a position at West Virginia's Marshall College (now Marshall University).

Although I enjoyed teaching I decided to jump into the 1958 congressional primary. I was labeled a "suitcase politician" (years later Bobby Kennedy and Hillary Clinton would have to overcome similar criticisms to win Senate races in New York) who "hadn't paid his dues." I decided that, if I was going to lose, I might as well have fun and run a campaign based on what I deemed "the politics of niceness." I decided to stress what I stood for, never attacking my opponent; instead, I praised both my Democratic and Republican rivals.

And so it was. As part of my effort to run a personable and positive campaign, I asked four Marshall coeds to help me campaign by performing the then-popular McGuire Sisters song "Sugartime." The catchy song's lyrics included: "Sugar in the morning/Sugar in the evening/Sugar at supper-time."

In place of the word "sugar" they sang my name, "Hechler." They also substituted "election time" for "supper-time" at the end. People smiled, sang along, and remembered the name. It cost me $1 to get the copyright.

In later campaigns, I ran an ad on Valentine's Day asking voters to "be my valentine," an ad on St. Patrick's Day with Bing Crosby singing "my Irish eyes are smiling," and another parodying the hit song "Get Me to the Church on Time" but changed the words to "get me to the polls on time."

After shaking enough hands in my "nice" grassroots campaign, I won a surprise victory in the primary despite—and perhaps on account of—my refusal to accept any contributions from the political machines in West Virginia. Anything is possible, especially in congressional elections, as was still evident during the 2008 elections. I also learned that the candidate mattered and, with the right campaign strategy, it was possible to overcome seemingly insurmountable barriers. This too is also true in congressional elections today. My run that year was labeled by the Associated Press as "the shrewdest personal electioneering" in over two decades. I decided to continue the "nice" campaign strategy and take it to the next level. So, after securing the Democratic nomination I ran an ad in the newspapers congratulating Congressman Neal on winning the Republican nomination. The response to such a courteous ad was overwhelming and positive.

Neal was a kindly eighty-one-year-old obstetrician who had served as mayor of Huntington, the largest city in the district. Plus, as the press often said of my opponent, "Neal had been bringing West Virginia babies into the world for more than 50 years." The candidate himself liked to say "I delivered you, now you deliver the votes!" It would be another uphill battle. To make matters worse, after gaining momentum, I suffered what appeared to be a devastating negative attack.

When I taught at Princeton in the 1940s, I used to contact famous politicians and put them on speaker phone in my classroom so my students could talk to them. We spoke to many Republicans, including the ex-president, Herbert Hoover. *Time* magazine picked up on it as a human interest story and described me as an effective professor and left-of-center Republican. My opponents in West Virginia used the story, alleging that I was a secret operative for the Republican Party and had worked for them while claiming to have been an aide to President Truman. In a panic, I called

Clark Clifford, one of Truman's top advisors, who got quite a laugh out of the story. Clifford agreed to write a public letter testifying to the good work I did for Roosevelt and Truman. It read: "If Ken Hechler was good enough for Democratic Presidents Roosevelt and Truman, I'm sure he's good enough for West Virginia Democrats."

The letter received a lot of attention and the entire incident ended up helping me. I learned that all things shall pass, even negative moments on the campaign trail.

In addition to an effective strategy and emphasis on the grassroots, often a single big event or story will make or break the campaign. The 2008 elections were no exception to this rule. The key is to seize such an opportunity and make it work for you. Two such moments helped me. One was a visit by President Truman to endorse me. The other was less obvious but equally as helpful.

I had written a new book titled *The Bridge at Remagen*, which would become a best seller and be made into a Hollywood movie. The book chronicled a critical incident in World War II and was based on my experiences there as an army combat historian. I decided to take advantage of the book's notoriety by handing out free, autographed copies everywhere I went, especially at the gates of factories and plants full of rank-and-file laborers. I was invited to speak to schools, clubs, churches, and on the radio, not as a candidate but as an author, thus receiving ample free publicity. A war book also blunted the criticism by conservatives that I was too liberal. The best investment I ever made was buying 10,000 copies of the book. It cost me $1,000, less money than I would have spent on a glitzy ad campaign, PR firm, or political consultants.

That November, I upset Congressman Neal by 3,500 votes. Anything is possible in congressional elections.

I'd like to think that if two astute scholars had decided to produce a book similar to *The Roads to Congress* about the 1958 campaign my race might have been intriguing and unpredictable enough to have been profiled in it. At the same time, had such a book been available before I ran for office, I believe it would have been helpful for me to have read it. *The Roads to Congress 2008* is an easy read and is full of important and keen insights into congressional campaigns. My students would have enjoyed—and benefited from—such a book when I was teaching courses on American politics and elections.

The book will be an important addition to scholarship on Congress and, more importantly, an invaluable tool for the classroom because it offers a unique approach to studying the topic. I found that my most useful lessons into congressional campaigns came not from a theory or textbook, but from either participating in them or analyzing the details of a particular campaign. This book offers the latter.

As I hope I have emphasized in this foreword, upsets happen in campaigns and by-the-book campaigns sometimes lose. Each campaign takes on its own dynamic and it is thus important to study the "ins and outs" of individual races rather than simply aggregate data on national elections. After all, the candidates themselves as well as the campaign strategies matter.

After winning seven straight elections I was thrown a curveball in 1972. After the 1970 Census, West Virginia lost one congressional district. At the same time, my independence and opposition to machine politics had caught up with me. Accordingly, in 1972 I was redistricted out of a seat and forced to run in a different district with new communities and new voters. The far majority of the counties in this new district had been friendly to the Democratic incumbent, whose mother and father before him had represented the district for forty years!

Once again, I emphasized my "nice" approach but had to tailor my strategy to the new circumstances. Also, a few key and unpredictable factors ended up influencing the race. One was the surge in environmentalism after Earth Day was established, with the corresponding impact of the momentous Clean Air and Clean Water acts of 1972. The timing was fortuitous, as I had been a supporter of the environment and had made a name in West Virginia opposing the polluters and the practice of mountain-top removal, and fighting for safer, cleaner mines and wilderness areas. My opponent's record was anything but green. Consequently, unlike in previous elections, a groundswell of environmental groups from around the country and outdoorsman from my state came out in support of me.

One of my best campaign ideas came from that race and courtesy of a waitress who suggested that I publish a table contrasting my votes on key issues to my opponent's. While doing so, I noted that my opponent was frequently absent from votes (he missed nearly one-third of all votes), whereas I had a perfect record on casting votes over the same ten-year period. As such, I ran an ad saying "Would you rather have a 100% congressman or a 68% congressman?" My opponent responded that he had a more important committee assignment than I, so I simply pointed out that it didn't matter because his attendance record in committee was equally as inexcusable. He recognized the damage and the threat I posed so he stepped up his campaigning in the district. But to do so he had to miss even more votes. My response was to go public with joking pleas for him to "please come back to Washington to vote tomorrow on this important bill that will [do such and such]." I won that race too.

My political career began as a young idealist who upset an eighty-one-year-old veteran of Congress. It ended in 2004 when I was defeated by a much younger woman in my bid for a fifth term as West Virginia's secretary of state, in part because of the perception that, at age ninety, I was too old.

When I lost in 2004, I was a decade older than my very first political opponent. You are never too young or too old to get involved in politics, because anything is possible.

Serving in Congress was a great responsibility and great honor. Members of Congress have the ability, on one hand, to help an individual with a problem and, on the other hand, to serve the entire country. While in Congress I always remembered advice I received from Harry Truman, who used to encourage his staff to follow Thomos Jefferson's adage of "equal rights for all, special privileges for none." This lesson stayed with me and, in the 1960s, I was a member of a committee on the space program and was charged with leading a junket for my fellow committee members to the Kennedy Space Center. However, I learned that Martin Luther King Jr. was preparing an important march from Selma to Montgomery that coincided with my congressional business. So, I made the rash decision to skip the congressional junket in order to stand with Dr. King in Alabama. I was the only member of Congress to do so and, as we now know, the march shaped history. Even though my decision did not sit well with my West Virginia constituents, it is a moment in my congressional career that I am particularly proud of.

Long ago as a graduate student at Columbia I was taught that legislation in Congress is the product of compromise among all the members. However, as a congressman I learned that "compromise" is often a veil for adding pork or appeasing special interests, and that there are times when one must make a stand on principle and rally the conscience of other members and the public. So too must one be able to move beyond a fight or defeat. Too many members of Congress today strike me as holding grudges, fighting for the sake of fighting, and refusing to share credit with the other side. When I served, I tried to treat my colleagues from the perspective that "today's opponent is tomorrow's ally."

Over my long career I developed other "rules for campaigners." Although it might lack the verbosity and sophistication of an academic thesis, I stand by them. My list includes simple and seemingly obvious advice to "pay attention to the average person," "be true to your personality," and "venture forth around the district every day . . . don't be deskbound." I wager that these rules still apply today as they did a half century ago when I was campaigning. In this book, Professors Watson and Dewhirst, and the contributing authors, have put forth their own lessons from the 2008 election, and I wager that they will prove most illuminating.

It is obvious that Watson and Dewhirst have produced a strong book and thorough examination of some of the most interesting and important races of 2008. Readers of this book will gain an understanding of the nuances, unpredictability, and dynamic nature of campaigns probably not offered by most standard textbooks.

Preface

Robert P. Watson and Robert Dewhirst

Every two years the pageantry of American politics unfolds when all 435 seats in the U.S. House of Representatives and roughly one-third of those in the U.S. Senate are up for election. These elections provide voters with an opportunity to evaluate their members of Congress and the institution as a whole and, in so doing, continue the American experiment in popular democracy. They also offer a regular and frequent barometer for the health and practice of American democracy. The 2008 election cycle, in particular, was in many ways one of the most intriguing and pivotal elections in many years and for many reasons, which are explored in this book.

Although a number of solid books have been produced about Congress and elections, this book is unique in that it analyzes several individual House and Senate races during the 2008 election. *The Roads to Congress 2008* offers readers detailed accounts of the campaigns, candidates, key issues, and outcomes of over one dozen of the most important and interesting races of 2008. This includes both House and Senate campaigns, contests from all regions of the country, and seats held by Democrats and Republicans, as well as open seats.

Much effort was made to produce a highly readable book. The cases are succinct but detailed and are written in lively prose. Each case shares the same general format and topics covered so as to permit comparisons among the cases, improve readability, and link together the themes explored in the book. For instance, in every case readers will find information on the district or state such as voting trends and profiles of voters, key factors in the campaign such as media coverage and fund-raising, and an analysis of the results. Each case presents basic lessons learned from the race, and an introductory chapter and conclusion place the cases and election cycle in both contemporary political context and historic perspective. So too are there data in the form of several tables in the appendix that will further assist the reader in understanding and drawing conclusions about the cases and state of congressional elections.

Another feature of the book is the quality of the contributing authors, all of whom reside in the state or district about which they are writing and all of them have expertise in American politics, the Congress, and elections. We thank them for participating in this book and for the time it took to research each particular race. A special thanks to Dr. Ken Hechler for agreeing to write the foreword to our book and for providing invaluable insights from the vantage point of someone with experience on all sides of congressional races—he is a former congressman who ran (and won) many races, a former state chief elections official who reformed the electoral process, a former political science professor who studied elections, and someone who has been voting since the Great Depression! Ken is a national treasure.

We would also like to thank Joseph C. Parry, Tawnya Zengierski, Julia Loy, and Abigail Graber, and the staff at Lexington Books for their assistance and support with this book. A warm thanks to our families (especially Alessandro and Isabella) for their patience during the time it took to produce this book.

The 2008 election was historic and will impact Congress and the American political landscape for years to come. We hope our readers will gain insights into how congressional campaigns work, the factors that influence the outcome of congressional elections, and the significance of this important election.

I
INTRODUCTION

1

The 2008 Congressional Elections

The "Other" Democratic Victory of 2008

Robert P. Watson

The U.S. Congress is the world's most venerable, powerful, and longest-running democratic legislature. In the American political system it has played a central role in many of the nation's most important decisions and was envisioned by the Founders as the primary branch of government, as indicated by their decision to devote Article I of the U.S. Constitution to the Congress. Many of its members are well known around the world and are household names within their home states or districts. Some have served for decades, leaving indelible marks on both the institution and the country. So too are the Capitol Building and the Congress it houses important symbols of democracy and integral components of the American political tradition.

At the same time, however, Congress has suffered through a number of high-profile scandals and a declining lack of confidence by the American public. Of course, scandal is nothing new for Congress. However, some recent Congresses have been among the most corrupt and ineffective in history. In particular, the 109th Congress (2005–2007) was thought to have been one of the worst in American history.[1] For example, during the 2006 calendar year the Congress was in session a total of less than one hundred days and passed not a single significant piece of legislation despite the presence of a number of serious problems at home and abroad. So too was it wracked by several particularly shameless scandals involving House members such as: Tom DeLay (R-TX), whose take-no-prisoners approach to legislating and penchant for retribution earned him the nickname "The Hammer" and resulted in an indictment on several criminal charges; Randall "Duke" Cunningham (R-CA), who accepted millions of dollars in bribes from lobbyists and pleaded guilty to mail fraud, wire fraud, tax evasion, and more; William Jefferson (D-LA), who was indicted for repeatedly taking bribes and whose office was raided by federal officials who found $90,000 in cash in his freezer; and Mark Foley (R-FL), who was caught sending sexually explicit messages to teenage boys and male congressional pages.

Things have not improved. The 110th Congress (2007–2009) had a public approval rating even lower than the worst numbers experienced by President George W. Bush, whose approval dropped to one of the lowest points in modern times.[2] As a result, in recent years Congress has been viewed by the public as incompetent, corrupt, and in the pocket of special interests.[3] Polls measuring the public perceptions of various occupations reveal that Congress suffers from lower levels of support than nearly every other occupation, including such distrusted professions as stockbrokers, building contractors, and real estate agents, and such maligned vocations as bankers, journalists, and even lawyers. The only jobs held in lower esteem today than Congress are the insurance industry and automobile sales.[4]

According to Congressman David Price (D-NC), a former professor at Duke University, "Congress bashing" has become something of a national pastime.[5] Cries of "throw all the bums out" are now heard during every election cycle, and bumper stickers saying "Reelect no one" can be found on cars throughout the country. Indeed, Americans seem to have a love-hate relationship with Congress insofar as they like their representative and their state's senators but want the rest defeated at the polls.[6] This attitude extends to seemingly minor complaints such as how much time members of Congress spend in the capital city versus time spent back home. While trying to juggle these two conflicting demands, Congressman Price describes a catch-22 whereby if a member stays in Washington, they are accused of forgetting the voters who sent them there, but if a member spends a lot of time back in the district, they are accused of failing to do the work the people sent them to do![7] The old adage that "you can please some of the people sometime, but you can't please all of the people all the time" certainly applies to Congress.

THE PEOPLE'S CONGRESS

This quandary is, of course, part of the conflicting views the public has about Congress. People want someone to serve their interests, but they detest the process often required to promote such interests.[8] What one voter might deem as serving constituents, another might label as pork barrel politics. Midwestern farmers want their subsidies protected, but the rest of the nation sees it as a waste of their tax dollars. Instances of such pork and earmarks were taken to new highs (or, perhaps more accurately, new *lows*) by the 109th Congress and were again apparent in the 110th Congress.

To be sure, much of the anger with Congress results from the inherent paradoxes found within, and the public's limited understanding of, the legislative process. For instance, members of Congress often find themselves in conflict over serving their constituency, representing their district, pursuing their own interests, supporting their political party and leaders, and following their own beliefs and conscience. How does one vote? All of the aforementioned factors are potential points to consider when voting. Then, depending on how the vote is cast, members of Congress must consider which important base of support might be alienated.

Partisan politics and bicameralism (two houses), which is a part of the checks and balances embedded in the Constitution, are simultaneously and inescapably part of the necessary design of the system and part of the headaches of legislative inertia and gridlock. The Senate and House of Representatives have different rules and norms of conduct—and often different priorities—and are but one of the three branches of government. The efforts of one chamber might be thwarted by the other, while a bill designed to address a pressing issue might fall victim to a presidential veto. Add to that the fact that each senator is but one of 100 members, while each representative is but one of 435 members and it is easy to see why the majority of bills introduced never become law. Moreover, the legislative process—like the problems Congress faces—is unwieldy, complicated, and time-consuming. Rarely is any action designed by committee the best or most expedient way to solve a problem; but nor is an imprudently rushed solution the best approach either.

The composition of Congress has been another enduring problem, in that many critics allege it has been anything but representative. The "people's house" contains a degree of the rainbow tapestry that is the American public—in the past three decades many blacks and Hispanics have been elected through the creation of "majority minority" districts—but it is not proportionately representative. On the other hand, the Senate remains a far more elite and homogenous institution, comprised almost entirely of older, wealthy white men who were educated at elite schools and came from only a handful of occupations such as law, business, banking, and public service. Very few skilled and unskilled laborers are found in either chamber, while Congress counts among its members dozens of millionaires. Aside from Hawaii, who sends one Asian and one Pacific Islander to the Senate, only one other minority served in that chamber in the 110th Congress, along with just over a dozen women.[9]

All these issues have exacted a terrible toll on the American body politic. The public has lost confidence in Congress, partisan bickering is alarmingly high while voting turnout has been abysmally low, and the institution seems incapable of conducting the nation's business. This is the backdrop for the historic 2008 congressional elections and the challenges waiting for the 111th Congress.

ENDURING DILEMMAS AND NEW CHALLENGES

Every Congress confronts the challenge of how to resolve the conflicting goals inherent within the design of the legislature and legislative process as well as the often contrary expectations held by voters. But the 111th Congress will face much more. Given the partisan gridlock, prevalence of scandal, and public distrust of the institution, Congress found itself at a crossroads going into the 2008 election. The country needed a Congress that works and one that is truly representative.

The stakes were high in 2008. The country was in the grip of skyrocketing gas and energy prices, foreign oil dependence, a mortgage crisis, a devalued dollar, a weakened economy, and an American public atypically pessimistic about its future. The Bush White House's record included two unpopular wars, a stalled peace process in the Middle East, record budget and trade deficits, a ballooning national debt, the nation's reputation abroad at an all-time low, a record number of 47 million Americans without health insurance, and virtually no significant international agreements or treaties to point to. The next Congress found a full plate waiting for them in January of 2009 when they were sworn in.

Congressional Elections and the Top of the Ticket: The Presidential Election

Every four years, congressional elections are conducted along with the campaign for the White House. The year 2008 was such a year. Presidential campaigns often introduce several additional, and at times incalculable, factors which can frustrate the plans of congressional candidates. Many candidates find themselves adapting their campaign strategies around the shape of the presidential race. Sometimes winning presidential candidates have been known to have "coattails," which have been enough to carry congressional candidates to victory who otherwise probably would have lost. This happened in 1980 when Ronald Reagan's landslide victory swept Republicans from all across the country and from an assortment of races into office with him. On the other hand, Bill Clinton's affairs with Gennifer Flowers and Paula Jones, coupled with an aggressive and highly effective campaign by future Republican Speaker Newt Gingrich, allowed Republicans to nationalize the 1994 election against Clinton. Near record numbers of Democrats were defeated, and the Republicans gained control of both houses of Congress for the first time in years (see appendix B) by running against Clinton's "reverse" coattails. Similarly, experts had predicted—and Republicans had worried—about voters' negative reactions to the Bush record in 2008. Sure enough, Republicans around the country suffered defeat in 2008's election in part because of Bush's unpopularity and the Republican Party's poor record on the economy.

In addition, some presidential campaigns have soaked up vast amounts of donations which otherwise might have gone to eager congressional candidates. The campaigns of George W. Bush and Bill Clinton, in particular, raised heretofore unimaginable amounts of money. But the 2008 presidential race would top even these well-funded campaigns, as Barack Obama's campaign raised well over half of a billion dollars, becoming the most expensive in history.

Having a presidential contest at the top of the ticket has been demonstrated to increase overall voter turnout by roughly 15 percent. This has tended to impact House and Senate races, in that some voters tend to vote only in presidential election years or tend to vote along straight party lines. The 2008 presidential race appears to have provided yet another example of these trends, especially with Democrat Barack Obama's ability to "get out the vote," which he did during the primary election and general election. Voter turnout in 2008 is estimated to have been roughly 64 percent, which represents a large increase over the 2006 midterm turnout and the turnout during the past few presidential elections.

The anticipated closeness of the 2008 election also led political activists in both parties to direct extra energy and funds toward increasing turnout among their bases. Christian evangelicals and gun-rights groups sought to mobilize their supporters for Republican candidates while civil rights, environmental, and labor groups launched get-out-the-vote efforts for Democrats. There is always an emphasis on turnout in key swing states, necessary to winning the presidency. This was the case in 2002 and 2004, orchestrated by GOP strategist, Karl Rove, which helped Republicans to win. In 2008, a number of swing states were in play such as Virginia, Florida, Ohio, and Pennsylvania.[10]

Twenty-first Century Political Connections: The Internet

The 2008 campaigns introduced new words to the nation's political vocabulary such as chat rooms, blogging, and text messaging. The Internet has emerged as a major force in American politics over the past four years, and every party nominee campaigning for a seat in Congress during 2008 had a website and an Internet presence. Most campaigns had elaborate and interactive websites that included email, online donations, blogs, photographs, and more. So too did all major interest and citizen groups have an online presence in 2008. Whether it was holding online meetings, raising campaign funds, exchanging ideas, or making important announcements, the Internet impacted the 2008 elections and allowed candidates to reach a far wider audience of citizens and voters than ever before in history.

The New Colors of American Politics

Color-coded political maps of the United States remained the rage throughout the election year. States which Republicans tended to win were colored red, while those dominated by Democrats were represented as blue. Political talk became spiced with references to "red states" and "blue states." Red Republican states were those found in the southeastern United States plus the Great Plains states and Rocky Mountains. The blue Democratic states included the west coast, the Northeast, and New England.

Not surprisingly, the Democratic and Republican congressional delegations of both chambers tended to come disproportionately from states identified by America's political map. Moreover, befitting the deep political divisions that existed in the nation in 2008, the combined population of the red states was nearly equal to that of the blue states. This was true even though distinct geographic and demographic patterns were identified with both parties and, in 2008, the old complaint that there was no difference between the parties was certainly not true. The parties had different perspectives on many important issues.

At the same time, the new term of "purple states" was added to the political lexicon. Some states have become neither red nor blue, and a bit of both. These were key states in both the presidential election and congressional elections and included a number of states such as New Hampshire in New England, Virginia in the South, Ohio, Missouri, and Minnesota in the Midwest, and Colorado, Nevada, and New Mexico in the West, to name a few. In 2008, Democrats were able to make inroads into several traditionally red states such as Colorado and Virginia both in the presidential election and congressional races.

The Impact of Money and 527s

The phrase "527 groups" burst onto the national stage during the 2004 campaign with the group MoveOn.org on the political left and the "Swiftboat Veterans for Truth" on the right spending millions of dollars on the election. The same phenomenon occurred in 2008, although the national impact of such advocacy groups was not as profound as it was in the elections of 2004 and 2006. Such groups earned their name because of section 527 in the pertinent federal code pertaining to campaign financing. These groups raised money in order to influence the results of select congressional elections. A number of powerful 527s again pumped significant resources into electing or defeating specific members of Congress.[11]

THE 2008 ELECTION

On November 4, the public went to the polls to elect the new 111th Congress. All 435 members of the U.S. House (plus the delegates from U.S. territories) were up for election, as is the case every two years, and approximately one-third of the U.S. Senate faced the voters. Going into the election, the Democrats held a 236-199 advantage in seats in the House and the Senate was deadlocked at 49-49, with two independents serving, Joseph Lieberman of Connecticut and Bernie Sanders of Vermont. Because both Independents aligned with the Democratic Party, Democrats technically had control of the Senate but lacked the necessary majority to easily push legislation, override President Bush's vetoes, or limit a filibuster or other procedural mechanisms.

In the 2006 midterm elections, Republicans had lost majorities that they had held in the House since 1995 and in the Senate for the same time frame, with the exception of a one seat majority held by the Democrats for part of 2001 and 2002. Moreover, the Republican Party had gained control of the majority of state legislatures in 2002 for the first time in a half century and controlled the majority of governorships and many key mayoral seats. The previous decade appeared to be part of a conservative realignment nationally and corresponded to the rise of Christian conservative voters within the party and proliferation of conservative news outlets such as Fox and right-wing radio talk shows. Accordingly, the Republican Party might have been expected to reclaim majorities in both chambers or at least have this as an objective going into the 2008 election.

However, given the unpopularity of President Bush and a problematic record for the party—two unpopular wars, high gas prices and economic woes, record deficits and debt, high profile scandals—most analysts predicted big gains by the Democrats in 2008.[12] More realistically, Republicans were simply trying to slow the bleeding. It was not whether the Democrats would win, but by how many seats and whether the Democrats would get to the magical number of sixty seats in the Senate—enough to have a "filibuster-proof" advantage. Even without such a majority, even a one seat majority brings with it the advantages of majority party status including the Speaker of the House, chairmanship of committees, control of the legislative agenda, and so on.

Not only did Democrats win the White House, with Obama winning the Electoral College by a count of 365-173 (270 votes are needed to win), but they gained seats in both the House and Senate, giving them comfortable majorities in both chambers. The Republicans were unable to limit the losses for many reasons, including public dissatisfaction with President Bush, the party's generally poor record over the preceding four years, the economic downturn (which a majority of voters blamed on the Republicans), and Barack Obama's ability to bring voters to the polls. But Republicans also struggled in the 2008 congressional races because of retirements and open seats, which will be discussed below.

Special Elections

In the year 1974, the Republican Party was struggling from backlash by the voters on account of an unpopular war in Vietnam, high gas and energy prices, and the Watergate scandal that drove President Richard Nixon from office. During the lead-up to the November election several defeats in special elections—including the symbolic loss of the former seat in Michigan of Gerald Ford, the House minority leader and new president—foreshadowed the difficulties the party would face in November. That fall the Democrats picked up a net of three seats in the U.S. Senate and a whopping forty-nine seats in the U.S. House.

In 2008, the Republican Party again faced the wrath of voters angry about high gas and energy prices, an unpopular president mired in scandal, and not one but two unpopular wars. Accordingly, as was the case in 1974, the Democrats swept several high-profile special elections held in the months prior to the 2008 elections. This included another parallel to 1974 when Republicans lost the minority leader's seat in 1974, but this time the party lost the Illinois seat formerly held by retired Dennis Hastert, Republican Speaker of the House.

Other Democratic upsets in special elections to replace retiring Republicans included victories in the Republican-dominated Deep South, including Louisiana's District 1 seat and the state's District 6 seat. After Roger Wicker resigned on December 31, 2007, to accept an appointment to Mississippi's open Senate seat, his former House seat in District 1 was also taken by a Democrat.

In addition to picking up seats long held by Republicans, the Democrats successfully defended their open seats. In California's 12th District another Democrat was elected to replaced Tom Lantos, a popular congressman and Holocaust survivor who died in 2008. The 7th District seat in Indiana also stayed in Democratic hands when the late Julia Carson's grandson was elected to her former seat. The writing was on the wall for the Republican Party going into the November 2008 election.

Incumbents and Open Seats

In any given election, the number of seats in the U.S. House that are truly competitive numbers only about three dozen. The reasons for this include the advantage played by incumbency—more visibility, experience, name recognition, and the ability to raise money. Reelection rates have exceeded 90 percent over the past twenty-five years (see appendix D). Far less than one hundred incumbents have lost their party's nomination in the last twenty-five years. Indeed, the sad joke among many Congress watchers has been that a member is more likely to die in office than be defeated. Incumbency brings many advantages, perhaps most important among them the amount of money raised. This is true in both the House and Senate. It is a rare incident in Congress when a better-funded candidate loses.

One of the main reasons for the lack of competitiveness in House races is the manner in which congressional seats are reapportioned. After the decennial census is taken, state legislatures redraw congressional districts to account for shifts—gains and losses—in population that occurred over the preceding decade. For instance, after the 2000 Census, Arizona, California, Florida, Georgia, North Carolina, and other states gained seats, whereas Illinois, Massachusetts, New Jersey, New York, Ohio, Pennsylvania, and other states lost seats in their congressional delegations. Sadly, the practice of "gerrymandering" has been so compromised by politics—in that districts are designed purely for political purposes in order to benefit a particular party or group—that the district boundaries resemble modern art. An example is North Carolina's infamous and odd-shaped 12th District, designed in response to reverse the historic underrepresentation by minorities by establishing "majority minority" districts. However, the 12th District twisted for 160 miles along Interstate 85 in order to connect as many black communities as possible.[13] The process has served to create an abundance of safe districts for one party or the other, contributing to the high reelection rates.[14]

However, going into the 2008 election, more seats were in play in both the House and Senate than are normally competitive. In addition to a less than stellar record by Republicans and an unpopular president in the White House, the party had to defend many open seats. In fact, the gap between the parties in open seats was the largest in a half century. There were thirty-three retirements in the U.S. House prior to the election, and fully twenty-six of them were Republicans. Of the seven Democrats not running for reelection in the House, four of them were campaigning for Senate seats. Accordingly, part of the early legacy of George W. Bush might prove to be his role in sparking a flood of retirements from public life within his party.

Republicans also faced the burden of defending more seats than the Democrats. Rather than the usual number of thirty-three Senate seats up for election, 2008 saw thirty-five seats up for grabs on account of two special elections. With twenty-three of their seats being contested—as opposed to only twelve by the Democrats—the Republicans were in a predicament of defending nearly twice as many seats.

There were also five prominent retirements in the U.S. Senate this election cycle, all by Republicans. Colorado's Wayne Allard had promised only to run for two terms. Adding to the challenge for Republicans was that his home state, formerly a GOP stronghold, was considered to be competitive in 2008.[15] The Republicans also faced competition from the retirement of two of the most senior members of the Senate—Virginia's John Warner and New Mexico's Pete Dominici. Seats that had been safe for several election cycles were now in play. Moreover, Dominici's fall from grace on account of an investigation into his role in the Bush Justice Department's firing of U.S. attorneys on alleged grounds of partisanship and retribution.

Although Idaho remained a solidly Republican seat, Senator Larry Craig's resignation due to charges that he solicited sex from an undercover male police officer in an airport bathroom did nothing to help his party nationally; nor did the senator's ham-fisted and unapologetic handling of the affair and the hypocritical twist that Craig had been a staunch opponent of gay rights. The scandal was an explosive media story for months. Also retiring was Chuck Hagel from Nebraska. Even though Nebraska would remain solidly in GOP hands, the former veteran's departure denied the party of an important and respected voice on national security.

The result was that the Democrats picked up twenty-two seats in the House and seven seats in the Senate, giving them a margin of 255–175 in the 111th House of Representatives (up from 233–202 in the 110th) and a margin of 58–40 in the 111th Senate (up from 51–49 in the 110th). The Republican Party did manage to win three House seats formerly held by Democrats. But two of those—Tom Delay's old seat in Texas and Mark Foley's old seat in Florida—had traditionally been controlled by Republicans. Both seats went to the Democrats in 2006 only because of embarrassing scandals by the Republican incumbents. But the Republican gain of three seats was more than offset by the fact that the Democrats picked up twenty-four seats that were in the hands of Republicans. While the Republicans retained twelve of their seats in the Senate, they lost seven Senate seats to the Democrats in the 2008 election. On the other hand, the Democrats also retained twelve Senate seats but lost not a single seat to the Republicans in that chamber.

To make matters worse for the Republicans, shortly after the election, longtime senator Arlen Specter (R-PA) announced he was switching parties and becoming a Democrat. Some pundits suggested Specter did so to help his chances of retaining his seat in the 2010 midterm election, as the state of Pennsylvania has moved slightly to the political left and many Republicans both in Pennsylvania and around the country were frustrated by Specter's moderate views on the issues and independent-minded voting behavior. Others suggested Specter's move was not so surprising, in that his relations with many Republicans in Congress had been souring for years and he was the brunt of many attacks by right-wing radio shock jocks, intolerant of his moderation and independence. As the party moved further to the right and newer members of the party showed both less and less respect for the seniority system and no patience for anyone not lockstep with them on the issues, Specter was a frequent target of their wrath. Even the Bush-Cheney White House was known to pressure Specter more than is the norm, and former Republican leader in the House Tom Delay (R-TX) and his supporters had been very critical of Specter. Specter's abandonment of the GOP gave the Democrats a 59th seat in the Senate.

Fully eight months after Election Day, the final Senate race was decided. In July of 2009, it was announced that Al Franken would be Minnesota's junior senator. Franken and incumbent, Norm Coleman (R-MN), had been locked in a bizarre and contested recount, reminiscent of the 2000 presidential debacle in Florida. Shortly after the polls closed, it was announced that Coleman was ahead by an ever so slim margin. Coleman postured that the tight race should be decided, but Franken, independent observers and the press, and state officials continued to recount the ballots. As Coleman warned Franken about opposing the initial count, the count changed to put Franken ahead. After months of wrangling by the courts and elections officials—and after months of Coleman's about-face refusal to accept the recount—Minnesota swore in their second member of the chamber. Al Franken's victory gave Democrats a sixty-vote, filibuster-proof majority in the U.S. Senate. It did not rain for the Republican Party, it had poured.

IN THIS BOOK

The cases selected for inclusion in this book constitute a broad cross section of some of the more intriguing and important races of 2008. Four criteria were used in selected cases for this text. The first was to select races from both chambers: four Senate races and ten House races are profiled. The second criterion used by the editors was to select for the book a mix of open seats, Democratic-held seats, and Republican-held seats. The third criterion was to profile races that cover a geographic cross section of the country, from New York to Florida to California, and points in between. The final criterion used in selecting cases was to consult prominent analysts such as *Congressional Quarterly* and the *Cook Report*. These sources compiled lists of "races to watch" such as those thought to be important, in that they were swing seats, seats that would likely change parties, and races that were among the tightest in the country. They also listed intriguing races, such as those with scandals and those with unusual primaries.

In using these four criteria for races to profile, the cases reflect the broader experiences of congressional candidates across the country, and many of the lessons from these races are applicable to other congressional races. All in all, the 2008 congressional elections might very well prove to be as historic and important to the path the United States takes during the pivotal years ahead as the presidential election.[16]

NOTES

1. In 2006, Roll Call produced a list under the heading of "Probing the Hill" of federal investigations into sitting members of Congress that revealed eighteen investigations by the Department of Justice. See www.rollcall.com. See also *USA Today's* "Columnists' Opinions," a series on the record number of scandals and poor performance of the 109th Congress at www.usatoday.com/news/opinion/editorials/2006-10-18-forum-congress_x.htm.

2. Polling Report provides a list of all major polls on Bush's approval over time at www.pollingreport.com/BushJob.htm. The University of Minnesota offers another source for comparing polls of Bush, including the Gallup, Zogby, Quinnipiac, Harris, Fox, CBS/NYT, CNN, Pew, NBC/WSJ, ABC/WP, and Newsweek polls. See www.hist.umn.edu/~ruggles/Approval.htm.

3. John R. Hibbing and Elizabeth Theiss-Morse, *Congress as Public Enemy* (New York: Cambridge University Press, 1995), 1–4.

4. Gallup Poll Monthly, December 1997, p. 2008.

5. David E. Price, *The Congressional Experience*, 2nd ed. (Boulder, CO: Westview Press, 2000), 6.

6. Glenn R. Parker and Roger H. Davidson, "Why Do Americans Love Their Congressmen So Much More Than Their Congress?" *Legislative Studies Quarterly*, February 1979, 52–61.

7. Price, *Congressional Experience*, 191–92.

8. For a good discussion, see the classic work by David R. Mayhew, *Congress: The Electoral Connection* (New Haven, CT: Yale University Press, 1974).

9. Norman J. Ornstein, Thomas E. Mann, and Michael J. Malbin, *Vital Statistics on Congress* (Washington, DC: CQ Press, 1998), see tables 1.9 through 1.13.

10. For a more thorough discussion, see Paul S. Herrnson, *Congressional Elections: Campaigning at Home and in Washington*, 3rd ed. (Washington, DC: CQ Press, 2000).

11. *Congressional Quarterly* tracks fund-raising for congressional races. See "Campaign Finance" on *CQ*'s Money Line (www.cqpolitics.com).

12. There are a number of respected reports that project congressional elections. See Larry Sabato's Crystal Ball at the University of Virginia (www.centerforpolitics.org/crystalball) and the *Cook Political Report* (www.cookpolitical.com).

13. Holly Idelson, "Court Takes a Hard Line on Minority Voting Blocs," *CQ Weekly Report*, July 1, 1995, pp. 4–5.

14. Roger H. Davidson, Walter J. Oleszek, and Frances E. Lee, *Congress and Its Members*, 11th ed. (Washington, DC: CQ Press, 2008).

15. *Congressional Quarterly*'s "Races to Watch" reports predicted which Senate races would be competitive (www.cqpolitics.com).

16. CQ handicapped races on their CQPolitics site (www.cqpolitics.com) and *Congressional Quarterly Weekly News* (www.cq.com); the *Cook Report* did the same at www.cookpolitical.com.

II
HOUSE ELECTIONS

2

Mississippi District 1 Race (Childers v. Davis)

Three Elections and a Stunning Upset

Tom Lansford

Travis Wayne Childers
Age: 50
Sex: Male
Race: Caucasian
Religion: Baptist
Education: B.S., business administration (University of Mississippi, 1980)
Occupation: Real estate broker
Political Experience: Chancery clerk (1991–2008)

Charles G. "Greg" Davis
Age: 42
Sex: Male
Race: Caucasian
Religion: Southern Baptist
Education: B.S., civil engineering (Mississippi State University, 1989)
Occupation: Engineer; public official
Political Experience: Mayor of Southaven (1997–present); state representative (1991–1997)

There were actually three elections for the Mississippi 1 District in 2008. In 2007, Senator Trent Lott (R-MS) announced his intention to retire. Then Representative Roger Wicker (R-MS) was named by Governor Haley Barbour (R-MS) to replace Senator Lott, creating a vacancy for the House seat. A special election was held on April 22, 2008, to replace Wicker, but no candidate received more than 50 percent of the vote as required by Mississippi law. As a result, a runoff election was held on May 22, followed by the general election on November 4.

CHARACTERISTICS OF THE DISTRICT

Like other areas of Mississippi, District 1 trends conservative on most issues, especially social matters and national security. Republican presidential candidates have won Mississippi in every presidential election since 1980. Moderate or "Blue Dog" Democrats have had success at the state and local level by embracing fiscal conservatism and populist campaigns that emphasize independence from the national Democratic party on several key social and economic issues. In addition, the leadership of the state Democratic Party remains moderate to conservative. As a result, in Mississippi there tend not to be significant policy differences between candidates of the two parties. Demographic divides within the district, especially between urban and rural voters and between the eastern and western areas of the district, are often as important as party affiliation to voters.

District 1 includes many communities stretched over twenty-two counties and portions of two others.

Party Balance

The once solidly Democratic region that comprises the district has become more diversified as the urban and suburban population increased. From 1873 to 1995, the seat was held by a succession of Democrats, but from 1995 to 2007, a Republican, Representative Wicker, dominated any Democratic challenger. Republicans had steadily increased their numbers within the district over the past thirty years; however, Democrats are still the majority among registered voters. In the district, prior to the 2008 special election, 31 percent of voters were registered Republicans while 38 percent were registered Democrats.

Voting and Electoral History

As is the case with other Southern states, party affiliation is not always a major determinant of voting patterns in state or national elections. The district has leaned Republican in national elections for the past decade. Senator Wicker, who represented the district in the U.S. House of Representatives from 1995 to 2007, won election each of his campaigns in the district with more than 60 percent of the vote. In addition, the district has voted Republican in both senatorial and presidential balloting for more than twenty years, including in the 2008 Senate and presidential races. Not surprisingly, it was considered a safe Republican seat by state officials and most pundits.

In the 2007 state elections, the majority of the counties in the district followed the overall trend in the state that saw Republicans secure seven of the eight statewide offices, including the governorship and lieutenant governorship. This particular election ran counter to broader political patterns across the nation in 2006 through 2008 in which Democrats performed increasingly well at the state and local level. Republicans did lose three seats in the state Senate, but there was no net gain for either party in the House of Representatives. The sole Democrat elected to statewide office was Attorney General Jim Hood who won reelection.

Demographic Character of the Electorate

The demographics of Mississippi's 1st District have changed considerably over the past decades. Originally a rural state and a rural district, the western counties have developed into suburbs of the greater Memphis metropolitan area. These areas tend to be more affluent, lean Republican, and have larger populations than their rural counterparts. Suburban De Soto County alone has 15 percent of the district's total population. The population of these areas continues to grow faster than the other areas of the district. The eastern areas of the district remain mostly rural, and they have a larger African American population. They trend Democratic, in large part because of the large African American population.

The district's total population was approximately 762,000 prior to the 2008 elections. The average age was 34.5 years old. Some 70.5 percent of the population was white, 27.2 percent was African American, with a small, but growing Hispanic population of just under 2 percent. Median household income was $35,831, considerably lower than the national average. The poverty rate was 16.4 percent, which varied across the counties, as did the unemployment rate. For instance, in 2007, De Soto County, on the northwestern edge of the district, had the lowest unemployment in the state at 4.1 percent, while Monroe County on the western side of the district faced an 11.4 percent unemployment rate. Only 14.3 percent of the population had a bachelor's degree, which is lower than the national average, but higher than the state average of 12.5 (De Soto County had the highest rate of bachelor's degrees in Mississippi at 21.6 percent). About 38 percent of the population was considered urban and the same percentage considered rural.

Key Voting Blocs

There are three main voting blocs in the district. The first is the Republican-leaning suburbanites in counties on the western side of the district. Like their counterparts in other areas of the Deep South, the suburban Mississippi Republicans are conservative on economic and social issues, as well as national security. The second major bloc is the traditional, rural Southern Democrats. They also tend to be conservative on social issues, including abortion, affirmative action, capital punishment, gun control, and homosexual rights. The Mississippi Democrats are less conservative on economic issues, and various party figures have demonstrated a willingness to challenge President George W. Bush's foreign and security policy, especially the 2003 Iraq War. The third and final bloc is the African American community which is overwhelmingly Democratic (about 90 percent of the African American voters in the district voted Democratic in the 2008 House balloting), making them a reliable base for the party.

Major Urban Areas and Employment/Occupational Characteristics

The city of Southaven in De Soto County had a 2007 population of approximately 42,000, making it the fifth largest city in Mississippi. Tupelo, best known as the birth place of Elvis Presley, in rural Lee County, had some 36,000 inhabitants, while Olive Branch, also in De Soto County had 30,600; Columbus, in Lowndes County, had 25,900; Grenada, in Grenada County, was home to 14,800 people; and Corinth, which is in Alcorn County, had a population of 14,050. More than 56 percent of the district's population works in white-collar or management occupations. Meanwhile, 30.4 percent are employed in manufacturing or agriculture, and 13.1 percent work in the service sector. Southaven and Olive Branch are bedroom communities within the Memphis metropolitan statistical area, and each has a large and affluent community that works in Memphis. In 2007, Toyota announced that Tupelo would be the site of a new manufacturing plant, which would provide an economic development stimulus for the area. However, the 2008 economic downturn repeatedly delayed the opening of the plant.

THE CANDIDATES

Both of the main candidates in the succession of elections were native-born Mississippians who had successful political careers at the state or local level. They were also well-known figures in their respective communities. Despite their party differences, there were few substantial policy disagreements between Democrat Travis Childers and Republican Greg Davis. The main difference was geographic: Childers was from the eastern, rural side of the district, and Davis was from the west.

Greg Davis

Charles G. "Greg" Davis was born in Southaven on February 22, 1966. Davis graduated from Mississippi State University and became an engineer. He married Suzann Savage in 1991 and has three children. Davis entered politics at a relatively young age when he was elected to the Mississippi House of Representatives in 1991. At the time, Davis was the youngest member of the House and developed a reputation for his hard work and ability to work "across the aisle" with Democrats. Despite his relative inexperience, Davis was given a seat on the powerful appropriations committee as a testament to his abilities.

Davis served in the House until 1997 when he successfully campaigned to be mayor of Southaven. Davis was reelected twice, in 2001 and 2005, and remained in office when he launched his bid for Senator Wicker's former congressional seat. As mayor, Davis was in office during a period of substantial economic growth. He was praised for his fiscal conservatism and led the effort to implement a tax-rebate program for Southaven, the first of its kind in Mississippi. Davis also oversaw the enactment of rules that made it impossible to raise local taxes without a supermajority of the city council.

Davis faced two opponents in the Republican primary on March 11, Glenn McCullough and Randy Russell. McCullough, the former head of the Tennessee Valley Authority (TVA) and a former mayor of Tupelo, was the most significant challenge for Davis. McCullough was popular in the Western areas of the district and argued that he could attract Democrats and independents. However, the majority of Republicans were located in the Western counties and ended up supporting Davis, who won the close-fought election with 17,082 votes to McCullough's 16,161 and Russell's 10,688.

Travis Childers

Travis Childers was born on March 29, 1958, in Booneville, in Prentiss County. He attended a local junior college before graduating from the University of Mississippi in 1980. Childers became a realtor and married Tami Gibson in 1981. The couple has two children. Childers built a highly successful realty firm.

In 1991, he was elected chancery court clerk for Prentiss County, and was reelected in the next five elections. In Mississippi, chancery clerks serve as the secretaries and treasurers for county governments. The clerks also oversee the recording and storage of all public documents. Childers became a well-known figure in Democratic politics in the Eastern counties of the district. He effectively used his position to form relationships with the leading local and state politicians. In addition, as chancery court clerk, he regularly interacted with leading members of the business community.

Initially, many Mississippi Democrats believed it unlikely that the party could reclaim the seat. As a result, some leading figures in the district declined to campaign. However, other Democrats, including Childers, believed the GOP was vulnerable because of the unpopularity of the administration of President George W. Bush. Childers faced a crowded field of four other primary opponents, including Mississippi House of Representative member Steve Holland and Marshall W. Coleman, an alderman for Calhoun City. During the primary, Childers emphasized his conservative credentials and bipartisanship. He won the primary with 40,919 votes (41.4 percent of the vote). His closest opponent was Holland with 30,274 votes (30.6 percent).

CAMPAIGN ISSUES

The combination of a special election, runoff, and general election meant that there were actually three campaigns between the two candidates, although the main campaign issues remained constant through the matches. Both Childers and Davis had very similar policy positions on the majority of issues, especially on social matters. For instance, both favored a constitutional amendment to define marriage as between a man and woman and declared themselves to be pro-life on the question of abortion. Both publicly courted the National Rifle Association (NRA) vote by endorsing gun rights. There were, however, some notable differences on healthcare and Social Security.

Two events did influence the contests and led to some alterations in message and campaign strategy. The first was the selection of Barack Obama as the Democratic presidential nominee. This played out mainly in the campaign itself, not on policy issues. The second was the expanding downturn in the nation's economy and the federal reaction to the recession, which led Childers to be more critical of the Bush administration's economic policies.

Childers's campaign message revolved around four issue areas: job creation and economic growth, better healthcare for seniors, enhanced access to affordable healthcare, and an emphasis on bipartisan or "progress before politics," as the campaign described it. Davis endeavored to frame his campaign around four areas: enhancing national security by "winning" the conflicts in Afghanistan and Iraq while improving homeland security, reducing energy costs through greater domestic oil and energy production, the defense of traditional family values, and reductions in federal taxation and spending. In spite of the efforts of the candidates to frame the issues, three factors emerged during the campaign that dominated the others: the economy, national security and the Iraq War, and Social Security and Medicare.

The Economy

Both candidates campaigned as fiscal conservatives who sought to reign in federal spending. Davis argued that the successive tax cuts enacted by the Bush administration should be made permanent and that Congress should undertake further tax reductions as a means to stimulate the sagging economy. Specifically, the Southaven mayor campaigned to eliminate the federal taxes on estates after a person died. Davis did support the original Bush stimulus package and argued that other federal efforts to jumpstart the economy had to be targeted toward specific industries or sectors. Among the priorities of the federal government should be greater efforts to open foreign markets to U.S. products through free trade. He consistently advocated a balanced federal budget and argued in favor of spending reductions as the best means to cut spending. Davis announced that he would work for a federal balanced budget amendment.

Childers also strongly supported the need for a balanced federal budget and pledged to vote for a federal balanced budget amendment. While careful not to appear supportive of tax increases, the Democrat asserted that some of the tax cuts, especially those targeted at the wealthy or corporations, should be allowed to expire in 2010 as a means to balance the budget. Concurrently, Childers declared that he would support Obama's plans for middle-class tax reductions. He came out as critical of "corporate welfare" programs, including subsidies for energy companies. Instead, Childers argued that the federal government should devote resources to promote economic development in rural areas and spur job creation. Finally, Childers contended that many of the free trade arrangements enacted over the past two decades had been disadvantageous to American workers and that future trade deals had to be negotiated more carefully (he described his philosophy as supportive of "fair" trade over free trade).

National Security and the Iraq War

Both candidates pledged to support efforts to enhance homeland security and to maintain a robust national defense. Davis endorsed the Bush administration's management of the war on terror and criticized the antiwar wing of the Democratic Party. He also asserted that the conflicts in Iraq and Afghanistan formed the "front lines" of the war on terror and that the United States had to win these conflicts in order to reduce its vulnerability to future terrorist attacks or challenges from potential global rivals such as China or Russia. Davis further argued that the Democrats in Congress had played "politics" with national security and had not provided the military with the resources necessary to accomplish its missions. He forcefully stated that the military commanders should determine strategy and tactics, not Congress.

The Republican also linked homeland security to immigration policy and contended that the nation needed better management of its borders and a more strict and tough immigration policy in order to deter future domestic terrorist strikes. He backed an expansion of the border patrol and stronger measures to deter illegal immigration. Davis also supported the troop surge in the Iraq War in late 2007 and argued that the strategy of deploying an additional 30,000 troops had been responsible for a decrease in violence in Iraq throughout 2008.

Childers, the Democrat, was more critical of the Bush administration's oversight of the war on terror. While he supported ensuring that the forces in Afghanistan and Iraq had adequate resources and weaponry, Childers sought a measured end to the U.S. presence in Iraq. He endorsed the plan advocated by Senator, and later vice presidential candidate, Joe Biden (D-DE) that called for the division of Iraq along sectarian lines. Childers was careful, however, to distance himself from the antiwar wing of his party and did not endorse a timetable for withdrawal. Like Davis, Childers tied homeland security to better border security. The Democrat argued for more resources for first responders, including local police and fire fighters. He also contended that the conflicts in Iraq and Afghanistan had hurt the nation's domestic security capabilities since so many first responders were in the National Guard and had either been, or were, deployed overseas during the past five years. Childers called for revisions to military policy to reduce the burden of overseas deployments for Guard and Reserve units.

Social Security and Medicare

One major issue that produced significant differences between the candidates was Social Security and Medicare. Childers argued that Social Security and Medicare were part of the foundations of the contemporary American political system. He asserted that the programs were a larger covenant between workers and the government and that Washington had an important duty to ensure that the programs remained solvent. Childers opposed any effort to privatize Social Security and he stated that he favored measures to extend the program's solvency, although he was vague as to the nature of these steps. The realtor and his wife owned two elder-care, assisted living facilities, and Childers pointed out that he was intimately familiar with the problems faced by the elderly. Through the campaign, he asserted that Medicare needed to be reformed to expand programs for in-home care for patients.

Davis, on the other hand, argued that Social Security and Medicare were unsustainable in their current state, since both faced looming financial crises. The Republican advocated the approach developed by the Bush administration which, in the case of Social Security, involved retaining the current system for those retired or about to retire, but privatizing a portion of the system for future retirees. He condemned Congress for not acting to protect the retirement and elderly medical systems. Yet, Davis declared that he would oppose any effort to increase the retirement age or raise taxes on employees to shoreup the system.

CAMPAIGN STRATEGY

Both campaigns endeavored to highlight the sometimes minor differences in policy between Childers and Davis and to exploit linkages with the candidates' respective national parties. They also sought to emphasize their candidates' respective experience. For instance, Childers repeatedly emphasized the fact that he oversaw sixteen years of balanced budgets as chancery clerk. Meanwhile, Davis underscored his efforts while mayor to promote economic development and attract new business and industry to Southaven. The Davis and Childers campaigns remained fairly consistent through the succession of three elections.

During the primaries, both Davis and Childers ran campaigns that appealed to conservative factions within their respective parties. However, Davis linked himself to Bush and the mainstream of the Republican Party, while Childers emphasized his willingness to break ranks with the Democratic Party, especially on social issues. In McCulloch and Russell, Davis faced opponents who endeavored to outflank him on conservative issues, forcing the Southaven mayor to the political right on most major issues during the primary campaign, positions he maintained after the primary and which were likely close to his personal political philosophy. Childers faced both conservative and liberal opponents in his primary, allowing him to chart more of a centrist course through his early campaign.

In the initial special election in April and then again in the general balloting in November, Davis and Childers faced a Green Party candidate, John M. Wages Jr., and an independent, Wally Pang. Wages captured the small wing of extremely liberal voters, while Pang, whose political leanings were close to the Libertarian Party, captured some of the voters on the political far right, especially on issues such as immigration and economic regulation.

Media

Both campaigns made extensive use of print and broadcast media. Mississippi politics is often dominated by small events such as rallies and town celebrations, rather than large campaign photo opportunities. Both Davis and Childers made obligatory appearances at a series of local events and venues, including county fairs, fish fries, and local political events.

Both candidates developed a Web presence. Davis had a more traditional approach that included a website and pages on both MySpace and Facebook, while Childers utilized a website, MySpace, Facebook, YouTube, and Flickr. Prior to the polling in each of the elections, both campaigns used automated phone messages urging citizens to vote for their respective candidates.

Image and Advertising

Childers endeavored to convey an image of a self-made man who understood the economic and social trials experienced by the working poor of the district. His campaign prominently relayed his personal history: the candidate's father died when Childers was sixteen, and the young man became the head of his household, working after school and on the weekends to take care of his mother and sister. Although he had an impoverished youth, Childers enjoyed a true Horatio Alger story in that he became a wealthy real estate broker.

The Davis campaign endeavored to emphasize their candidate's experience as both a state legislator and a mayor. The campaign also sought to emphasize family values and present Davis as a staunch defender of what it termed as "Mississippi Values" (a succession of conservative stances on social matters, centered on support for gun rights and opposition to abortion). As the economy worsened, Davis argued that increased trade and further tax relief were the best tools through which to stimulate the troubled economy.

Initially, following the March primary, Davis aired positive ads which featured endorsements by leading Republicans, including Wicker and the very popular U.S. senator Thad Cochran (R-MS), who would go on to win reelection in 2008 with more than 60 percent of the vote. After the April special election, the Davis campaign began airing negative ads which endeavored to link Childers to Obama and the more liberal factions of the Democratic Party. This was part of a broader strategy on the part of the Republican Party in Southern and conservative districts.[1] Meanwhile, Childers retained an issue-oriented campaign through the April special election and the May runoff. However, he began to respond to Davis attack advertisements ahead of the November balloting.

Because of the succession of elections, many voters reported campaign fatigue and it was unlikely that the negative advertisements of either candidate were particularly effective by the time of the general election. Nonetheless, the Childers campaign took the advertisements very seriously. The Davis campaign and its surrogates ran ads which highlighted comments by Obama and the Reverend Jeremiah Wright that were critical of the social and religious values of conservatives and specifically questioned Childers for not publicly condemning Wright's controversial comments. Spots also linked Childers to Senator John F. Kerry (D-MA), the 2004 Democratic presidential nominee who lost the district by more than twenty-five points. In addition, other anti-Childers advertisements falsely claimed that Obama had endorsed the Mississippi Democrat. In response to this inaccurate charge, Childers took the unusual step of issuing a public disclaimer that he had not been endorsed by Obama and that, in fact, his campaign had not interacted with the Illinois senator's staff. Childers's statement read "Sen. Obama hasn't endorsed my candidacy, I have not been in contact with his campaign, nor has he been in contact with mine."[2]

The Childers campaign then produced and ad that chided Davis for the attack and noted that Childers had never even met Obama. Childers had to pursue a delicate balance. On the one hand, he did not want to alienate conservative voters in the district by aligning himself with Obama and certain factions of the Democratic Party. On the other hand, he needed a large African American turnout in order to win. Meanwhile, Childers's camp ran targeted ads that linked Davis with certain unpopular policies of the Bush administration, including the administration's management of Hurricane Katrina in 2005 and Bush's veto of the State Children's Health Insurance Program (S-CHIP). S-CHIP legislation, which would have expanded insurance coverage for the many disadvantaged children of the district, was a highly popular program in Mississippi.

Finance

Both political parties devoted considerable resources to the election. Initially viewed as a safe Republican seat, after the April balloting, the GOP found itself in danger of losing the district while the Democrats saw an opportunity to not only pick up the seat but damage the Republican brand ahead of the November general elections. Through the series of elections, Davis raised $1.53 million, of which $365,000, or 24 percent, was from political action committees (PACs). His campaign spent $1.44 million.

Childers outraised and outspent his opponent in overall terms, although Davis outspent Childers during the runoff campaign. The Democrat received more than $1.83 million in contributions ($1 million or 55 percent from PACs), and spent $1.79 million. Davis collected more small-money contributions, while Childers received larger and more concentrated donations. Childers also received more funding from out-of-state sources, reflecting the new prioritization of the district seat by the national Democratic Party and the dissatisfaction with President Bush and the national Republican Party.

The national and state Democratic Parties spent or contributed about $1.9 million for the Childers campaign, while the Republicans provided approximately $1.29 million in support for Davis. The Republican money disadvantage was particularly acute following the May runoff. As the campaign for the general election commenced, Davis had just over $53,000 in cash, while Childers had more than $160,000. Furthermore, following Davis's defeat, the Republican Party reduced the amount of funding they provided, although independent groups continued to supply advertising on behalf of Davis and run ads critical of Childers.

Childers signed a pledge that his campaign would not accept contributions from pharmaceutical companies and that he would not take money from the industry if elected. He contended that the sector had created artificial barriers to patient care that caused rising prices and reduced availability of drugs and medicine.

Grass Roots

Childers had significant grassroots support in the Eastern counties and was able to align that enthusiasm with the more structured efforts of the local Democratic Party groups. Davis faced two daunting challenges in motivating supporters at the grassroots level. First, although the Bush administration remained more popular in the district than in other areas, Davis was confronted with the general malaise that affected many Republicans and generally depressed party turnout, especially in the November balloting. Second, the Republican primary had been a bitter contest with both Davis and McCullough running negative ads about the other. In addition, McCullough raised almost as much money as Davis, forcing the eventual Republican candidate to spend considerable resources. Many local analysts subsequently blamed the nature of the primary campaign for the relatively low levels of grassroots support for Davis.

Since Childers ran a campaign that emphasized his independence from the more liberal wing of the party, he did not endeavor to bring in national figures or leaders to help his campaign. He did share the stage with former president Bill Clinton at a Tupelo event, but otherwise Childers downplayed his party affiliation. The Davis campaign attempted to increase enthusiasm at the grassroots level by bringing in state and national leaders of the GOP. Popular Mississippi governor Haley Barbour stumped for Davis, as did Vice President Dick Cheney, Senator Cochran, and former senator Lott. However, Republican efforts were unsuccessful in motivating the party's base to turn out in the succession of balloting.

Bases of Support

Each candidate had significant political and geographic bases of support. For Childers, he was able to turnout the traditional Democratic base that included blue-collar and working-class Democrats and the African American community. Davis was supported by the suburban Republicans, but was unable to overcome low voter turnout in the majority Republican counties. The candidates divided the important evangelical community within the district with neither gaining a distinct advantage.

Prior to the November 2008 election, Childers was endorsed by the NRA. This was a major victory for the campaign and undercut efforts by Davis to portray Childers as a liberal Democrat. Childers was one of the authors of the Second Amendment Enforcement Act which overturned a Washington, DC, measure that restricted handgun ownership in the aftermath of the 2008 Supreme Court decision which overturned earlier gun control laws in the nation's capital. For his efforts, Childers was given an "A" rating by the NRA. Among the rural hunters and outdoorsmen of the district, the NRA support was viewed as a significant endorsement. It was also one that Davis had endeavored unsuccessfully to gain for his campaign.

ELECTION RESULTS

Through the succession of elections, Davis faced the same obstacles. He was outspent and had a difficult time motivating the Republican and Republican-leaning base in the district, especially during the November election when there was significant enthusiasm for the Democratic national ticket within the district. Meanwhile, Childers ran a near-flawless campaign that won him the endorsements of the region's major newspapers, including the Tupelo-based *Northeast Mississippi Daily Journal*, the *Commercial Dispatch* of Columbus, and the *Commercial Appeal* of Memphis.

The Primaries and Special Election

The Democratic primary united the party behind Childers. Holland, his main opponent, endorsed Childers and campaigned on his behalf, and the rest of the state and national party rallied around the winner. The Republican primary left the party divided and dispirited. Some leading Republicans maintained that McCullough was the more electable of the two candidates, others argued that the former Tupelo mayor's stint as head of the TVA made him seem an outsider in Mississippi politics. In the three elections, it is important to note that Davis underperformed in the city of Tupelo and in Lee County, McCullough's home. Many Republicans increasingly voiced concerns that their candidate was from the wrong geographic region within the district.

In the April 22 special election, Childers received 49.4 percent of the vote, while Davis placed second with 46.3 percent. Wages and Pang each received about 1 percent, as did Holland and McCullough, whose names remained on the ballot even though both candidates had withdrawn after their defeats in their respective party's primary. There were only three weeks before the runoff, and both campaigns embarked on aggressive advertising and a flurry of public appearances. Davis's negative ads seemed to backfire and, instead of mobilizing Republicans, the strategy alienated voters.

In the May 13 runoff, Childers received 53.7 percent of the vote, while Davis secured 46.3 percent. Childers improved his showing across almost all sectors. He increased his vote share in eighteen counties, and roughly maintained his number in three other counties. Davis improved in only two counties. He expanded his margin of victory in Lee County but, more significantly, Childers increased his numbers in De Soto, Davis's home county and the heart of the Republican base, rising from 17 percent of the vote to 25 percent.[3] The Democratic victory in Mississippi, when combined with other special election losses in Illinois and Louisiana, affirmed the party's strategy of running moderate to conservative candidates in Republican-leaning districts and was a prelude to the 2008 general election.[4]

The General Election

The runoff victory meant that Childers would have the advantage of incumbency, albeit only a moderate boost given the short period of time he would be in office ahead of the November election. Still, his aforementioned sponsorship of the anti-gun control legislation affirmed his conservative status among voters. He also championed efforts to pass new S-CHIP legislation. Consequently, Childers was able to shoreup both his conservative and liberal bases. The Democrat was praised for his workman-like style in Congress and again won the endorsements of the leading newspapers in the region. The *Northeast Mississippi Daily Journal* wrote:

> We endorsed Childers in the special election last spring, and have had no regrets through the first few months of his service in Washington. He has already demonstrated the pragmatism characterizing generations of effective Mississippi House members. He has lived up to his word to reach across party lines and to vote his convictions on what is best for the district he represents.[5]

Childers maintained the central elements of his campaign. He continued to focus on healthcare and the economy in his stump speeches and advertisements. The Childers campaign did increase its criticism of Bush's economic policies.

After his defeat in the runoff, Davis reorganized his campaign and brought in new staff members. The Southaven mayor and his closest advisors sought to reinvigorate the campaign. Davis issued a series of statements apologizing for the negative nature of his advertising and pledged to lead an issues-oriented campaign for the general election. He wanted to reenergize the party's base and increase Republican turnout in November. However, after losing two elections to Childers, Davis found it difficult to raise funds for the general election. Despite the earlier pledge, his campaign again resorted to negative ads, especially following the Democratic and Republican national conventions. Davis's campaign believed that Obama's candidacy would increase African American turnout, and thus he desperately sought to balance that increase by motivating the white Republican base.

Davis was unable to close the gap with Childers. On Election Day, Childers expanded his lead for a third time, defeating Davis 54 percent to 44 percent (Wages and Pang each received about 1 percent of the vote). In Davis's De Soto County, Childers increased his percentage of the vote by 10 percentage points, rising to 35.2 percent, thanks to increased African American turnout. Including De Soto, Davis won only four of the district's twenty-two counties.

Republican efforts to link Childers to Obama and the liberal wing of the Democratic Party failed again in the November balloting. Key to Davis's defeat was the internal divisions within the district between the rural east and the suburban west. Political analyst Stuart Rothenberg argued that polling data suggested that Davis was a strong candidate among suburban Republicans, but that he was unable to reach out to independents and conservative Democrats because of the geographic divide among the counties. Rothenberg wrote that the "results demonstrate that Republicans nominated a candidate from the wrong part of the district."[6] In addition, Childers's victory did not represent a dramatic shift in the overall voting patterns of the district. Republican presidential candidate Senator John McCain (R-AZ) won majorities in eighteen of the twenty-two counties in the district, including in Childers's home county, Prentiss, where the GOP candidate won 70.4 percent of the vote (a greater margin than Bush's 65.8 percent in 2004).[7]

NOTES

1. Alexander Mooney, "Dem Beats Republican in a Race That May Predict November," CNN, May 14, 2008, http://www.cnn.com/2008/POLITICS/05/13/miss.election/index.html.

2. Mark Preston, "Republicans Use Obama as the Bad Guy in Negative Ads," CNN, May 4, 2008, http://edition.cnn.com/2008/POLITICS/05/04/obama.ads/index.html.

3. Reid Wilson, "GOP Stunned by Loss in Mississippi," *Real Clear Politics*, May 14, 2008, http://www.realclearpolitics.com/articles/2008/05/gop_stunned_by_loss_in_mississ.html.

4. Ken Dilanian, "After Losses, Republicans Fear Public Has Lost Confidence in Party," *USA Today*, May 15, 2008, sA6.

5. *Northeast Mississippi Daily Journal*, "Editorial: Our Endorsements," October 29, 2008, http://www.djournal.com/pages/archive.asp?ID=281213.

6. Stuart Rothenberg, "Mississippi Special: Why Childers Won and Why Davis Lost," *Roll Call*, May 15, 2008.

7. Greg Giroux, "Reach Exceeds Grasp—Again—for Most Candidates," *CQ Politics*, December 1, 2008, http://www.cqpolitics.com/wmspage.cfm?docID=news-000002992110.

3

Missouri District 6 Race (Barnes v. Graves)

"Change" Comes Up Short against a Negative "Values" Campaign in a Rural District

Daniel E. Smith

Kay Waldo Barnes
Age: 70
Sex: Female
Race: Caucasian
Religion: Unlisted
Education: M.A., secondary education (University of Missouri, Kansas City, 1960); B.A., secondary education (University of Kansas, 1959)
Occupation: Professor; retired business owner
Political Experience: Mayor of Kansas City (1999-2007); City Council of Kansas City (1980-1999); Jackson County Commissioner (1974-1979)

Samuel B. "Sam" Graves
Age: 45
Sex: Male
Race: Caucasian
Religion: Baptist
Education: B.S., agronomy (University of Missouri, Columbia, 1985)
Occupation: Farmer
Political Experience: U.S. House of Representatives (2001-present); Missouri State Senate (1995-2001); Missouri State House (1993-1995)

CHARACTERISTICS OF THE DISTRICT

The most important characteristic of Missouri's 6th Congressional District is not partisan makeup, employment patterns, or demographics, but its geographic dimensions. The district extends from the suburbs of Kansas City to the northwestern corner of Missouri, and eastward across the northern regions of the state for over 100 miles. It encompasses 13,000 square miles—larger than eight states—includes 26 counties, 200 cities and towns, and 111 school districts. Just under two thirds of the district's population, estimated at 655,000, resides in four counties: Buchanan, Clay, Platte, and the eastern portion of Jackson; the remaining 34 percent are scattered across 22 counties comprising 98 percent of the district's land area.[1]

The sprawling nature of the district forces the candidates and their campaigns to rely more extensively on grassroots support, from local party organizations and civic and community organizations. But candidates also rely on interpersonal relationships between supporters and their neighbors. In the urban portions of the district like St. Joseph and the Kansas City suburbs, television and radio advertisements reach large numbers of people, making the investment worthwhile; but the same is not true in the vast rural expanses of the district. And because those rural areas contain a third of the population, candidates cannot afford to ignore them. Of course, as discussed below, media advertising was terribly important in the 2008 race. But even with such advertising, the only way to effectively campaign district-wide is through a network of volunteers and existing local organizations. Capitalizing on these grassroots relationships, often irrespective of party, is critical to electoral success in the 6th District, where significant face-to-face contact by the candidate is physically impossible. In these ways the district compels campaigns that more closely resemble statewide campaigns than a typical district race.

The physical structure of the district not only shapes the type of campaigns, it also magnifies incumbent advantage. In most elections, the incumbent, particularly one with long-standing ties to the district, has greater name recognition, an established support network, and a significant head start in forging positive relationships with local groups.

Demographic Character of the Electorate[2]

There is diversity, and then there is *diversity*. Compared to the rest of the state, particularly other districts with large rural components, the district is quite diverse in economic disparity, industry, and education. It is remarkably homogeneous, however, in the racial, ethnic, and religious makeup of the population.

Median household income was $41,225, based on the 2000 Census; per capita income in 2007 was $25,388, several thousand dollars above the statewide figure for designated rural areas. Only 1.3 percent in the district have incomes over $200,000, whereas nearly 10 percent are below the poverty line, and 8 percent receive food stamps or some other form of public assistance. The vast majority of the district's residents, 72 percent, own their own homes.

While 21 percent of the district hold bachelor's degrees and 6.7 percent hold a graduate degree, another 10 percent (above twenty-five years of age) did not complete high school.

Based on the 2000 Census, the district is 92 percent white, non-Hispanic, with minority populations far below the statewide average of 16 percent. To break it down further, the district's population is 3 percent African Americans, 2 percent Hispanic, 1 percent Asian, and a total of 1.9 percent foreign-born. Four percent of the population speaks a primary language other than English.

The district is also remarkably homogeneous in its family units. Of the total population, including those under twenty-five years of age, married couples comprise 56 percent, and 24.9 percent of the district's residents are married with children. Those self-identified as having same-sex partners comprise 0.4 percent.

While figures are not available regarding religious affiliation, the district is also above national and statewide averages regarding the standard measure of religiosity; 50 percent of the district's residents attend religious services regularly, and 26 percent attend occasionally.

Major Urban Areas and Employment/Occupational Characteristics

As noted above, the district includes two major urban and suburban areas: portions of the Kansas City suburbs, including Blue Springs, Liberty, and Gladstone; and the City of St. Joseph, located approximately 50 miles north of downtown Kansas City. The rest of the district is predominantly rural, with towns ranging from under 50 to just over 10,000 in population. Therefore, it is not surprising that the district has a diverse employment base, with significant numbers of blue-collar (26.8 percent), white-collar (58.6 percent), and service employees (14.6 percent); and a significant number of both agricultural and jobs.[3]

Party Balance and Electoral History

The 6th District is best described as historically balanced, but conservative and increasingly Republican. Before Sam Graves won the seat in 2000, it had been held by Democrat Patsy Ann "Pat" Danner, for four terms. Danner announced in 1999 that, for health reasons, she would not seek reelection, and Mr. Graves narrowly defeated her son Steve Danner to win the seat. Historically, the U.S. House seat has swung back and forth between the two major parties without a clear partisan preference. However, the district has a decidedly conservative bend—Pat Danner, for example, held conservative positions on social issues such as abortion and sexual orientation—and has become increasingly Republican in national and statewide elections since backing Bill Clinton for president in 1992 and 1996.[4] Voters in the district backed President George W.

Bush by wide margins in 2000 and 2004, and preferred John McCain over Barack Obama by ten points in the 2008 presidential race. In 2006, the district backed Senator Jim Talent (R-MO) over the victor, Claire McCaskill (D-MO). At the state level, voters in the district have sent a majority of Republicans to the House and Senate for the past several terms.[5]

As is fairly common at the local level, partisanship matters less. With over two dozen counties and literally hundreds of towns and small communities scattered throughout the district, local elections are often dominated by one party for years, irrespective of how the same voters decide statewide and national elections. As noted shortly before the election by political scientist Robert Dewhirst of Northwest Missouri State University, "There are a lot of Democrats in the district, but many are conservative Democrats. On social issues in particular, they'll vote Republican."[6]

Key Voting Blocs

Key voting blocs in the 6th District are closely tied to the demographic character of the populace. Because there is no dominant industry or demographic, the candidates must be wary in focusing on particular voting blocs. Certain general patterns do emerge, however. Covering the rural northern expanse of the district is the rural/agricultural bloc, and its members demand attention to their economic needs, receiving $1.6 billion in farm subsidies between 1995 and 2006.[7] This group of voters is also motivated by socially conservative issues such as abortion and family values. The Kansas City suburbs are heavily white collar and in the service occupations, with higher per capita incomes and a greater focus on economic issues.

District-wide, there is a sizable senior citizen population, representing over 13 percent of the public (and a higher percentage of likely voters).[8] In addition, due to the lack of racial, ethnic, and cultural diversity, candidates can, and often feel compelled, to treat the socially conservative white majority as a voting bloc. This manifests itself in candidates touting socially conservative credentials and assailing even the slightest deviation from those values. It also makes issues like gay marriage—which was banned by a state constitutional amendment in 2006—immigration, and foreign terrorist threats far more prevalent in campaigns than one might expect, given those issues' marginal impact on rural Missouri as a practical matter.

THE CANDIDATES

Sam Graves

Samuel B. "Sam" Graves sought his fifth consecutive term as the representative for the 6th District in 2008. A native and lifelong resident of Tarkio,

Missouri, a small town in the far northwestern corner of the district, Graves attended the University of Missouri at Columbia, earning a B.S. degree in agronomy. While he owns a family farm and prides himself as being a sixth generation farmer and small business owner, he has spent much of his adult life serving as an elected official. Graves was elected to the State House of Representatives in 1992 and the State Senate in 1994 and 1998, before running successfully for the U.S. House in 2000.

At the time of the election, Graves was the ranking member of the House Subcommittee on Public Buildings, Economic Development, and Emergency Management. He served on the Agriculture, Small Business, and Transportation Committees, leaving himself well-positioned to serve his rural and suburban constituents.[9]

In Congress, Graves has been, for the most part, a loyal Republican, voting with his party over 95 percent of the time, and supporting President Bush's domestic and foreign policy agendas with few exceptions. Two significant exceptions to his loyalty to president and party are his opposition to school vouchers (his wife is a teacher, which may have influenced his views on the issue) and his support for enormous agricultural subsidies, which is a virtual necessity for a representative from the heavily agricultural district.[10] Normally, when he opposes his own party, he does so from further to the political right, advocating deeper tax and spending cuts, and harsher immigration restrictions. For the most part, however, Graves has kept a low profile in Washington and in the district. He sponsors few bills, has few legislative highlights, and avoids the spotlight. His three most prominent acts in Congress have been his amendment to mandate that 95 percent of funds for the No Child Left Behind program be spent in the classroom, which gained bipartisan support; his uncharacteristically vocal opposition to the bailout of financial institutions in October 2008; and his dubious use of nearly $275,000 in education funds to address the problem of "Goth culture" in Blue Springs, Missouri, schools, which was publicly ridiculed by the group Citizens Against Government Waste and Senator McCain.

The incumbent is described by friends and colleagues as a dedicated family man, who is unpretentious, unassuming, and almost shy.[11] Yet he is also known to be ambitious and a fierce and, at times, ruthless, campaigner. A 2004 article in *The Pitch*, a Kansas City news publication, documented some of the more colorful exploits of the Graves campaign team over the years, particularly those of Jeff Roe, his former campaign manager and chief of staff.[12] Roe's modus operandi is to go on the attack early, focusing as much as possible on wedge issues and character rather than substance, and to use all available means to win. In Graves's 2000 campaign, he accused his opponent, Steve Danner, of having been sued for unpaid hospital bills; however, the bills in question belonged to another man named Steve Danner, a fact Graves eventually acknowledged but never apologized for.[13] In 2006, the Graves campaign ran advertisements labeling his opponent, a sixty-three-year-old grandmother, Sara Jo Shettles, a pornographer. The basis for the claim was that Shettles had once sold advertisements for the science magazine *Omni*, whose parent company at the time also owned *Penthouse* magazine.[14]

Graves has developed a reputation for aggressive negative campaigning, and has had success doing it. These efforts have not always come without a price, however. Graves is known to have a less-than-friendly relationship with Missouri's powerful senior senator, Kit Bond (R-MO).[15] He and his campaign staff have also angered fellow Republicans at the state and local level, leading to formal complaints, at least one lawsuit being filed, and Republican officials crossing the aisle to support his Democratic opponents.[16] Most recently, Missouri's Republican Speaker, Ron Jetton, lent at least tacit support to Mayor Barnes's campaign.[17] Nonetheless, Graves remains a formidable incumbent, popular in his district, with a political future still very much on the rise.

Kay Waldo Barnes

Kay Barnes has had a long, distinguished professional career in politics and in the private sector. A native of St. Joseph, and cousin of the legendary Walter Cronkite, she has spent most of her adult life in the Kansas City area. After receiving a B.S. from the University of Kansas, and an M.S. from Missouri–Kansas City, both in secondary education, Barnes started Kay Waldo, Inc., a human resources consulting firm. In 1974, she was one of the first two women ever elected to the Jackson County Commission. She subsequently was elected to the Kansas City Council in 1979. She is best known, however, for her two terms as the first female mayor of Kansas City, from 1999 to 2007. During her tenure, she oversaw the revitalization of the city's downtown area, and led the effort to develop the Sprint Center.[18]

When her second term ended, Mayor Barnes accepted a position as Distinguished Professor of Public Leadership at Park University. At almost the same time, however, she was being recruited by congressional Democrats to challenge Graves. She did, announcing her candidacy in May 2007.

The former mayor brought a great deal of political capital and heavy hitters to the campaign. As a recently retired mayor with a generally positive record, she was viewed from the start as a serious contender, unlike Graves's three previous general election opponents. Highly regarded in the Missouri Democratic Party, she also could point to a bipartisan track record, praise from local media outlets, and a wealth of experience as a legislator, executive, and, most important, as a tough campaigner. She was endorsed early by EMILY's List and was reportedly promised significant financial assistance by the DCCC.[19]

Barnes did not, however, enter the 6th District race without some obstacles. While a native of St. Joseph, she has far stronger ties to the Kansas City urban center, which does not endear her to the core of the 6th District. While the district does include portions of the Kansas City suburbs, they are predominantly Republican areas, which weakened her strategy of winning in the urban centers to offset the incumbent's rural strength. Her message of change, an attempt to tie her opponent to the unpopular policies of President Bush and the Republican Party while linking herself to the national Democrats, was also problematic. First, the district is less receptive to the change message in general. Second, 6th District voters are passionate about the "values" campaigns run by Graves. Third, Barnes's record was sufficiently and demonstrably progressive so as to provide Graves a great deal of ammunition. For example, EMILY's List raised money for the candidate, but it also labeled her pro-choice in a decisively pro-life district. Fourth, Barnes is twenty-five years older than Graves, making the pitch for change and a fresh face difficult.

CAMPAIGN ISSUES

A number of policy issues were addressed by the candidates in the campaign. Serious discussion of the issues, however, never really occurred, and even when raised took a back seat to what devolved into a campaign of generalizations and personal attacks.

Energy Policy, Particularly Oil Prices

Early in the campaign, Barnes seized on the skyrocketing cost of oil and gasoline to call for changes to energy policy and launch attacks that Graves was "in the pocket of big oil." Noting that her opponent accepted significant campaign contributions from the oil industry, she accused him of opposing reasonable measures to curb speculation in the oil market and curb excessive profits by energy companies. In a particularly harsh criticism, Barnes attacked Graves's September 2008 vote against the Renewable Energy and Job Creation Act as putting loyalty to his party and contributors ahead of the needs of his constituents.[20] Environmental groups supporting the challenger added their criticism of the incumbent's votes to protect oil and gas companies' royalties and tax incentives, as well as his voting record in opposition to clean energy initiatives.[21]

For his part, during the August 2008 recess, Graves joined a group of Republican legislators keeping the House technically in session to force a vote on expanding energy drilling. When the House subsequently let expire the long-standing moratorium on off-shore drilling, Graves hailed it a major step toward energy independence, and attacked his opponent for standing with Nancy Pelosi in opposing increased oil exploration.[22]

Breaking through the campaign rhetoric and name-calling, the candidates' positions were actually carbon copies of their parties' and presidential candidates' positions; both supported a comprehensive energy plan, with the Republican placing greater emphasis on oil and natural gas exploration, and the Democrat favoring greater focus on alternative, renewable sources. Barnes initially gained some traction with her focus on high gasoline prices. However, the price of oil declined at the very end of the campaign to roughly $2.00 per gallon from a high of nearly $4.00 in Missouri, which ended her momentum on the issue.

Cultural Issues

Consistent with his prior campaigns, Graves attacked his opponent early and often as a liberal, focusing attention on her support for gay rights and abortion. He also used his opposition to immigration as a cultural issue by framing it as an "us versus the invaders" argument. This position appealed to many of the district's constituents, who were also leery of any "disruptive" change. In its first significant campaign advertisement, in May 2008, Graves gained national notoriety by tying Barnes to House Speaker Nancy Pelosi and "San Francisco values":

> "In San Francisco, Nancy Pelosi's throwing a party for Kay Barnes," the ad's narrator says, over a groovy disco score. "Barnes, it seems, subscribes to those notorious San Francisco values, meaning: Yes to same-sex marriage. Yes to abortion. Yes to amnesty for illegal immigrants."

During that recitation of liberal stances, the ad shows a multiracial trio dancing suggestively in front of a bar. The trio is comprised of a man wearing a cowboy hat and two women, one of whom has terrible hair. It is not clear whether the ad is implying that one or all of them are homosexual or illegal immigrants, but it is suggested.[23] The advertisement was criticized as homophobic, xenophobic, and racially tinged, prompting criticism from both sides of the political aisle and suggestions that, this time, Graves's harsh tactics might backfire. The Barnes campaign hit back aggressively with its own ad attacking the "Sam Graves' negative campaign. It's sad. . . . A pathetic record. A pathetic campaign."[24]

But the Graves campaign simply continued its efforts to depict Barnes as not sharing 6th District values, and the Barnes campaign became increasingly less effective rebutting the attacks. Regarding immigration in particular, Barnes never conveyed a clear, decisive position even though these issues were not before the voters in Missouri or even on the legislative agenda in Congress in 2008. Yet, in the long term, the Graves campaign was effective in communicating its message. Graves may not have convinced voters that Barnes was evil incarnate, but it certainly questioned her "values" and painted her as not in sync with the district's voters.

The Economy and Financial Crisis

As she did with energy, Barnes sought to focus early and often on economic policy, especially the failure of the Bush administration to control spending, pay for its tax cuts, or provide meaningful supervision over the excesses of the market. The financial meltdown in the fall of 2008 should have been a boon for the Barnes campaign, as it was for so many other Democratic campaigns around the country. Yet, as with cultural issues, the challenger never quite found her voice. As early as spring 2007, Mayor Barnes decried the Bush administration's hands-off approach to regulating the markets and the explosion of the national debt. Labeling Graves as complicit in these failures, Barnes compared him in an October 16, 2008, debate to the "least productive employee in a failed company."[25] But her own plans for righting the economy often lacked substance, focusing rather on generalities such as "improving oversight and regulations," and "helping the middle class."

Thus, while the challenger was able to keep on the offensive for much of the campaign regarding the economy, she was unable to translate this offensive into votes. By the time the financial crisis hit full tilt in the fall of 2008, the Barnes campaign had lost steam and the candidate seemed less sure of what approach she should take to the deepening economic gloom. At this point, Graves made a tactical decision to oppose Bush's bailout plan and to do so publicly and emphatically. Barnes took much longer to arrive at an opinion on the bailout, and her lukewarm statements did not resonate. There was little movement in the polls due to the candidates' positions on the bailout, but the Barnes campaign's failure to take the lead on the issue likely cost the candidate her last opportunity to cut into Graves's lead.

CAMPAIGN STRATEGY

Barnes entered the race determined to accomplish three things: (1) depict the incumbent as a loyal foot soldier in a failed, cynical Republican regime; (2) appeal to voters as a commonsense advocate for new policies; and (3) connect with voters as one of them. Graves's campaign seemed to have two goals: (1) attack his opponent as a liberal outsider; and (2) emphasize his strong ties to the district.

Media

As a race identified early on as high-stakes, the campaigns relied heavily on broadcast advertising, as well as mass mailings. As documented below, both campaigns raised record funds for the 6th District, enabling more extensive media buys. After an initial flurry of negative ads in the late spring of 2008 and the subsequent lull through the barely contested Democratic primary, the two campaigns began bombarding the local media with messages emphasizing their preferred messages. Given the characteristics of the 6th District, however, media buys were strategically employed to create favorable caricatures of the candidates and to reinforce grassroots campaign efforts. The media messages—radio and television alike—were simple, simplistic, and often biting. Graves contrasted his "salt of the earth," long-standing ties to the community with a caricature of his opponent, who he said was a "liberal, pro-gay, pro-immigration, tax-and-spend big city mayor." He did not try to explain his own near-record deficit spending; it was simply ignored.

Barnes sought to establish her 6th District bona fides through family images, while trying to promote a caricature of Graves as a lackey of corporate America, particularly big oil, and a blind partisan supporter of an unpopular president. When these caricatures were not enough, the candidates simply lowered the bar further.

Image and Advertising

This campaign was never about substance. It was a war of attrition between candidates that disagreed on policy and shared a palpable disdain for each other. Issues were merely vehicles to launch personal, often petty and distorted attacks on the opponent's character or qualifications.

Regarding energy policy, the Barnes campaign repeatedly accused Graves of taking money from the oil companies, then voting time and again to give them tax breaks even though the industry was posting record profits. The campaign also cited the Graves family's investments in several ethanol plants, implying that the incumbent could reap financial benefits from his support for ethanol subsidies. For its part, the Graves campaign equated Barnes's hesitancy on off-shore drilling as the Nancy Pelosi position—connecting the issue attacks on Barnes's liberalism. Graves also claimed that both candidates received oil industry money, "but she launders it through congressmen who take money from oil companies and then donate to her campaign."[26]

Economic policy was a vehicle for allegations of financial wrongdoing, mismanagement, tax evasion, and poor oversight. Most notable among these efforts were the Graves campaign's assertions that Barnes was responsible for the failure of Fannie Mae because she had served on its advisory board, and that her campaign manager orchestrated a sweetheart deal with City Hall to buy out a failing corporation, an allegation the Mayor flatly denied. These allegations were raised at the candidates' October 16 debate, as well as in campaign ads. The Barnes campaign offered its own attacks. The campaign seized upon news reports that the incumbent had accepted free airline travel from a contractor in the district, and that his family was personally benefiting from his legislative support for biodiesel. In perhaps his most successful television spot of the campaign, Graves responded to these allegations by appearing with his young daughter, who touted his endorsements by teachers and firefighters, noted he still does chores on the farm, and closed by saying, "I trust you."[27] During the final weeks of the campaign, the Barnes team also attacked Graves over allegations he had multiple airplanes for which he had neither declared nor paid property taxes, and that his family had an illicit arrangement with the Tarkio airport. The claims were largely debunked by local officials and media, but they lasted several news cycles before fading.[28]

Finance

The 6th District campaign, while ordinary in many respects, was hardly ordinary from the financial perspective. Graves raised over $2.58 million and spent $2.56 million on his campaign. Barnes raised and spent even more: $2.77 million and $2.75 million, respectively. The campaigns combined raised nearly $5.4 million. By contrast, Graves raised and spent approximately $1.2 million in 2006, and his opponent raised a paltry $131,000; in 2004 the figures were $1.7 million and $861,000, respectively, meaning the 2008 campaign more than doubled previous campaign spending in the district, shattering the old record by nearly $3 million.[29]

Total independent expenditures supporting or opposing the two candidates totaled another $1.86 million. On the Graves side, just under $69,000 was spent supporting his effort, and nearly $579,000 was spent in negative attacks on Barnes; most of these expenditures were by the NRCC, which spent only $16,000 supporting their incumbent, but almost $573,000 attacking his opponent. On the Barnes side, over $235,000 was spent in support of the Barnes campaign, and just under $204,000 was spent in negative attacks on Graves; the bulk of these expenditures were incurred by the DCCC, which spent $200,324 supporting their candidate and opposing the Republican. When independent expenditures are accounted for, the challenger's monetary advantage evaporates.[30]

Nor were the funds unlimited or used equally. As polling data showed the race slipping away in the final month, the DCCC cut off additional funds for Barnes. The Graves campaign, despite being outspent overall, was able to spend more money in the final weeks before the election, enabling the candidate to close particularly strong.

Grass Roots

As previously noted, grassroots support is critical to running a successful campaign in the 6th District. The Graves campaign had been developing a support network for years. Therefore, the keys to a serious challenge to Graves were for Mayor Barnes to develop a competing network and to win big among conservative Democrats, young people, and independent voters looking for an alternative to the status quo. Her inability to exploit Graves's vulnerabilities in the district, and present herself as a viable alternative, was a matter of both style and strategy. Despite her obvious prowess as a fundraiser and proven capabilities as a mayor, the challenger never warmed to campaigning in the district.

A case in point: For reasons unknown, Graves had long refused to appear on the campus of Northwest Missouri State University. Northwest, located in Maryville, the largest population center north of St. Joseph, serves over 6,000 students and is the largest employer in the district north of St. Joseph. During the campaign, Graves refused to hold one of the candidate debates at Northwest, and declined invitations to appear at either of the candidate forums on campus or in the town of Maryville, or to schedule another event to meet Northwest students and/or answer constituents' questions in a campaign setting. This refusal presented a golden opportunity for the Barnes campaign to make inroads into the heart of the district. Rather than attend one of the events to highlight her willingness to appear, the campaign simply issued a statement regretting that a debate would not be held in Maryville, and relied upon student and community activists to express disappointment. The opportunity to depict Graves, who was dependent on his close relationship to the district, as unwilling to even speak with constituents in one of the largest towns in the district, should not have been passed up. Moreover, when Barnes did schedule an appearance, her staff selected a late Friday afternoon time, thereby guaranteeing a tiny, less than enthusiastic audience.

A second example is that, on multiple occasions, Barnes appeared ill-at-ease and somewhat ill-prepared when speaking with different groups in the district. On one such occasion, she spoke to a group of students and faculty at a local university. In her remarks, she never once mentioned education, did not have a position on other issues, and offered vague, canned statements, leading one attendee to comment, "[i]t seemed like she saw corn on the drive into town, and decided, 'there's corn here; time for my agricultural stump speech.'" The end result of such performances was to deflate enthusiastic Democratic supporters, reduce the potential volunteer pool, and to give some voters little reason to support her on

Election Day. Running against a seasoned incumbent, one can ill-afford this type of lost opportunity.

Bases of Support

In addition to their perceived demographic strengths—Mayor Barnes in the Kansas City suburbs and Representative Graves in the rural north—the candidates were able to rely on a number of key support groups, both local and national. Graves, as always, received significant financial and logistical support from rural organizations, including the Missouri Farm Bureau, business and political interest groups who have helped support his campaigns over the past two decades, the local, statewide, and national Republican Party, and a vast array of community organizations. The state and county Republican party organizations opened campaign headquarters throughout the district beginning midsummer 2008, with offices in the smaller towns opening up to a month before the election. These offices served to recruit and coordinate campaign volunteers and support the party's "get out the vote" efforts. Graves was bolstered by campaign appearances by President Bush and Vice President Cheney, and received the endorsement of the *St. Joseph News-Press*, the most widely read newspaper in the district north of Kansas City.

The Barnes campaign was also able to solicit aid from a number of diverse sources. The chief differences were that the Republican presidential campaign was folded into the party network, whereas the Obama organization remained largely independent of the state Democratic Party apparatus and that the Barnes campaign did not have nearly the physical volunteer base that the Graves campaign was able to put together in the district. However, the challenger had an impressive array of endorsements, including Republican and Democratic mayors, the *Kansas City Star*, community and business leaders in the Kansas City area. She also was a beneficiary of the DCCC's inaugural "Red to Blue" program, which provided logistical and financial support to selected candidates in competitive congressional races.[31]

ELECTION RESULTS

The Numbers

Ultimately, despite early signs of trouble for the incumbent, the race was not close. Graves was reelected by a comfortable margin, receiving just under 60 percent of the vote (see table 3.1).[32] This was the first time since his initial election to the House in 2000 that he received less than 60 percent, a benchmark number which for some election experts is viewed as a sign of eroding support. One must remember, however, that despite the district being quite conservative and, certainly of late, reliably Republican in statewide and national races, a drop-off of a few percentage points is to be expected in an election like 2008, where the Republican brand took a serious hit due to the unpopularity of President Bush and his party. With a substantial number of low- and middle-income voters, it is not surprising to see a slight decline in support for a Republican incumbent when Republicans are blamed for a bad economy. Nonetheless, Graves won by only a slightly smaller margin of the vote than in 2002, 2004, and 2006, when he faced far less threatening opponents in terms of fund-raising, experience, and name recognition.[33]

Notably, as shown in table 3.2, Barnes did not benefit from this decline; the transfer of votes from the incumbent was reflected as much in gains by the Libertarian candidate (compared to past elections) as by the Democratic challenger.

Analysis

In an exceedingly difficult year for Republicans, and with the challenger raising and spending more money than the incumbent, this race was none-

Table 3.1. Vote Totals

Candidate	Total Votes	Percentage of Votes
Sam Graves (REP)	196,526	59.4%
Kay Barnes (DEM)	121,894	36.9%
Dave Browning (LIB)	12,279	3.7%

Table 3.2. Comparison of Voting

Candidate	Total Votes	Percentage of Votes
2002		
Sam Graves (REP)	131,151	63.0%
Cathy Rinehart (DEM)	73,202	35.2%
Erik Buck (LIB)	3,735	1.8%
2004		
Sam Graves (REP)	196,516	63.8%
Charles Broomfield (DEM)	106,987	34.8%
Erik Buck (LIB)	4,352	1.4%
2006		
Sam Graves (REP)	150,882	61.6%
Sara Jo Shettles (DEM)	87,477	35.7%
Erik Buck (LIB)	4,757	1.9%
Shirley Yurkonis (PRO)	1,679	0.7%

theless nowhere near as competitive as many experts, including party insiders and both campaigns, anticipated. Why? First and foremost, in congressional elections, incumbents win, and they win in increasingly higher percentages. In recent elections incumbents have won at rates as high as 98 percent of the time; even in decisive "change" elections—most recently in 1994 and 2006—incumbents seeking reelection still won approximately 94 percent of the time.[34] Despite the initial excitement engendered by Mayor Barnes entering the race, polling consistently showed Rep. Graves with a comfortable lead, extending across geographic and demographic categories. Only in the July Survey USA poll did the race appear competitive; every other poll showed at least a nine-point gap, which steadily widened throughout the fall campaign.[35]

It is often said that the financial advantage incumbents have is a primary reason for their success in retaining office. This election, however, runs afoul of that theory, as incumbency quite clearly remained the ultimate trump card. Graves entered the race a four-term incumbent, with all the tangible and intangible advantages incumbency yields. He was far better known in the district, dramatically so as one moved further away from the Kansas City suburbs. While Barnes was born and raised in the district, most of her adult professional life was spent in the Kansas City area which, while geographically proximate, is in many ways a world apart from the northern extremities of the 6th District. By contrast, Graves spent most of his adult life there, and has represented the district as a state and national legislator for the past sixteen years. Like most successful incumbents, he has cultivated strong personal, family, and political relationships in the district, giving him a significant head start against even a well-positioned challenger. In towns like Lancaster and Chillicothe, the high-profile former mayor of Kansas City could be dubbed the "big city mayor" and viewed as a virtual alien, while her attacks on Graves's cozy relationships with oil executives lacked staying power when presented to voters who already viewed him as one of their own. This is true notwithstanding the challenger's ability to match the incumbent's media buys. Put simply, Graves invested years into defining himself to the district's voters, both as their representative and as one of their own, before Barnes entered the game.

Additionally, Barnes did not run an effective campaign, particularly in the rural third of the district where Graves won by huge margins, as shown in table 3.3. Given the unpopularity of the Republican Party in 2008, Graves's slim legislative accomplishments, and his heavily partisan legislative record, Barnes had an opportunity to tie her opponent to unpopular policies in Washington, DC. She also had sufficient funds to do so. But absent a scandal, it takes more than an unpopular president and political party to bring down an entrenched incumbent, even in that rare case where the challenger has a funding advantage. It is critical for the challenger to present herself as a viable alternative, in terms of policies, capabilities, and most important, a sense of familiarity. Kay Barnes entered the race with impressive credentials as a former Kansas City mayor, but particularly outside the Kansas City area she was largely unsuccessful connecting with voters, and even in the Kansas City suburbs, thought to be her base, she did not win a majority of the vote. The task was a tall order given the incumbent's inherent advantages; but the Barnes campaign lacked a consistent, compelling message that resonated with the district's voters or effectively undermined the incumbent's strengths, and the candidate herself never appeared to "find her voice" during the campaign.

The negative tone of the campaign also played to the incumbent's strengths and accentuated the challenger's difficulties. To begin with, personal attack campaigns and wedge issues are Graves's style and that of his advisor, Jeff Roe. The Graves campaign's "San Francisco values" commercial did create some negative backlash, even receiving criticism from the *Washington Post*, but it helped establish two of the campaign's key negative themes: (1) homophobia and, more generally, (2) the challenger as having "liberal values" out of touch with the district. The Graves campaign returned often to homosexuality as an issue, accusing the challenger of promoting a "homosexual agenda" in September.[36] Barnes played into the negative tone with attacks on Graves for ties to lobbyists, undeclared travel benefits, and alleged tax evasion. But, although clearly negative, the Barnes attacks lacked the audacity and viciousness of the Graves's ads. In the battle of negative attacks and labels, Graves won.

More important than winning the battle of negative attacks, however, was the substitution of attacks for substance. This also played to the advantage of the incumbent. It is difficult for a challenger to create a positive image while engaging in what is widely perceived to be a negative campaign. The War in Iraq was a dominant issue early in the campaign, only to be replaced by the nation's economic woes and the financial crisis. Voters were not debating the candidates' positions on the war or the economy; they were hearing about personal attacks. As for those voters disgusted with the tenor of the campaign, presented with a choice between two negative campaigns with little substance, they not surprisingly opted for the "devil they knew."

Furthermore, as noted above, issues played a remarkably small role in the voters' decisions. Other than the occasional high-profile event—Graves's vote and statements on the financial bailout and the candidates' formal debates—neither candidate focused on policy specifics nor presented many concrete legislative proposals. The incumbent had strategic reasons for avoiding detailed policy discussions, namely, it would highlight his party's unpopularity, and policy substance has never been his forte. For her part, the challenger was content to focus on generalities, to avoid attacks from the opposition and because her positions were not clearly defined. Policy specifics can be dangerous for a candidate, exposing her to criticism and negative attacks. However, lack of substantive policy debate made it far more difficult for the challenger to build the case for change which is necessary to unseat an incumbent.

Finally, the challenger did not benefit from any coattail effect from the presidential race. Consistent with nationwide trends, voter turnout was up in 2008, due to the historic nature of the race, as well as the simple fact that presidential races always produce higher turnout. As was the case nationwide, more votes were cast for president than Congress, but the number was less dramatic than elsewhere; 4,202 more votes were cast for president (excluding Jackson County, only a portion of which is included in the district), a difference of 1.4 percent.

A challenger might not expect to reap much benefit from the Obama phenomenon in a district known for backing conservative Republicans for statewide and national office. Indeed, Senator McCain won the district by six points. Mayor Barnes, however, ran nearly ten points behind President-Elect Obama throughout the 6th District, losing badly in St. Joseph while Obama actually won Buchanan County; losing Nodaway County by a two-to-one margin, while Obama lost by ten points; and losing by larger margins than the president-elect in twenty-five of twenty-six counties. Only in Howard County did Barnes receive a result similar to Obama.

This disparity is also not surprising. As discussed above, U.S. House races are, except in rare cases, dominated by incumbency; national trends rarely have significant impact on an incumbent's ability to win reelection. Even in elections where one party wins decisively, incumbents running for reelection have a 94 percent success rate. Dissatisfaction with President Bush, and concerns about the U.S. economy, did not translate into votes for the challenger, nor were 6th District voters anxious to blame their representative even for policies they disliked.[37]

CONCLUSION

The Missouri 6th District race illustrated that the more things may appear to change, the more they stay the same. How a district is configured—geographically, demographically, politically—matters as much, if not more, than anything candidates do. The power of incumbency is magnified by the district's size and layout, which make the task of introducing a challenger to the voters daunting even to a skilled campaigner. The residents of the district are not significantly issue-driven, making it that much more difficult to make inroads against an established incumbent. And negative campaigning, while a preferred tool of incumbents and challengers alike, including

Table 3.3. County Votes

County	Graves, Sam REP	Barnes, Kay DEM	Browning, Dave LIB	Total Votes 6th District U.S. House	Total Votes 6th District President	McCain REP	Obama DEM
ANDREW	5,855	2,597	258	8,710	8,790	5,279	3,345
ATCHISON	2,112	780	83	2,975	2,976	1,936	1,000
BUCHANAN	21,487	15,866	1,477	38,830	39,031	19,110	19,164
CALDWELL	2,967	1,321	218	4,506	4,560	2,654	1,814
CARROLL	3,227	1,166	122	4,515	4,538	2,955	1,535
CHARITON	2,290	1,738	107	4,135	4,213	2,339	1,799
CLAY	59,916	42,940	4,460	107,316	109,399	54,516	53,761
CLINTON	6,121	3,731	437	10,289	10,452	5,709	4,545
COOPER	4,704	2,855	234	7,793	8,026	4,902	2,996
DAVIESS	2,521	1,077	170	3,768	3,786	2,263	1,400
DEKALB	3,086	1,382	185	4,653	4,683	2,889	1,692
GENTRY	2,136	1,022	124	3,282	3,292	1,964	1,235
GRUNDY	3,296	1,216	175	4,687	4,740	3,006	1,580
HARRISON	2,800	969	133	3,902	3,915	2,512	1,287
HOLT	1,982	552	76	2,610	2,631	1,794	802
HOWARD	2,591	2,033	156	4,780	4,817	2,708	2,036
JACKSON	21,532	13,069	1,168	35,769	185,632	92,883	90,722
LINN	3,595	2,113	183	5,891	5,927	3,140	2,638
LIVINGSTON	4,384	1,951	166	6,501	6,552	3,993	2,435
MERCER	1,271	399	60	1,730	1,748	1,169	519
NODAWAY	6,699	3,081	335	10,115	10,219	5,568	4,493
PLATTE	26,660	17,378	1,756	45,794	46,472	24,460	21,459
PUTNAM	1,667	532	51	2,250	2,339	1,591	695
SCHUYLER	1,154	692	37	1,883	1,983	1,139	775
SULLIVAN	1,709	1,070	63	2,842	2,869	1,607	1,173
WORTH	764	364	45	1,173	1,174	707	427
TOTAL	196,526	121,894	12279	330,699	484,764	252,793	225,327
Percentage	59.40%	36.90%	3.70%	—	—	52.10%	46.50%

Source: County-by Country Results, November 4, 2008, General Election Results, Missouri Secretary of State Office, www.sos.mo.gov/enrweb/raceresults.asp?eid=256&oid=56165&arc.

both candidates in this race, works much more effectively when combined with something else—familiarity, community ties, clearly defined and acceptable positions on core issues and values.

Finally, the 2008 election showed that Sam Graves is entrenched as the 6th District's man in the U.S. House of Representatives. It will take a rare challenger to unseat or even seriously threaten him. Kay Barnes, despite being a seasoned politician with ample financial resources, simply was not that challenger.

NOTES

1. Ken Newton, "Sprawling 6th District a Unique Challenge for Candidates," *St. Joseph News-Press*, September 14, 2008.
2. Demographic data in this section is taken from "U.S. House, Missouri 6th District," *CQ Quarterly 2008 Election Guide*; data not from the 2000 Census was cited in Newton.
3. *CQ Quarterly 2008 Election Guide*.
4. Maria Sudekum Fisher, "Key U.S. House Race in Missouri Heats Up," Associated Press, September 29, 2008. www.usatoday.com/news/politics/2008-09-29-214921733_x.htm.
5. Archived General Election Results, Missouri Secretary of State Office.
6. Fisher, "Key U.S. House Race."
7. Newton, "Sprawling 6th District."
8. *CQ Quarterly 2008 Election Guide*.
9. "About Sam Graves," www.Gravesforcongress.com/about.
10. Project Vote Smart, Representative Samuel B. "Sam" Graves, www.votesmart.org/voting_category.php?can_id=9425.
11. David Martin, "Goon Squad," *The Pitch*, May 13, 2004.
12. Martin, "Goon Squad."
13. Martin, "Goon Squad."
14. Russ Purvis, "The Convenient Truth," *The Landmark* (Platte County newspaper), June 6, 2008.
15. Stuart Rothenberg, "Graves vs. Barnes: A Royal Rumble in Kansas City," *The Rothenberg Report*, January 23, 2008m www.realclearpolitics.com/articles/2008/01/graves_vs_barnes_a_royal_rumble.html.
16. Martin, "Goon Squad."
17. Rothenberg, "Graves vs. Barnes."
18. "About Kay Barnes," www.kay4congress.com.
19. Rothenberg, "Graves vs. Barnes."
20. Ken Newton, "Graves Celebrates Expiration of Drilling Moratorium," *St. Joseph News-Press*, September 27, 2008.
21. Ken Newton and Alyson E. Raletz, "Political Notebook: Environmental Group Takes on Rep. Graves," *St. Joseph News-Press*, August 13, 2008.
22. Newton and Raletz, "Political Notebook."
23. Ben Pershing, "Capitol Briefing: Pelosi and Her San Francisco Values," *Washington Post*, July 28, 2008, blog.washingtonpost.com/capitol-briefing/2008/05/Pelosi_and_her_san_francisco_v.html.
24. Fisher, "Key U.S. House Race."
25. Ken Newton, "Good Manners, Sharp Words," *St. Joseph News-Press*, October 17, 2008.
26. Newton, "Good Manners, Sharp Words."

27. *National Journal*, "The Hotline," October 15, 2008, www.nationaljournal.com/hotline/hr_20080916_7895.php.

28. Ken Newton, "Airport Issue Spills into Final Debate," Prime Buzz, "Graves: The Great Plane Debate: Are They Planes or Junk?" *St. Joseph News-Press*, October 26, 2008.

29. Open Secrets, "Total Raised and Spent: Missouri District 06." Rep. Graves raised far more money, 47 percent of his total, from Political Action Committees, compared to just 21 percent of Mayor Barnes's total. On the other hand, while both candidates raised virtually the same amount of money in-state, the mayor raised substantially more from out-of-state donors.

30. Open Secrets, "Independent Expenditures."

31. Ken Newton, "Barnes Candidacy Gets Help from Washington," *St. Joseph News-Press*, July 26, 2008.

32. November 4, 2008, General Election Results, Missouri Secretary of State Office, www.sos.mo.gov/enrweb/raceresults.asp?eid=256&oid=56165&arc=1.

33. Archived General Election Results, Missouri Secretary of State Office.

34. Alan I. Abramowitz, Brad Alexander, and Matthew Gunning, "Incumbency, Redistricting, and the Decline of Competition," Charlie Cook, "Looking Back at 2006," *Journal of Politics* 68, no. 1 (2006): 75–88.

35. Pollster.com, "2008 Missouri CD-06 General Election: Graves (R-i) vs. Barnes (D)."

36. *National Journal*, "The Hotline," September 16, 2008, www.nationaljournal.com/hotline/hr_20080916_7895.php.

37. Ryan Richardson, "Biden Talks Change at Western," Griffon News, October 21, 2008, www.thegriffonnews.com/2008/10/21/biden-talks-change-at-western/.

4

Illinois District 14 Race (Foster v. Oberweis)

A National Proxy Fight for a Special Election and a Former Speaker's Seat

Jeffrey Ashley and Justin Sinner

Bill Foster
Age: 52
Sex: Male
Race: Caucasian
Religion: Not Stated
Education: Ph.D., physics (Harvard, 1984); B.S. (University of Wisconsin, 1975)
Occupation: Cofounder, Electronic Theater Controls (1975); scientist, Fermi Lab (1984)
Political Experience: None

Jim Oberweis
Age: 61
Sex: Male
Race: Caucasian
Religion: Roman Catholic
Education: MBA (University of Chicago, 1980); B.A. (University of Illinois, 1968)
Occupation: Chair, Oberweis Dairy (1986); chair of Oberweis Asset Management (1978)
Political Experience: Unsuccessful campaign for Senate (2002, 2004); unsuccessful campaign for governor (2006)

The 14th Congressional District has often been characterized as having two competing identities. The first is a historically Republican area with Downstate Illinois roots, and the second is a sprawling urban community close to the Chicago metropolitan area. The district has traditionally adhered to its Republican values and its downstate identity. When one thinks of the 14th they generally envision small towns in the west and safe and conservative suburbs in the east that are separated from the hurry and strife of Chicago politics. Despite the district's history, population growth and urban sprawl in the western counties of the district—particularly Kendall County—have intensified the conflict between these two identities.

CHARACTERISTICS OF THE DISTRICT

Party Balance

The district has been labeled a Republican stronghold for decades. The counties of Whiteside, Bureau, and Henry have historically been among the strongest Republican territories in the nation. The early formers of the Republican Party and the Grand Army of the Republic were from northern Illinois, and many of their descendents remain Republican today.[1] Thus it was no surprise that, in 2006, the Cook Partisan Voting Index for the district scored a R+5. George W. Bush won the area twice, garnering 54 percent in 2000 and 55 percent in 2004.[2]

Voting and Electoral History

Dennis Hastert (R-IL) was first elected to Congress in 1986, the only year he received fewer than 60 percent of the vote. His average margin of victory for eleven terms was 67.9 percent. Sometimes referred to as the "accidental speaker" because he was not originally vying for the position, Representative Hastert ended up serving in that position from 1999 to 2007 and was the longest serving Republican Speaker of the House in history. During his tenure as Speaker, it is well known that the district received certain benefits. For instance, in 2003 the 14th District received 43 percent of all the projects earmarked for Illinois even though the district represents only about 5 percent of the entire state's population.[3] The pork he brought into the area solidified his support over the years. Thus, factors such as history, an incumbent in leadership, and pork barrel politics have ensured that the 14th District remained in Republican control for years.

Demographic Character of the Electorate

The 14th District is 80.8 percent white and, except the eastern urban areas, is predominately upper-middle class with a median income that is

$25,546 higher than the national average of $50,740. Kendall County is the fastest growing county in the nation. From 2000 to 2007, the population grew by 77.5 percent and is now at 805,046. Subdivisions and traffic are now a part of life for many residents, and this also creates new pressures for government to provide services.[4] The fastest growing congressional district in Illinois was certainly changing. With reports coming out that, after eleven terms, Hastert was ready to resign, many experts and commentators began to wonder how these demographic changes would affect future elections.[5]

Major Urban Areas and Employment/Occupational Characteristics

Illinois' 14th Congressional District is a string of eight counties stretching from the east to the west in northern Illinois. After redistricting, the 14th now extends as far west as Henry County, almost touching the Mississippi River, and as far east as Kane, Kendall, and parts of the western edge of DuPage County, approximately 30 miles from Chicago's Loop.[6]

The district has a fairly large portfolio in terms of industry. Educational services and health care are at the top with 18.3 percent, but these are followed closely by manufacturing at 17.5 percent of all industry. No industry completely dominates the economy with occupations that are 59.4 percent white collar, 26.6 percent blue collar, and 14 percent service related.[7]

The district is also home to parts of the Fox River Valley, where the manufacturing cities of Aurora and Elgin are located.[8] Aurora has now surpassed Rockford as the second largest city in Illinois with a population that has reached 170,855 residents. Finally, the district includes the DeKalb area, which is home to Northern Illinois University and boasts some of the richest soil in the world.

Key Voting Blocs

The biggest voting bloc in this election became unaffiliated (independent) voters. While the district leans naturally Republican, Democratic enthusiasm for presidential candidate Barack Obama and changing demographics increased the number of unaffiliated voters who could be convinced to vote either way. Kane County was Hastert's old stronghold, but data indicated that the fastest growing segment in the county was independent voters.[9] The county also has seen a dramatic increase in its Hispanic population, which grew from 137,000 in 2000 to 770,000 in 2006.[10] In major cities such as Aurora and Rockford, the Hispanic population comprises approximately 40 percent of the population.[11] This is important because Hispanics are generally believed to be a key swing voting bloc.

THE CANDIDATES

Hastert announced his retirement in mid-November of 2007. This meant that a special election would have to be scheduled to determine who would finish out Hastert's 2006 term. Essentially, the winner would serve until the year's end. Then, the regular November 4 election would determine who served the next full term. Whoever won the special election would benefit from a year serving in the House of Representatives and would gain a significant incumbent advantage for the November regular election. Hastert most likely retired early hoping that his chosen Republican successor would handily win the special election. The winner would ultimately become a de facto incumbent and ensure that the district remained in Republican hands.

The Confusing Primary

While seemingly simple, the primary is where things started to get confusing for the voters. Even though the special election and the regular election were to be held on separate days, Republican and Democratic voters had to decide which candidates would receive their party's endorsement for both elections in a single primary. Why is this confusing? Basically, on February 5 voters decided who would face off in both the March 8 special election and in the November 4 general election. The conventional wisdom was that whoever won the primary for the special election would also almost surely win the later primary for the general election. Although this is ultimately what happened, it appeared, for a time, that the Democrats might be running different people in each of the elections.

The Democrats

Four Democrats—Bill Foster, John Laesch, Jotham Stien, and Joe Serra—vied for their party's nomination, but Foster, a Geneva physicist and businessman, and Laesch, Hastert's unsuccessful 2006 opponent, emerged as the main contenders. Foster ultimately won the party's nomination for the special election, 49 percent to 43 percent. Foster would run to finish out Hastert's term. But voters were also deciding who would run in November, and the winner for the party's nomination in the regular November election was unclear. Unofficial results showed that only a few hundred votes separated Foster and Laesch.[12]

Foster claimed victory in both primaries, and the campaign proceeded with its plans. Laesch refused to concede and immediately began combing precincts for irregularities or uncounted provisional ballots.[13] With the results at 42.4 percent to 42 percent (a difference of only 355 votes), the

Laesch campaign decided that there were enough provisional and absentee ballots still to be counted to forgo conceding.[14] The Laesch camp continued to pursue their legal options for over a month after the primary election. The campaign eventually conceded two days after the special election was held. On March 10, 2008, Laesch told his supporters that he had directed his attorneys to withdraw the recount petitions. He pointed to the results of the special election and the overall costliness of the recount process as his main reasons for conceding.[15]

The Republicans

Five Republicans—Kevin Burns, Rudy Clai, Mike Dilger, Jim Oberweis, and Chris Lauzen—were vying for their party's nomination. Like the Democrats, the Republicans saw two clear front-runners emerge. Oberweis, of Sugar Grove, and State Senator Lauzen, from Aurora, were spending large amounts of money and were constantly on the attack. Only Lauzen and Oberweis made it to the special election primary ballot. Lauzen had asked Hastert not to endorse any Republican primary candidate, in part because Hastert and Lauzen were not close and Hastert had endorsed Oberweis in his 2002 run for the senate. Despite Lauzen's request, the coveted endorsement from Hastert went to Oberweis.[16]

In the face of the Hastert endorsement, Lauzen had to rely heavily on a grassroots campaign. Since he was not accepted by the Republican establishment, his campaign portrayed him as the little guy without money and political clout. The "no money" theme was actually fairly accurate. Lauzen had put $325,000 of his own money into the campaign, but he was outspent over four to one by Oberweis, who contributed $1.6 million of his own fortune.[17]

The race between the two Republican front-runners was cutthroat and even comical at times. Lauzen consistently compared his fifteen years in the Illinois State Senate to Oberwieis's lack of political experience. He threw a punch right away when his campaign sent out flyers with dead cows that were meant to represent dairy owner Oberweis's failed political campaigns. (This may have been the first-ever dead cow political mailer in history!) Oberweis responded by having his "spokescow" send out a news release calling the ad an act of desperation.[18] Oberweis slammed Lauzen for taking too long to return a $100,000 campaign contribution from an owner of a business that was being sued for widespread sexual harassment and possible fraud. He called the delay a lack of judgment.[19]

Lauzen was ultimately fighting an uphill battle. Not having the endorsement of the Republican establishment and low funds would prove to be too much to overcome. Oberweis won both the special election and the regular election primaries with over 57 percent.[20] The Republican infighting between

Lauzen and Oberweis is important to the outcome of the special and general election. The bitter fighting between the two would eventually lead Lauzen to refuse official support for Oberweis in his general election run.

Putting It All Together

After the confusing, heated, and sometimes comical primaries, the voters finally decided on two millionaires. Foster, the Democrat, and Oberweis, the Republican, faced each other on March 8 to decide who would finish Hastert's term through the year. Then, both candidates would have a rematch on November 4 to determine who would represent the district for the 2008 term. The Democrats narrowly avoided running separate candidates in both elections. This would have negated any incumbency advantage that would be gained if their candidate won the first election.

Oberweis was fairly well known throughout Illinois. He had mounted unsuccessful bids for U.S. Senate and governor in the past. In addition, he was the chair of Oberweis Asset Management and chairman of Oberweis Dairy, a family-run company started by his grandfather in 1915. At the time of the election there were over forty-three Oberweis ice cream stores throughout the 14th Congressional District and larger Chicago.[21] It is safe to say that he did not suffer from a lack of name recognition, but it was unsure how much political baggage the name carried. He had a reputation for using aggressive television advertising. For instance, he was known for an ad during his Senate bid where he flew a helicopter over Soldier Field and claimed that 10,000 illegal immigrants, enough to fill the football stadium, enter the country each week.[22] He was also accused of using fake news headlines in ads during the gubernatorial primary.[23]

Conversely, Democrat Bill Foster was a political newcomer. He and his brother made millions when they started a company that is now the world's leader in theatre lighting equipment. After leaving the business, he attended Harvard and graduated with a doctorate in physics. Before deciding to get involved in politics he worked at Fermi Lab in Batavia for thirteen years. He took a leave of absence to consider a possible campaign, eventually deciding to work for Democrat Patrick Murphy in a suburban Pennsylvania district not unlike Illinois' 14th. Foster's get-out-the-vote computer software quickly earned him the nickname "Campaign Physicist."[24]

CAMPAIGN ISSUES

In terms of the issues, both national parties made the 14th District special election a proxy war. From the start, Foster heavily aligned himself with the Democratic playbook and pushed for the pullout of troops in Iraq, universal healthcare, and rolling back the Bush tax cuts. He was critical of all things Bush and attempted to tie Oberweis to Bush whenever possible. Oberweis also relied on his party's national themes. He supported keeping troops in Iraq until commanders on the ground said otherwise. He also took an early strong stance against illegal immigration and supported the Bush tax cuts.[25]

Iraq War

The Iraq War was an issue that transcended the primaries and both elections. Some in the Democratic Party felt that antiwar sentiment had reenergized the party. It certainly was the number one issue at the primary debate where the candidates argued who was the most antiwar. Foster came out in the middle and said he would only support appropriations that included a timetable for withdrawal. Throughout both the special and general election campaigns, Foster criticized the Bush administration for mismanaging the war, calling it one of the greatest foreign policy blunders in history.[26] He continuously stated that Congress should take away President Bush's blank check to run the war. In mailings, on the radio, and in television ads Foster expressed support to withdraw troops and charged that Oberweis's message was just an echo of the failed Bush policy.

Some of Oberweis's earliest attacks were about Iraq. Since Foster said we would vote against funding if a timetable was not present, Oberweis immediately accused him of cutting troop funding and raising the white flag.[27] Oberweis was against a specific timetable for troop withdrawal because it would give the enemy an advantage that could ultimately put soldiers in danger. He consistently talked about how the troop surge and General Petraeus's plan were reducing levels of violence and that the generals on the ground—and not politicians—should ultimately decide troop levels. Oberweis also accused Foster of being too vague about how he planned on getting troops home.[28]

Health Care

Health care affordability and coverage was a salient issue in both the special and general elections. Foster believed that all Americans could have affordable and comprehensive basic healthcare through a universal healthcare system that incorporated government and free enterprise.[29] Oberweis pushed for free market solutions that could drive down rising health care costs such as tax-free health savings accounts and having small businesses and the self-employed join together in a trade association to provide coverage. Statewide exchanges could then be created for them to purchase lower-cost policies.[30]

Both candidates readily attacked each other on their healthcare stances. The Oberweis campaign accused Foster of supporting a single-payer, big government system that would ultimately reduce the quality of healthcare. Foster responded by making it known that his plan is a public-private hybrid. On the other side, the Foster campaign accused Oberweis of supporting a complete ban on employer-based health insurance, which would then mean that everyone would have to fend for themselves.[31] Oberweis never called for the complete elimination of employer-based health insurance and was also charged with advocating an insurance plan that helped only the healthy and wealthy.[32]

Energy and the Economy

The rising costs of energy and the mortgage crisis took center stage in the final months of the campaign. Soaring gas prices in the summer and the sub-prime mortgage crisis in the fall of 2008 took precedence over other issues, like illegal immigration, that were salient early in the campaigns. At an October 8 forum, both candidates agreed that the government needed to take more initiative in discovering new ways to become energy independent. Oberweis, however, accused Foster of flip-flopping on the issue of drilling. Oberweis also supported suspending the gas tax.[33] Both of their plans were similar, but Oberweis focused more on producing energy at home while Foster focused more on global warming.

Gas prices fell and the mortgage and credit market crises took center stage near the end the race. Foreclosures were racking up before the special election, and both candidates disagreed on the proper response. Foster supported a New Deal–style approach similar to the Homeowners Loan Corporation that was created in 1933. Oberweis supported a more limited government approach that brings lenders and borrowers together voluntarily.[34] The credit crisis prompted congress and the president to agree on a $700 billion bailout package for the mortgage industry, which Foster supported as an imperfect but necessary action but that Oberweis opposed.[35] The economy was one of Oberweis's perceived strengths, and the campaign took advantage of the situation by hammering Foster on his support of the final bailout bill. Oberweis even called the bailout bill a worse decision than the rush into war in the Middle East.[36]

SPECIAL ELECTION CAMPAIGN STRATEGY

After the confusing primary, the candidates only had about a month to campaign for the March 8 special election. In one sense it would seem that the situation favored Jim Oberweis, a Republican who was well known all over the district versus an unknown Democrat who had only a few weeks to introduce himself to the public. Taking into account the support of Speaker Hastert, it just seemed Oberweis would win. But this was no ordinary election.

Media

The special race was a proxy for the national fight between the Republicans and the Democrats. A Foster win in such a Republican district would be used by the Democratic Congress as a referendum on President Bush and the War in Iraq. Also, since this was a special election, it received an unusual amount of attention. One observer called the special election a short and nasty campaign dominated by negativity and television attack ads.[37]

Since both campaigns had such a short amount of time, they put a lot of money into a media blitz that utilized television airings, flyers, and robo-calls. Certain flyers were targeted for specific areas and were distributed via mail and by hand. The tone was negative right away, and the Foster and Oberweis campaigns simply made outrageous back-and-forth attacks until Election Day.

Foster's first ad made his campaign's television strategy very clear. They were following the national democratic formula of tying Republicans to President Bush. In his first ad children were shown growing older and then the narrator stated that Oberweis wanted to stay in Iraq for ten years and the war would still be raging while the kids would be in college. Next, images of Oberweis and Bush were shown while the candidate was accused of following Bush's "stay the course" strategy and agreeing with Bush on most issues.[38] The Foster campaign repeatedly accused Oberweis of being Bush. Additionally, in the weeks prior to the special election, Oberweis was accused of hiring illegal immigrants, sending American jobs to China, and being a man who was willing to smear anyone who got in his way.[39]

The Oberweis campaign mainly used television attack ads to paint Foster as a big government, tax-and-spend liberal. As one reporter put it, if all of the Oberweis advertisements were true then Foster would spend everyone to the poor house, take away the ability to see their doctor, surrender to terrorists, and allow their daughters to get an abortion without telling anyone.[40] A National Republican Congressional Committee news release connected Foster with House Speaker Nancy Pelosi and it used the word "liberal" thirteen times.[41] One of Oberweis's more famous ads showed Foster saying that there is nothing in life you cannot improve by throwing money at it.[42]

Even though most people tend to focus on the candidate's television advertisements, the most outrageous and even comical attacks were in the form of flyers and "robo-calls." Most residents of the 14th District were bombarded with expensive flyers from both campaigns. These mailings were specifically targeted to certain neighborhoods depending on the type of audience the candidate was targeting. The Foster campaign was accused of purposely sending flyers to Hispanic communities that made Oberweis seem to be anti-immigrant. Foster fired back by pointing out that some of Oberweis's flyers attacking him had pictures of families who did not even reside in the 14th District.[43]

The Oberweis campaign further accused Foster of being a big government liberal through mailers. One flyer had "tax raiser" stamped on Foster's face. Another flyer had a photo of a baby on it, and it claimed that even infants will pay higher taxes under Foster.[44] The Foster campaign also utilized a large amount of flyers that were humorous and outrageous, and capitalized on the rift that occurred in the local Republican Party during the primaries. The dead cow flyers State Senator Chris Lauzen used to depict Oberweis's failed campaigns were brought back by the Democrats. One accused Oberweis of hiring illegal immigrants and believing that the cows would keep it secret.[45] Another Foster flyer depicted a mother holding a little girl at the doctor's office, and it accused Oberweis of wanting to eliminate employer-based healthcare.[46]

Both campaigns utilized robo-calling to attack each other and also remind voters about the unique Saturday election. A famous robo-call from the Democratic Congressional Campaign Committee accused Oberweis of hiring illegal immigrants at his dairy stores. Some individuals claim they received as many as six calls after 8:30 PM. Another resident claimed he had eleven robo-calls on his answering machine on the day of the special election.[47] (So many Illinois voters complained about these automated phone calls that lawmakers are seeking to ban them.)

Image and Advertising

The Foster campaign faced a serious challenge. They only had four weeks to introduce an unknown physicist to voters. Conventional wisdom suggests that Oberweis's name recognition was an advantage, but Oberweis has often been characterized as a polarizing figure who ran unsuccessful attack-driven campaigns, and many worried he would prove to be too unlikable. For instance, he never reconciled with State Senator Chris Lauzen, who had many grassroots Republican supporters in the eastern urban areas of the district.

The Foster campaign utilized the national message of change of both Hillary Clinton and Barack Obama. A new fresh face during this election proved to be an advantage. Even though Foster made plenty of attack ads, the campaign also made an effort to portray Foster as "above the fray" right from the start. Two ads during the primary touted Foster as an outsider. One of the ads featured two young boys fighting and bickering. Foster then compared those children to the bickering in Congress.[48] Foster also received a huge boost when Democratic presidential candidate Barack Obama endorsed him a in a thirty-second commercial right before the special election. Obama told voters that they did not have to wait until November to vote for change. They could vote for Foster in the Saturday special election.[49]

Finance

The campaigns received hundreds of thousands of dollars in contributions, but Foster and Oberweis had the added advantage of being millionaires. Federal filing indicated that the candidates were heavily funding their own campaigns in the run up to the special election. As of a few weeks before the campaign, Foster had loaned himself $1.3 million and Oberweis loaned himself $2.3 million.[50] Given the symbolic nature of the special election, the national parties also invested a large amount of funds into the campaigns. Both the National Democratic and Republican Congressional Committees spent over a million dollars on mailers and ads to help their respective candidates.[51]

Grass Roots

Even though the special election campaign is most remembered for nasty mailers and television ads, there was a significant grassroots effort in the race. Foster employed the same high-tech get-out-the-vote software he had invented in Patrick Murphy's Pennsylvania congressional campaign. The program was designed to make canvassing more efficient and the campaign asserted that it was very effective. On the day of the special election, the campaign had 725 people knock on doors, and they estimated that they reached 100,000 doors in total. Foster also benefited from the support of Chicago volunteers caught up in the Obama buzz.[52]

Oberweis, on the other hand, lacked a strong grassroots effort. Oberweis's main contender in the Republican primary was a grassroots candidate who was widely perceived as having been treated unfairly by the party and former Speaker Hastert.[53] The infighting led Lauzen to not support Oberweis's candidacy, possibly resulting in many of Lauzen's supporters staying home on Election Day. For example, a total of 43,000 Republican votes were cast in Kane County, Lauzen's home town, for the February 5 primary. However, Oberweis only received 28,000 votes there in the special election. Thus, some argue that the Oberweis nomination sidelined a powerful grassroots organization.[54]

SPECIAL ELECTION RESULTS

In a stunning upset, the political newcomer Bill Foster defeated Jim Oberweis in the special election. Foster received 53 percent to Oberweis's 47 percent in the traditionally Republican 14th District.[55] Foster enjoyed a great deal of support from the northern and eastern parts of the 14th District. He won the majority of the vote in Dekalb County and he garnered 65 percent of the vote in the traditionally Democratic Aurora. He also won slim majorities in the Eastern Counties of Kane, Kendall, and Dupage.[56] Democrats had been asserting that the demographic changes in the eastern part of the district had created a more Democratic-leaning population. The suburban sprawl spreading from Chicago and the increasing Latino immigrant population in the east appears to have helped Foster. Given the results and the fact that Foster's grassroots support was centered in this area, they may have been right.

A district, however, does not just change its political leanings overnight. Many other factors can be attributed to Oberweis's loss besides demographics. Many will tell you that the problem began with Oberweis, who was simply not likable. He had a large personal piggy bank and name recognition, but his name carried significant political baggage. One Illinois Republican politician complained that the party has focused too heavily on candidates who are rich enough to finance their own campaigns.[57]

Oberweis's negative playbook and reputation did not resonate with voters during a time when people in Illinois were captivated by the message of change that was being delivered by the Democratic candidates. The rise of Barack Obama was a significant threat to the Oberweis campaign. It created momentum and provided support for Foster. Obama's endorsement also allowed Foster to attach himself to the message of change. He was portrayed as an outsider who would stop the bickering in Washington. Additionally, Foster's nonconfrontational demeanor when contrasted to Oberweis's reputation helped the Democrats avoid being labeled as negative. The Foster campaign produced plenty of negative ads, but they always managed to come out more positively in the eyes of the public

Speaker Hastert's midterm resignation may have also caused more harm than good. First of all, the special election cost the counties in the district over a million dollars.[58] Many believed that if Hastert had served out his term and had a normal primary without intervention, the Democrats would not have taken the seat. It is generally party policy to not support candidates in the primary, but Hastert endorsed Oberweis anyway. The endorsement helped him win the primary, but it also aligned Oberweis with the politics of the past, which ended up hurting the Republicans.

GENERAL ELECTION CAMPAIGN STRATEGY

The general election rematch was significantly toned down from the short attack-driven special election campaign. Despite reports and calls for Oberweis to step down after his crushing defeat, his campaign assured the public that he would be running again. There was still some hope for Oberweis to win the general. The turnout for the special Saturday election was low. Only 25 percent of registered voters showed up to the polls.[59] Also, many Republican voters did not turn out. Despite the rift in the Republican Party created by the primary, it was the hope of the Oberweis campaign that many Republicans and Lauzen supporters would wake up after the stunning defeat.[60]

Media

Unlike the primary, the candidates and national parties decided not to spend millions of dollars on television advertising. Instead, the money was diverted to more inexpensive and issue-based cable ads. Both campaigns realized that the aggressive robo-calls, mailers, dead cows, and radio and television ads really turned many voters off. Oberweis now lost his fourth race (third senate attempt) where he utilized hard attacks. After his defeat, he vowed that the general election campaign would be as positive as possible, and issue-focused.[61]

Oberweis believed that the many voters just knew the stereotyped version of him. The drastic change in the tone of the Oberweis campaign was best exemplified by his first two ads. The ads portrayed him as an everyday family man and never mentioned his opponent. His daughters are laughing in the backyard and describing their dad while Oberweis is cooking on a large grill. Another ad took place in a barber shop where his two sons were getting haircuts. They explain how great their dad is and how he instilled good values in them. Then Oberweis's head pops up from a newspaper and he says, "it's nice to know they are listening." Even when Oberweis attacked Foster for voting for the economic bailout package, he used words like "respectfully" and did it with a smile.[62]

Foster also refrained from harsh attacks on his opponent. His first ad never mentioned Oberweis and focused on his work in Washington. He was portrayed as a problem solver who worked with both parties to get things done. Foster touted what he termed to be a tie-breaking vote for ethics reform, and his efforts to create a new GI bill. His second ad also did not mention his opponent. Foster blamed Wall Street for the economic crisis and he told viewers that we would pull through it together. Foster did throw in a quick attack in his last ad right before the election. He accused Oberweis of jeopardizing Social Security by supporting Bush's plan to privatize it. It was reminiscent of the special election because it placed an unflattering picture of Oberweis right next to President Bush. The attack was placed very quickly in the middle of the ad that was overall fairly positive, and, therefore, did not seem so bad.[63]

Image and Advertising

The Oberweis campaign focused a lot of effort on changing his image. The goal was to make him more likable and tout his knowledge of the economy. It was almost as if Oberweis was running against himself—or at least against the stereotyped mean-spirited attack dog of his own creation. The strategy simply was to make him seem like an everyday family guy who was pretty nice. In addition, once the issue of the economy took precedence over the Iraq War, healthcare, and immigration, Oberweis touted his business credentials. Oberweis had worked on Wall Street and he runs an asset management company. He hammered Foster for supporting the $700 billion bailout plan, and he produced his own three-step economic plan. In one interview Oberweis pointed out how Foster has less experience dealing with the market. He went on to say that Foster was better suited for answering questions on nuclear physics, but not when it came to the economy.[64]

Foster was still portrayed as above the fray and as a fresh newcomer who could bring change to Washington, but this time he was using his voting record to prove it. Foster now had the remaining seven months of Hastert's term to take of advantage of his incumbency status. Most importantly, he would be able to build up a voting record on the issues. The Foster campaign now portrayed their candidate as a political independent who looked at the issues factually. He joined a small group of sixteen democrats and voted against the proposed Democratic budget.[65] He also tried his best to bring benefits to 14th District, including funds to the district's Fermi National Laboratory, which allowed the facility to operate without layoffs.[66] He was not just a well-known physicist, but now a well-known congressman.

General Election Finance

Oberweis spent more than $5 million on both campaigns. He financed $3.8 million himself. The remainder was mostly picked up by business associates. Foster used up $4.5 million and was outspent. One report does note, however, that Oberweis amassed most of his funds before the special election. Once that is taken into account, Foster actually had a two-to-one spending lead in the general election campaign, and he ended up with more cash-on-hand in the end.[67] Foster's incumbency advantage also gave him considerable benefits in terms of finance. For instance, speaking to constituents, sending mailers and newsletters, and collecting contributions could now be paid for with tens of thousands of dollars of taxpayer funds. Foster would also benefit from having offices and staffers throughout the district.[68]

General Election Grass Roots

After his special election loss, some had complained that Oberweis did not do enough old-fashioned campaign work to convince voters that he was the best candidate. Phone calls and mailers were obviously not effective. Oberweis needed to build a repertoire with the community by knocking on doors and attending clubs and dinners.[69] The campaign recognized this need and asserted that one of their biggest changes from the last campaign was how they communicate with voters.[70] Consequently, Oberweis held a series of town hall meetings. The first set of twelve meetings were scheduled throughout the summer and were focused on soaring gas prices. The campaign continued this strategy throughout the race, and eventually changed the theme of these meetings to address the credit crisis and the bailout bill.

Foster spent every weekend in his district and held more than twenty "Congress on your corner sessions." He would simply set up a card table and talk with constituents at grocery stores.[71] New voters and swing voters were the key to Foster's grassroots success, and the Obama effect helped a great deal in terms of enthusiasm. Foster continued the heavy grassroots effort in the general election campaign. The campaign estimated that they knocked on over 50,000 doors to determine which voters were on-board and which ones remained undecided. They then had a follow-up campaign that targeted any undecided voters and continued the education and push to get out the vote all the way through Tuesday's election.

Bases of Support

The Republicans enjoy a natural advantage in the district and there are no true bases of support beyond the typical union support for the Democrats. Thus, the key voting block for the Foster campaign became unaffiliated (independent) voters. While the district leans naturally Republican, there are a huge number of these unaffiliated voters that can be convinced to go either way. In fact, this district had more "independent" voters than anything else. For example, Kane County was Hastert's old stronghold, but data indicated that the fastest growing segment in the county was independent voters.[72] These new voters in the east were targeted through a massive grassroots effort.

GENERAL ELECTION RESULTS

Bill Foster beat Jim Oberweis 57 percent to 43 percent in the general election. Oberweis only won a majority in the counties of Bureau, Lee, and Henry. Foster, now the incumbent, increased his margin of victory from the special election by 4 percent. The Oberweis campaign was optimistic since only 22 percent of Republicans came out to vote for the special election. They were hoping that Republican voters would hit the polls hard after losing the district to a Democrat for the first time in decades. Although turnout was higher in the general election, it was not in Oberweis's favor. Despite the "nicer" tone of the general election, Oberweis never fully reconciled with State Senator Chris Lauzen who referred to the attacks he received in the primary as unnecessarily inflicted wounds.[73] The Lauzen conflict destroyed Oberweis's ground game, and it is possible that many Lauzen supporters switched their support to Foster. Hastert's intervention also effectively killed Chris Lauzen's campaign, and many were not happy with the way he was treated. One resident called the Republican primary nasty and mean.[74] By not leaving the situation alone, Hastert created a rift in the party which the Democrats exploited.

Perhaps more importantly, the rise of Barack Obama produced a swell of new voters that were drawn to Foster's candidacy. In the last four weeks of the presidential campaign, Barack Obama had surged in the polls as the economy declined. Locally, the polls began to show that Kane County, Hastert's Republican stronghold county, was going to go to a Democratic presidential candidate. Obama ended up carrying Kane at 55 percent, and Foster won it with a surprising 59 percent of the vote. Obama enthusiasm countered any hopes of higher Republican turnout. About a week before the election, the Oberweis campaign had admitted that Obama's home-state strength made it hard to gain traction against Foster.[75]

NOTES

1. Michael Barone with Richard E. Cohen, *Almanac of American Politics 2008*, 574.
2. Barone, *Almanac of American Politics 2008*.
3. Al Kramen, "District in Illinois Known for Its Hogs," *Washington Post*, December 12, 2003.
4. "Kendall County Is Fastest Growing City in the Nation," *Daily Herald*, March 20, 2008.
5. Rick Pearson, "Former Speaker Hastert Will Not Seek Re-election, Sources Say," *Chicago Tribune*, August 14, 2007.
6. Barone, *Almanac of American Politics 2008*, 574.
7. United States Bureau of the Census, 2006 American Community Survey, factfinder.census.gov/servlet/ADPTable?_bm=y&-geo_id=500$50000US1714&-context=adp&-ds_name=ACS_2007_1YR_G00_&-tree_id=307&-_lang=en&-_caller=geoselect&-format/.
8. United States Bureau of the Census, 2006 American Community Survey.
9. Paul Merrion, "Obama Tilts Suburban Contests," *Crain's Chicago Business*, October 27, 2008.

10. Deanna Bellandi, "Beleaguered GOP Knows It Has Work to Do before November Election," *Associated Press State and Local Wire*, March 15, 2008.
11. United States Bureau of the Census, 2006, American Fact Finder, factfinder.census.gov, see Aurora and Elgin.
12. James Kimberly, "Jim Oberweis Already Campaigning, Though Opponent in Doubt," *Chicago Tribune*, February 7, 2008.
13. Kimberly, "Jim Oberweis Already Campaigning."
14. *Daily Gazette*, "Laesch Waiting on Results," February 9, 2008.
15. "A Message from John Laesch," www.john08.com/?p=299.
16. James Kimberly, "Hastert Backs Oberweis, Burns Drops Out: Geneva Mayor Exits GOP Primary Race," *Chicago Tribune*, December 14, 2007.
17. James Kimberly and Susan Kuczka, "Oberweis Far Outspends GOP Foe," *Chicago Tribune*, January 25, 2008.
18. Lisa Smith, "14th Hopefuls Go on the Attack with Ad Campaigns," *Chicago Daily Herald*, January 12, 2008.
19. James Kimberly, "Oberweis Slams Lauzen, Citing Delay in Return of Campaign Contribution," *Chicago Tribune*, January 16, 2008.
20. Kate Thayer, "Oberweis Wins; Democrats too Close to Call," *Daily Chronicle*, February 6, 2008.
21. Jim Oberweis for Congress, "About Jim," www.jimoberweis.com/index.php?PageID=20.
22. Lisa Smith, "Oberweis Dumps Helicopter for Fireplace in New TV Spot," *Chicago Daily Herald*, November 16 2007.
23. Andy Shaw, "Oberweis under Fire for Campaign Ads," ABC Local, March 1, 2006, abclocal.go.com/wls/story?section=news/local&id=3952977.
24. Leslie Hague, "Innovator, Scientist and Now, Politician, Bill Foster's Curiosity, Ideas Generate His Multiple Careers," *Chicago Daily Herald*, March 23, 2008.
25. James Kimberly, "Turnout Poses Big Challenge in Race to Succeed Hastert," *Chicago Tribune*, February 28, 2008.
26. Bill Foster for Congress, "The War in Iraq," www.foster08.com/2007/12/the_war_in_iraq.html.
27. James Kimberly, "Oberweis, Foster Duel Iraq in Race to Succeed Hastert," *Chicago Tribune*, February 12, 2008.
28. Deanna Bellandi, "Candidates in Race to Replace Hastert Debate," February 22, 2008.
29. Bill Foster for Congress, "Affordable and Comprehensive Health Care for America," www.foster08.com/2007/12/medical_care_sm.html.
30. Jim Oberweis for Congress, "Making Healthcare Affordable and Accessible," www.jimoberweis.com/index.php?PageID=25f.
31. Bill Foster for Congress, "Durbin, Foster Say Cut Health Care Cost, Don't End Employers Paying for Health Care," February 21, 2008, www.foster08.com/2008/02/durbin_foster_s.html.
32. Deanna Bellandi, "Illinois Congressional District Gets Ready for Rookie in Special Election to Replace Hastert," *Associated Press State and Local Wire*, March 9, 2008.
33. Erika Wurst, "Candidates Tangle on Economy, Iraq War, Energy," *Batavia Sun*, October 8, 2008.

34. James Kimberly, "Candidates Differ on Mortgage Crisis; Oberweis, Foster Seek to Finish Hastert's Term," *Chicago Tribune*, March 2, 2008.
35. James Kimberly, "Foster, Oberweis Clash on Bailout Package," *Chicago Tribune*, October 6, 2008.
36. James Fueller, "Oberweis Makes Economic Bailout Suggestions," *Daily Herald*, October 2, 2008.
37. James Kimberly, "Foster Takes Seat from GOP," *Chicago Tribune*, March 9, 2008.
38. James Kimbery, "Rival Ad Links Obreweis, Bush; Democrat Fires Salvo While Dairy Magnate's TV Spot Touts Expertise," *Chicago Tribune*, February 8, 2008.
39. Susan Sarkauskas, "Both Camps Blasting Away but What in Foster, Oberweis Ads Is True?" *Chicago Daily Herald*, March 6, 2008.
40. Sarkauskas, "Both Camps Blasting Away."
41. Tony Scott, "Special Election Campaign Heats U.S.," *Oswego Ledger-Sentinel*, March 6, 2008.
42. Scott, "Special Election Campaign."
43. James Kimberly, "Campaign Mailings Heat Up 14th Congressional Race," *Chicago Tribune*, March 6, 2008.
44. Lisa Smith, "Campaign Sees Return of the Cows," *Chicago Daily Herald*, March 1, 2008.
45. Smith, "Campaign Sees Return."
46. Sarkauskas, "Both Camps Blasting Away."
47. Sarkauskas, "Both Camps Blasting Away."
48. Bill Foster for Congress, Videos, "Bill Fosters Second TV Ad: Bicker," December 17, 2007.
49. James Kimberly, "Foster Airs TV Ad Featuring Obama," *Chicago Tribune*, March 5, 2008.
50. James Kimberly, "2 Candidates in the 14th District Heavily Fund Own Campaigns," *Chicago Tribune*, February 26, 2008.
51. Joseph Ryan, "Oberweis Likely on His Own in Rematch, Spokesman Doubts GOP Will Give Him More Money," *Chicago Daily Herald*, March 14, 2008.
52. Mose Buchele, "Foster's 14th District Victory: A View from the Ground," *Progress Illinois*, March 14, 2008.
53. Tony Scott, "What Can Oberweis Do to Win in November?" *Oswego Leger-Sentinel*, March 20, 2008.
54. Rick Pearson, "Foster Win a Big Blow to GOP; Loss of Hastert's Seat, Obama Rise Could Further Hurt Party in Other Races," *Chicago Tribune*, March 10, 2008.
55. James Kimberly, "Foster Takes Seat from GOP," *Chicago Tribune*, March 9, 2008.
56. Kimberly, "Foster Takes Seat."
57. Bellandi, "Beleaguered GOP."
58. Paul Dailing, "Officials Frown on Timing," *Kane County Chronicle*, October 20, 2008.
59. Kate Thayer, "14th District Election Sees Low Voter Turnout," *Northwest Herald*.
60. Mike Murray, "IL 14th: Dairy King's Change of Victory Has Curtailed," *Illinoize*, November 3, 2008.
61. "Hastert's Old District Up for Grabs," *ABC Chicago News*, October 28, 2008.

62. Jim Oberweis for Congress, Multimedia, www.jimoberweis.com/Multimedia.php.

63. Bill Foster for Congress, Videos, www.foster08.com/videos/.

64. Dennis Conrad, "Democrats Looking to Hold on to Hastert's Old Seat," *Chicago Tribune*, October 4, 2008

65. Conrad, "Democrats Looking to Hold."

66. Martha Quetsch, "Foster, Oberweis Meet in 14th Congressional Race," *Elburn Herald*, October 3, 2008.

67. Murray, Mike, "IL 14th: Dairy King's Change of Victory Has Curtailed," *Illinoize*, November 3, 2008.

68. Conrad, "Democrats Looking to Hold."

69. Tony Scott, "Cross: Oberweis Needs to 'Really Hit the Ground,'" *Oswego Leger-Sentinel*, March 20, 2008.

70. Erin Sauder, "Oberweis vs. Foster: Take Two," *Geneva Republican*, October 21, 2008.

71. Sauder, "Oberweis vs. Foster."

72. Paul Merrion, "Obama Tilts Suburban Contests," *Crain's Chicago Business*, October 27, 2008.

73. Tony Scott, "Cross: Oberweis Needs to 'Really Hit the Ground,'" *Oswego Leger-Sentinel*, March 20, 2008.

74. Tony Scott, "What Can Oberweis Do to Win in November?" *Oswego Ledger-Sentinel*, March 20, 2008.

75. Scott, "What Can Oberweis Do?"

5

New York District 13 Race (McMahon v. Straniere)

A Congressman's Fall from Grace Turns a Red Seat Blue

Jeffrey Kraus

Michael McMahon
Age: 50
Sex: Male
Race: Caucasian
Religion: Roman Catholic
Education: J.D. (New York Law School, 1985); A.A. (Heidelbog University, 1983), B.A. (New York University, 1979)
Occupation: Attorney
Political Experience: New York City councilman (2002–2008)

Robert Straniere
Age: 67
Sex: Male
Race: Caucasian
Religion: Jewish
Education: J.D. (New York University, 1965; B.A. (Wagner College, 1962)
Occupation: Attorney
Political Experience: New York State assemblyman (1981–2005)

> Last night I made an error in judgment. As a parent, I know that taking even one drink of alcohol before getting behind the wheel of a car is wrong. I apologize to my family and the constituents of the 13th Congressional District for embarrassing them, as well as myself.
>
> —statement issued by Representative Vito Fossella, May 1, 2008

Shortly after midnight on May 1, 2008, Representative Vito Fossella (R-NY) ran a red light in Alexandria, Virginia. Fossella had attended the White House celebration for the Super Bowl champion New York Giants and then spent the evening at a dinner with other New Yorkers before ending up at Logan's Tavern, a Washington bar. He and another patron were asked to leave.

Arrested for driving while intoxicated, Fossella initially told police he was on his way to visit his sick daughter (which seemed odd since Fossella's family remained on Staten Island while the House was in session). According to the Alexandria Police Department, Fossella's blood-alcohol level was 0.17, more than double the legal limit in the Commonwealth of Virginia.[1]

Following his arrest, the congressman issued an apology to his family and constituents, a ritual that has become routine for public officials who find themselves in this situation. What happened in the days that followed was far from routine, even for a politician in trouble. Fossella, a married father of three young children, admitted that he had maintained a secret relationship with Lieutenant Colonel Leslie Fay, a retired female Air Force officer whom he met while she was a military liaison to Congress, and that he was the father of her three-year-old daughter. Fay's relationship to Fossella only became known to the public when it was reported that the congressman had been released to her custody following his arrest.[2]

On May 20, less than three weeks after his arrest, Fossella announced that he would not seek reelection, placing on hold what had once had been seen as a promising political career. In his statement, Fossella said that, "I have made the decision not to seek reelection to the United States House of Representatives this November. This choice was an extremely difficult one, which was balanced between my love of service to our great nation and the need to concentrate on healing the wounds that I have caused my wife and family."

Fossella's decision not to seek reelection triggered an incredible contest for the open seat. The local Republicans, reeling in the face of the Fossella scandal, had difficulty finding a candidate to take up their standard. The candidate they would eventually recruit died suddenly, opening up the race for a former member of the State Assembly who had been driven from office by the Richmond County Republican Party and had moved to Manhattan to become a lobbyist and operate a hot dog business. The Democrats would turn to a term-limited member of the New York City Council, who had planned to run for Staten Island Borough president in 2009. However, he would first have to win a primary against Fossella's 2006 opponent.

Minor parties would also play a role in the race. At first, they attempted to fill the vacuum in the Republican Party by offering candidates who would accept Republican positions on the issues. When the Republicans rejected their entreaties, the Conservative and Independence Parties, which had cross-endorsed Fossella in the past, nominated candidates of their own. Even this turned out to be out of the ordinary, as the original Conservative Party candidate, who had sought the Republican Party's endorsement, would withdraw and be replaced on their ticket by a Republican who had briefly sought his party's nomination before bowing out of that contest.

CHARACTERISTICS OF THE DISTRICT

The 13th District includes all of Staten Island (the most suburban of New York City's five boroughs), and the southwestern Brooklyn neighborhoods of Bay Ridge, Bensonhurst, Dyker Heights, and Gravesend. The district had been represented by Fossella since his victory in a 1997 special election.[3] Fossella succeeded Susan Molinari, who resigned after seven years in the House to join CBS News. She had replaced her father, Guy V. Molinari, who had represented Staten Island and parts of Brooklyn from 1981 to 1990, when he resigned following his election as Staten Island Borough president. The Molinaris, like Fossella, were Republicans, meaning that the election of 2008 could result in the election of a Democrat from a Staten Island–centered congressional district for the first time since 1978.[4]

Party Balance

While Fossella and other Republicans had represented the district for more than a quarter of a century, party enrollment favored the Democrats. According to the New York State Board of Elections, enrolled Democrats outnumbered Republicans by a substantial margin.

However, while Democrats constitute a plurality of the electorate within the 13th District (see table 5.1), more than 91,000 of the 358,000 registered voters (25.4 percent) are registered in third parties or are not registered in any political party. In contrast, the other twelve congressional districts that

Table 5.1. Voters by Party (Registered Voters as of March 1, 2008)

County	Status	Democrats	Republicans	Third Parties	Blanks	Total Voters
Kings	Active	45,225	22,060	3,508	21,098	91,921
Kings	Inactive	3,470	1,797	350	1,874	7,491
Kings	Total	48,725	23,857	3,858	22,972	99,412
Richmond	Active	109,720	74,579	11,533	48,688	244,520
Richmond	Inactive	6,529	4,027	858	3,265	14,679
Richmond	Total	116,249	78,606	12,391	51,953	259,199
13th Congressional District	Total	164,974	102,463	16,249	74,925	358,611

Source: New York State Board of Elections, *NYS Voter Enrollment by Congressional District, Party Affiliation and Status; Voters Registered as of March 1, 2008.*

include portions of New York City have overwhelming Democratic majorities, making the 13th Congressional District the only competitive district in the region.

Staten Island, where about 70 percent of the voters in the district live, has elected a number of Republicans. In addition to providing majorities to Fossella and the Molinaris before him, Republicans have controlled the borough presidency since 1989. John Marchi, who was the Republican Party's candidate for mayor of New York in 1969 and 1973, served as a state senator from Staten Island from 1956, when he defeated a Democratic incumbent, until his retirement in 2006. He was then succeeded by another Republican, Andrew Lanza. Two of the three members of the council's delegation to the New York City Council are Republicans (McMahon being the sole Democrat), and Staten Island has voted Republican in the last five mayoral elections, giving Michael Bloomberg 77 percent of the vote in both the 2001 and 2005 elections. In presidential politics, Staten Island has voted Democratic three times since 1952 (1964, 1996 and 2000), giving Republican George W. Bush 57 percent of the vote in 2004. In contrast, Democrat John Kerry carried the other four boroughs of New York City, 77 to 22 percent. David Wasserman, a political analyst with the *Cook Political Report*, explained that Staten Island's "political heritage is one of conservatism. Staten Island does not like to pay high taxes for city services that go to other boroughs that are typically in more need of government assistance."[5]

The Brooklyn neighborhoods of the district, while more Democratic-leaning than those on Staten Island, tend to be conservative. The only Republican elected to any office from Brooklyn represents most of this area in the New York State Senate. The neighborhoods delivered large majorities to Republican Rudolph Giuliani in the 1989, 1993, and 1997 mayoral elections.

Voting and Electoral History

Notwithstanding the Democratic plurality, this Staten Island-centered congressional district has sent Republicans to Congress since 1980. The large number of "Independent" and third-party voters as well as "Reagan Democrats" has often ensured comfortable majorities for Republican congressional candidates. Fossella has been elected with 61.3 (1997), 64.8 (1998), 64.6 (2000), 69.6 (2002), 59 (2004), and 56.8 (2006) percent of the vote.

Fossella's 2006 victory, while impressive, came against a candidate (Stephen Harrison) whom he outspent, $1.7 million to $130,000.[6] Given his Democratic opponent's respectable showing on a shoestring budget, there was speculation that Fossella might be vulnerable in 2008.

In March 2008, the Democratic Congressional Campaign Committee (DCCC) released its target list. Fossella was one of five Republicans from New York on the DCCC list. The National Republican Congressional Committee placed Fossella on their Regain Our Majority Program (ROMP) list, this consisted of vulnerable Republicans they were defending as well as targeted Democratic and open seats.

Demographic Character of the Electorate

According to the Census Bureau's 2000 Census, the district had a population of 654,361. In many ways, the 13th Congressional District is atypical among New York City's congressional districts. The Census Bureau found that 76.8 percent of the district's residents were white; 9.2 percent Asian and 6.9 percent black. (By comparison, citywide the population was 36.3 percent white, 25.5 percent black, 27.4 percent Hispanic, and 10.8 percent Asian.) Roughly one-quarter of the residents of the district were foreign-born, compared to 36 percent of the city's overall population. The median household income in the District was $50,092, with 54 percent of the district's residents living in owner-occupied housing—this in a city where more than two-thirds of the population lived in rental housing in 2000.[7]

Key Voting Blocs

The 13th District contains a large Italian American and a predominantly Roman Catholic population on Staten Island and the Brooklyn neighborhoods of the district. The 13th actually has the highest percentage of Italian-Americans of any congressional district in the nation.[8] This has given the district its social conservative orientation. There are also a large number of senior citizens in the district (13.3 percent of the district's residents are sixty-five years of age or older). More than 45,000 residents of the district are veterans of the Armed Services.[9]

The Brooklyn side of the district includes a growing Asian population (9 percent) and a number of Arab Americans. According to CQ Politics, the district contains the second highest concentration of Arab-American voters in the country.[10]

Employment/Occupational Characteristics

The Census Bureau found that 283,413 residents of the district were part of the employed civilian population in 2000. According to the 2000 census, 65 percent of the workforce was employed in white-collar positions; 18 percent in blue-collar jobs, and 16.6 percent in services. Twenty-four percent of the district's adult residents held college degrees with about 9 percent holding graduate degrees. The 2000 Census found that health care and social assistance was the largest employer of the district's residents (39,944), followed by finance and insurance (33,795) and retailing (26,207).

While many of the district's residents travel to Manhattan for employment, there are some significant employers within the 13th. The district is home to Fort Hamilton, the only active duty military base in New York City, which is located in Brooklyn. Major employers on Staten Island include the Staten Island University Hospital and the Richmond University Medical Center, as well as the stores located at the Staten Island Mall, a large regional shopping center.

THE CANDIDATES

Following Fossella's announcement that he would not seek reelection, both the Democrats and Republicans sought out new candidates for the seat. The DCCC spoke to a number of local Democratic office-holders, including State Senator Diane Savino, State Assemblyman Michael Cusick, and City Council members Domenic Recchia and Michael McMahon. Savino and Cusick would have had to give up "safe" seats in order to run and decided to seek reelection. Recchia, a term-limited council member, had been exploring a candidacy for the seat prior to Fossella's arrest. According to Federal Election Commission (FEC) records, Recchia had raised $352,740 for a race. However, Recchia is from Brooklyn, and the conventional wisdom was that a candidate from Staten Island would run a stronger race.

Savino, in commenting on the viability of Recchia's candidacy and that of Steve Harrison, Fossella's 2006 opponent, said "I've told them this, their biggest problem is that they don't live on Staten Island. . . . One thing about Staten Islanders, they will vote for anybody on any line if they're from Staten Island versus someone who's not."[11] McMahon, a political moderate who had run with the backing of the Conservative Party and left-leaning Working Families Party in past races, was planning to run for Staten Island Borough president in 2009 and had not considered a run for Fossella's seat prior to the congressman's arrest. While the DCCC normally does not endorse candidates involved in primary contests, DCCC chair Chris Van Hollen announced they would support McMahon because the district was in play following Fossella's withdrawal from the race. McMahon was placed in the DCCC's "Red to Blue fund-raising program," which would provide him with financial support following the primary. McMahon was also endorsed by Kings County (Brooklyn) Democratic leader Vito Lopez and the Richmond County (Staten Island) Democratic County Committee. The Working Families Party also announced their support for McMahon. Notwithstanding the organizational backing received by McMahon, Harrison announced that he would stay in the race.

On the Republican side, the Staten Island Republican Party had difficulty recruiting a replacement for Fossella, as all of the party's local elected officials passed on the race. At one point, Curtis Sliwa, a conservative radio talk show host known for forming the Guardian Angels crime fighters group, said that he would run if no one from the district stepped forward.[12] The party then turned to Fossella's finance chairman, Frank Powers, a sixty-seven-year-old retired Wall Street executive and member of the Metropolitan Transportation Authority (MTA) board who had been a major contributor and fund-raiser for the party.

Staten Island Republican chair John S. Friscia explained the Powers selection as "We endorsed a dark-horse candidate. Frank is well-known to the Republican Party county committee, and he is a contributing member of the community, with a wealth of volunteer work."[13] Powers received the support of the Kings County (Brooklyn) Conservative Party, which circulated nominating petitions on his behalf.[14]

However, support for Powers was not unanimous. The Richmond County Conservative Party favored McMahon, who had been endorsed by the local party in his two successful runs for the council. However, McMahon was opposed by the Brooklyn Conservatives, and the State Conservative Party would not give McMahon permission to enter their primary against Powers.[15] The Brooklyn Republican Party was reluctant to support Powers, preferring to support Paul Atanasio, a member of the Conservative Party who had run for Congress in 1980, nearly defeating the incumbent Democrat, Leo Zefferetti. Despite their misgivings, the Brooklyn Republicans eventually agreed to support Powers.

Dr. Jamshad Wyne, the Richmond County Republican Committee finance chair, announced that he would run in the primary against Powers, and began collecting petition signatures. Like Powers, Wyne was a first-time candidate known more for his fund-raising efforts on behalf of the party. A medical doctor, Wyne had been fined $5,000 and placed on probation for three years in 2003 by the New York State Department of Health's Board for Professional Medical Conduct. The board found he had practiced "with negligence on more than one occasion."[16] The race became even more muddled when Francis M. Powers, the Republican candidate's son from his first marriage, announced that he would seek the nomination of the Libertarian Party for the seat. The Libertarians instead selected another candidate, Susan Overeem.[17]

On June 22, less than three weeks before the filing deadline, Powers died suddenly. This threw the Republicans into total confusion. Robert Straniere, a former State Assembly member (1981–2005) who no longer lived in the district (not a requirement as members of the House of Representatives must "be an inhabitant of that state in which he shall be chosen"), having moved to Manhattan, announced that he would be a candidate and began circulating designating petitions. He explained that he was running in order to save New York City's last Republican seat in the U.S. House of Representatives. Straniere, who since losing his Assembly seat in the 2004 election, had opened a hot dog restaurant near City Hall in lower Manhattan, claimed that he "really had retired from being active in partisan politics, but I feel this is a call of duty under the circumstances. . . . It's absolutely essential that there be a Republican congressman from our city."[18]

Wyne continued his campaign and two non-Republicans entered the contest. Conservative Paul Atanasio had the support of the Kings County (Brooklyn) Republican Organization, although Straniere was backed by Arnaldo A. Ferraro, a one-term State Assembly member (1985–1987) with his own political club, the Fiorello LaGuardia Republican Club, in the Bensonhurst neighborhood of Brooklyn. Carmine Morano, father of the leader of the Richmond County Independence Party, announced that he too would circulate petitions for the Republican nomination. Both Atanasio and Morano faced the challenge of obtaining 1,250 signatures in less than three weeks and then obtain permission from the Republicans to participate in the Republican primary.

McMahon and Harrison filed petitions for the Democratic nomination, while Straniere, Wyne, Atanasio, and Morano would all file for the Republican nomination. The Richmond County Republican Party organization filed a petition for Powers which contained signatures gathered prior to his death. Under the New York State Election Law (Section 6-148), Powers's "Committee to Fill Vacancies" would be able to select a replacement candidate if the petition was not challenged or was found to contain the requisite number of valid signatures. That committee designated Straniere as Powers's replacement, giving him the support of the Staten Island Republicans. John S. Friscia, the party chairman, said that Straniere "has the following, the name recognition and the verve and the drive."[19] The Republicans did not grant the Wilson-Pakula waivers to Atanasio and Morano, ending their efforts to appear on the Republican Primary ballot. Morano, the Independence Party candidate, vowed to continue as a write-in candidate for the Republican nomination.[20]

The Primaries

The Republican Primary turned into a rancorous affair, as candidates traded accusations. Wyne claimed that Straniere had tried to persuade him to make illegal campaign contributions to his unsuccessful 2001 campaign for Staten Island Borough president. The allegation was that this was done by distributing money to his relatives who would then make $250 contributions to Straniere's campaign. Straniere would then, under New York City's public finance program, have received $1,000 in matching funds for each $250 contribution. Straniere denied the allegation, asking "Why would he make these accusations for the first time, seven years after that campaign?"[21] Straniere answered his own question:

> What he's trying to do is avoid the issues because he doesn't understand any of the issues. He doesn't want to discuss his lack of experience. And he certainly doesn't want to deal with the ethically challenged facts about his medical practice.[22]

Straniere noted that Wyne's campaign literature referred to him as "Jim Wyne," which Straniere charged was an attempt by the doctor to conceal his Pakistani and Muslim background. Wyne asserted that Jim was easier for voters to remember. While questioning Wyne's ethics, Straniere had an ethical problem of his own. While working as an assistant counsel in the New York State Department of Health's New York City Office (for which he was paid $65,000 per year), Straniere took a full-time partnership with Kantor Davidoff, where he lobbied on behalf of some of the firm's clients. Straniere's firm defended him, arguing that he had only lobbied the New York City Council and city agencies, not any state government entities.[23]

Straniere's candidacy was also opposed by many Republican leaders. Guy Molinari, the former congressman and long a dominant figure in Staten Island politics was vehement in his opposition:

> If Straniere is the nominee, there will be prominent people who will be front and center opposing him. This man was a candidate for various offices for 20 years, and he brought nothing but grief to the Republican Party. We threw him out of office and got him off Staten Island. And we don't want him back.[24]

The Democratic Primary was less rancorous and focused more on the ideologies of the two candidates. Harrison, the more liberal of the two candidates, supported an immediate redeployment of American forces from Iraq and criticized McMahon for his support of Mayor Michael Bloomberg's proposal for congestion pricing. Harrison also charged that McMahon was not a "real" Democrat, citing the support that McMahon had received from the Conservative Party in his previous runs for the City Council, his opposition to gay marriage (he supports civil unions), and his vote against a New York City Council resolution calling for an end to the Iraq war. McMahon contended that, as a moderate, he would be a stronger candidate in the general election than the more liberal Harrison.

While McMahon had the support of most of the Democratic Party establishment (party leaders, labor unions, and public officials), Harrison received the endorsement of the National Organization for Women (NOW), the Progressive Democrats of America (PDA), former Brooklyn congressman Major Owens, and three local Democratic clubs: the Staten

Island Democratic Association, the Democratic Organization of the County of Richmond, and the Central Brooklyn Independent Democrats. McMahon was endorsed by the *New York Times*, the *Staten Island Advance*, and the weekly *Brooklyn Paper* and *Courier-Life* newspapers in Brooklyn.

McMahon and Straniere won the primaries (see table 5.2). McMahon defeated Harrison by a better than three-to-one margin. On Staten Island, McMahon's plurality was more than 8,700 votes, vindicating the assertion that Staten Islanders would be more inclined to support one of their own against a Brooklynite. In Brooklyn, McMahon edged Harrison by about 200 votes.

The Republican primary was closer, with Straniere winning by about 17 percentage points. The Republican turnout was very low, with only 6.4 percent of enrolled Republicans coming out (compared to 10.9 percent of the Democrats). Also notable was the number of write-in votes received by the Independence Party nominee, Carmine Morano. Actually, an argument can be made that Morano's vote was even higher: 106 of the remaining 158 write-in votes were cast for "Morano," with another 27 votes cast for "Carmine Marino" or some other variant of the name.

Following the primary, Wyne resigned as the Staten Island Republican Party's finance chair, claiming that he "was not given the nomination of the Republican Party because of my religion and ethnic background." The party's chair, John Friscia, denied Wyne's charge, stating that "the issue of his ethnicity was brought into play not by anyone in the party, but by Dr. Wyne himself."[25]

Table 5.2. Congressional Primary Vote

Democrats		
	Votes	Percent
Stephen A. Harrison	3,992	23.6
Michael E. McMahon	12,805	75.6
Write-ins	128	0.8

Republicans		
	Votes	Percent
Robert A. Straniere	3,324	53.8
Jamshad I. Wyne	2,246	36.4
Carmine Morano (write-in)	449	7.3
Other write-ins	158	2.5

Source: Board of Elections in the City of New York, *Statement and Return Report for Certification; Primary Election 2008-09/09/2008 Crossover—Republican Party*, September 23, 2008.

CAMPAIGN ISSUES

The campaign, like elsewhere, came to be dominated by the economy. As the general election campaign began, Straniere linked McMahon to Democratic presidential candidate Barack Obama and claimed that McMahon would support tax increases if he were elected to Congress. McMahon focused on the lack of support for Straniere's candidacy by the leaders and elected public officials from his party, suggesting that this lack of support would make Straniere an ineffective congressman.

Straniere also attempted to link McMahon to Congressman Charles Rangel (D-NY). Rangel, of Harlem, who was mired in controversy surrounding his renting of four rent-stabilized apartments and his failure to pay income taxes on rental income from a second home, had (according to the National Republican Congressional Committee) contributed (as of September 19, 2008) $60,582 to McMahon. In a press release issued by his campaign, Straniere called upon McMahon to "come clean and ask his good friend Charlie Rangel to resign his post and completely and fully cooperate with authorities."[26] Straniere also urged McMahon to return the contributions to Rangel's committees; a demand which McMahon chose to ignore.

The nation's growing economic crisis became the basis for a number of disagreements between McMahon and Straniere. Straniere asserted that tax increases would cripple the economy, and criticized McMahon for having supported an 18.5 percent real estate tax increase that had been proposed by Mayor Bloomberg in 2003. McMahon, who throughout the campaign offered no comment on the potential for new taxes, countered that he had supported the tax increase in order to stabilize New York City's finances after the 9/11 terrorist attack and that he had subsequently voted for tax reductions and rebates as New York's economy improved.

Straniere's effort to present himself as a "tax cutter" was challenged by the New York State Democratic Committee, which issued a press release on the "Real" Bob Straniere. They claimed that Straniere had voted for $2.35 billion in new taxes, including a $1.7 billion income and sales tax increase.[27]

They differed on the bank bailout bill. McMahon supported the bill and praised Congressman Fossella (the man he was seeking to replace) for voting yes on the bill. In a statement after the first bill was defeated in the House, McMahon said, "I applaud Representative Fossella for his vote today, and wish more had joined him." In response, Straniere praised the House Republicans who opposed the bill for refusing to "cave in to the doomsayers."[28]

Social Security privatization, not a major issue during this election cycle, assumed some prominence in the race. Citing the precipitous decline of the stock market, McMahon argued that this proved that the proposal, initially made by President George W. Bush in 2005, to allow individuals to invest a portion of their Social Security taxes in the stock market, was a bad idea. In a candidate forum sponsored by the AARP, McMahon asked, "Can you imagine what would have happened if Social Security had been privatized with the crashes in Wall Street? The system would be bankrupt."[29]

Straniere, a supporter of the Bush proposal, called for the creation of a five-year pilot program where younger workers would be allowed to invest some of their Social Security taxes into what he called "safe, conservative vehicles for investment."[30]

On the Iraq War, McMahon called for "responsible redeployment," saying, "We want our troops home safely and to get out of a situation that has become a quagmire."[31] Straniere took the position that "we won the war" because of the troop surge, and that the decision to redeploy troops should be left to the military commanders.[32]

Fossella: Would He or Wouldn't He?

Notwithstanding his May announcement, speculation continued that Congressman Fossella would jump back into the race. This speculation continued even after the primary and was fueled by a poll that was put in the field in mid-September, asking residents of the district questions about Fossella and whether they would vote for the congressman in a head-to-head race with McMahon.[33] Fossella issued a public statement denying interest in getting back in the race, stating that he was "deeply humbled by the outpouring of support that I have received from people throughout the district through these difficult times, but I am not a candidate for Congress."[34]

Notwithstanding Fossella's pronouncement, efforts to find a way for Fossella to be placed at the ballot continued, spearheaded by the former congressman, Guy Molinari. Molinari acknowledged that he, along with other Staten Island Republicans, were "making some last-ditch efforts to try to convince Vito Fossella to run and to create opportunities for him to run."[35] State Senator Andrew Lanza, a longtime ally of the congressman, asserted "that there are a lot of people out there who support him and would vote for him."[36]

The New York County (Manhattan) Republican Party then nominated Straniere for a State Supreme Court judgeship. This nomination was supposedly engineered by supporters of Fossella who hoped that Straniere would accept the nomination, freeing up the Republican nomination for the congressman. Straniere declined the judicial nomination and remained on the ballot as the congressional candidate.

Another possibility was that Fossella would take the Conservative Party's nomination following Paul Atanasio's withdrawal from the race. But, the Conservatives then nominated Timothy Cochrane, who had briefly sought the Republican nomination after Fossella's withdrawal. Michael Long, the state Conservative Party chair, when asked about the possibility of placing Fossella on the Conservative ticket, said:

> I worked with Vito for a lot of years. I'm very saddened by the position he's in. I don't think his career is over, but I would think it's over for this year. I think it's ill-advised for him to do anything else, and I take him at his word that he's not a candidate.[37]

And so, he wasn't.

CAMPAIGN STRATEGY

Media/Mail

McMahon's television commercial, which started airing on local cable outlets October 7, focused on trust, change, and experience. The spot's message was that McMahon had, as a councilman, worked hard for his constituents and that he would work as hard for them in Washington. The commercial's tag line was "Change We Can Trust."

McMahon's direct mail focused on his endorsements. One mailing featured Mayor Michael Bloomberg's endorsement of McMahon, while others featured testimonials from Senators Hillary Clinton and Charles Schumer and former mayor Edward Koch. Later mailings focused on his record in the Council, including his support for real estate tax cuts, recycling legislation, and education.

Straniere's limited advertising emphasized his experience in the State Legislature, stating that his prospective constituents knew who he was because of his twenty-four years in the Assembly. The slogan "Staten Island Knows. Brooklyn Knows." was featured. Straniere's advertising was limited to direct mail and print ads in the *Staten Island Advance*. Straniere linked himself to the national Republican ticket of John McCain and Sarah Palin, expecting that they would do well in the district.

As closely as Straniere attempted to associate himself with his party's standard bearer for president, McMahon often downplayed his support of Senator Barack Obama. While making public statements that were supportive of the Democratic presidential nominee, the Democratic congressional candidate's literature did not mention the Obama-Biden ticket. The sample ballot distributed by the McMahon campaign listed every Democratic candidate—except Obama. With an arrow pointing downward on the ballot, it read: "After you vote for president, vote for all of the most qualified an experienced candidates in our community."[38]

Media outlets serving the district endorsed the Democrat. The *Staten Island Advance*, influential with voters on the Island, endorsed Councilman McMahon, stating that:

Mr. McMahon has always been thoughtful and well-reasoned in articulating his positions, including on national and international issues. We have no doubt that this approach, which is all too rare in national politics these days, will enable him to make a seamless transition to the larger stage the House of Representatives affords.[39]

The *New York Times* and the *Brooklyn Paper*, a weekly, also endorsed McMahon.

Finance

McMahon, even with his late start in the race, enjoyed a tremendous fundraising advantage. Within three weeks of announcing his candidacy, he raised more than $500,000, demonstrating the commitment of his backers to his race.

McMahon would continue to enjoy this edge over his opponents. According to Federal Election Commission (FEC) filings, through October 15, 2008, McMahon had raised $1,156,438 while Straniere had raised only $123,443 (see table 5.3). As the campaign entered its final three weeks, McMahon had more than $284,000 in hand—more than twice the total raised by Straniere. Straniere had slightly more than $10,000 on hand with three weeks to go. With Fossella out of the race, the PAC money that would have normally flowed to the incumbent instead went to McMahon.[40]

The Republican's financial situation was so dire that the campaign was forced to use leftover primary campaign literature, recycling it by placing "Vote McCain-Palin-Straniere November 4th" stickers over the original primary date.

While McMahon raised about ten times the amount of money collected by Straniere, the disparity in PAC giving was far greater (see table 5.4). The

Table 5.3. Candidate Finances (through October 15, 2008)

Candidate Name	Net Receipts	Net Disbursements	Cash	Debt	Through
Vito Fossella*	$1,023,326	$816,400	$220,326	$0	09/30/2008
Stephen Harrison	$219,720	$201,159	$25,040	$2,745	09/30/2008
Michael McMahon	$1,156,438	$871,923	$284,514	$0	10/15/2008
Carmine Morano	$47,575	$48,622	-$999	$41,000	10/15/2008
Domenic Recchia*	$353,340	$191,351	$161,986	$0	09/30/2008
Robert Straniere	$123,443	$112,909	$10,533	$0	10/15/2008
Jamshad Wyne	$341,900	$311,477	$24,287	$300,000	09/30/2008

Source: Federal Election Commission, FEC Financial Summary Report.
*Not a candidate in either the primary or general election.

Table 5.4. Sources of Receipts (through October 15, 2008)

Candidate Name	Total Receipts	Individual	PAC	Party	Candidate	Other
Vito Fossella*	$1,023,326	$590,575	$422,050	$500	0	0
Stephen Harrison	$219,704	$207,815	$7,200	$1,500	$2,825	$364
Michael McMahon	$1,156,439	$592,290	$499,350	$5,000	$1,000	$58,799
Carmine Morano	$47,575	$6,450	0	0	$41,000	$125
Dominic Recchia*	$353,340	$326,690	$23,050	0	$3,000	$600
Robert Straniere	$123,444	$111,844	$11,600	0	0	0
Jamshad Wyne	$316,901	$16,835	0	0	$300,000	$66

Source: Federal Election Commission
*Not a candidate in either the primary or general election.

amount of PAC money raised by the Democrat was more than forty-three times the amount that Straniere received. PAC contributions represented slightly over 43 percent of McMahon's total receipts. In contrast, PAC donations accounted for nine percent of Straniere's funds. A number of PACs that had contributed to Fossella would contribute to McMahon.[41]

Straniere relied almost exclusively on individual contributions and found that many of the longtime financial backers for Staten Island–based Republican candidates would not support him.[42] Through October 15, 2008, Straniere had received 102 individual contributions; McMahon, 912 individual contributions. Straniere's poor finances were not limited to his campaign. The hot dog restaurant he had started near City Hall following his departure from elective politics closed and declared bankruptcy in September 2008.

Bases of Support

McMahon's prominent supporters included many of the city's labor unions, which endorsed his candidacy after the DCCC decided that they would back him for the seat. The New York City Central Labor Council, representing more than 400 unions and 1.3 million members, and the State AFL-CIO, an umbrella organization representing more than 2.5 million workers across the state, were early supporters of McMahon. Other unions supporting McMahon included the 200,000 member United Federation of Teachers (UFT); Local 1199 SEIU Health Care East; the United Food and Commercial Workers (UFCW); the Retail, Wholesale, and Department Store Workers Union (RWDSU); the Uniformed Firefighters Association (UFA), the Uniformed Fire Officers Association (UFOA), and virtually all of the law enforcement unions.[43]

McMahon received the endorsement of virtually every Democratic elected public official in the area. Senator Hillary Clinton (D-NY) appeared at a

September rally held for McMahon at Wagner College. He was also endorsed by Mayor Michael Bloomberg, the Democrat-turned Republican-turned Independent, and the Staten Island Borough president, James Molinaro, a Conservative Party member.[44]

Straniere was hampered by the lack of support that he received from Republican elected officials on Staten Island. Guy Molinari, the former congressman, endorsed the Conservative Party candidate, Timothy Cochrane. State Senator Martin Golden, whose Brooklyn District included portions of the 13th, also declined to endorse Straniere. Straniere did pick up the endorsements of Republicans from outside the district. Among those backing him were former governor George Pataki and Congressman Peter King, who represented portions of Long Island's Nassau and Suffolk Counties in the 3rd Congressional District. However, their support had little impact on the race.

McMahon's broad base of support was clear through the impressive field operation that his campaign put in place and their "get out the vote" (GOTV) effort in the run up to the election. His local campaign was augmented by operatives from prominent Democrats including Hillary Clinton, Senator Charles Schumer (D-NY), and Representatives Joseph Crowley (the leader of the Queens County Democratic Organization), and Steve Israel.

House Majority Leader Steny Hoyer and House Transportation and Infrastructure Committee chair James Oberstar both came to the district to campaign, demonstrating the DCCC commitment to the campaign. McMahon acknowledged the DCCC's role, "It's really been extremely refreshing and encouraging that they've done what they said they would do, that they were very serious about this race, and very serious about my candidacy."[45]

Union supporters also filled out the ranks. According to the campaign, their cadre of volunteers knocked on over 30,000 doors and made more than 100,000 phone calls to voters. In contrast, the Straniere campaign, lacking the support of local Republican officeholders, could not come close to matching the Democratic effort. On Election Day, the Straniere campaign did not even attempt to mount a get out the vote effort on the Brooklyn side of the district.

ELECTION RESULTS

The final tally was not even close. McMahon captured more than 60 percent of the vote (see table 5.5).

On Staten Island, McMahon polled 80,788 votes (60 percent) to Straniere's 45,724 (34 percent). In Brooklyn, McMahon won, 24,340 (61 percent) to 12,256 (31 percent) for Straniere.

Table 5.5. 13th Congressional District Vote

Candidate	Votes	Percentage
Michael McMahon, Democrat/Working Families	105,128	60.8
Robert Straniere, Republican	57,530	33.3
Carmine Morano, Independence	4,762	2.8
Timothy Cochrane, Conservative	5,525	3.2

Source: CQ Politics/District Detail: NY-13, www.cqpolitics.com/wmspage.cfm?docID=district-NY-13 (accessed November 27, 2008).

McMahon routed Straniere, winning 78 percent in the overwhelmingly North Shore neighborhoods of Staten Island that he represented in the City Council and garnered 55 percent of the mid-island neighborhoods that are considered "swing vote" areas. Only Staten Island's South Shore, the Republican bastion that Straniere represented in the State Assembly for twenty-four years, went for the Republican by a narrow margin: 47 percent to 45 percent.

McMahon was the first Democrat to represent this district in Congress in more than a generation. In the days that followed his election, the congressman-elect set forth his agenda: funding for mass transit improvements; increasing access to health care; and fostering economic growth and tax relief for the middle class families of the district.

In claiming victory, McMahon told his supporters, "I do think that the people were yearning to have someone of integrity and honor representing them, and I think that really helped us."[46]

Straniere, in his concession speech, contended that "the tides were against us, and due to events largely out of our control—including the severe downturn in the global economy and the declining support of the McCain-Palin ticket—things did not go as we had hoped." In a move that reflected his campaign, the congressional candidate held his own election night party, rather than joining with the other Republican candidates at their event. When asked why he did not join with the others, Straniere said, "I wanted to spend time with my family and with the people who have been supportive."[47]

The election was a unique double victory for the McMahons over the Straniere family. McMahon's wife, Judith, won a seat on the State Supreme Court on Staten Island, defeating Philip Straniere, the congressional candidate's brother.

Barring any serious missteps, McMahon should be a strong favorite to retain this seat in 2010. It is unlikely that any of the Republican officeholders who declined to run following Fossella's withdrawal will be inclined to run against an incumbent Democratic representative. Another factor that will deter them is the strong possibility that, even if they retook the seat, they would probably become the victims of redistricting following the 2010 census. The Democrats gained control of the State Senate in this election, giving the Democratic Party control of both houses of the State Legislature and the governor's office for the first time since the Great Depression.[48] If this remains the case after the 2010 election, the Democrats would control the redistricting process and could make the seat more hospitable to a Democrat.

And so, a traffic stop for a DWI on a street in Alexandria, Virginia, in May changed some lives and the course of politics in New York City's "red" congressional district. The Republicans, long dominant, are now in a state of disarray. The Democrats, who had not held the seat for more than a generation, ended up electing someone who, eight months before the election, was not even considering a race.

In 1850, Charles Dudley Warner, the editor of the *Hartford Courant*, wrote "that politics makes strange bedfellows." In 2008, bedfellows (Representative Fossella and his mistress) made for strange politics in New York's 13th Congressional District.

NOTES

1. Thomas DeFrank, Rich Schapiro, Mike Jaccarino, and Larry McShane, "Vito Fossella's Mystery Woman: Va Lady Who Sprung Him From Jail Lives Nearby," www.nydailynews.com/news/2008/05/03/2008-05-03_vito_fossellas_mystery_woman (accessed August 13, 2008).

2. Fossella met Fay while she was the Air Force liaison to the House of Representatives, an assignment she was posted to in July 2001. According to British Government records, Fossella and Fay attended an Air Force–sponsored dinner in the UK on July 27, 2003, along with other members of Congress. Fossella's wife was not in attendance. Fay and her husband, Gary Shoaf, divorced in December of 2003.

3. Fossella, then a member of the New York City Council, defeated Eric Vitaliano, a conservative Democrat who was a member of the New York State Assembly, 61.3 to 38.7 percent. The other four representatives in the area were Peter King (3rd District), Jim Walsh (25th District), Tom Reynolds (26th District), and Randy Kuhl (29th District). Walsh and Reynolds decided not to seek reelection. The DCCC could not recruit a viable candidate to challenge King, and took him off their list. Kuhl, who defeated ex-Republican Eric Massa by 6,033 votes out of more than 206,000 votes cast, was facing Massa again in 2008. Democrat Dan Maffei won Walsh's seat, and Massa defeated Kuhl.

4. Staten Island (along with adjacent communities in Brooklyn or Staten Island) had been represented in Congress from 1963 to 1981 by John M. Murphy, who was implicated in the Abscam scandal. While Murphy was not indicted by federal authorities, his reputation was irreparably damaged and he was defeated by Guy Molinari in 1980. Martin J. Golden was elected to the State Senate from the 22nd Senate District in 2002, defeating incumbent Democrat Vincent Gentile, 55 to 45

percent. Golden had represented part of this district in the New York City Council, having been elected from the 43rd Council District in 1997 and 2001.

5. Sara Jerome, "GOP Divisions Could Make Staten Island Blue," www.gothamgazette.com (accessed September 4, 2008).

6. Dana Rubinstein, "SI Dems Want Harrison," *Brooklyn Paper*, March 1, 2008.

7. The Furman Center for Real Estate and Urban Policy, *State of New York City's Housing and Neighborhoods 2007* (New York: New York University, 2007), 38.

8. Michael Barone, Richard E. Cohen, and Grant Ujifusa, *The Almanac of American Politics* (Washington, DC: National Journal Group, 2007), 1164.

9. During the campaign, Straniere promised to hire at least one-third of his Congressional staff from the disabled veterans within his district if he were elected. Straniere called this the "Wounded Warrior Workplace Initiative."

10. CQ Politics, "CQ 2008 Election Guide-13th Congressional District," www.cqpolitics.com (accessed October 26, 2008).

11. Elizabeth Benjamin, "Savino Awaits Decision from 'Hamlet on the Verrazano,'" *New York Daily News*, www.nydailynews.com/blogs/dailypolitics/congress/ (accessed on October 5, 2008).

12. David Saltonstall and Kenneth Lovett, "Curtis Sliwa Says He Might Run for Vito Fossella's Congressional Seat," *New York Daily News*, May 29, 2008.

13. Jonathan P. Hicks, "Republicans Back Ex–Wall Street Executive to Run for Fossella's Seat," *New York Times* May 30, 2008.

14. Under the New York State Election Law, candidates may appear on the primary election ballot only if they submit designating petitions containing a sufficient number of valid signatures from voters who are enrolled in their party (Section 6-118). Congressional candidates must submit designating petitions containing at least 1,250 signatures or a number equal to 5 percent of the party's enrollment in the congressional district, whatever is less (Section 6-136g).

15. Jonathan P. Hicks, "Republican Ex-Friends Do Battle in S.I. Congressional Contest," *New York Times*, August 19, 2008.

16. The New York State Health Department found that Wyne had treated at least two patients without recording adequate medical histories.

17. The Libertarian Party failed to qualify a petition in the 13th Congressional District and did not have a candidate on the ballot.

18. Special to the Sun, "Former Politicians Makes Bid for Fossella's Seat," www.nysun.com/new-york/former-politician-makes-bid-for-fossellas-seat/81207/ (accessed September 7, 2008).

19. Jonathan P. Hicks, "Republicans Pick a Party Rebel to Run for Fossella's Seat," *New York Times*, July 15, 2008.

20. Candidates who are not enrolled in a party can run in a primary only if they receive the permission of the party (New York State Election Law, Section 6-120). This is known as a "Wilson-Pakula," authorization.

21. Hicks, "Republicans Pick a Party Rebel."

22. Hicks, "Republican Ex-Friends Do Battle."

23. Bill Hammond, "Look Who's in a Pickle Now: Hot Dog Pol Lobbied While on the Public Payroll," *New York Daily News*, August 28, 2008; Straniere, as required by the Administrative Code of the City of New York (title 3; chapter 3; subchapter 2), registered with the Lobbying Bureau, a unit of the City Clerk's Office. From

January 1, 2007, until December 31, 2007 (he was employed in the State Health Department until March 2007, when he was fired by the new Democratic administration), Straniere represented the New York Metropolitan Retail Association, LLC; the New York Junior Tennis League; and the Sports and Arts in Schools Foundation. According to the NYC Lobbyist Search Database, Straniere and his partner (Lawrence Mandelker, an attorney who has been active in New York politics) received $72,000 in compensation from the three groups.

24. Hicks, "Republican Ex-Friends Do Battle."

25. Jonathan P. Hicks, "Loser in S.I. Race Quits G.O.P. Post," City Room-Metro-New York Times Blog, cityroom.blogs.nytimes.com/2008/09/11/loser-in-si-race-quits-gop-post/ (accessed September 14, 2008).

26. Bob Straniere for United States Congress, "Straniere Asks McMahon: 'Do You Stand with Rangel or Real New Yorkers?" press release issued September 19, 2008.

27. New York State Democratic Committee, "Bob Straniere: What Voters Need to Know about the Republican Candidate before They Head to the Polls," press release issued October 30, 2008.

28. Elizabeth Benjamin, "McMahon Praises Fossella on Bailout Vote (Updated)," *New York Daily News*, www.nydailynews.com/blogs/dailypolitics/congress/ (accessed on October 5, 2008).

29. Tom Wrobleski, "House Hopefuls Clash over Tax Policy," *Staten Island Advance*, October 7, 2008.

30. Wrobleski, "Staten Island House Candidates."

31. Jonathan P. Hicks, "Defying Political Labels, Staten Island's New Congressman Is Seen as a Pragmatist," *New York Times*, 17 November 2008.

32. Tom Wrobleski, "Staten Island House Candidates Asked about Ending Iraq War," blog.silive.com/politics/2008/10/staten_island_house_candidates_1.html (accessed November 27, 2008).

33. Tom Wrobleski, "Who Was behind Last Weekend's Surprise Telephone Poll?" *Staten Island Advance*, September 21, 2008.

34. Jonathan P. Hicks, "S.I. Republicans Press for Fossella on Ballot," cityroom.blogs.nytimes.com/2008/09/23/S.I.-Republicans-Press-for-Fossella-on-Ballot/ (accessed November 23, 2008).

35. Hicks, "S.I. Repbulicans."

36. Wrobleski, "Who Was Behind."

37. Elizabeth Benjamin, "NY-13 Mystery Deepens," *New York Daily News*, www.nydailynews.com/blogs/dailypolitics/congress/ (accessed on October 5, 2008).

38. Judy L. Randall, "An Eruption of Joy among Island Supporters," *Staten Island Advance*, November 5, 2008.

39. "For Congress: Michael McMahon," *Staten Island Advance*, October 30, 2008.

40. Larry Sabato, *PAC Power: Inside the World of Political Action Committees* (New York: Norton, 1984).

41. PACs that had contributed to Fossella in his prior campaigns and to McMahon in 2008 included the AFLAC PAC; Air Line Pilots Association PAC; Amalgamated Transit Union-COPE; America's Health Insurance Plans PAC (AHIP PAC); American Academy of Ophthalmology Political Committee (ORTHPAC); American Association for Justice PAC; American Health Care Association PAC; American International Group Employee PAC; American Pilots' Association PAC; Arent Fox LLP

PAC; AT&T Federal PAC; Carpenters Legislative Improvement Committee; the Dealers Election Action Committee of the National Automotive Dealers Association; the General Electric Company PAC; the Goldman Sachs Group, Inc., PAC; HIP Health Plan Federal PAC; I.U.O.E. Local 14-14B Voluntary Political Committee; I.U.O.E. Local 15 PAC; Independent Insurance Agents and Brokers of America PAC; International Association of Firefighters Interested in Registration and Education PAC; ILA-COPE; Keyspan Corporation PAC; Laborers' Political League; the Letter Carriers Political Action Fund; Met Life Inc. Employees' Political Participation Fund A; National Active and Retired Federal Employees Association PAC; National Air Traffic Controllers Association PAC; National Association of Chain Drug Stores PAC; National Association of Postal Supervisors PAC; National Association of Postmasters of the United States PAC; National Association of Real Estate Investment Trusts PAC; National Association of Realtors PAC; National Rural Letter Carriers' PAC; National Venture Capital Association PAC; New York Life Insurance Company PAC; Pfizer PAC; Price Waterhouse Coopers PAC; Seafarers International Union of North America; Sprint Nextel Corporation PAC; Transport Workers Union Political Contributions Committee; UNITE Here TIP Campaign Committee; United Transportation Union PAC; Verizon Communication Good Government Club; and the Waste Management Employees Better Government Fund.

42. Some prominent Staten Island Republicans contributed to McMahon's campaign. Jerry Cammarata, a frequent Republican candidate and political appointee in the mayoral administration of Rudolph Giuliani, contributed $2,500 to McMahon. Kathryn Rooney, a longtime aide to Republican state senator John Marchi, gave $500 to McMahon. Leticia Remauro, a former leader of the Richmond County Republican Party, donated $250 to McMahon's campaign.

43. These included the Patrolmen's Benevolent Association, Detectives Endowment Association, Captains Endowment Association, Lieutenants Benevolent Association, Sergeants Benevolent Association, and the New York State Court Officers and the New York State Supreme Court Officers Association. All of these groups had endorsed Fossella two years earlier.

44. Bloomberg's deputy mayor for health and human services, Linda Gibbs, is McMahon's sister-in-law. In 2001, Bloomberg contributed $1,000 to McMahon's City Council campaign. McMahon was a supporter of Bloomberg's congestion pricing plan, which would have required drivers to pay a fee for entering Manhattan south of 96th Street. McMahon supported this plan in the face of opposition from his Staten Island constituents, who would have been severely impacted by the plan given the paucity of public transportation options for Staten Islanders.

45. "House Majority Leader Steny Hoyer the Latest Congressional Heavyweight to Campaign Hard for Michael McMahon," *Staten Island Advance*, October 19, 2008.

46. Glenn Blain, "Democrat Michael McMahon Wins Vito Fossella's Scandal-Scarred House Seat," *New York Daily News*, November 5, 2008.

47. "Call Him Congressman McMahon," *Staten Island Advance*, November 5, 2008.

48. The last time the Democrats controlled the governor's office, the State Senate, and the State Assembly was 1935.

6

Texas District 23 Race (Rodriguez v. Larson)

A Vulnerable Candidate in a High-Profile Race . . . Proves to Be Neither

John David Rausch Jr.

Ciro D. Rodriguez
Age: 61
Sex: Male
Race: Hispanic
Religion: Roman Catholic
Education: M.S.W. (Our Lady of the Lake University, 1978); B.A., political science (St. Mary's University, 1973)
Occupation: College instructor; social worker; lobbyist
Political Experience: U.S. House of Representatives (1997–2005; 2007–present); Texas House of Representatives (1987–1997); trustee, Harlandale Independent School District Board (1975–1987)

Lyle Larson
Age: 49
Sex: Male
Race: Caucasian
Religion: Methodist
Education: B.B.A., marketing (Texas A&M University, 1981)
Occupation: Owner/CEO, American Consortium
Political Experience: Commissioner, Bexar County Commission (1997–2008); councilman, San Antonio City Council (1991–1995)

As populations grow and shrink, congressional districts must be reorganized to reflect changes in the population and to assure that every congressional district has roughly the same number of residents. For example, for much of the past three decades states in the Northeast such as New York,

New Jersey, and Pennsylvania have lost populations, whereas the populations of states in the "Sunbelt" such as Florida, Arizona, and California have grown. Accordingly, because the number of members of Congress remains constant at 435 (since 1929), some states loose seats while other states gain seats. The process of reapportionment generally occurs after the decennial census is taken and is performed by the legislature of the state impacted. Not surprisingly, state legislators try to advantage their own political parties and own political interests in what is known as "gerrymandering." At the same time, the Voting Rights Act and actions by the courts have tried to remedy the historic disadvantages faced by minority populations at the polls by creating so-called majority-minority districts—congressional seats containing a majority of nonwhite voters. One of the best examples of all these ingredients—population growth and change, gerrymandered seats, and majority-minority districts—is in the 23rd District of Texas.

CHARACTERISTICS OF THE DISTRICT

Party Balance

One of the nation's largest congressional districts and, in its current configuration, the newest congressional district in the country, the 23rd District was redrawn in 2006 as a result of a successful legal challenge to a congressional map drawn by Republicans in the Texas Legislature in 2003. In 2003, the Texas Legislature redrew the congressional map enacted in 2001 to increase the number of districts that would elect Republican members of Congress. In June 2006, the U.S. Supreme Court upheld most of the 2003 map, but ruled that that 23rd District was invalid because its 55 percent Hispanic population was insufficient to meet the protections for racial and ethnic minorities specified in the federal Voting Rights Act. After the Supreme Court's ruling, a federal court restored the district's Hispanic voting-age population to 65 percent by moving the south side of San Antonio to the 23rd from the adjacent 28th District.

Adding a larger Hispanic population reduced the Republican Party's strength in the district. Former representative, Ciro Rodriguez (D-TX), defeated Representative Henry Bonilla (R-TX) in a special election run-off in December 2006. According to several calculations, Republican governor, Rick Perry, would have won by 15 percent in the 23rd District configuration as drawn in 2003. In his 2006 reelection, Perry won by just 3.5 points. Republican presidential candidate John McCain defeated Democrat Barack Obama by nine points in the state of Texas. In the 23rd District, however, Obama received 56 percent of the vote. In the U.S. Senate race in 2008, John Cornyn (R-TX), defeated Democratic challenger Rick

Noriega, 54 to 44 percent. In the 23rd District, Noriega bested Cornyn by nearly 99,000 votes. After the 2006 redraw, the 23rd District became a safer district for Democrats.

Voting and Electoral History

From 1967, when the 23rd Congressional District was first created, until 1993, it was represented by a Democrat. In 1991, the Texas Legislature cut the new 28th Congressional District out of much of the 23rd District's original territory. The action left a heavily Republican section of San Antonio in the 23rd District. In 1992, Republican challenger, Henry Bonilla, defeated incumbent Albert Bustamante (D-TX) by charging that the incumbent was out of touch with the district. Even though the district maintained a slight edge in Democratic registrations, Bonilla, a television news personality, was very popular in San Antonio and did not face a serious Democratic opponent until 2002. Former Texas secretary of state Henry Cuellar, a Democrat, came within two percentage points of defeating Bonilla that year.

In 2003, the Republican-controlled Texas Legislature reconfigured a number of congressional districts in South Texas. The city of Laredo, historically one of the centers of the 23rd District, was drawn out of the 23rd District into the 28th District. Several heavily Republican San Antonio suburbs were added to the 23rd District, almost ensuring Rep. Bonilla easy reelection. The scenario changed on June 28, 2006, when the U.S. Supreme Court, in *League of United Latin American Citizens v. Perry*, ruled that the 23rd District violated the Voting Rights Act of 1965. The Court ordered a federal district court to redraw the 23rd District. The former representative, Rodriguez, defeated Rep. Bonilla in the December 2006 special election runoff with 54 percent of the vote.

Demographic Character of the Electorate

The 2000 Census recorded that the 23rd Congressional District had 651,620 people. The district is majority Hispanic with 55 percent of the residents. About 41 percent of the residents are non-Hispanic whites and slightly more than 2 percent are African American. Almost 16 percent of the population is foreign born. Slightly less than 51 percent of the population speaks a language other than English. Almost 30 percent of the residents are under the age of eighteen while 11 percent are over sixty-five.

Key Voting Blocs

The heavily Hispanic south side of San Antonio votes Democratic. Most of the white Anglo areas in the city's north side and in the western suburbs vote Republican. Other areas with strong Republican support include Medina County and Val Verde County, home to Laughlin Air Force Base. Maverick County and the city of Eagle Pass are overwhelmingly Hispanic areas on the district's southern border. Voters in these counties usually support Democratic candidates.[1]

Major Urban Areas and Employment/Occupation Characteristics

The 23rd Congressional District is about 700 miles long from eastern El Paso County in the west to San Antonio on the eastern edge of the district. It includes 700 miles of the border with Mexico on the Rio Grande. Nearly 60 percent of the residents live in San Antonio or in Bexar County. Slightly more than 294,000 residents of San Antonio reside in the part of the city that lies in the 23rd District. The other large cities in the district are Del Rio (33,867 population) and Eagle Pass (22,413).

The district has a high unemployment rate caused by seasonal employment, an influx of immigrants owing to the proximity to the border, and an abundance of cheaper Mexican labor. The district's unemployment rate during the early part of the decade was 6.5 percent. Of the employed residents, 71.8 percent work in the private sector, 19.4 percent are employed by government, and 8.4 percent are self-employed. Major industries include retail trade, education services, health care, and manufacturing. In 2006, Toyota opened a $1.2 billion plant in San Antonio. The plant which builds Tundra pickup trucks employs about 2,000 people. The median household income is $39,000.

There are two military bases in the district. Laughlin Air Force Base employs 1,420 military personnel and 1,800 civilians. Brooks City-Base (Air Force) employs 1,300 military personnel and 1,300 civilians. In 2005, the residents of the district learned that the Air Force's city-base would be closed by 2011.

THE CANDIDATES

Ciro Rodriguez

Ciro Rodriguez was born on December 9, 1946, in Piedras Negras, Coahuila, Mexico. His family moved to San Antonio, Texas, when he was a child. While he was in the ninth grade, Rodriguez's mother died and he dropped out of school. After a year working at a gas station, he decided to return to school, eventually graduating from Harlandale High School in Bexar County. After attending San Antonio College, he transferred to St. Mary's University in San Antonio where he earned a bachelor of arts in political science. He continued his education at Our Lady of the Lake University in San Antonio, earning a master of social work.

In 1975, Rodriguez was elected to the Board of Trustees of the Harlandale Independent School District where he served until 1987. During this time, he worked as an educational consultant for the Intercultural Development Research Association and as a caseworker for the Texas Department of Mental Health and Mental Retardation. Rodriguez also taught at Our Lady of the Lake University's Worden School of Social Work from 1987 until 1996.

Rodriguez served in the Texas House of Representatives from 1987 to 1997 and chaired the Local and Consent Calendar Committee, an important position as a gatekeeper for legislation in the House. He also served on the Public Health Committee and the Higher Education Committee. Among the bills he championed was legislation that guaranteed the top 10 percent of graduating students a place at a Texas four-year university.

In January of 1997, U.S. Representative Frank Tejeda (D-TX) of the 28th Congressional District died and a special election was called to fill the remainder of Tejeda's term. Rodriguez won the special election and was reelected in each election until 2004. In the House of Representatives, Rodriguez served as a member of the Armed Services, Veterans' Affairs, and Resources Committees. He also was the ranking member of the Veterans' Affairs Subcommittee on Health and, from 2003 through 2004, served as the chair of the Congressional Hispanic Caucus.

In 2003, the majority Republicans in the Texas Legislature redrew the districts drawn in 2001. Most of Laredo, a heavily Democratic area of the 23rd Congressional District, was moved into the 28th Congressional District. Rodriguez was now in the same district as Representative Henry Cuellar (D-TX), whose political base was Laredo. Rodriguez lost the March 2004 primary election to Cuellar by fifty-eight votes. After leaving the House in January 2005, he partnered with his former chief of staff to create a government relations firm that assisted clients in their relationships with local, state, and national government.

Rodriguez tried to regain his House seat in the 28th District in 2006. Running an underfinanced campaign, Rodriguez lost the March Democratic primary to Cuellar, carrying 48 percent of the vote. He was given another chance to run for Congress when the Supreme Court ruled in June that the 23rd District violated provisions of the Voting Rights Act. A federal court redrew the 23rd District to have a Hispanic voting-age population of 61 percent by attaching the south side of San Antonio to the 23rd District. The south side of San Antonio is Rodriguez's political base.[2] Rodriguez thus defeated Republican Representative Henry Bonilla with 55 percent of the votes cast in a special runoff election.

Lyle Larson

Representative Rodriguez's Republican challenger in 2008 was Lyle Larson. A native of San Antonio, Larson attended Anglo State University in San Angelo, Texas, before transferring to Texas A&M University, where he earned a bachelor of business administration in marketing. After working for a subsidiary of Johnson & Johnson, he opened his own business, a medical- and security-imaging company. In 1991, he was elected to the San Antonio City Council and served there until 1995. In 1997, Larson was elected to the Bexar County Commissioners Court, serving as the only Republican commissioner. As a commissioner, Larson served as chairman of the Military Transformation Task Force charged with protecting the military bases in San Antonio from closure. He also voted against and refused to accept all pay raises for county commissioners. When Larson left the commission, he was earning less than half the current pay of county commissioner. When he announced that he was entering the campaign to represent the 23rd District in Congress, Larson also promised that he would resign from the County Commission by June in order to devote his time during the summer to the congressional campaign. However, he did not follow through on this promise, although he did not seek reelection as a commissioner in 2008.

Before Larson could face Rep. Rodriguez in November, he had to defeat Francisco "Quico" Canseco in the March Republican primary. Canseco, a lawyer and the chair of Hondo National Bank, had been running for the seat since January 2007.[3] Larson did not officially enter the race until the filing deadline in January 2008. Canseco had the endorsement of many conservative political activists in the district as well as the Young Conservatives of Texas, Texas Right to Life, an anti-abortion group, and former representative, Bonilla.

Canseco promised to "empty his pockets" to defeat Rodriguez, but he never enjoyed the name recognition of his opponent. Canseco spent almost $1 million in the primary, about four times as much money as Larson was able to raise, but "everywhere that Canseco aired a radio or television ad, Larson went by car and met community leaders. Larson had just as many campaign signs as Canseco did dotting the landscape along Highway 90 West."[4] While Canseco could have attracted more Hispanic voters in the November general election, Larson was able to portray his primary opponent as a carpetbagger who moved from Laredo to San Antonio only a few years before entering the congressional race. Canseco responded by describing himself a nonpolitician, but Larson countered that Canseco had zero political experience.[5] Larson defeated Canseco with 62 percent of the Republican primary vote on the strength of his support in north Bexar County.

The Candidates' Ideologies

The candidates for the 23rd Congressional District exhibited complex ideologies. During his early terms in the House of Representatives, Rodriguez was considered one of the more liberal Democrats. In 2003, as the Representative from the 28th District, "he had an 80 percent rating in a *National Journal* survey or House votes, placing him in the top 20 percent of liberal-leaning congressman." He was the most liberal of the six Hispanic representatives from Texas.[6] But, later in the 2007 *National Journal* survey, Rodriguez rating dropped to a more moderate 59 percent. The new moderation exhibited itself in a number of votes against the rest of his party in the House.

Larson pointed out that even a 59 percent rating was too liberal for the 23rd District and presented himself to voters as a conservative. Throughout the campaign he told voters that, as a county commissioner, he worked to lower the tax rate seven times during his eleven years in office, saving taxpayers over $150 million. Larson accused Rodriguez as being too close to labor unions since the incumbent voted against free trade agreements.[7] On social issues, Larson maintained an anti-abortion position and support for traditional marriage and attempted to both attract those tired of politics as usual and distance himself from his unpopular party and president by regularly telling audiences that he was not interested in politics as a profession despite his years in San Antonio city government and Bexar County government. A central part of his campaign was a proposal to limit all members of Congress to twelve years in office.[8]

A Third Party Challenge: Lani Connolly

The 23rd Congressional District race included a Libertarian candidate, Lani Connolly, a San Antonio real estate agent. This was her first campaign for any political office and she did not really have much of an impact on the race.[9]

CAMPAIGN ISSUES

Military and Veterans' Spending

Military and veterans' spending is important to the residents of the 23rd Congressional District because it is home to two military bases and there are a number of other bases located near the boundaries of the district. Both candidates emphasized their work to maintain a military presence in the San Antonio area. The candidates also stressed the importance of veterans' rights. One area of primary concern for Rep. Rodriguez was the compensation received by American military personnel in war zones. In August 2008,

Rodriguez visited American forces in Baghdad. When he returned, he spoke about the inadequate compensation of American forces there, noting that employees of private firms contracting with the U.S. military were paid much more than American military personnel working in the same regions.[10] Larson also emphasized his role as chairman of the Military Transformation Task Force, claiming that he helped keep the military bases in San Antonio.

Relatedly, Larson highlighted the challenges faced by the approximately 55,000 military veterans living in the Rio Grande Valley. These veterans often have to travel long distances to get medical care at the Audie Murphy Hospital in San Antonio. He promised that veterans' health care would be a top priority after his election. Rep. Rodriguez reminded voters that he served on the House Veterans Affairs Committee and helped pass proposals to extend substance abuse treatment benefits and to expand access to health care for veterans who live in rural areas, which contrasted him from the record of his opponents' party.

Rodriguez was an early opponent of the war in Iraq, arguing that the money spent trying to build a democracy in Iraq could have been spent more fruitfully trying to improve government at the Texas-Mexico border. The Republican challenger stressed his belief that the U.S. military presence served as a stabilizing force in Iraq.

Immigration Policy and Border Security

Two other top campaign issues for the district were immigration policy and border security. This is not surprising considering that about 65 percent of district residents are Hispanic and the district encompasses about 700 miles of the border with Mexico along the Rio Grande. What was surprising was that both candidates advocated fairly moderate positions on immigration policy and border security when compared to their fellow partisans. Both candidates worked to distance themselves from the positions held by the majority in their parties.

For example, Rodriguez stressed the need to reform and restructure the Department of Homeland Security's approach to border security. He supported the Security through Regularized Immigration and a Vibrant Economy (STRIVE) Act of 2007, a bipartisan piece of legislation that would have established new programs for undocumented immigrants to achieve legal citizenship. He also supported the Secure America through Verification and Enforcement (SAVE) Act of 2007. With strong Republican support, this bill would have authorized the hiring of an additional 8,000 border agents over five years and would have required employers to use an electronic verification system to determine whether employees were undocumented immigrants. The only Hispanic House member supporting the bill, Rodriguez broke with House Democrats to support this bill, drawing the ire of Hispanic leaders in the district. He supported the bill because it would have provided federal funds to local governments that work with immigrants and it would have provided additional funding law enforcement efforts on the U.S.-Mexico border.[11]

Larson recognized Rodriguez's support for additional law enforcement on the border, but he argued that the incumbent was not doing enough. On his campaign website, Larson stressed that "the Congressman from this district must take ownership of the issue of border security and immigration to ensure that these concerns are finally addressed." He presented several specific proposals to address the issues of border security and illegal immigration such as creating a border guard comprised of all the members of Congress with border districts and the eight senators from the states along the border. This group would provide guidance to Congress on questions relating to the border. The members of the border guard would work with their counterparts from the Mexican government. To encourage the participation of Mexico, Larson suggested that the $1.3 billion of drug interdiction funding the United States provides Mexico would be contingent on their participation.

Larson advocated the expansion of Operation Streamline along the entire stretch of the U.S.-Mexican border. This program focuses on capturing, detaining, and incarcerating or deporting illegal immigrants and enjoyed public support. In fact, in a pilot project in the Del Rio area, illegal immigration was reduced by almost 70 percent. Larson also opposed granting amnesty to anyone who entered the United States illegally, a position he shared with many other Republicans. Instead of granting amnesty, he proposed an expansion of the Farm Visa program to other industries such as hospitality, food service, and construction. The expansion of the program would make it easier from employers to fill positions legally.

Neither candidate supported President George W. Bush's border fence. Larson was concerned that building the fence and then not properly manning the border would do little to stem illegal immigration or increase border security, and he, like many Republicans around the country, tried to distance himself from the unpopular president.

The Economy and Taxes

The candidates exhibited significant differences in their position on the economy and taxes. Larson stressed that he was a fiscal conservative and emphasized his experience as a tax-cutter while serving as a county commissioner where he led the process to get the commission to cut the county tax rate seven times, saving taxpayers over $500 million dollars. He also led the movement to freeze property taxes for county senior citizens while increasing the senior homestead exemption. He supported extending President Bush's tax cuts after their expiration date and proposed a simplification of the federal tax code largely by replacing the tax code with an alternative called the Fair Tax. The Fair Tax would replace all forms of tax collection (federal personal and corporate income taxes, gift, estate, capital gains, alternative minimum, Social Security, Medicare, and self-employment taxes) with a progressive national sales tax.

Rodriguez's campaign latched on to the Fair Tax proposal and created an advertisement attacking the proposal. Rodriguez suggested that Larson wanted to impose a 23 percent national sales tax. Larson proposed the sales tax to replace other federal taxes, but the Rodriguez campaign failed to mention this key fact.[12]

The campaigns also discussed the question of congressional earmarks. The Republican challenger indicated that he would work to eliminate all earmarks until the federal government achieved a balanced budget. He proposed that specific projects should be openly considered by Congress rather than be attached to bill as earmarks. Rodriguez responded by pointing out that the Democratic majority in Congress worked to reduce the amount of money spent on earmarks below that spent by previous Republican congresses, while also requiring that members of Congress attach their names to the earmarks added to pieces of legislation. Rodriguez stopped short of calling for a ban on earmarks, however, pointing out that there is funding for local projects contained in many budgets and bills. Among the "earmarks" was $5 million for the University of Texas at San Antonio (UTSA) to be used for Homeland Security projects and $5 million from the Department of Defense for UTSA to develop cyber security. Rodriguez pointed out that local companies would be expanding and hiring more employees because of the "disgraced" earmarks.[13]

Early in the campaign season, both candidates responded to significant economic challenges. With the rapid increase in gas prices and concerns about an economic downturn, the *San Antonio Express-News* reported that Rodriguez and Larson scheduled events across the district to discuss their economic plans and listen to constituents' concerns.[14]

Both men opposed the $700 billion bailout of financial institutions proposed by President Bush and considered by Congress in September 2008. Before the House of Representatives voted on the first proposal, Larson blasted the president's plan. He called for a less expensive, market-driven alternative that included lowering the capital gains tax. Larson also placed the blame for the failing financial institutions squarely on a complacent Congress, while trying to shift blame from his party.[15]

Rodriguez voted against the proposal in the House, acknowledging that politics played a role in his decision. His spokesperson told the media that Rodriguez opposed the bailout because his constituents did not like it. The

San Antonio Express-News hypothesized that the incumbent voted against the bailout because Larson publicly announced his opposition. Rodriguez "couldn't risk being on the wrong side of an angry electorate."[16] The *Express-News* endorsed Larson. Rodriguez blamed the Republican Party for the economic crisis because Republicans long supported less regulation of Wall Street firms.

CAMPAIGN STRATEGY

Media

Many political observers viewed the 23rd District as a swing district in 2008. Pundits believed Rodriguez could be reelected but could also be defeated by a quality Republican challenger. Conservative political activists in San Antonio believed that Rodriguez was lucky to win the seat from Bonilla in the special runoff election in December 2006. Consequently, both candidates would need strong media strategies to win in 2008. Because Rodriguez spent his first term as the representative of the 23rd Congressional District, and thus getting his name in front of his constituents, he enjoyed an incumbent's advantage in both media coverage and name recognition during the campaign.

The incumbent drew media attention to problems that plagued the district and its constituents—and thus to himself—through press conferences, photo opportunities, and various publicity stunts. In early May, the Rodriguez campaign combined "National Train Day" with a whistle-stop "Get Economy Back on Track" event. Unfortunately, the Amtrak train was three and a half hours late arriving in El Paso. An appearance at the rodeo in Del Rio had to be cancelled, but the representative spent the time aboard the train visiting with elected public officials from different parts of the district. He also discussed economic problems.[17]

As an incumbent county commissioner, Larson was able to capitalize on earned media in San Antonio. In fact, it is possible that one of the reasons Larson did not resign from his commission seat during the campaign for Congress was to continue to get free media coverage in the crucial San Antonio media market. Because of his limited campaign resources, he also had to rely on a grassroots effort that involved visiting communities to the west in the sprawling district. Larson employed a strategy similar to the one used in his successful campaign against a wealthy opponent, Canseco, by emphasizing the grass roots and taking the campaign on the road. In addition to the traditional media, the campaign was also fought in the news media. One subject that had bloggers buzzing was Rodriguez's refusal to endorse a presidential candidate until late in the nomination process. As an elected public official, Rodriguez was a "superdelegate" to the Democratic National Convention. In April, the Republican Party of Texas issued a press release asking Rodriguez to announce who he was supporting for president. Rodriguez finally endorsed Senator Hillary Clinton (D-NY) in May, shortly after it appeared as though Senator Barack Obama (D-IL) had taken the lead in the delegate count. Rodriguez said that he endorsed Clinton because "the district went overwhelmingly for Sen. Clinton in the primary."[18]

Larson was endorsed by the *San Antonio Express-News*. Rodriguez was endorsed by a number of interests and individuals including the Business Industry Political Action Committee and the Texas Farm Bureau.

Image and Advertising

Rodriguez entered the 2008 election cycle high on the Republican Party's list of targeted Democrats. Local Republicans regularly referred to him as "Zero" Rodriguez. Although he had defeated incumbent Bonilla in December 2006, most Republicans believed that Rodriguez had stolen their seat. Rodriguez also had a history of being slow in raising funds.

The Rodriguez campaign received a gift when Republican primary voters nominated Larson and not Francisco Canseco. While Canseco's political experience was nonexistent, he could have caused significant trouble for the incumbent. Canseco was a conservative Hispanic with significant personal financial resources to bring to the campaign. Canseco was also somewhat effective in making a case to primary voters that Republicans needed a Hispanic nominee to beat Rodriguez in the general election.[19] When the Republicans nominated Larson, however, national Democrats calculated that Rodriguez had improved his chances for reelection.

The campaign largely focused on constituent service and ideology with Rodriguez discussing how he had benefited the district since being elected in 2006 and Larson pointing out how the incumbent was too liberal for most residents in the district. Larson's campaign developed a television commercial to stress his opposition to congressional earmarks. The ad showed Larson on a farm while pigs fed at a trough. The candidate compared the federal government to the swine and resulted in some of the harshest exchanges of the campaign. The Democratic Congressional Campaign Committee, allegedly acting independently of the Rodriguez campaign, filed a complaint with the Federal Election Commission because Larson mistakenly failed to note that he approved the ad.[20]

The Rodriguez campaign ran a number of ads focusing on Larson's support for the Fair Tax national sales tax proposal. In one ad, Rodriguez claimed that Larson supported a 23 percent increase in the sales tax even on groceries. Larson responded that the Rodriguez campaign was spreading misinformation because it did not explain that the sales tax would replace other federal taxes including the income tax.

At the end of the campaign, Larson criticized Rodriguez for the campaign's negative tone. He complained about the misinformation presented in the Democrat's attack ads on taxation. Larson also criticized the incumbent for refusing to engage him in a debate of the issues.[21]

Finance

Financial resources are important in every congressional campaign. In a district as expansive as the 23rd, money becomes even more vital. Rodriguez received significant financial support from the Democratic Congressional Campaign Committee. His Republican challenger received significant empty promises from national Republican organizations.[22] According to the Center for Responsive Politics, Rodriguez raised $2,333,425 and spent $2,265,087. Larson raised $814,616 and spent $803,714.

Rodriguez raised 56 percent of his financing from political action committee (PAC) contributions and individuals provided 42 percent of his funding. Whereas, Larson, received 86 percent of his funds from individual contributions while PACs contributed only 14 percent. Larson stressed his reliance on individual contributions in press releases and other statements.

The National Republican Congressional Committee targeted Rodriguez as one of several vulnerable Democratic incumbents but, because it was a difficult election for Republicans across the country, the NRCC failed to provide enough money to Larson. The DCCC spent more than $700,000 on television advertising.[23]

Grass Roots

As a challenger lacking substantial campaign funds, Larson focused on personal appearances, following his successful strategy from the Republican primary. He regularly appeared before community meetings and other groups, especially in the heavily Hispanic areas in Bexar County, Rodriguez's political base. Late in the campaign, there was some apprehension among Rodriguez's advisors that Larson's grassroots campaign might have been changing voters' minds. But Rodriguez relied less on a grassroots strategy. Instead he reminded constituents about his ability to serve them as a member of the House of Representatives. He remarked that his office had created a model for outreach to constituents. From the time he took office in 2007 until the November 2008 election, for example, Rodriguez met with more than 100 small groups on the Republican Northwest Side of San Antonio.[24]

Bases of Support

Both candidates worked hard to maintain their bases of support while also trying to secure votes in neighborhoods far from their traditional bases. The candidates focused most of their attention on the two-thirds of the district's residents who live in Bexar County. In one incident, Larson related how, as a member of Bexar's Commission, he worked with Sergio "Chico" Rodriguez, who was a precinct commissioner and happened to be Rodriguez's brother, to deliver projects to the South Side of San Antonio. Larson was endorsed by a number of South Side political leaders including Lillie Tejeda, the mother of the late Democratic representative Frank Tejeda Jr.; former councilwoman Lynda Billa Burke; and Lisa Salazar, board president of the Southside Independent School District. Perhaps more importantly, he earned the support of former commissioner Robert Tejeda, who was defeated in Precinct 1 by Chico Rodriguez in 2004.[25]

ELECTION RESULTS

The 23rd District race was expected to be competitive. Rodriguez was targeted by national Republicans and had a history of lethargic fund-raising. Even some local Democrats did not think he was an effective member of Congress. As late as October 25, just days before the election, local political experts still saw the district as competitive, reflected by the sizable contributions coming in late in the campaign.[26] Bexar County Democrats continued to highlight the possibility of Rodriguez's defeat during the two-week early voting period when voter turnout in North Side precincts far outstripped the turnout in the heavily Hispanic south. Democrats in Bexar County typically vote on Election Day.

In the end, Rodriguez was easily reelected, defeating Larson 56 percent to 42 percent. The Libertarian candidate picked up just 2 percent of the vote. Before the election, both campaigns identified their bases of support, with Larson running stronger in conservative areas such as northwest San Antonio, Val Verde County, and the smaller rural towns that dot the district. The largest concentrations of Democrats supporting Rodriguez were in south San Antonio, Eagle Pass (Maverick County; across the Mexican border from Rodriguez's birthplace, Piedras Negras), and Presidio in Presidio County. A review of the county-level vote illustrates that Rodriguez had support in almost every county in the district (see table 6.1). Rodriguez carried the precincts in Bexar County with 52 percent of the vote. He also won 66 percent of the vote in Val Verde County, the home of Laughlin Air Force Base and a key conservative stronghold. Larson carried Edwards County with 55 percent of the vote, Medina County with 58 percent, and Sutton County with 52 percent.

Table 6.1. Votes in Congressional District 23

County	Rodriguez (D)	Larson (R)
Bexar	52%	45%
Brewster	55%	41%
Crockett	50%	49%
Culberson	72%	25%
Dimmit	82%	17%
Edwards	43%	55%
El Paso	76%	21%
Hudspeth	62%	34%
Jeff Davis	52%	44%
Kinney	51%	47%
Maverick	87%	12%
Medina	40%	58%
Pecos	50%	48%
Presidio	82%	17%
Reeves	70%	28%
Sutton	45%	52%
Terrell	54%	43%
Uvalde	56%	42%
Val Verde	66%	33%
Zavala	89%	10%

Note: Totals do not equal 100 percent because of the votes received by the Libertarian candidate.

Larson explained Rodriguez's victory as one result of the "Obama wave." The presence of Obama at the top of the ticket brought an "unprecedented number of straight-ticket Democratic voters" to the polls in the 23rd District. In fact, Obama's popularity in the district affected a number of other races. Even though Republican presidential nominee, John McCain, defeated Obama by nine percentage points in Texas, Obama won 56 percent of the votes in the 23rd District. In the race for the U.S. Senate, Republican incumbent, John Cornyn, defeated Democratic challenger, Rick Noriega, 54 percent to 44 percent, but Noriega received 99,000 more votes in the 23rd District. The importance of straight-ticket voting was apparent in Texas and, remarkably, there have even been legislative efforts to try and ban it.

NOTES

1. Gary Martin, "Money Keeps Coming in Hot Race for 23rd Congressional District," *San Antonio Express-News*, October 25, 2008, 4A.

2. Greg Giroux, "Rodriguez's Upset Win in Texas 23 Yields Another Seat for Dems," *New York Times*, December 12, 2006.

3. Greg Jefferson, "Larson in No Rush to Toss Hat in Ring," MySanAntonio.com, www.mysantonio.com/news/MYSA120907_01B_District_23_2b7e89f_html9683.html (accessed November 11, 2008).

4. Gebe Martinez, "Rodriguez Tests Ninth Life in West Texas Race," Politico.com, March 11, 2008.

5. Jamie Castillo, "Larson Has Work to Do in GOP Primary, Let Alone in November," *San Antonio Express-News*, January 7, 2008, 1B.

6. Gary Martin, "Rodriguez More Moderate since Capturing New Post," *San Antonio Express-News*, September 15, 2008, 1A.

7. Martin, "Rodriguez More Moderate."

8. Gilbert Garcia, "Playing by Earmark," *San Antonio Current*, September 24, 2008, www.sacurrent.com/printStory.asp?id=69355 (accessed November 21, 2008).

9. Gustavo Reveles Acosta, "District 23 Race Pits 2 against Incumbent," *El Paso Times*, October 19, 2008.

10. Garcia, "Playing by Earmark."

11. Martin, "Rodriguez More Moderate since Capturing New Post."

12. Jamie Castillo, "Watch Out, the Socialists Are Coming—or Is It the Fascists?" *San Antonio Express-News*, October 30, 2008, 1B.

13. Garcia, "Playing by Earmark."

14. Gary Martin, "House Candidates Focus on Gas, Economy," *San Antonio Express-News*, April 25, 2008, 3B.

15. Scott Stroud, "Re-election Bid in Time of Crisis Has Rodriguez Laying Blame," *San Antonio Express-News*, October 4, 2008.

16. Stroud, "Re-election Bid."

17. Lynn Brezosky, "Riding the Rails a Lesson in Patience for Congressman," *San Antonio Express-News*, May 4, 2008.

18. Scott Stroud, "Rep. Rodriguez Throws His Support Behind Clinton—in His Own Time," *San Antonio Express-News*, May 10, 2008, 14A.

19. Martinez, "Rodriguez Tests Ninth Life."

20. Garcia, "Playing by Earmark."

21. Gary Martin and Guillermo X. Garcia, "Rodriguez Wins 2nd Term in High-Profile Campaign," *San Antonio Express-News*, November 5, 2008, 5A.

22. Martin and Garcia, "Rodriguez Wins 2nd Term."

23. Martin and Garcia, "Rodriguez Wins 2nd Term."

24. Greg Jefferson, "Who Can Raid Whose Base?" *San Antonio Express-News*, October 29, 2008, 1B.

25. Jefferson, "Who Can Raid Whose Base?"

26. Martin, "Money Keeps Coming."

7

California District 26 Race (Warner v. Dreier)

Anti-Republican Sentiment Proved No Match for Money and Incumbency

Marcia Godwin and Richard Gelm

Russ Warner
Age: 58
Sex: Male
Race: Caucasian
Religion: Methodist
Education: Attended Cypress Junior College
Occupation: CEO, Warner International Periodical Services (magazine distributor) (1986–present)
Political Experience: No prior political experience

David Dreier
Age: 56
Sex: Male
Race: Caucasian
Religion: Christian Science
Education: M.A., American government (Claremont McKenna College, 1976); B.A., political science (Claremont McKenna College, 1975)
Political Experience: U.S. House of Representatives (1986–present)

Like the vast majority of congressional districts, California's 26th is represented by a long-entrenched incumbent. Republican David Dreier has represented the district since 1980 when, aided by the landslide victories by Ronald Reagan and the Republican Party, he defeated Democratic incumbent, James F. Lloyd (D-CA), with 52 percent of the vote. Dreier has also benefited in each subsequent election by redistricting plans in California that protect most incumbents whether Democrat or Republican.

Yet, Democrats have held out hope of defeating Dreier since he secured his reelection in 2004 by only a 54 to 43 percent margin against a novice opponent and after a popular conservative radio program criticized his record on immigration. While there continue to be more Republicans than Democrats in the district, the gap has narrowed and a large bloc of independent voters could impact future election outcomes.

As the 2008 race began, Dreier appeared to be facing a relatively well-financed candidate, businessman Russ Warner, for the first time in his tenure. Ultimately, resources to mount a serious general election challenge did not materialize for Warner. Warner did not attempt to capitalize on the pro-Obama sentiment and tide of anti-Republican, anti-incumbency sentiment sweeping the nation. These national trends did not have a profound impact on voting in the district. Dreier won by a large margin, but with only 53 percent of the vote because of the presence of a Libertarian candidate on the ballot. The district may be one to follow in future elections because liberal independent political committees based in Los Angeles have targeted the district and the 26th is one of only two potentially competitive congressional districts in the Los Angeles metropolitan area.

CHARACTERISTICS OF THE DISTRICT

By all measures the 26th District has been safe Republican territory, although the Republican margin steadily declined in the 1990s. Reapportionment after the 2000 census, with Rep. Dreier taking a lead role in protecting Republican incumbents, was designed to secure the district as a safe seat for the next decade. However, by 2008 the percentage of registered Republicans declined to 41 percent, as shown in table 7.1, raising the possibility that a combination of Democrats and independent voters could vote Dreier out of office.

California's 26th Congressional District is nestled along the Southern rim of the San Gabriel Mountains of Southern California and spans across twenty-four communities from eastern Los Angeles County to western San Bernardino County. The district lacks a true urban center, and mass media outlets are based to the west in Los Angeles, hampering efforts by any challenger to gain name recognition. To the extent that the district has any common identity, it is that it is a collection of fairly affluent suburbs of Los Angeles that are bisected by the 210 Freeway.

The district is predominately white, professional, and conservative, but with growing Hispanic and Asian American populations. Asian American professionals, especially Chinese and Koreans, are now a significant part of the population in the district, especially in the San Gabriel Valley portion of Los Angeles County. Republican Jay Kim, the first Korean American in Congress, represented the adjoining 41st District for three terms from 1992 to 1998.

Table 7.1. Partisanship and Elections in California's 26th Congressional District

	Voter Registration				Election Results	
	Republican	Democrat	Decline to State			
2000	41%	40%	15%	President:	Dreier 57%	Nelson 40%
					Bush 53%	Gore 44%
2002	47%	34%	15%		Dreier 64%	Mikels 34%
2004	45%	34%	17%	President:	Dreier 54%	Matthews 43%
					Bush 55%	Kerry 44%
2006	44%	34%	18%		Dreier 57%	Matthews 38%
2008	41%	35%	20%		Dreier 53%	Warner 40%
					McCain 47%	Obama 51%

Source: California Secretary of State, *Report of Registration* and *Statement of Vote* documents, available at www.sos.ca.gov. Registration does not include minor party registration, which has remained at 4 percent of the electorate.

THE CANDIDATES

David Dreier

Dreier's roots are in Kansas City, Missouri, where his family continues to reside; his mother passed away in Kansas City in the middle of the 2008 campaign. Dreier moved to Southern California to attend Claremont McKenna College (formerly Claremont Men's College), one of the Claremont Colleges, which is located in the middle of the district. Dreier was elected to Congress while still in his twenties and held onto the district in 1982 when reapportionment resulted in a primary campaign against a fellow Republican incumbent.

With droll wit, the *Almanac of American Politics* concluded that "Dreier evidently decided never to be pressed for funds again; he raised plenty and spent little, which takes more self-discipline than one might imagine."[1] With a campaign balance of $2 million deterring serious challengers, Dreier was able to build up seniority on the House Rules Committee and initially did not seem to place much emphasis on maintaining a high profile or in pork-barrel politics.

Dreier was a loyal lieutenant of House Speaker Newt Gingrich (R-GA) during the 1990s and placed in charge of reforming the committee structure of Congress in 1994. He became chair of the Rules Committee in 1999 and continued until the Republicans lost their majority in 2006. As chair, Dreier assumed a more public persona and actively sought funds for the district, including earmarks for groundwater remediation efforts in the western part of the district and funding for a prominent senior center in the City of Rancho Cucamonga that was then named in his honor. During the 2003 gubernatorial recall election against unpopular Democrat Gray Davis, he toured with Arnold Schwarzenegger during his successful run for governor and headed Schwarzenegger's transition team.

After media speculation about a possible 2004 run against Senator Barbara Boxer (D-CA), Dreier chose to remain in the House, and his star may have somewhat faded. Dreier had unexpected opposition in 2004, most notably a concerted radio station campaign against him for his less than aggressive stance against illegal immigration. He since has become a more vocal advocate of a border fence and tighter immigration restrictions. Dreier's opponent in 2004, Cynthia Matthews, was an underfunded political novice who had never held prior political office. Nonetheless, Matthews garnered 43 percent of the vote.

Although he was briefly considered for the post of majority leader in 2005 after Tom Delay (R-TX) resigned, Dreier's perceived moderate views and potentially scandalous rumors about his personal life led the more conservative members of the Republican caucus to side with John Boehner (R-OH).[2] Instead of the leadership post, Dreier was given additional party duties and asked to lead ethics reform efforts.[3] For the 2006 election, Dreier ran a much more aggressive campaign. According to Federal Election Committee reports, he spent close to $2 million and donated over $600,000 to the National Republican Congressional Campaign Committee during the 2005–2006 election cycle. Dreier was still able to carry over a fund balance of about $2 million to the next election because of extensive fund-raising efforts.

Dreier had been an early supporter of Republican presidential candidate Rudy Giuliani in 2008. When Giuliani's campaign failed, Dreier was not as actively involved with the McCain campaign; he did donate $2,000 from his campaign coffers to McCain, however. Following the Democratic takeover of the Congress in 2006, Dreier became the ranking minority member of the Rules Committee. No longer in the House majority and without a committee chairmanship, Dreier has faced a considerably more challenging environment for securing government funding and earmarks for his district in recent years.

Russ Warner

The 2008 race pit Dreier against a political newcomer, Russ Warner. Warner had contested the 2006 Democratic primary, but lost to 2004 nominee Cynthia Matthews. Warner was a longtime resident of the district who began his business career as a distributor for *U.S. News & World Report* before founding his own magazine distribution company, Warner International Periodical Services. His company also employed his wife, Kris, and two of his sons.

Warner made the war in Iraq a centerpiece of his campaign and often spoke about how his eldest son, Greg, had convinced him to run after Greg's experience in Iraq as an army soldier. Warner garnered several high-profile endorsements including one from retired general Wesley Clark, a 2004 Democratic presidential candidate. Warner spent over $160,000, mostly through self-funding and donations from immediate family members. Matthews spent less than $20,000 for the entire 2006 campaign, but won the 2006 primary by a 47 to 38 percent margin over Warner, about a 3,000 vote difference. (A third, largely unknown candidate garnered 15 percent of the vote.) Dreier then easily defeated Matthews in the 2006 general election.

Warner kept his campaign committee active and quickly began campaigning and fund-raising for the 2008 election. During the 2008 primary season, Warner sent out a number of mailers to Democratic households that highlighted his endorsement by the California Democratic Party and a platform that called for ending the Iraq War, helping the economy, and supporting energy independence. Warner also compared and contrasted his record with Dreier's, using the label of "Bush Rubber Stamp" that was also adopted by independent committees and Democratic activists.

Warner easily won the primary this time around, receiving just over 67 percent of the vote against his opponent, Cynthia Matthews. Warner clearly did not want to take any risk of losing the campaign and may have felt that the June primary was close enough to the general election that sentiment would carry over to the fall campaign. As discussed later in this chapter, the heavy primary spending seriously depleted Warner's campaign coffers and Warner was not able to spend as much on the general election campaign in 2008.

CAMPAIGN ISSUES

Immigration

As a border state with a large Hispanic population, immigration and border issues are visible in California politics. Immigration issues have been a part of Dreier's campaign message since the 2004 campaign when he was criticized by conservatives for not being a strong advocate of border security. Dreier faced primary challenges in both 2006 and 2008 from a conservative critic, Sonny Sardo. Sardo has not come close to unseating Dreier, but his candidacy has had the effect of keeping sustained pressure on Dreier to publicly advocate and defend his conservative record.

Dreier's campaign literature clearly anticipated immigration as a concern. One general election mailer to Republicans touted Dreier's own record while criticizing Warner's views on driver's licenses and amnesty for undocumented immigrants. The mailer also criticized Warner's business practices related to filing taxes. Warner did not make immigration a focus of his own campaign, so immigration was, surprisingly, mostly a nonissue in the general election.

The Iraq War and Support for Veterans

Warner initially ran in 2006 on a mostly anti–Iraq War platform and would have had a compelling message if he had advanced to the general election then. As a businessman with a son in the army, he could have been very persuasive in opposing the war while supporting those serving in the military. Voter surveys from the 2006 election indicated that voters' opinion on the Iraq War was a strong predictor of votes for House challengers.[4]

By 2008, the apparent success of the "surge" in lowering casualties in Iraq led Warner, independent committees, and bloggers to shift criticism from the war to Dreier's votes on veteran's benefits. These arguments were similar to those made by the Obama and McCain presidential campaigns. While technically true that Dreier had voted against veteran's benefits, there had been numerous bills in Congress that included veteran affairs issues, with Republicans opposing some bills and amendments while Democrats opposed others. To ward off criticism, Dreier made support for veteran's benefits one of his spotlighted issues in both official correspondence and campaign literature.

President Bush's Record and the Economy

A key message made by Democratic activists and the Warner campaign was that Dreier was too closely aligned with the unpopular Bush administration. This message was highly effective in 2006 congressional races, but was overshadowed by the economy in the 26th District as local economic conditions worsened in 2008. IndyMac Bank, headquartered in the district, was seized by federal regulators in the summer. PFF Bank and Trust (Pomona First Federal), the largest local bank in the eastern part of the district and a Dreier campaign contributor, also suffered from home foreclosures, the slowdown in new construction, and a run on its deposits; PFF first negotiated a buyout by another bank, but was seized by regulators and sold to a different bank just before the election.

Some of Dreier's mailings were adapted to include reassurances about his efforts to deal with the economy. One postcard listing awards from organizations also had a statement that Dreier is "an effective and recognized leader who will fight to help get our economy back on track." Two other mailings had first-person comments from Dreier that he was working hard to put the economy back on track, although these multipage flyers mostly covered a variety of other issues.

Warner seemed unable to capitalize on the issue of the economy. As a wealthy businessman, Warner was not well-positioned to promote himself as a champion of the middle or working classes, usually core Democratic and independent voter constituencies, but he should have been able to tout his own business credentials. With Dreier able to send out more mailers to independents and also accusing Warner of unfair business practices, many voters did not know whether Warner was, in fact, qualified to deal with economic issues. Warner responded mainly through interviews with local newspapers. The Warner campaign tried to turn the tables by criticizing Dreier's support for the $700 billion bailout legislation as a last-minute change of heart, but Warner added that he would have voted for the bailout as well.

Warner could have linked his candidacy more to the Obama campaign or more directly criticized Dreier's acceptance of donations from corporate PACs, many of whom either filed bankruptcy or were beneficiaries of the government bailout. Obama ended up winning California by a 61 to 37 percent margin over McCain. Yet, Warner included Obama's picture and endorsement in only one of the few mailers he was able to afford for the general election. While local Democratic groups assisted with the Warner campaign, the noncompetitiveness of the California presidential race may have actually hurt local grassroots efforts; many Obama volunteers and staff from California were sent to nearby Nevada to campaign.

There is some sense, though, that if the campaign had gone longer, the momentum of the Obama candidacy and voter anger about the economy would have led to additional campaign donations to the Warner campaign and a closer outcome. During the last few weeks of the campaign, news reports began circulating that even safe Republican incumbents could be at risk. Dreier was specifically mentioned in several of these articles, although Warner was still given slim odds of winning.[5]

CAMPAIGN STRATEGY

Campaign Finance

Data compiled from campaign finance reports to the Federal Elections Commission illustrate a crucial gap in monetary resources between Dreier and Warner. As shown in table 7.2, Warner actually came close to Dreier in individual donations, trailing by only $73,000, and Warner's total contributions were just over a respectable $1 million. However, Dreier raised an additional half million dollars from political action committees (PACs), including a wide variety of corporate PACs, compared to a little over $40,000 donated to Warner from Democratic organizations and labor groups. Warner partially made up the difference by personally donating over $180,000 to his campaign and also loaned money to his campaign. However, Dreier ended up with a $400,000 fund-raising advantage for the election cycle and outspent Warner by $800,000 by drawing upon funds accumulated in past elections. Even with donating over $1 million to the Republican Congressional Campaign Committee and running an aggressive campaign, Dreier ended the 2008 election cycle with a fund balance of over $900,000. This fund balance is not as large as might appear; Dreier will completely exhaust his campaign account if he maintains similar fundraising levels and spends as much in 2010 as he did in 2008.

Campaign expenditure details indicate that Warner may have been hampered not just by total funds available, but by questionable spending priorities. Warner spent almost $650,000 through the end of primary season, going through almost all of the funds raised to that point. Warner actually spent less in the general election campaign, a little over $400,000, than he had in the primary. Dreier's expenses appeared to have been similar for the primary season, but he was actually more frugal because a portion of his expenditures were for taxes and accounting services related to his large campaign account balance.

Table 7.2. Campaign Finance Summary, Rep. David Dreier (R) v. Russ Warner (D)

	David Dreier (Incumbent)	Warner (Challenger)
Cash on Hand		
Jan. 1, 2008	$1,964,514	$239,980
Nov. 24, 2008	$918,144	$8,951
Contributions		
Individual	$886,747	$814,012
PAC Donations	$546,806	$41,150
Candidate	None	$184,643 $10,000 loan outstanding
Total Contributions	**$1,433,553**	**$1,038,805**
Operating Expenditures		
Through Primary Election	$706,774	$648,804
Through General Election	$1,157,528	$414,653
Total Expenditures	**$1,864,302**	**$1,063,457**
Contributions to Other Campaigns	$1,022,500 National Republican Congressional Committee $2,000 Giuliani Campaign $2,300 McCain Campaign	None

Source: Federal Elections Commission, www.fec.gov.

Table 7.3 details that Dreier had a more streamlined campaign organization compared to Warner. Even with keeping his campaign manager on retainer for $1,000 per month and then paying her $5,000 per month during active campaign periods, Dreier only spent a total of $50,000 on salaries. Warner paid his campaign manager a similar salary, but had several other paid staff members and, thus, spent over four times as much on staff as Dreier.

Warner also spent considerably more on consultants. A portion of Warner's campaign consultant expenditures may overlap with fund-raising services. However, some expenses seemed excessive, such as $1,500 per month paid to a public relations firm. Warner spent about $80,000 for services provided by Hildebrand and Tewes, a top campaign management consulting firm based in South Dakota and Washington, DC, whose founders had major roles in the Obama campaign. Services were also provided by two other political consulting firms. The use of premium consultant services raises questions about Warner's use of funds, but may simply reflect that the campaign geared up to run a large-scale campaign and anticipated general election donations from Democratic Party sources and other donors that did not come to fruition.

Table 7.3. Major Campaign Expenditures, Rep. David Dreier (R) v. Russ Warner (D)

	David Dreier (Incumbent)	Warner (Challenger)
Campaign staff	$50,000	$211,000
Contribution to organizations for election support	$3,000	n/a
Campaign consultants	$61,000	$173,000
Fund-raising consultants	$36,000	$16,000
Fund-raising expenses	$48,000	$19,000
Survey research	$79,000	$68,000
Mailers/postage	$1,109,000	$452,000
Printed materials/T-shirts	$30,000	$5,000
Slate mailer/advertising	$15,000	$2,000
Telephone calls	$10,000	$9,000
Website/Internet	$21,000	$31,000
Yard signs	$10,000	$2,000
Campaign office	$16,000	$21,000
Telephone charges	$10,000	$2,000
Accounting services	$107,000	$33,000
Candidate reimbursement/in-kind reimbursement	$72,000	$18,000
State and federal taxes	$167,000	n/a

Source: Federal Elections Commission, www.fec.gov. Expenses compiled by M. Godwin and rounded to nearest $1,000.

Regardless of the reasons for his spending decisions, Warner was able to spend only about $230,000 for campaign mailers for the general election, very similar to the $211,000 he spent on mailers for the primary. By reducing spending in other areas, Warner might have been able to fund a few more mailers in the fall. It should be noted, though, that Dreier spent in excess of $900,000 for mailers for the general election and could have spent more if needed.

Alternately, Warner could have focused his campaigning efforts more internally by doing a lot more grassroots organizing and locally based fundraising, but again it is doubtful whether a more effective campaign strategy would have affected the outcome.

Local Elected Official and Newspaper Endorsements

Dreier received the endorsement of prominent Republicans and some Democratic elected officials in the district. Dreier sent out a "Democrats for Dreier" mailing in July and also mailed postcards listing endorsements from other local leaders. Newspaper endorsements followed from the regional papers such the *San Gabriel Valley Tribune* and *Inland Valley Daily Bulletin* and finally from the Southern California powerhouse *Los Angeles Times*. Touted as a seasoned veteran who delivered for his district and had worked with Democrats, the papers' endorsements argued that Dreier should and would be reelected, while acknowledging that "at last, Democrats have fielded a challenger worthy of consideration."[6]

Targeted Constituencies

The fall general election campaign was a tale of different constituencies, almost as if there were two different districts. Democratic voters might not have known there was a contested race as they received *no* campaign literature. Independent voters received several mailers from Warner and numerous mailers from the Dreier campaign, which also sent many of the mailers to Republican households.

Dreier's mailers emphasized broad-based concerns like public safety, traffic congestion, senior issues, tax code simplification, and health care. Two postcards attacked Warner directly: One criticized Warner's views as "being out of the mainstream" and another focused on some apparent tax filing and business license problems, concluding that Warner should not be trusted with "our tax dollars." A mailer on immigration issues was apparently sent only to Republican households.

In a tough election year for Republicans, it was unsurprising that the Dreier campaign did not want to remind Democratic constituents that the incumbent was a Republican; it was wise to avoid signaling to Democrats that Dreier felt threatened. Appeals to the Republican base and to independents did not have the same risks. What was puzzling was that Warner targeted only independent households during the general election. As discussed earlier, Warner could only afford a few mailings and had to limit the total number of households per mailing, but could have adjusted his strategy to include Democrats or even reprinted a compare/contrast brochure from the primary that effectively mixed concern for the economy with the case for change.

Instead, the general election literature mostly attempted to raise ethical concerns. Two mailings to independents accused Dreier of having donated in the past to Congressional colleagues under investigation. A third mailing had a cover of Dreier in a tuxedo holding a cigar and claiming that he had spent his career favoring special interests. It also called Dreier a "Bush rubber stamp" and briefly mentioned PAC contributions. It included a more pro-Warner message and a picture of the Democratic presidential nominee, with Obama's endorsement, but the overall tone was much more negative than positive.

Independent Committee Involvement

Several independent political organizations targeted Representative Dreier as a potentially vulnerable incumbent. These groups aggressively used limited funding to criticize Dreier, but did not make the case for voting for Warner due to legal restrictions against directly endorsing candidates.

Working Families Win, a project of the liberal Americans for Democratic Action interest group, was the first independent political organization to become involved. Although its website, www.workingfamilieswin.org, says that it was involved in other states in 2008, Working Families Win made a series of recorded telephone messages to voters in the 26th District during the summer of 2008. These were classic "informational" messages criticizing Dreier's voting record and asking voters to contact Dreier on issues such as the Iraq war, veterans, the economy, and price gouging by oil companies.[7] These calls apparently were intended to soften up voter opinion leading into the fall campaign.

Interestingly, Dreier took advantage of the congressional franking privilege (free mailing) to saturate the district with high-quality mailers that addressed similar issues at the same time. Federal law prohibits members of Congress from using the franking privilege for mailers sixty days before an election and Dreier took full advantage of the window between the primary and general election to send out four mailers at taxpayer expense. Three were full-color mailers that touted his commitment to war veterans, his efforts in support of energy exploration, his support for tax reform, his telephone town hall conference calls, and constituent services provided by his office. Dreier also mailed out a 4th of July letter that featured his own handwriting, a format he has used throughout his congressional career.

The Courage Campaign, founded in 2005 as an independent organization under Section 527 of the Internal Revenue Code and based in Los Angeles, took a more active role than Working Families Win in criticizing Dreier. As of late 2008, the organization had seven staff members, including a former campaign staffer for Democratic candidate, Jerry McNerney, in his successful campaign against Republican incumbent, Richard Pombo (R-CA) in 2006. The Courage Campaign has been involved in a variety of politically liberal issues, but is best known for its opposition to Proposition 8, a ballot initiative passed by California voters in the 2008 general election that reimposed a ban on same-sex marriage. The Courage Campaign received nationwide media attention for its controversial video advertisement showing Mormon missionaries entering a home and taking wedding rings from a lesbian couple.[8]

According to a telephone interview with founder Rick Jacobs, the 26th Congressional District was the only district targeted by the Courage Campaign in 2008.[9] The Courage Campaign spent a little over $50,000 on its efforts, including about $15,000 on video advertisements and a website, www.bushrubberstamp.com, that included videos, statements about Dreier's votes in Congress matching President Bush's views, and advice for writing letters to newspapers to inform voters about Dreier's record.

The Courage Campaign based its activities on information obtained from focus group research, conducted in May 2008 in the western (Pasadena) and eastern (Rancho Cucamonga) portions of the district with persons who had voted for Dreier in the past. The Courage Campaign found that most participants thought that Dreier had voted with Bush 50 percent of the time. Many were very surprised to hear it was 93.6 percent of the time and did not initially believe the results, even when given a list of Dreier's votes on particular bills. The Courage Campaign used these results in crafting the "Bush Rubber Stamp" message and in creating cable/Internet ads that, in the opinion of the campaign, "had a clear message that we knew would make sense." These ads received limited airplay and may not have changed voter perceptions about Dreier's voting record. Dreier's campaign manager called the ad amateurish and negative in an interview with the *Los Angeles Times*.[10]

Courage Campaign staff also had communication with local Democratic groups, including an umbrella organization in San Fernando Valley. The Warner campaign itself used the phrase "Bush Rubber Stamp" in one mailing, and several letters to the editor used the slogan against Dreier, but these seemed to come mostly from members of local Democratic organizations rather than the general public. Late in the campaign, the Courage Campaign issued a statement asking for Dreier to oppose Proposition 8 and delivered the message to his office; this action received no response from the Dreier campaign and did not appear to attract the attention of local newspapers. According to Rick Jacobs, the Courage Campaign intends to continue to provide information on Dreier to his constituents and "to hold him accountable."

The tactics of the Blue America Political Action Committee, located in Los Angeles, were much more controversial. A PAC, rather than an independent 527 committee, its actions were subject to Federal Election Commission reporting requirements and were more obviously campaign-oriented. The Blue America PAC was led by Howie Klein, an openly gay political blogger and activist who has written for the *Huffington Post*. Blue America spent about $20,000 for a mailer sent to Republican households the weekend before the election alleging that Dreier had a same-sex partner who is a staff member and had traveled with Dreier on numerous international trips at taxpayer expense. The flyer included stock photos of two men lying on a beach and also accused Dreier of never having an outside job. The flyer appeared to compile unsubstantiated information that is easily obtained from Internet searches using Dreier's name and from his 2008 Wikipedia profile.

Capitol Weekly, a well-known newspaper covering California political issues, was the only major media source to report on the Blue America PAC mailer.[11] Its article referenced long-circulating rumors about Dreier's sexual orientation, but questioned the wisdom of a Democratic PAC sending an attack piece to Republicans or whether there was any hypocrisy by Dreier since he had voted against a proposed constitutional amendment prohibiting same-sex marriage. Groups supporting gay rights, including Rick Jacobs from the Courage Campaign, also expressed concerns about the anti-gay tone of the mailer.

ELECTION RESULTS

Dreier won the election with his lowest percentage ever in a general election, 53 percent, but Warner received only 40 percent of the vote. Libertarian candidate Ted Brown, who has run for several elected offices, received the remaining 7 percent. Brown's website touted himself as "Defender of the Constitution" and "Advocate of Limited Government." He accused Dreier of being "an apologist for the most spectacular growth of government in two generations," and supporting a national ID card.

An analysis of political scientist Paul Hernnson's regression models for predicting incumbent and challenger votes in House elections, shows that votes for the Libertarian candidate were largely at Dreier's expense.[12] Hernnson's model for challengers, based on past elections, was very close in predicting Warner's actual vote. For Warner to win, he would have had to have received media endorsements *and* spent several times more money on advertisements. Hernnson's model for incumbent vote share predicted a higher vote share for Dreier (58 percent) than the amount (53 percent) he actually received. Therefore, the difference seems mostly attributable to having a Libertarian candidate on the ballot as an alternative for conservatives.

Although national trends have favored Democratic challengers in the 2006 and 2008 elections, these results show that the advantage of incumbency still has relevance. In addition, this race can be evaluated in terms of whether Warner fits the definition of a quality challenger, as defined by elections scholar Gary Jacobson.[13] Warner was able to self-fund initial expenses to hire staff, consultants, and fund-raisers. He also presented a positive image as a distinguished, personable candidate and established name recognition as a two-time candidate. Nevertheless, Warner has not held prior public office and, as has been documented in this chapter, could have raised and spent his funds more effectively.

In contrast, in District 44 in California, which is located just southeast of Dreier's district, incumbent Ken Calvert (R-CA) defeated by only two percentage points a longtime school board member. There was a stronger Republican partisan advantage, and the challenger spent only $180,000 compared to Calvert's $1 million. Calvert faced a more typical quality challenger and received negative media attention for his interactions with lobbyists and ethical concerns related to his land development business dealings. Ironically, Calvert's vulnerabilities may protect Dreier in the future as Democratic donors and strategists are very likely to target Calvert more than Dreier in 2010.

Nevertheless, the 26th Congressional District remains one to watch. Dreier's ability to replenish his campaign funds and continue to donate surplus funds to the RCCC will be an important gauge of Dreier's influence as he goes into another term as chair of the California Republican Congressional Delegation. Independent political groups and donors based in Los Angeles are likely to continue to be involved with local congressional races. Russ Warner has announced that he will run again in 2010.

Finally, this campaign illustrates how changing forms of political communications and campaign strategies are affecting elections, even in districts with long-serving incumbents in relatively safe districts. Dreier has benefited from telephone town hall technology to speak directly to voters, even as he continues to periodically send copies of handwritten newsletter updates to constituents. Dreier critics have also made use of newer technology by posting video ads on the Internet, creating their own websites, and blogging. Yet, the strategy that may have the most potential is grassroots organizing, effectively used by the Obama presidential campaign for mobilizing young voters and connecting supporters to opportunities for online campaign contributions. Any serious challenger in the 26th District will need both organization and fund-raising skill to be successful, while Dreier may need to shift his own fund-raising strategies away from corporate PAC contributions and toward more individual donors.

ACKNOWLEDGMENTS

The authors especially appreciate the contributions made by graduate assistant Teresa Martinelli-Lee in researching campaign mailings and newspaper coverage of this race.

NOTES

1. Michael Barone with Richard E. Cohen, *The Almanac of American Politics 2008* (Washington, DC: National Journal, 2007), 230.
2. Advocate.com, "Barney Frank: Dreier's Orientation Cost Him the House Leadership," *The Advocate*, October 15–17, 2005.
3. Barone with Cohan, *Almanac of American Politics 2008*.
4. Gary C. Jacobson, "The President, the War, and Voting Behavior in the 2006 House Elections," in *Fault Lines: Why the Republicans Lost Congress*, ed. Jeffrey J. Mondak and Dona-Gene Mitchell (New York: Routledge, 2009), 128–46.
5. Dan Morain, "GOP Faces Fierce Fights for California Congressional Seats," *Los Angeles Times*, October 27, 2008, B1; Erica Werner, "More Calif. House Seats May Be in Play in November," *The Associated Press State & Local Wire*, October 23, 2008.
6. *Inland Valley Daily Bulletin* (Ontario, CA), "Retain Dreier," October 15, 2008, A15.
7. Personal observation, Marcia Godwin. Calls received in July and August, 2008.
8. Jessica Garrison and Joanna Lin, "Prop. 8 Protesters Target Mormon Temple in Westwood," *Los Angeles Times*, November 7, 2008.
9. Jacobs, interview with Marcia Godwin, November 10, 2008. Information verified with follow-up interview on December 12, 2008.
10. Dan Morain, "New Group Faces Uphill Challenge of GOP Rep. David Dreier," *Los Angeles Times*, July 8, 2008.
11. Malcolm Maclachian, "Gay Rights Groups Angered by Attack Mailer from Democratic Group," *Capitol Weekly*, November 20, 2008
12. Paul S. Hernnson, *Congressional Elections: Campaigning at Home and in Washington* (Washington, DC: CQ Press), 246–58.
13. Gary C. Jacobson, *The Politics of Congressional Elections* (New York: Pearson Longman, 2009).

8

Ohio District 16 Race (Boccieri v. Schuring)

One of the Nation's Most Competitive Open Seats

William Binning and Sunil Ahuja

John Boccieri
Age: 37
Sex: Male
Race: Caucasian
Religion: Roman Catholic
Education: MPA (Webster University, 1996); AB (St. Bonaventure University, 1992)
Occupation: Politician
Political Experience: Ohio State Senate (2007–2008); Ohio State House of Representatives (2001–2006)

Kirk Schuring
Age: 55
Sex: Male
Race: White
Religion: Unknown
Education: Attended Kent State University
Occupation: Politician
Political Experience: Ohio State Senate (2002–2008); Ohio House of Representatives (1993–2002)

The 2008 race for the 16th Congressional District in Ohio, an open seat, was very competitive. This congressional seat had long been held by Republican congressman Ralph Regula, who was elected to the seat in 1972. Before Regula, the seat was held by Republican congressman Frank Bow, who was elected in 1952. Regula did not run in 2008. Although the seat had long been held by Republicans and President George W. Bush carried the district by 56 percent in 2004, this congressional seat was viewed as competitive and a very good opportunity for the Democrats to pick up a seat.

When Ohio's 16th District seat became an open seat, Chris Cillizza, *Washington Post* writer of the column "The Fix," ranked Ohio's 16th district as the number one seat in the country that would likely change party hands from the Republicans to the Democrats.[1] In an earlier column, Cillizza wrote that the key to the Democrats' chance of winning the Ohio 16th was the quality of the candidates. He noted that the Democrats "have one of their best recruits in the country in Ohio State Senator John Boccieri, a conservative lawmaker who has been in the race for months." Cillizza went on to say that "Republicans privately express concern about State Senator Kirk Schuring who appears to be their likely standard bearer."[2] The *Cook Political Report* ranked the Ohio 16th as a toss-up in 2008.[3] By mid-October, it moved to Leans Democratic in the *Cook Political Report*. The Cook Partisan Voting Index for the Ohio 16th was R+4. In September, an essay in *Real Clear Politics* listed congressional races in order of their likelihood to change party control, and the Ohio 16th was listed as ninth in the nation. The authors wrote that "[w]hile the seat leans Republican, the well financed and highly touted moderate state Sen. John Boccieri (D) is well positioned against fellow state Sen. Kirk Schuring."[4]

CHARACTERISTICS OF THE DISTRICT

The 16th congressional district in Ohio is made up of the entirety of Stark County; the major city in that county is Canton, which gained political fame with the front porch campaigns of President William McKinley. At one time, Stark County was a national and state "bellwether," but no more. With the recent and significant losses in manufacturing jobs, it has tended to become a red county. Loss of jobs at Timken Steel and the decline in the presence and the sale of the renowned Hoover vacuum sweepers to an overseas buyer were symbolic of the loss of manufacturing in this area. Although President George W. Bush won Stark County in 2000, he lost it in 2004. The other counties in the Ohio 16th are Wayne County and parts of Ashland and Medina counties. Wayne County is the home of Smuckers, the food company, and includes the largest Amish settlement in the world. Ashland County is very conservative and has Ashland University, with the well-known Ashbrook Center for Public Affairs, a promoter of conservative thought. In the fall of 2008, Ashland-based Archway Cookies declared bankruptcy, likely putting 100 employees out of work. This was not seen as good news for the Republican candidate who needed a big plurality in this conservative county. In addition to Ashland and Wayne counties, the district now includes the southern two-thirds of Medina County, which had been Sherrod Brown's district before he was elected to the U.S. Senate. These counties west of Stark define the district as predominantly rural and small town.

Congressman Regula was one of the most senior members of the Republican caucus in the House and, as a ranking member of the Appropriations Committee, had secured a great deal of benefits for his district. However, the 2006 election was a landslide for the Democrats in Ohio and an indication that Regula's hold on the district was weakening. In 2006, he was challenged in the Republican primary by Matt Miller, an Ashland County commissioner. In that primary, Regula won only 58 percent of the vote. In the general election of 2004, Regula garnered 67 percent of the vote, but in the 2006 general election his vote dropped to 58 percent against an unfunded Democratic opponent. The Democrats began to think that they missed an opportunity to pick up a seat in the 2006 election cycle and should have given this district more attention. There was speculation that Regula was grooming his son to take his congressional seat, but that plan went awry when Richard Regula was defeated for county commissioner in 2006.

THE CANDIDATES

The Democrats moved very early in the 2008 election cycle to test Regula's strength in the 16th District, suspecting that a strong challenge might encourage the eighty-three-year-old Regula to retire if he had to battle to retain a seat when there was little likelihood that the GOP would regain the majority in the House of Representatives. State Senator John Boccieri, whose State Senate district was primarily in neighboring Mahoning County, wasted little time in announcing his candidacy. The Democrats courted the young, personable Air Force reservist Boccieri, who was married with a young family but, at the beginning of the campaign, did not actually live in the 16th Congressional District. Boccieri graduated from St. Bonaventure University and had played minor league baseball for a year in the Frontier League. He entered electoral politics in 2000 by defeating a very conservative Republican for the 61st Ohio House seat. Many attributed that victory to Boccieri's strong support of the Second Amendment. In 2006, he was elected to the Ohio Senate. His Senate seat was not up in 2008, so he would retain his seat if he did not win the congressional seat.

Boccieri is ambitious; he had weighed running for Ohio's 6th Congressional District in 2006 and also explored the possibility of running for various statewide administrative offices in 2006. He has a very close relationship with former congressman and now Ohio governor, Ted Strickland. In May 2007, he was thirty-seven years old when he announced that he was running for the 16th District and made it clear that it did not matter if

Regula sought reelection or not. Based on polls, Boccieri's campaign believed that, if they got his personal story out, he would win.[5] For a long time, it appeared that Boccieri would be unopposed for the Democratic primary; however, Canton city councilwoman Mary Cirelli filed for the race at the last minute but she had few resources and there was very little doubt that Boccieri would win the Democratic nomination.

Boccieri represented the eastern part of Stark County for eight years, first as a state representative and more recently as a state senator. He is a member of the Air Force Reserves who had flown air cargo planes for various missions in Afghanistan and Iraq and was keenly interested in issues that impact on veterans. In his announcement for Congress, he said the election was about changing the direction of the country, citing the job losses in the district. The candidate stated his respect for Regula but that it was time for change. Boccieri's announcement was met with what would become the central theme of the Republican campaign when outgoing GOP state chairman Bob Bennett said "Sen. Boccieri is a carpetbagger who doesn't understand the district."[6] Boccieri had been heavily courted by Rahm Emmanuel, the chair of the Democratic Congressional Campaign Committee (DCCC).

The Republican field was more muddled, and the nomination ended up being quite competitive. Matt Miller, the County Commissioner from Ashland, who had run against Regula in the Republican primary in 2006, said he would run for Congress again no matter what Regula decided to do. The other GOP candidates were more respectful of Regula and gave Regula time to determine his political future.

State Senator Kirk Schuring, who was fifty-five years old, filed papers for an exploratory committee with the Federal Election Commission (FEC) in June of 2007. He was then allowed to raise money that could be used for a federal campaign. His exploratory committee had some very notable local business, finance, and political supporters, including Ward J. Timkin Jr., chairman of the board of Timkin, a long-time influential Stark County and Ohio Republican family. Also on his list was Bill Belden of Belden Brick, a notable Stark County business. Powerful supporters from Wayne County included Richard and Tim Smucker, the president and chairman of the J. M. Smucker Company. When he formed the committee, Schuring said that "the congressman (meaning Regula) knows we are doing this and gave his permission." Schuring said, "I am running in concert with his making a decision. If he decides to run, I would take whatever political apparatus I have and fold it into his."

The Ohio Democratic Party filed a complaint with the FEC claiming that Schuring's exploratory committee was a violation of the reporting requirements because Schuring is "accumulating funds in vast excess of what can reasonably be expected to be used for exploratory activity."[7] The complaint went on to say that the funds were being collected to promote an actual candidacy. Mark Braden, Schuring's Washington attorney, who had Ohio roots, said Schuring could raise and spend as much as he wanted for such things as polling, travel, and other expense associated with "testing the waters." Braden maintained the Democrats' complaint would not amount to anything.[8] He was proven to be right.

Schuring said he respected Boccieri but that he knew the problems of the district because he lived in the district.[9] Schuring was a lifelong resident of Stark County and he was a resident of Jackson Township, one of the largest townships in Ohio. He had been involved in a family insurance agency, which he sold in 1990. A community and civic leader before becoming a legislator, Schuring was a former president of the Canton Jaycees and active in the Chamber of Commerce. He attended Kent State University, did not serve in the military, and was married with two children. Schuring had been in the Ohio State Legislature for eighteen years, serving in the Ohio House from 1993 to 2002 and was elected to the State Senate in 2002.

Schuring had tried to launch a school funding initiative for primary, secondary, and higher education but was unable to get a hearing for his proposal in the Republican-dominated Ohio State Senate.[10] The school funding initiative was seen as part of his overall congressional campaign plan. Schuring did try to play to the public school interests when he voted against vouchers for families of special education students. He said he had a "longstanding practice" of opposing money for programs better suited for public school systems.[11] With this vote, he was voting against the position of the Republican caucus on this issue and described himself as a "pragmatic conservative."

On October 11, 2007, Ralph Regula announced he would not seek what would have been his nineteenth term in the U.S. House. He denied that his decision was based on the fact that his party had failed to select him to chair the Appropriations Committee in the last Congress or that his party was now in the minority. He said he was asked to run again by the GOP House leadership. Congressman Regula was characteristically gracious and humble in his remarks about his retirement, saying he would not endorse a successor and would support the Republican nominee selected in the primary. His announcement set off a flurry of activity by prospective candidates on the Republican side.

In addition to Schuring, there were other notable Republican candidates in consideration. The mayor of Canton, Janet Creighton, received encouragement to run from Bob Bennett, the outgoing state party chair. Creighton refused to fuel this speculation and said she was not interested in the congressional race. She said her interest was in the office of mayor, for which she was then running for reelection. She was subsequently defeated in that race and received an appointment in the Bush administration. Another

GOP prospect was Scott Oelslager, a longtime political figure in Stark County. He was in the Ohio Senate from 1985 to 2002, and because of term limits, was forced out of the Senate and took a House seat in 2003. Oelslager had long considered how to position himself to succeed Ralph Regula.[12] At one time, he had worked for Regula as an aide. However, he did not actively pursue the open seat nomination, saying, "Republicans have a tough campaign challenge ahead of them."[13] He did not say whether that meant Boccieri was a particularly tough candidate or that it was now a difficult environment for Republicans in this congressional district. Oelslager was on good terms with some typically Democratic-leaning interest groups like the Ohio Education Association (OEA) and was unopposed for his reelection to the Ohio House. Another credible candidate was State Senator Ron Amstutz, who was ineligible for another term in the State Senate because of term limits. He eventually decided not to run for Congress and ran for a seat in the Ohio House, which he won.

Kirk Schuring ended up with only two primary opponents. A talk show host and perennial candidate, Paul Schiffer, who had lost a number of campaigns, filed to run for the 16th congressional seat as a Republican. Schiffer was a somewhat controversial figure. He had been the literary agent who helped get the book *Unfit for Command*—a smear of Democratic presidential nominee John Kerry's service in Vietnam—published in 2004.[14] The finance reports available at the time showed that Schuring led the Republicans with a total of $115,000, Miller with $53,000, and Schiffer with zero funds. Schuring was endorsed by the Stark County Republican Executive Committee and by most of the major newspapers in the district, including the *Canton Repository* and *The Akron Beacon Journal*. Despite those apparent advantages of money and newspaper and party endorsements, Schuring won a narrow victory. The results are presented in table 8.1 below.

Schuring was able to win the nomination with the margin he received in his home county. As shown below, he lost the other three counties in the district to Matt Miller. There is no evidence that special problems were cre-

Table 8.1. Republican Primary Results

County	Matt Miller	Paul R. Schiffer	Kirk Schuring
Ashland	5,044	307	699
Medina	6,075	2,220	3,244
Stark	11,020	3,358	25,524
Wayne	7,587	1,563	4,067
Total	29,735	7,448	33,534
Percentage	42.05%	10.53%	47.42%

Source: www.sos.state.oh.us/SOS/elections/electResults/2008ElectionResults/prusrep.aspx

ated by this close primary victory. Although he was seen as the more moderate and pragmatic candidate in the field, there is no evidence that he would not enjoy the support of economic and social conservative groups.

Boccieri said he did not care which Republican won the primary. He entered the primary season with more campaign cash than any of the other candidates in the field, with a total of $170,650. He tried to define the issues for the forthcoming general election during the Democrat primary, saying the campaign was "about jobs and the number of jobs lost through unfair trade agreements." He said many jobs have been shifted overseas and "it concerns me that so many families have been so adversely affected by the decisions makers in Washington."[15] It is somewhat ironic that the Democratic candidate took the protectionist position in what was essentially the district once held by Republican William McKinley, who was an ardent protectionist. Boccieri also tied all GOP candidates to President Bush and former Ohio governor Bob Taft.

Boccieri had an easier time in the primary than his eventual Republican opponent, Kirk Schuring. Mary Cirelli did not run a very active campaign, and Boccieri won the Democratic nomination with 64 percent of the vote and carried all of the four counties in the district.

Campaign finance reports filed at the end of March, after the Ohio primary, showed that GOP candidate Matt Miller spent almost all of the $121,000 he had raised. Schuring spent almost $387,210 of the $490,687 he had received. On the Democratic side, Boccieri spent $441,496 of the $692,020 that he had raised.[16] The Boccieri campaign spent the money to secure the Democratic base for the general election.

CAMPAIGN ISSUES

Residency

One of the first issues that surfaced in the general election campaign between the two nominees was the attention Schuring gave to Boccieri's residency. Schuring would often point out that he was a lifelong resident of the district and Boccieri was not. This was done to draw attention to the fact that Boccieri initially did not live in the district. In fact, Boccieri never lived in the congressional district, even though he represented a small part of it as a state legislator. His home was in New Middletown, Ohio, which is on the eastern border of Mahoning County. The county seat of Mahoning is Youngstown, which has a history of unsavory politics, which Schuring tried to exploit against Boccieri. The U.S. Constitution does not require that candidates live in the district, only that they reside in the state they represent. However, the issue of Boccieri being a carpetbagger eventually caused him to move to the city of Alliance on the eastern part of Stark County, which is in both the 16th Congressional District and his State Senate district. Ohio congressman Charlie Wilson lived outside the 6th Congressional District in Ohio and won easily. However, Boccieri was very uncomfortable about the criticism and traction Schuring was getting by emphasizing that issue. After Boccieri moved, his supporters claimed the residency issue was over, and that it was the only issue that the Schuring campaign had. However, the Republicans did not see it that way. P. J. Wentzel, a Schuring campaign operative, said they were happy Boccieri moved into the district. "Even though he is a politician from Youngtown, he'll find the 16th Congressional District is a great place to live."[17]

The local Stark County Republican Party referred to Boccieri as "Youngstown John," a reference to the central city of Mahoning County, where Boccieri went to high school. Schuring and his allies continued to raise the issue throughout the campaign. On his website, Schuring had a day counter displaying the number of days since Boccieri had filed to run for the nomination but had yet to register as a voter in the district. After Boccieri finally registered from his new address in Alliance, the Schuring campaign made the number of days since Boccieri was eligible to vote in the district the central element on their website. As late as July 27, 2008, in the *Canton Repository*, the biggest paper in the district, there was a major story entitled "Boccieri counters residency questions."[18] In early October, the Boccieri campaign complained about Republican party mailings that called Boccieri "a Youngstown politician" and that he had links to the disgraced former Ohio attorney general, Marc Dann, who was forced to resign from office in 2008 for an array of improprieties, including having an affair with a staffer. Dann had been an attorney in the Youngstown area before being elected to office and had served with Boccieri in the Ohio Senate. Schuring emphasized his lifelong residency, ties to the district, and the "Youngstown John" label in his television ads.

In the final two weeks of the campaign, Boccieri ran a radio ad with female voices expressing concern about the negative campaign of Kirk Schuring and saying that John Boccieri lives in the district and has represented the district. The ad also said Schuring voted for the biggest tax hike in Ohio history because Bob Taft asked him to. The other campaign theme in the ad was that Boccieri was looking out for the middle class and Schuring was not.

Guns

The two candidates tried to outdo one other in their support for guns and the Second Amendment. The gun issue resonated for Boccieri in the past with rural and conservative voters. His first state legislative election was a surprise to many; he defeated a very well self-financed, arch conservative

Republican incumbent. The key to that victory was Boccieri's strong support of the Second Amendment. He was against virtually any type of gun control. When the U.S. Supreme Court came out with its strong defense of the Second Amendment against gun control in the Washington, DC, case, Boccieri sent out a press release stating:

> Every day that I strap myself into that $30 million C-130 airplane, I put my life on the line for all the Amendments in the U.S. Constitution. I applaud the Supreme Court for affirming our individual Second Amendment rights, not only as a gun owner but as a member of the military. The court has shown that the Constitution still protects Americans' rights and liberties.[19]

The Boccieri campaign pointed out that he earned the Ohio Sportsman's Association's "Legislator of the Year" award in 2006 and earned an "A rating" from the National Rifle Association.

Schuring also applauded the U.S. Supreme Court's decision to strike down Washington, DC's thirty-two-year ban on handguns, calling it a victory for those who cherish the Second Amendment. Later in late September, he told a group of Ashland sportsmen that "the Second Amendment is one of the most important provisions of our Constitution. It is the very protection that ensures our life won't be threatened and our property will be protected."[20] These two candidates tried to outdo each other in their support of the right to bear arms. The National Rifle Association did not endorse either candidate since both were favorable to their issues.

Energy

The candidates disagreed on energy, with both supporting their respective party's positions. Trying to gain voter attention, the candidates stepped into what was arguably the number one issue in the summer of 2008—the rising price of gasoline. Boccieri was the first to address this salient issue. He called a press conference at a local Sonoco station to decry the "skyrocketing gas prices," declaring "enough is enough." He said, "We need a congressman who's going to stand up and say 'no' to big oil." He said attention must be given to alternative energy sources and criticized Schuring for voting for an increase in the Ohio gasoline tax. Boccieri said the Republican call for more drilling would not solve the problem and that he would crack down on oil companies and speculators.[21]

Schuring was aware of Boccieri's press conference and held a press release of his own. He said he had a plan to increase supply and decrease demand that included offshore drilling and drilling in ANWR. Schuring argued that Democratic proposals, supported by Boccieri, requiring oil companies to drill on land where they had existing federal leases, was tantamount to requiring them to drill in dry holes.[22]

The candidates continued to press the energy issue, which was on the minds of voters. They each wrote a guest column for the *Canton Repository* on Sunday, July 20, 2008. Taking their respective issues from their national parties, Schuring pushed for drilling offshore and ANWR, but Boccieri said drilling in ANWR would not yield any oil for ten to twenty years. He called for releasing fuel from the Strategic Petroleum Reserve and said oil companies should be required to drill for oil on the land they already have. In his column, Boccieri tried to tie Schuring and his plan to President Bush.[23] Schuring took comfort from the fact that the Democratic Congress allowed the twenty-five-year offshore drilling ban to expire that year. He reminded voters that he was also for drilling in ANWR.

The gasoline price issue drew Freedom Watch, a conservative advocacy group launched by Ari Fleischer, a former Bush administration press official, into the Ohio 16th District to conduct "robo-calls" against Boccieri. The robo-call message was "Hi, this is an emergency gas price alert from Freedom Watch. Did you know Ohio gas taxes add more than 28 cents to every gallon of gas? 28 cents!" The call then asked what Boccieri was doing about it? "Nothing" was the robo-call answer to its question.[24] Boccieri responded to the Freedom Watch robo-calls by arguing that Schuring was the one who voted to raise the gas tax in Ohio, not him. He challenged Schuring to a debate, maintaining that Schuring was "hiding behind third parties" and "should agree to debate our energy future in a one-on-one or in a neutral forum."[25]

Employee Free Choice Act

Another thing the two candidates disagreed about was the issue of the Employee Free Choice Act. Schuring criticized Boccieri for "his disdain for area workers" by supporting "a radical change to American labor law." Schuring said, "Workers should not live in fear of intimidation." The legislation he referred to is the Employee Free Choice Act, also known as the "card check" legislation. The bill would allow for a card check method instead of a secret ballot election for union representation. The National Labor Relations Act would be required to certify a union after a majority of workers had signed the union cards. Schuring criticized the proposed law for denying the right to a secret ballot.[26]

The Boccieri camp responded quickly to Schuring's criticism of his support for the Employee Free Choice Act. Boccieri said that Schuring's alleged support for workers can now "Rest in Peace." The Boccieri camp went on to say that it took Schuring a mere three weeks to abandon his effort to paint himself as a promoter of workers' rights and a friend of organized labor. Boccieri's statement said Schuring threw workers and their families under the bus by opposing the Employee Free Choice Act and that Schuring was "deafening silent" on the bailout of Wall Street but did not hesitate to deny workers their rights during these very difficult times. Boccieri defended his position on the EFCA and received vocal support from organized labor during this response to Schuring.[27]

The two issues of drilling for oil and the union card check proposal continued to be discussed and to divide the two candidates. At a well-attended Alliance Chamber of Commerce breakfast in mid-October, the two candidates made a joint appearance, and even though it was not billed as a debate, they both brought up the aforementioned two issues. Schuring continued to support more domestic oil drilling, while Boccieri pushed alternative fuels and "green" programs to create jobs rather than increased drilling. Boccieri said he favored the employee-based healthcare program advocated by Barack Obama. The candidates gave their divergent views on card check union organizing. The large size of the crowd at the event was seen by the moderator of the program as an indication of the interest in this congressional election.[28]

Financial Crisis and the Bailout

Boccieri took up the issue of the massive federal bailout of Wall Street with one of his first TV ads in the fall campaign, saying: "When Washington is pushing for a $700 billion bailout of irresponsible Wall Street corporations while American taxpayers get nothing but the bill, it is time for a change. It's time for leaders who will fight to put the middle class first again."[29] Schuring's position on the bailout was much more tempered. On his website, he expressed opposition to taxpayer monies being used to finance any severance packages for CEOs.

On the first failed vote for the bailout package, Boccieri said the House did the right thing in voting the package down. He said that the proposal did not do enough to safeguard taxpayers' money and did not address the greed which was at the root of the meltdown. Boccieri said this was why he was running against Washington. Schuring's early position was that officials in Washington needed to cooperate. Rather than buy equity in these companies, the government should loan them money to be paid back later. He also said the House was right to vote against the first bailout package. In a debate on October 5 at the Canton Veteran of Foreign Wars Post 3747, the two candidates were asked about their views of the bailout after it was passed. Boccieri went first and said, "Too often representatives pay too much attention to special interests while middle-class families are struggling. Greed and avarice on Wall Street caused the problem." He said giving a blank check with little oversight was the wrong move. Schuring was more supportive.[30] He said while the bailout might anger people, it was necessary. Boccieri said if he could change the package, he would use the money to help those who are going through home foreclosure, and help them renegotiate their mortgages. He wanted enforcement of existing regulations. Schuring also called for more regulatory reform.

CAMPAIGN STRATEGY

Gotcha

With widespread recording technology, YouTube, and the Internet, candidates for public office are always vulnerable to being caught on tape in a misstatement. Schuring got caught. He was the featured speaker at an Ashland rally for John McCain, where he spoke on behalf of McCain, saying, "so the other thing I know is that Ashland County has a rich history and tradition of rallying around Republicans and I was telling people earlier, where I come from we could never have a rally like this in the center of Canton. If we did, we might get shot at."[31] Even though the event was covered by local press, these remarks did not gain any attention until someone who had used a cell phone camera put them on YouTube. Bloggers gave Schuring a bad time about his remark.

State Democratic communications director Alex Goepfert said that "it was appalling to witness Kirk Schuring speaking with such venom and disdain toward the very individuals he is seeking to represent in Congress."[32] Schuring said it was an attempt at humor, and Canton is a safe city. The incident did receive some press but did not have the political life of the 2006 "macaca" remark by Senator George Allen (R-VA), which arguably cost him his seat. Each of the candidates was followed by and taped by people from the other camp with video cameras. Welcome to the modern campaign! Boccieri's spokesperson said of the videotaping, "I think it's just quickly become a fundamental part of modern campaigning."[33]

Another incident occurred that involved both the residency issue and the use of new technology. The Ohio Democrats had an employee trail Schuring during the campaign and tape any public remarks he made. The Schuring camp complained about this frequently as an invasion of privacy. In one instance, the person was asked to leave the Stark County Fair by the Fair Board. The Schuring campaign made a video and accused Boccieri of using "Youngstown tactics" in his campaign while playing music from the "Untouchables." This attempted to both label Boccieri as a carpetbagger and tie him to the reputed mob influence in Youngstown.

There was further controversy over charges by Schuring that Boccieri's agents stormed Schuring's headquarters with the demand for a debate challenge. One of the figures involved in this was Boccieri's campaign manager, Ian Walton. Schuring claimed this was desperation by the Boccieri campaign.[34]

In midsummer, the Schuring campaign released a Terrance Group poll that showed that Schuring was ahead with 40 percent. Boccieri was at 34 percent, with 26 percent undecided. Schuring was pleased with the poll results, and Boccieri said that those results were arrived at before the voters found out that it was Schuring who had raised the gas taxes.[35]

The July campaign finance report filings showed that Boccieri continued to lead in this important indicator of candidate strength. In that report, Boccieri had raised $391,237, for a total of $1,081,509, and a balance of cash-on-hand of $531,015. Schuring raised $329,237 in the same period and showed a balance of cash-on-hand of $348,939. Boccieri made the argument that his money was from small donors, while Schuring said his money came from inside the district, trying to again emphasize the fact that Boccieri's support, like Boccieri himself, was from outside the district.[36] Boccieri privately told one of the authors of this essay that he hoped these reports, which would show him over $1 million, would show weak support for Schuring and that national Republicans would abandon him. There is no evidence at this point that had occurred.[37] They did abandon Schuring later in the campaign, however.

The Schuring campaign tried to keep the Boccieri campaign off balance with a continuous drumbeat on the issue of residency. Schuring had a number of radio ads out in the summer which focused on various issues, but invariably all ads had the voice of a local political figure with the theme that Schuring lived his whole life in the district.

The Ohio Republican Party introduced a character-related issue in late July. It charged that, four months after the primary, Boccieri was still claiming endorsements from the primary on his website that he had not yet collected for the general election. The party's press release said that Boccieri claimed an endorsement from the *Akron Beacon Journal*, the National Rifle Association, and the Buckeye Firearms Association. These entities had not yet endorsed for the general election, and the Republicans claimed Boccieri was presenting them as if he had already collected them for the general election against Schuring. The state chair of the Ohio GOP said, "Either John Boccieri doesn't understand the law or he's intentionally trying to deceive voters." The GOP called for an immediate removal and an apology.[38]

A final "gotcha" moment occurred at the very end of the campaign. The candidates answered special interest group questionnaires sent to them. The candidates often respond with what they think the interest group wants to hear in order to collect endorsements, and so the Boccieri camp was able to get their hands on Schuring's answers to the National Association of Manufacturers' questions on whether he would support a repeal of the court case *Ledbetter v. Goodyear Tire and Rubber Company*, which supports equal pay for equal work. Schuring answered in the questionnaire that he would support legislation to overturn that ruling. In the final days of the campaign,

Boccieri made a campaign issue out of Schuring's support for overturning equal pay for equal work. The Ohio House Republicans had warned their candidates about answering these interest group questionnaires since the Democratic caucus was getting access to the responses and airing them.[39]

Endorsements

The various interest group endorsements for the candidates fell along fairly predictable lines but each side tried to mitigate the impact of their opponent's support. The Hall of Fame Council of the AFL-CIO and the Canton Firefighters endorsed Boccieri, while the Fraternal Order of Police in Canton endorsed Schuring. In order to draw attention away from the strong labor support for Boccieri, Schuring announced that he had a coalition of labor supporting him, including one current and one former union leader in the area. The major business organizations lined up behind Schuring, including the U.S. Chamber of Commerce and the National Federation of Independent Businesses. In order to check that, Boccieri lined up ten business people in the district and claimed that business backed him. The Ohio CPAs endorsed Boccieri. Boccieri was awarded the Buckeye State Veterans advocacy award. He served fourteen years in the Air Force, flying cargo planes, and was asked to give the Memorial Day radio address for the national Democratic Party. He was a ceaseless advocate for veterans' interests and enjoyed the support of a variety of veterans' organizations. To try to counteract that record and support, Schuring rounded up some area veterans and put out a press release that he enjoyed the support of a veterans' coalition. In mid-October, Schuring received the endorsement of the Move America Forward's Freedom PAC, which is a pro-troop organization and featured a mother who lost her son in combat as their spokesperson. Schuring also received the Friend of Agriculture award from the Ohio Farm Bureau, while Boccieri countered with an endorsement from the National Farmers Union. The Ohio Federation of Teachers endorsed Boccieri, and so did the Ohio Education Association (OEA). But the Ohio Right to Life and the national Right to Life Political Action Committee endorsed Schuring. Boccieri also held pro-life positions, which helped him in this socially conservative district. In September, Boccieri campaigned with First Lady Francis Strickland at the home of, as they released it, "a lifelong Republican." Schuring countered a few days later with a coalition of Democrats for Schuring headed up by a former Democratic Canton city councilman.

There are benefits a candidate receives from an interest group's endorsement. Gary Carlile, a communication and political action consultant for the OEA, said that after the primary Boccieri was screened and recommended by the National Education Association (NEA) and his seat was designated a targeted race. The NEA Fund for Children and Public Education then donated $5,000 to Boccieri. The NEA also sent four mailings to OEA members in the district specifically promoting Boccieri's candidacy. Boccieri was included in two OEA mailings recommending candidates; one mailing sent just prior to early voting and one prior to the general election. Boccieri was also featured in the OEA's Election Guide, which was available for all its members. In the month of October, OEA volunteers made 9,620 phone number dials and spent over 2,500 minutes calling members to promote Boccieri for Congress.[40]

The major newspaper in the district, *The Canton Repository*, endorsed Schuring on October 5, 2008, stating "Schuring meets the 'one of us' test and like Regula has shown a capacity for rising above partisanship." About Boccieri, it said he was passionate and articulate, "[b]ut we're concerned that his proposals reflect more awareness of packaging a marketing message than of the 16th District itself." It went on to say that "Boccieri has benefited in this campaign far more than his opponent from the help of officially unaffiliated outsiders—'help' that we think has coarsened and cheapened the campaign." It specifically mentioned DCCC mailers. The overall theme of the endorsement reflected the Schuring campaign's effort to define Boccieri as an outsider and Schuring as "one of us." On October 16, the *Medina Sun* endorsed Boccieri, saying he "has more detailed and well-thought out plans to help the district." The well-respected *Akron Beacon Journal* endorsed Schuring. It said of Boccieri: "His record in office is thin, his campaign little more that a collection of pre-packaged talking points." The *Massillon Independent* also endorsed Schuring.

Debating the Debates

The two candidates initially argued over the number of debates they would participate in and whose fault it was if a debate was not held. One of the debates was held at the regional campus of the University of Akron, sponsored by the Ray C. Bliss Institute of Applied Politics. It was taped for broadcast on the regional public television channel. There was one debate broadcast by a radio station. A debate scheduled by the Chamber of Commerce was cancelled because Boccieri refused to participate because the moderator was the editorial page editor of the *Canton Repository*, a newspaper seen as being favorable to Schuring and to Republicans. Schuring refused an AARP-sponsored debate and a debate offered by the Time Warner cable station. The cable station manager reported that Schuring wanted to be interviewed but he did not want to engage in a televised debate.[41] One of the first face-to-face and more spirited debates took place in Wooster, sponsored by the Wooster Area Chamber of Commerce. Boccieri used his opening remarks to criticize the policies of the last eight years as the cause of the economic problems in the nation. He said what was needed were incentives to bring jobs back to this community. Schuring said that he firmly believed that what was needed was "a representative who understood the needs of the 16th district." Again, he was focusing attention on that fact that he was the person who had lived in the district.[42] Schuring issued a "fact check" statement after this debate to point out the mistakes that Boccieri had made in his remarks.

By the end of the campaign, the candidates agreed to more joint appearances. They were not usually debates but joint appearances, where each one would speak for ten minutes after a dinner and would often take questions. None of these debates or joint appearances impacted significantly on the outcome of this competitive race. In the joint public appearances, Boccieri liked to talk about "strengthening the middle class." He also liked to point out that Schuring was for privatizing Social Security. Schuring preferred to emphasize his local roots and that he was objective when it came to political philosophies and noted that he preferred working together to solve problems.

Help from Washington

The DCCC at various points provided support to the Boccieri campaign through independent money. It financed a mailing and phone banking in the district, with a total expenditure at this point of $32,000. This campaign said Schuring voted to raise his salary by $9,000, which was misleading. Schuring denounced the mailer as misleading and called on Boccieri to ask third party interests to stay out of the race. Schuring inserted the carpetbagger charge by saying that "[i]t is not surprising that someone from Youngstown wouldn't understand the important issues facing people in the 16th District." In mid-September, the DCCC spent $83,000 for a media buy on behalf of Boccieri, including TV time and production costs. In late September, the DCCC spent another $7,717 for direct mail for Boccieri.[43] In addition to the support from the Democratic caucus, the Boccieri camp received help from another outside group, the Patriot Majority, an advocacy organization which, according to FEC filings, was spending $200,000 on ads to attack Schuring. The money for the Patriot Majority came from the American Federation of State County and Municipal Employees. Both Democratic House Speaker Nancy Pelosi and Rahm Emmanuel came to Cleveland in October for Boccieri's fund-raising events. Boccieri enjoyed the support of and visits from several Democratic members of Congress, including Speaker Nancy Pelosi (D-CA) and Rahm Emmanuel (D-IL).

This was not the case for Schuring, who received little support from the National Republican Congressional Campaign (NRCC), a campaign arm of House Republicans. One of the few efforts to support Schuring was a visit to the 16th District by the chair of that committee, Representative Tom Cole, a three-term congressman from Oklahoma, who stopped in the district on October 22 as he made a three-week tour of House races around the country. The NRCC reserved $800,000 worth of television time for Schuring. That was later reduced to $500,000. In the end, the campaign reports show that the NRCC did not spend anything in support of Schuring. However, the third quarter financial disclosure reports show that Boccieri benefited from at least $1.6 million by the DCCC on his behalf.

Polling

There were not many polls made available to the public during the general election race in the 16th District. Schuring had released a Terrance group poll in the summer showing him with a lead. However, in September, Survey USA released a poll of a sample of 775, of those 625 were determined to be likely voters and the poll was based on their preferences. The poll was conducted for *Roll Call*, and was done September 19–21, 2008. It showed Boccieri leading Schuring by 49 to 41 percent. Boccieri was leading primarily from female support, 57 percent to 37 percent for Schuring. Males support was even at 47 percent each. The poll also showed that McCain led Obama by a mere 48 to 46 percent in the district, evidence of the problems McCain and Republicans were having in this part of battleground Ohio.[44] George W. Bush carried this district by 8 percent four years prior.

A second public poll was conducted by Research 2000 between September 30 and October 1. Of a sample of 400, it gave Boccieri a 10-point lead, with Boccieri at 48 percent and Schuring at 38 percent. In this poll, Boccieri enjoyed a 5 percent lead among men, a 15 percent lead among women, and 13 percent advantage among independents.

The widely respected *Rothenberg Report* on September 30, 2008, listed the Ohio 16th as Toss Up/Tilt Democratic, a listing that likely diminished national financial support for Schuring, particularly when the national prediction late in the 2008 campaign estimated an overall Democratic gain of ten to twenty House seats.

Money for the Endgame

Boccieri raised $415,738 in the third quarter; his campaign had $464,474 in cash-on-hand for the final weeks of the campaign, bringing to a total of $1.5 million for him. Schuring raised $298,032 for the same period for a total of $1.11 million and a balance of $127,606 in cash-on-hand for the final weeks. Those funds combined with the spending of outside groups, which was reported to be $1.6 million for Boccieri, coupled with no support for Schuring by the NRCC pointed to the problems for the Schuring

Table 8.2. Results

Candidate	Stark	Wayne	Medina	Ashland	Total
Boccieri	97,475	24,431	30,287	8,701	160,894
Schuring	72,917	24,304	24,012	9,037	130,270

campaign and for the GOP congressional candidates around the country in 2008. While Boccieri was spending money and receiving support from the DCCC in the final days, Schuring rented a bus to campaign in the district. The Schuring camp claimed it knocked on 4,500 doors all over the district the first weekend of the bus tour.[45] Schuring was able to introduce Republican vice presidential candidate Sarah Palin at a Canton rally on November 2, 2008, where he said McCain and Palin were the "comeback kids and will win on Tuesday."[46] Boccieri closed out his election by visiting factories, restaurants, and other venues in all four counties in the district the Monday before Election Day.

The Boccieri campaign had extensive network TV buys in the Cleveland media market six weeks out from Election Day. The ads were all positive. Boccieri stuck to his game plan devised before he entered the race: Get Boccieri's story out to win, and they did.[47] Schuring never placed enough ads in the costly Cleveland TV media market.

BOCCIERI WINS: TAKES LONG-HELD GOP SEAT

Boccieri won the election easily with 55 percent of the vote. Table 8.2 gives the results by county.

Boccieri said in his victory announcement that his top priorities were "renegotiating free-trade agreements to stimulate the national economy, closing tax loopholes that benefit companies that leave the country, and invest in companies that stay in America."[48] Many pundits point to Boccieri's dynamic personality in order to explain his win, while other factors included his military record, conservative positions on guns and abortion, and a nationwide disapproval of President Bush and the Republican Party.

NOTES

1. Chris Cillizza, "The Fix," January 18, 2008, blog-washingtonpost.com/thefix/2008/01/the_line_senate_and_house.html.

2. Ohio Daily Blog, www.ohiodailyblog.com/node?page=40.

3. Cook Political Report, "2008 Competitive House Race Chart," March 6, 2008.

4. Reid Wilson and Kyle Trygstad, "Top 25 Competitive Congressional Races," Real Clear Politics, September 8, 2008, www.reaclearpolitics.com/printpage??url=realclearpolitics.com/articles/2.

5. Phone interview with Anthony Trevena, campaign advisor to Boccieri, November 13, 2008.

6. Paul E. Kostyu, "Boccieri Seeks Regula's Seat," May 9, 2007, www.cantonrep.com/index.php?Category=9&ID=353244&r=13&subCategoryID=.

7. Paul E. Kostyu, "Democrats Claim Schuring Is Being a Candidate," CantonRep.com, August 1, 2007, www.cantonrep.com/printable.php? ID=368026.

8. Kostyu, "Democrats Claim."

9. Paul E. Kostyu, "Schuring Ponders Run for Congress," CantonRep.com, June 8, 2007, www.cantonrep.com/printable.php? ID=358857.

10. Paul E. Kostyu, "Buzz Is Negligible for Sen. Schuring's School Amendment," CantonRep.com, January 29, 2008, www:cantonrep.com/printablephp? ID+397115.

11. Paul E. Kostyu, "Schuring Opposes Vouchers," CantonRep.com, May 8, 2008, www.cantonrep.com/printable.php? ID=411305.

12. In the early 1990s, he had expressed an interest in the Regula seat to the lead author of this chapter.

13. Paul E. Kostyu, "Schuring Has More in Coffer than GOP Foe," CantonRep.com, October 17, 2007, www.contonrep.com/printable.php? ID=381719.

14. Tom Botos, "Three Republicans Eye Regula's Spot," CantonRep.com, February 19, 2008, www.cantonrep.com/printable.php? ID=400088.

15. Kelli Young, "Schuring, Boccieri to Square Off in Race to Replace Regula," CantonRep.com, March 5, 2008, www.cantonrep.com/printable.php?ID=402176.

16. Congressional Elections: Ohio District 16 Race: 2008 Cycle/OpenSecrets, www.opensecrets.org/races/summary.php?cycle=2008&id=OH16.

17. David DeWitt, "Dems Fire at Schuring for Canton 'Might Get Shot at' Remarks during Ashland Rally," http://www.politickeroh.com/democrats-hit-schuring-canton-remarks-ashland-rally.

18. Edd Pritchard, "Boccieri Counters Residency Question," July 27, 2008, www.cantonrep.com/index.php?ID=422820&Category=9&fromSearch=yes&subCategoryID=0.

19. john4congress.blogspot.com/search, June 26, 2008.

20. David DeWitt, "Schuring Pitches Support for Second Amendment," October 1, 2008, politickeroh.com/daviddewitt/schuring-pitches-support-second-amendment.

21. David DeWitt, "Schuring Pre-empted Boccieri Gas Station Event with Statement," July 2, 2008, politickeroh.com/schuring-pre-empted-boccieri-gas-station-event-statement.

22. David DeWitt, "Schuring Camp Hits Boccieri for Wanting to Drill in 'Dry Holes,'" July 18, 2008, politickeroh.com.

23. David DeWitt, "Boccieri Calls Schuring Energy Plan 'Gimmicks' from Bush Playbook," July 21, 2008, politickoh.com/boccieri-calls-schuring-energy-plan-gimmicks-bush-playbook.

24. Alex Isenstadt, "Freedom Watch Target Boccieri, Driehaus with Robocalls," politickeroh.com.

25. "OH 16-Freedom Watch Smears Boccieri (D) over Gas Tax Schuring Voted For," Ohio Daily Blog, www.ohiodailyblog.com.

26. David DeWitt, "Schuring Camp Says Boccieri 'on Wrong Side of Workers' Rights,'" September 23, 2008, politickeroh.com/da.viddewitt/schuring-camp-say-boccieri-wrong-side-worker-rights.

27. David DeWitt, "UPDATED: Boccieri Now Delivers Blow to Schuring over Employee Free Choice Act," September 25, 2008, politickeroh.com/daviddewitt/boccieri-now-delivers-blow-schuring-over-employee-free-choice-act.

28. Edd Pritchard, "Boccieri, Schuring Trade Jabs at Chamber Breakfast," October 11, 2008, www.cantonrep.com/index.php?ID=435660&Category+9&subCategoryID.

29. Ohio Daily Blog, www.ohiodailyblog.com, September 23, 2008.

30. "Schuring, Boccieri Debate on Issues Posed by Veterans' Groups," *Canton Repository*, October 5, 2008.

31. DeWitt, "Dems Fire at Schuring."

32. DeWitt, "Dems Fire at Schuring."

33. Edd Pritchard, "Lights, Camera, Campaign Action: Videographers Roll When Schuring, Boccieri Stump," *Canton Repository*, July 20, 2008.

34. Buckeye State Blog, www.buckeyestateblog.com.

35. See politickeroh.com/internal-poll-schuring-sixpoints-boccieri.

36. David DeWitt "Schuring Camp Hitting Boccieri for Money Taken from outside of District," politickeroh.com/schuring-camp-hitting-boccieri-money-taken-outside-district.

37. Interview with Boccieri, July 2008.

38. David DeWitt, "UPDATED: Ohio Republican Party Calls on Boccieri to Remove Endorsements from Web Site," July 28, 2008, politickeroh.com/ohio-republican-party-calls-boccieri-remove-endorsements-web-site.

39. Jim Siegel, "Ohio GOP Gets Earful for Answers on Survey," *Columbus Dispatch*, November 1, 2008.

40. Gary P. Carlile, "NEA/OEA Support for John Boccieri for Congress (OH-16)," memo November 15, 2008.

41. Edd Pritchard, "16th Congressional Candidates Set, Reject Debates," *Canton Repository*, August 22, 2008.

42. David DeWitt, "Boccieri and Schuring Square Off in Wooster Debate on the Economy and Jobs," October 9, 2008, politickeroh.com/da viddewitt/boccieriand-schuring-square-wooster-debate-economy-and-jobs.

43. David Dewitt, "DCCC Puts Another $7K into 16th, This Time Direct Mail," September 30, 2008, politickeroh.com/da viddewitt/dccc-puts-another-7k-16th-time-direct-mail.

44. Results of Survey USA Election Poll #14404, www.surveyusa.com.

45. David DeWitt, "Schuring Camp Talks Up Bus Tour Weekend," October 27, 2008, politickeroh.ohcom/node/1949.

46. David Dewitt, "Schuring Introduces Palin at Canton Rally," November 2, 2008, www.politickeroh.com/daviddewitt/schuring-introduces-palin-canton-rally.

47. Phone interview with Anthony Trevena, November 13, 2008.

48. David Skolnick, "Gerberry, Alliance Official among Those Eyeing Boccieri's State Post," *Vindicator*, November 6, 2008.

9

Florida District 21 Race (Martinez v. L. Diaz-Balart) and Florida District 25 Race (Garcia v. M. Diaz-Balart)

The Change in "Little Havana" That Did Not Happen

Sean Foreman

Raul L. Martinez
Age: 59
Sex: Male
Race: Hispanic
Religion: Roman Catholic
Education: B.S., criminal justice (Florida International University, 1977); A.A., Miami-Dade Community College (1968)
Occupation: Public relations; politician
Political Experience: Mayor of Hialeah (1981–2006); Hialeah City Council (1977–1981)

Lincoln Diaz-Balart
Age: 54
Sex: Male
Race: Hispanic
Religion: Roman Catholic
Education: J.D. (Case Western Reserve University, 1979); B.A., international relations (New College of University of South Florida, 1976)
Occupation: Lawyer; politician
Political Experience: U.S. House of Representatives (1993–present); Florida Senate (1989–1992); Florida House of Representatives (1986–1989)

Joe Garcia
Age: 45
Sex: Male
Race: Hispanic

Religion: Roman Catholic
Education: J.D. (University of Miami, 1991); B.A., political science (University of Miami, 1987)
Occupation: Public servant
Political Experience: Chair, Florida Public Service Commission (1992–2000); executive director, Cuban American National Foundation (2000–2004); chair, Democratic Party of Miami-Dade County (2006–2008)

Mario Diaz-Balart
Age: 47
Sex: Male
Race: Hispanic
Religion: Roman Catholic
Education: Attended University of South Florida (1979–1982)
Occupation: Public relations; politician
Political Experience: U.S. House of Representatives (2002–present); Florida Senate (1992–2000); Florida House of Representatives (1988–1992); aide to the mayor of Miami (1980)

The old adage is that "all politics is local," but in Miami political debates are often international. Miami-Dade's three main congressional seats (Districts 18, 21, and 25) are held by popular Cuban Americans as are many county and municipal positions. The two main challengers for Districts 21 and 25 in 2008 were also Cuban Americans. Moreover, politics in Miami often focuses on debates about U.S. foreign policy toward the island nation located 90 miles from Florida's southern coast. In many ways, Miami politics has been an extension of Cuban politics ever since Fidel Castro's revolution caused a major exodus of Cubans to Miami in 1959. Forty years later, the first Cuban American was elected to Congress.

Ileana Ros-Lehtinen, the first Cuban American and first Hispanic woman elected to Congress, won a special election in August 1989 to succeed longtime member of Congress Claude Pepper (D-FL). The campaign between Ros-Lehtinen and Democrat Gerald F. Richman, a Jew, was one of the most ethnically polarizing in U.S. history. In the race, Republican National Committee chair Lee Atwater called the seat a "Cuban American seat," to which Richman replied in the Democratic primary that it was an "American seat."[1] Ros-Lehtinen won 53 to 47 percent, with 94 percent of the Hispanic vote. Ros-Lehtinen was followed to Congress by Lincoln Diaz-Balart in a newly created district (District 21) in 1992. Ten years later, his brother, Mario Diaz-Balart, was elected to another newly created seat in District 25. These three Republican representatives became popular incumbents in seats with majority Republican voters and in an environment where policies focusing on Cuba dominated the campaign discussions. As such they often skirted contenders for their seats, and when they did draw opponents, they were usually inexperienced and underfunded challengers.

CHARACTERISTICS OF THE DISTRICTS

In examining the national map for House seats that might be vulnerable, Democrats decided that the time might be right to crack the dominance of Miami's Republican Cuban Americans. The rise of registered independent voters, the increase in younger Cuban Americans for whom the issues of Fidel Castro and the U.S. embargo on Cuba are less pressing, and the sharp increase in number of non-Cuban Hispanics in Miami meant that the Cuban American stranglehold on these three south Florida congressional districts could be vulnerable. The Democratic Congressional Campaign Committee (DCCC) started targeting these Miami Cuban American seats more than a year before the 2008 election by running ads on Spanish-language radio in October 2007 critical of the Republican trio's votes against the State Children's Health Insurance Program (SCHIP).[2] The ads attacked the representatives as abandoning American children and for their votes with President George W. Bush. These were primary reasons why Colombian-born businesswoman Annette Taddeo challenged Ros-Lehtinen in District 18, the least vulnerable of the three seats.

Miami-Dade County Democrats sought to recruit tough candidates to take on the powerful Diaz-Balart brothers. They found the high-profile former mayor of Hialeah, Raul Martinez, to run against Lincoln Diaz-Balart in District 21, and Joe Garcia, former director of the Cuban American Foundation, who was serving as chair of the county party organization, to challenge Mario Diaz-Balart for District 25. By the summer, Martinez and Garcia were running strong and making a good showing in polls. It prompted the *New York Times* to ask, "Will Little Havana Go Blue?" The DCCC put these races on their "Red to Blue" website.

Party Balance

Once solidly Republican, District 21 voter registration shifted between 2006 and 2008. When Martinez announced he was challenging Lincoln in January 2008, there was a 124,744 to 101,267 advantage for Republicans over Democrats in voter registration. That was a decrease in Republican voters by 4,558. Independent voters in the district grew by 71,208 during that same time.[3] The Miami-Dade part of the district showed 114,586 Republicans, 93,357 Democrats, and 59,841 NPA (with 11,112 other party registrations). In Broward County (Fort Lauderdale) just to the north, there were 28,337 Democrats and 18,195 Republicans, with 13,550 NPA (and 2,471 others) in 2008.

District 25 was created to favor Republicans, but their voter registration advantage was diminishing by 2008. In Miami-Dade there were 119,920 Democrats, 119,177 Republicans, and 78,476 NPA (with 14,467 other party registrations).

Voting and Electoral History

Since District 21 was created in 1992, it has been occupied by Lincoln Diaz-Balart. Lincoln first considered running for Congress in 1989 but was talked out of running against Ros-Lehtinen in District 18 by Jorge Mas Canosa of the Cuban American National Foundation. Lincoln waited until the 21st District was created.[4] Challenged by Javier Soto, also a Cuban-born Florida senator, Lincoln won the primary by 69 to 31 percent and was unopposed in the general election. He has held the seat since then.

District 25 was created after the 2000 census awarded Florida two additional House seats. Mario Diaz-Balart, serving in the state House after being term limited out of the state Senate, chaired the redistricting committee that drew the 24th District in central Florida around Orlando to favor Republican Florida Speaker of the House Tom Feeney, and the 25th District in southwest Miami-Dade to favor himself.[5]

District 21 supported Bush (104,888) over Gore in 2000 (76,322) by a 57 to 43 percent margin in 2000. In 2004, Bush (127,326) won by a 58 to 42 percent margin over Kerry (96,232) in the district. The 25th District voted 55 to 45 percent for Bush (88,308) over Gore (72,050) in 2000 and 56 to 44 percent for Bush (122, 342) over Kerry (95,001) in 2004.

Demographic Character of the Electorate

The three main voter groups in District 21 are Cuban Americans, non-Cuban Hispanics, and whites (Anglos). Blacks number only 6.5 percent of the voters. Voter registration breaks down to 56 percent of Hispanic origin, 29 percent Anglo, and 7 percent black. Cuban Hispanics outnumbered non-Cuban Hispanics by 270,000 to 190,000 in 2008. A race for District 21 is largely fought in the Spanish-speaking part of the community on talk radio and in Cuban cafes.

District 25 is comprised of 62 percent Hispanic, 24 percent Anglo, and 10 percent black. Like Miami-Dade County as a whole, it is largely a Hispanic and bilingual district. Roughly 30 percent of the households speak English only. The difference in this district is found between the Cuban and non-Cuban Hispanic vote. Cuban Americans tend to vote more Republican while the non-Cuban Hispanic population has been divided between Nicaraguans and Venezuelans who tend to vote Republican and Puerto Ricans, Dominicans, and others who are likely to vote Democratic. Anglos are largely split by party affiliation with black voters (there is a large Haitian, Bahamian, and Caribbean population) strongly favoring Democrats.

Key Voting Blocs

The main issue in these districts has traditionally been U.S. policy toward Cuba, in terms of the embargo, family travel, and sending money to the island. Although the anticommunist policies are conservative, the Cuban population has been peculiarly liberal on social issues and more likely to take positions favored by Democrats even as they vote for Republican representatives to go to Washington to fight the Castro regime in Cuba. Lincoln and Mario have often been ridiculed by opponents as "one-trick ponies" for being singularly concerned with Cuba, even to the exclusion of doing much constituent work to bring funding home to the region or dealing with socioeconomic concerns in the community. The issue has always been Cuba for the Diaz-Balart brothers and many Cuban Americans, but this year focused more on mainstream issues closer to home like the economy, record home foreclosures, and rising unemployment. Given the mild changes in party registrations, the strong anti-incumbent and anti-administration mood, and the perceived changes in the concerns of the local electorate, Democrats placed significant effort toward cracking the Republican dominance over Little Havana's congressional delegation.

Major Urban Areas

District 21 sprawls through the middle of Miami-Dade County from north to south. It is a thin but dense district with a northern tip in Broward County that runs south to the Cutler Ridge area of Southern Miami-Dade County. A few miles west of downtown Miami, it is basically the suburbs of Greater Miami that serve as the buffer between the beach areas on the east side in District 18 and the Florida Everglades to the west in District 25. It includes communities like Hialeah, Miami-Lakes, and Doral near the airport and the Kendall, Pinecrest, and Cutler Ridge neighborhoods in the south. This district originally only included parts of Dade County until it was redistricted in 2000. That added a part of western Broward County to the north, including parts of the towns of Miramar and Pembroke Pines.

West of District 21, District 25 encompasses a sprawling swath of land across southwest Florida including parts of Miami-Dade, Collier (Naples on the Gulf Coast), and Monroe (the Florida Keys) Counties. The large land area includes the Florida Everglades and has a population that is mainly from Miami-Dade County (87 percent) with about 13 percent in Collier County. The Collier territory is largely a suburb of Naples in areas that straddle the Everglades and are conservative. The Miami-Dade part of the district represents areas west and south of the downtown area and was the fastest growing district in Florida in the 1990s with 52 percent population growth during the decade.[6] District 25 is the least Cuban of the three Cuban American districts in Miami.

In the northern part of Miami-Dade County, the district includes Cuban and non-Cuban Hispanic areas like Hialeah Gardens and Tamiami as well as southwestern parts of the district including South Miami Heights, Cutler Ridge, Princeton, Naranja, and south to the town of Homestead. District 25 is an exurb in West Miami-Dade County.

Employment/Occupational Characteristics

District 21's west-central swath through Miami-Dade County includes the Miami International Airport and has an employment base related to air travel and trade and the large seaports. It houses several universities and hospitals and has service, tourism, and sales jobs. District 25 to the west and south contain similar employment characteristics. What is different is the large area of the protected Florida Everglades that is in that district.

THE CANDIDATES: DISTRICT 21

The District 21 race shaped up to be a clash of the titans since the day Raul Martinez announced that he would challenge Lincoln for the seat. Martinez, the twenty-four-year mayor of Hialeah, the second largest city in Miami-Dade County, is a well-known public servant and powerful force in Hialeah and Miami-Dade politics. But he also has a checkered background of courtroom battles and controversies. In an anti-incumbent year, with Republicans that could easily be tied to the Bush administration, and amidst talk that the Cuban American community was becoming less conservative and interested in issues beyond Cuba, some pundits thought Lincoln could be unseated.[7]

Lincoln Diaz-Balart was born in Havana, Cuba, in 1954. His father Rafael Diaz-Balart was a legislator in Cuba. Rafael's sister was once married to Fidel Castro and "is the mother of Castro's only recognized child."[8] Despite this rich heritage with Cuba roots, Lincoln does not note on his congressional website or his campaign biography that he was born in Cuba. His biography begins by stating that he attended public schools in South Florida and high school in Madrid, Spain.

Lincoln earned his B.A. in international relations from New College of University of South Florida and his J.D. from Case Western Reserve University before practicing law in Miami. He worked for Legal Services of Greater Miami doing free legal work for the poor before becoming assistant state attorney in Miami and then a partner in a law firm. Lincoln ran for the Florida House of Representatives as a Democrat in 1982 and lost. In 1986, Lincoln and his brother, Mario, switched their party affiliations to Republican. He was elected to the State House in 1986–1989 and then to the Florida Senate in 1989 before winning the newly created seat in the U.S. House of Representatives in 1992.

Lincoln's reputation in Congress is that of a staunch supporter of the Cuban embargo and a hard-liner against the communist regime. Through his efforts, the Cuban embargo was strengthened in 1996. Although Lincoln is a loyal Republican vote in Congress, he was one of three Republican incumbents not to sign the 1994 Contract with America because it called for cutting benefits to legal immigrants. The issue of Hispanic immigration is one of the few issues beyond the Cuban embargo where Diaz-Balart has demonstrated legislative leadership. He voted against the 1996 Republican-backed welfare reform bills that denied welfare to illegal immigrants and the next year he sponsored a bill to provide disability benefits and food stamps to illegal immigrants who were denied aid by the 1996 welfare reform law. In 1998, Lincoln sponsored legislation to help more than 150,000 Central Americans stay in the United States and gain legal residency.

Lincoln Diaz-Balart was placed on the House Foreign Affairs Committee as a popular freshman and then he was given a plum appointment as the first Hispanic to be named to the powerful Rules Committee. He was reelected twice with no opposition (but for six write-in votes). Lincoln faced a Democratic challenge in 1998 from Patrick Cusack, but carried 75 percent of the vote. He was again unopposed in his 2000 reelection (except for thirty-five write-in votes). After redistricting was completed for 2002, he was still unopposed. In 2004, Lincoln defeated Democrat Frank J. Gonzales by carrying 75 percent of the vote, but his margin of victory over Gonzalez in the 2006 race was reduced to 60 percent.

What was significant about the 2006 race was that Diaz-Balart's numbers dipped in Broward County from 64 percent to only 43 percent of the vote. While the Broward area is a small part of the district, people there were growing dissatisfied with Lincoln. Seen as being too focused on Cuba and too closely linked with President Bush, interest began to grow for a legitimate challenger. Democrats needed someone with name recognition to run; they found that person when Raul Martinez declared in January 2008 that he would run for District 21.

Raul Martinez was born in Santiago de Cuba a decade before Fidel Castro came to power, and he moved to the United States in March of 1960. He graduated from Miami Senior High School, the former Miami-Dade Junior College (now Miami-Dade College), and then Florida International University with a B.S. in Criminal Justice. Martinez took up residence in Hialeah in the 1960s and with his father started a Spanish-language newspaper.

After being appointed to the city's Personnel Board in 1976, he was elected to the city council the next year. From there Martinez ascended to the mayor's office and was reelected eight times, serving for twenty-four years. Hialeah proclaimed the title "City of Progress" due to its economic and social transformation, which occurred largely because of Martinez's guidance. Hialeah's City Hall was renamed for him in 2005 and, two years later, the State Legislature renamed the main street through Hialeah as "Mayor Raul L. Martinez Street." Many wondered what was next for the married fifty-nine-year-old public servant with two adult children.

Martinez was considered a candidate for Congress in 1989 when it was reported he would challenge Ros-Lehtinen in District 18. While he was considering the race, Martinez was investigated on public corruption charges that ended any campaign. The investigation was led by acting U.S. attorney Dexter Lehtinen, husband of Ileana Ros. Martinez was charged with eight counts of extortion and racketeering and was ultimately convicted of six counts and sentenced to ten years in prison. His appeal was granted based on flawed jury instructions and jury misconduct. The appeal ended with a hung jury in March 1996. A third trial brought an acquittal on one of the extortion charges and an eleven-to-one jury vote favoring acquittal on the other charges. A new U.S. attorney appointed by Democratic president Bill Clinton dropped the remaining charges.

Martinez's 1993 reelection as mayor was decided by 273 votes, but the result was thrown out by a judge who found that campaign workers had forged absentee ballots in favor of Martinez. He won a special election in 1994 and was reelected twice more before stepping aside in 2005 to serve as a consultant and on the 2007 Miami-Dade County Charter Commission. Martinez is one of the rare breed in elected Miami-Dade politics: a Cuban American Democrat. Saying he believes in affordable housing, helping the disadvantaged, universal healthcare, and a humanistic approach to politics, Martinez positioned himself in the centrist wing of the Democratic Party.[9] Martinez positioned himself for a run for Congress since his 1989 charges by pointing to his record of economic development in Hialeah. Martinez's political connections in Washington and to the Democratic Party, and his gregarious nature, made him a strong candidate to challenge Lincoln. It would turn out as one of the nastiest races in recent history.

THE CANDIDATES: DISTRICT 25

Mario Diaz-Balart was elected to represent District 25 in the U.S. House of Representatives in 2002. Mario worked as an aide to Xavier Suarez, the mayor of the City of Miami, after briefly attending the University of South Florida. He was elected in 1988 to the Florida House of Representatives and, in 1992 at age thirty-one, became the youngest person elected to the Florida Senate. He rose to be a party leader and a respected budget hawk, even earning the nickname "The Slasher" for his cuts as chair of the Senate Ways and Means Committee. Term limited out of the Senate, he won a seat back in the State House and chaired the redistricting panel that drew the legislative districts, including two new ones awarded to Florida after the 2000 Census. District 25 was tailor-made for Mario.[10]

Mario eliminated his primary opponents through court challenges and then won the general election with 65 percent of the vote over State Representative Annie Betancourt, a widow of a Bay of Pigs veteran and a former social worker and educator. Mario's well-financed campaign received the endorsement of the teachers' union and other unions. Even though Bentancourt called for an end to the Cuban embargo, a dangerous move in a Miami-based campaign, Mario did not exploit the comment and instead focused on gaining the support of the non-Cuban Hispanics in the district. In 2004, Mario ran unopposed and, in 2006, easily won reelection with 58.5 percent of the vote against Michael Calderon, a computer programmer from Miami.

Joe Garcia announced in February 2008 that he would challenge Mario Diaz-Balart in District 25. Garcia had been the Executive Director of the Cuban American National Foundation (CANF) and was serving as chairman of the Democratic Party of Miami-Dade. Garcia was born in Miami Beach in 1963 to parents who had fled Castro's Cuba. He attended a top Miami prep school, Miami-Dade Community College, and then earned both his bachelor's and law degrees from the University of Miami. In 1993, the late founder of CANF, Jorge Mas Canosa, asked Garcia to head Project Exodus, a refugee resettlement program that reunited more than 10,000 families and brought Cuban refugees stuck in other countries to the United States.

Garcia was appointed as chairman of the Florida Public Service Commission by Democratic governor Lawton Chiles. In that role he regulated the energy and utilities industries. From 2000 to 2004, he headed CANF, a powerful lobby group that traditionally held strong views against communist Cuba. Garcia later joined the New Democrat Network (NDN), a Washington-DC-based, centrist policy institute to lead Hispanic outreach efforts, and was elected as county party chair in 2006.

Garcia was not a resident of District 25, instead living in neighboring Miami Beach (in District 18). When asked about it, he would say that Mario has been absent from the district while Garcia had been born and raised in the community and that he would move to the district if elected. "What matters is not where I live, but how the people in that congressional district live," Garcia told local ABC political reporter Michael Putney on his Sunday morning show. At a time when economic issues and not Cuba policy dominated the discourse, Garcia rallied the party to his side in his run at Mario in District 25.

CAMPAIGN ISSUES

Lincoln and Mario have been very popular in the Cuban conservative community and among moderate Whites. Martinez appealed to his Hialeah city base and to liberal Democrats. Garcia appealed to progressive Democrats and more liberal Cubans and non-Hispanic Cubans.

This campaign came down to three basic issues with some additional ones on the periphery: the record of the Bush administration; Cuba policy; and the character of each candidate pertaining to various ethical scandals and corruption charges on both sides. To a lesser degree, the housing foreclosure and financial crises also were discussed by the Democratic challengers, as Districts 21 and 25 had some of the highest foreclosure rates in the nation. The protection of the Everglades was a minor issue in the District 25 race and there was also a debate over candidate debates. In the end, the negative campaign ads and voter uncertainty about Martinez and Garcia tipped the electorate toward the Diaz-Balart brothers.

The Bush Administration

Both Democratic challengers claimed that the Diaz-Balarts were closely tied to President Bush and tried to tie them together whenever possible. A liberal 527-group called the One South Florida Media Fund sent out a mailer showing Mario as a "mini-Bush" in a play on the Austin Powers "mini-me" movie character. It stated that Mario voted with Bush 96 percent of the time. Garcia ran a commercial showing Mario saying "George W. Bush is right today" on the House floor and claiming that Mario voted with the president 93 percent of the time. These and other ads tied Mario to Bush on the economy, energy, health care, and war spending.

The Martinez campaign also highlighted Lincoln's links to Bush. Their main ad showed Lincoln as a bobble-head, rubber stamp for Bush. The Lincoln bobble-head stamped "Yes to Bush!" on top of $2 billion a week for the Iraq War, and support for the president's economic, energy, budget, and health care plans. It also noted that Lincoln once said "I thank God for George Bush" and ends with the phrase "We need leaders, not rubber stamps."[11]

The DCCC added an ad that described the Diaz-Balart brothers as "Loyal to Bush. Not to us" for voting with the president on the war, on tax cuts, and on the children's health insurance program. The ad also claimed that the Diaz-Balart brothers had voted themselves five pay raises in Congress and cited the vote numbers on the bottom of the screen. The Diaz-Balarts countered the claims that they voted with Bush more than 90 percent of the time. They noted that the numbers were actually lower over the entire Bush presidency and included some important votes on which they had differed with the president. Both brothers voted against the economic stimulus package favored by the president. While Mario is a rank-and-file Republican, Lincoln has a slightly more moderate record and has voted against his party on immigration issues.

The Cuba Issue: "One-Trick Pony"

It was no surprise that Cuba was one of the first and most acrimonious issues to be raised in this campaign. In 1998, Lincoln was named one of the fifty most effective members of Congress by *Congressional Quarterly*. In their write-up, they called him a "niche player . . . known, first and foremost, for his crusade against Castro's Cuba."[12] Lincoln took offense to the charges that he was a "one-trick pony," pointing to his website which listed non-Cuba issues as all but one of his top ten legislative achievements.

Lincoln counterpunched with the claim that Martinez's candidacy was supported by Castro sympathizers in order to weaken or end the Cuban embargo. "I do not think that we should weaken the embargo on Cuba. I would work to increase the amount of funding to dissidents on the island," Martinez said in his defense during his announcement. Lincoln further accused Martinez of being willing to give "concessions to the Cuban dictatorship." Martinez's spokesman, Jeffery Garcia, replied by saying, "You expect Lincoln Diaz-Balart to call anyone who disagrees with him to be a communist."[13]

Garcia posted videos online calling Mario a "one-trick pony" and playing the Paul Simon song in the background. It showed Mario and Lincoln shouting "Fidel Castro" and "communist" while waving their hands on the floor on Congress. In response, Mario put out a video showing him speaking on a variety issues in the House. The brothers also played up their support of other Hispanic groups. Mario told a group of Venezuelan Americans, "People say the Diaz-Balarts are too focused on international issues. Well, as the saying goes, I can walk and chew gum at the same time." Lincoln told reporters, "This is who I represent. I don't represent Iowa," as he shook hands with supporters at a Colombian restaurant.[14] Both Diaz-Balarts took to Spanish radio with paid ads painting their opponents' stances as weak on the Cuban regime.[15]

Martinez, Garcia, and the Democrats argued that the electorate was more interested in such economic issues as state insurance and housing rather than Cuba. Polling suggested that Cuba was, in fact, low on voter's minds.[16] In the end, the Cuba issue was as predominant as it usually is in Miami campaigns. While the campaign was bitterly fought among a host of surrogates on Spanish-language radio, the lack of Cuba as an issue in the presidential race and the dominance of the economy as the issue in Miami both relegated Cuba policy to the sidelines and pointed to change within the Cuban American community.

Character and Corruption

Questions of corruption, ethics, and fitness for office dominated both campaigns. Ethics became the biggest issue in the District 21 race and was an issue in District 25. On the day Martinez announced his candidacy, Lincoln was campaigning with Republican presidential candidate John McCain. "I think he's unfit to be trusted with public office and his record shows that," said Lincoln. "His record is not only of corruption but also vulgarity."[17] Republican Party of Florida (RPOF) chair Jim Greer added, "This campaign will likely be [a] very contentious one, considering Raul Martinez has a history of corruption and indecency." Greer called it "the ultimate in hypocrisy" to have Martinez run on "a record of corruption, crude behavior and offensive rhetoric."[18]

Greer had previously criticized Martinez for holding a fund-raiser for Hillary Clinton at his house in February 2007. Martinez replied in a telephone interview with a reporter with an obscenity-laced response saying: "I would debate any f—— Republican about my past. We'll have a *mano a mano* if they want to take me on. I'm a businessman. I'm a Democrat. Why shouldn't I raise money at my house? I will get on the horse, and I will beat the s—— of out them."[19]

The day after the August 25 primary election (the candidates were unopposed in the primaries), Lincoln started running advertisements on cable TV. The new ad campaign effectively rehashed the Martinez controversies and scandals and disgusted many voters. A few ads highlighted some of Lincoln's legislative accomplishments. For instance, one thirty-second spot began with Lincoln talking about caring for others and creating jobs. But during the second half of the spot the screen and music went dark and showed Martinez. The ad accused him of insults, vulgarities, and a conviction without full acquittal.

From there it went downhill. Ads claimed Martinez threatened a city employee's life, spit in a rival's eye, had "a history of disrespecting women," and assaulted a "defenseless young man." Martinez's behavior was labeled "horrifying" and footage was aired from an incident in 1999 when the 6'4", 275-pound Martinez punched a skinny twenty-one-year-old butcher named Ernesto Mirabal. Mirabal and hundreds of others were blocking the Palmetto Expressway, one of the more important roads in Miami, while protesting the U.S. Coast Guard treatment of Cuban rafters. The stunning video showed in slow motion twenty seconds of Martinez landing five punches to the face and abdomen of Mirabal as police officers tried to pull the mayor off him. Martinez claimed to be coming to the aide of his police chief who was allegedly hit in the head with a rock by Mirabal. Battery charges were brought against Mirabal but were later dropped.

Perhaps the catchiest and most damaging commercial was called "Raul Martinez's Wheel of Corruption." In a play on the television series *Wheel of*

Fortune, a wheel spinning to snappy music landed on several past scandals while accusing Martinez of using his influence to get government jobs for his family and friends, taking $1.2 million of taxpayer money for legal fees and back pay, and "being prosecuted for racketeering and extortion." It ended with a mug shot of Martinez and the line "We know Raul Martinez is corrupt enough for Washington, but that doesn't mean we should send him there." The Republican Party was responsible for the ad.[20]

A similar ad run by Lincoln's campaign started with the Martinez mug shot and a mention of the indictment. It then accused Martinez of using his office to become a millionaire, and stated that he was featured in the movie *Cocaine Cowboys*. But Martinez's indictment, though true, is only half of the story. On appeal Martinez was acquitted on some charges and others resulted in a hung jury. Federal prosecutors eventually dropped the charges, and he never spent a day in prison. Martinez did take the $1.2 million owed to him and claims to have made any additional money through legitimate real estate deals. Martinez's picture was shown in the documentary about drug trafficking in South Florida but he was not mentioned in the film.[21]

On October 30, an ad featuring an ex-Hialeah police captain, Bill O'Connell, was released. In it O'Connell spoke to the camera saying of his former boss, "Raul Martinez is the poster child of everything wrong in politics" and "Raul Martinez is the most corrupt politician you will see in your life." The ad aired extensively on local and cable stations. Martinez held a press conference and denounced the former officer's comments but did not respond on air. Ultimately, his campaign could not match the negative onslaught from Lincoln.

Lincoln was not without his own ethics questions. He was fined by the Federal Elections Commission (FEC) in 2000 and paid $30,000 in fines for various campaign finance violations. An eighteen-page report was issued after a year-long investigation into the 1997–1998 campaign cycle. The report documented the failure of Lincoln's campaign to report $45,000 in contributions, how the FEC made him refund $30,000 in illegal contributions, the presence of $45,000 in uncashed checks to vendors, and showed a $144,000 discrepancy in campaign funds.[22] Lincoln was also fined $5,500 for filing late campaign reports in early 2000. Despite the ugly details of the campaign violations report, the Democrats did not capitalize on Lincoln's woes in the 2002 or 2004 elections. Martinez hoped to resurrect it as an issue in the 2008 campaign.[23]

In October, the *Miami Herald* reported on federal earmarks that Lincoln secured for small defense-contracting groups based in his district. They suggested a quid pro quo relationship between campaign contributions from company employees in exchange for more than $10 million in earmarks, spending for specific projects inserted into larger budget bills. Their report uncovered a total of $41,000 in campaign contributions to the Diaz-Balart brothers' campaigns and to their joint leadership political action committee, Democracy Believers, between 2003 and 2006. Lincoln defended the earmarks saying that he was working to create jobs in the community and to promote the development of military technology to help the South Florida economy.[24]

Also that month, Democratic officials alleged that Lincoln had taken illegal cash contributions from Puerto Rican politicians. It was reported that Puerto Rican senator Jorge de Castro Font, who was indicted on thirty-one counts of federal extortion, and Luis Fortuno, later to become Puerto Rico's resident commissioner in Congress, delivered money to Lincoln in Miami in 2005. The amount was alleged to have been $50,000 in cash in a suitcase from a prominent Puerto Rican family. Lincoln admitted that he received $400 and reported two $200 checks from one family member in 2006.[25] In Puerto Rico, de Castro Font was heard on video saying that they brought money to Diaz-Balart and claimed in a radio interview that the money went toward the congressman's reelection campaign. Democrats used the scandal in ads against Lincoln's "crooks" and "dirty deals," but it did not gain traction because the Puerto Rico allegation was remote and the earmarks were for the good of the district.

No major questions were raised about Mario's ethics or past dealings. The toughest charges against him were voting for tax breaks for oil companies while taking thousands of dollars in campaign contributions from their executives. Mario's campaign tried to raise flags about Garcia, running ads calling him "Enron Joe" and saying that he "begged" convicted Enron CEO, Kenneth Lay, to help him get a job on a regulatory commission. The ad highlights Enron's failings, even though Garcia was not involved. The ad also states that Garcia supported a huge utility rates hike, although Garcia was not on the panel that voted for the increase. Most observers thought Mario was starting to look desperate.

Debates

An issue in the campaign from the beginning was that of debates. The Democratic opponents challenged the incumbents to many public debates. The Diaz-Balarts, though seasoned debaters, limited their appearances. They rejected or simply ignored many requests for public forums and even missed some scheduled events with their opponents. Empty seats or podiums sat next to Garcia and Martinez as they discussed the issues in several appearances.

In May, the Democratic candidates invited the three Republicans (the Diaz-Balarts and Ros-Lehtinen) to a three-day series of debates, one in each district to be hosted by the South Florida AFL-CIO. The union, which had endorsed the three Republican candidates in 2006 when all three had marginal challenges, hosted debates in recent years for various offices. Both Diaz-Balarts initially agreed to the events, but backed out citing scheduling conflicts a few days later. Ros-Lehtinen never answered the invitations. Lincoln Diaz-Balart claimed that the date and place of his debate was changed.[26] The Democrats egged on the Republican trio in press releases, and the AFL-CIO held "meet the candidate" forums without the candidates.

The candidates did make some joint appearances in October. The first was a Monday night "meet and greet" at the Kendall Federation of Homeowner Associations. It was mostly cordial until Mario attacked Garcia for not living in the district and Garcia responded by saying that Mario dropped out of college. Then, on October 8, all six candidates from the District 18, 21, and 25 races appeared at a Greater Miami Chamber of Commerce event. The contention began over the format. Michael Putney, WPLG-ABC 10 political reporter, was supposed to moderate the event. But when the candidates received copies of the questions prior to the event, Putney refused to moderate, calling the event "a farce."[27] Putney had hoped to ask unscripted questions but was told that some of the candidates wanted to see the questions in advance (all of the candidates later denied that it was them). Chamber officials stated that the questions were handed out first because they were questions their constituents wanted to hear. In the three candidate forums, the District 18 candidates were the most heated while the D21 and D 25 events were less quarrelsome. For the most part, the candidates spoke to the audience rather than to each other.

Mario and Garcia held a low-key debate with Generation Engage on August 23 in Coral Gables. Lincoln and Martinez had two other debates. One was a lively, televised debate and the other was held at Miami-Dade College. At both events, it was the off-stage comments after the debate that dominated the news. During side-by-side dueling media interviews, the candidates accused each other of saying one thing in Spanish and another in English.

Polls

Districts 21 and 25 were identified as "Red to Blue" seats by the Democratic Party. Public opinion polls showed that the races tightened during the summer. A July poll conducted by Bendixen & Associates showed Lincoln (41 percent) slightly ahead of Raul (37 percent) with 22 percent undecided. The same poll showed Mario (44 percent) ahead of Garcia (39 percent) with 17 percent undecided. By late August, respected pollsters listed the races as "toss-ups" or leaning Republican. One Washington-based *Roll Call* poll put Martinez up by two points. In October, the Rothenberg Political Report called the race a "pure toss-up" with momentum on the side of Democrats.[28]

National attention was focused on these races, and speculation grew that the Diaz-Balarts might finally be defeated. The *New York Times* and *Huffington Post* suggested an end to the Diaz-Balart dynasty. The races had tightened, but the Diaz-Balarts and the Republicans then began to play hardball. Closer to home, a poll by the Metropolitan Center of Florida International University in late October showed results that would be similar to the election outcome. The poll suggested reelection of the Diaz-Balarts with 42 percent of independent voters and 90 percent of Cuban Americans favoring Lincoln. "It was these pollsters who wanted to create this clash of titans. Being a Democratic mayor of a Republican city looks good on paper, but it was not the reality on the ground," said Ana Carbonell, Lincoln's campaign manager and a veteran member of his congressional staff. "When people realized who Raul Martinez is and what he has done, they did not feel comfortable voting for him," added Carbonell.[29]

CAMPAIGN STRATEGY

Media

The *Miami Herald* endorsed Martinez on October 14, two-and-a-half weeks before the election. Their support was terse and barely mentioned Lincoln. They noted that both candidates were "strong advocates of a free Cuba" but pointed out their differences on Iraq and tax cuts. "Mr. Martinez is firmly grounded in reality. He has a broad agenda and a hands-on style of leadership. His penchant for devising practical solutions to political problems would be an asset to the district."[30] The paper also noted that a vote for Martinez represented the changing nature of Miami's Hispanic community and Republican voting bloc.

The *Miami Herald* endorsed Mario but applauded Garcia's impressive public record. They described the race as "a referendum on the Bush administration" but recommended Mario based on "his overall record of engagement on policy issues and for delivering resources and jobs to the district."[31] The endorsement mentioned Mario's record of bringing funding to the district for local transportation and infrastructure projects and his support for Everglades restoration, Israel, and trade with Colombia. An issue in the campaign was a free trade agreement with Colombia. District 25 has the largest Colombian population in the United States and is home to large Colombian flower import and distribution businesses.

Image and Advertising

Lincoln's advisors knew that Martinez was vulnerable to ethics and corruption charges. Thus, their strategy was to portray Martinez as corrupt and vulgar and to present their candidate as respected and possessing a record beyond his Cuba accomplishments. Mario tried to present Garcia as a typical politician and tried to tie him to the Enron scandal. Martinez and Garcia attempted to take advantage of the anti-Bush and anti-incumbent moods by making the Diaz-Balarts out to be close associates of Bush. They also painted the Diaz-Balarts as being concerned only with Cuba, to the exclusion of issues closer to home including home prices, job losses, and the general economy.

Lincoln suffered an early public relations blunder when his campaign released a list of twelve local unions that endorsed his reelection in the spring. But two on the list, a transport union and longshoreman union affiliated with the AFL-CIO, said they did not endorse the incumbent. A longshoreman union official said that they had a good relationship with the Republican incumbents but that they could not endorse them because more than two-thirds of the state AFL-CIO had voted to endorse the Democratic challengers. The transport union indicated that they considered the Diaz-Balarts to be their friends in Congress and that Lincoln had helped to steer money home recently for a local labor studies center but that they had to stick with the decision of the statewide body.[32]

Martinez and Garcia enjoyed a temporary bump from an appearance at the Democratic National Convention. Excitement over Obama carried over to other Democratic candidates. Lincoln was scheduled to speak on Monday of the Republican National Convention in Minnesota, but his appearance was cancelled due to an abbreviated convention in response to Hurricane Gustav.

Mario appeared with John McCain during a June visit to the Florida Everglades. McCain was criticized by Floridians for voting against a water bill in late 2007 that included millions of dollars for Everglades restoration. President Bush vetoed the bill but was overridden by Congress. Mario, who helped to get the Everglades funding into the bill, was thus in the awkward situation of having to back off his support for the bill and the Everglades in order to support his party's candidate for president.

Finance

Lincoln raised $2.3 million in this election cycle—$1 million from individual contributors and $621,000 from PACs—and spent nearly $3.3 million. His top contributors included foreign and defense lobbyists, law firms, real estate, health professionals, and leadership PACs. Martinez raised almost $1.9 million—$1.5 million from individuals and $233,000 from PACs—and spent nearly all of it. Mario brought in about $2 million (and spent $2.5 million), while almost $1.9 million was raised and spent by Garcia. Mario's contributions flowed evenly between individuals and PACs.

Garcia, like Martinez, raised much more from individuals ($1.2 million) than from PACs ($258,000).

Add to these totals about $2.6 million from the national Republican Party and about $2 million from the Democrats, and these were two of the top funded and ad-saturated campaigns in the nation. The GOP spent more on Lincoln than on any other congressional candidate in the nation.[33]

Grass Roots

Each of the candidates worked tirelessly walking their districts and frequented early voting sites. Lincoln spent a lot of time working on the Broward part of his district while Mario did outreach in each corner of his district. Garcia walked neighborhoods knocking on doors each weekend and both challengers showed up at numerous public forums and rallies. The incumbents kept their appearances limited to higher-profile events. Lincoln and Mario appeared at rallies for John McCain both at Florida International University and at the University of Miami. At the FIU event, Mario was demonstrative, amusing the crowd when he dove to the stage and simulated a referee in a wrestling match "counting out" Democratic vice presidential candidate, Joe Biden, in his debate with Governor Sarah Palin. During McCain's midnight concert held two days prior to Election Day at the Hurricanes' convention center, Mario joked "This is the house of the 'Canes most of the year—tonight it is the night of the McCains!" and then fired the crowd up by shouting the record of his brother in Spanish.

While Obama made several South Florida appearances and mentioned Martinez and Garcia on the stump, he did not actively campaign for their candidacies. Both Martinez and Garcia tapped into some of the new channels of fund-raising opened by Obama. It was presumed that Obama's real impact would be in turning out newer and younger voters that would vote for other Democrats on the ticket. "I'm the Democrat in the race," Garcia told district residents. "My name will be listed right below Barack Obama's."[34]

Bases of Support

The Diaz-Balart brothers are two charismatic Cuban politicians. Because of their popularity in the Cuban exile community and their hard-line stances on Cuba, they have reliably depended on the Cuban American and the Republican votes. Their challengers needed to mobilize Anglos, African Americans, and non-Cuban Hispanics and make inroads into their Cuban votes to catch the incumbents. Because Lincoln served for eight terms and Mario had been elected to three terms, the brothers had all of the advantages of incumbency that make them difficult to defeat.

The Martinez camp had assistance from an independent group called Patriot Majority, funded by labor unions, that ran ads and send out mailers against Lincoln. In the ads, a series of veterans claim they served in several battlefields and then described some of their injuries. They said Lincoln voted against military veterans while voting five pay raises for himself. The Patriot Majority spent $550,000 in September attacking Lincoln and over $1 million in total.[35] The Patriot Majority attack prompted Lincoln to tape a two-minute video message that was available on his website and on YouTube. In it he explained that he has faithfully supported the troops and military salary increases and that he never once voted to raise his own salary, explaining that it was a federal COLA increase, and that he even returned more than $1 million in office funds to the taxpayer. He also created a fact check section on his website and encouraged people to contact him.

Nancy Pelosi made a high-profile visit to Miami's Little Havana to raise money for the three Democratic challengers (Martinez, Garcia, and Taddeo) in late October. Pelosi said the Democrats needed them in Congress and suggested that her candidates had momentum and a message that appealed to the middle class. The House Speaker noted that she, like the three candidates, opposed Bush's decision to tighten travel restrictions and remittances to Cuba. Standing with Pelosi in support of the three candidates was Debbie Wasserman-Schultz (D-FL) and Kendrick Meek (D-FL), two local Democrats who earlier had stayed neutral in the races against their Republican colleagues in Congress.

Both Mario and Garcia ended up working the same precinct for ten hours on Election Day. In the closing hours of the polls, they walked the line of voters outside South Kendall Community Church, a busy double precinct. Garcia handed out homemade sandwiches, soft drinks, water, and chocolate to make sure people would stay in line and vote. Turnout was relatively high but did not produce the record-breaking numbers that some had predicted. In the end neither Martinez nor Garcia was able to unseat the popular incumbents, and Garcia came closer out of the two.

ELECTION RESULTS

Hard work and heavy fund-raising helped keep the incumbents in office. Both Diaz-Balarts campaigned vigorously and paid attention to key parts of their constituencies. They also benefited from the goodwill they had built up with voters over the years. Voters decided to stick with the candidates they knew and who know their way around both Miami and Washington politics.

Lincoln Diaz-Balart easily held on to his seat by a 58 to 42 percent margin. He won 113,987 to 76,521 in Miami-Dade County and barely lost in Broward 23,255 to 23,239. Lincoln led absentee votes with a 32,469 to

14,791 margin and had a narrow edge in early voting at 30,220 to 29,004 in Miami-Dade. While Democrats usually enjoy an advantage in early voting in Miami-Dade, this number showed that Martinez was in trouble heading into Election Day.

The *Miami New Times* said, "It was perhaps the most dramatic reversal in the most dramatic election in American history."[36] That piece of hyperbolic boosterism aside, it was an impressive victory by the Diaz-Balarts, who appeared to be on the ropes and to finally have worthy challengers. In the end, it may be that Martinez was too tainted of a candidate to take on the popular, sophisticated, and well-funded incumbent. Republicans were able to hurt Martinez early with the ethics and corruption charges. They used a well-funded campaign styled out of Lee Atwater's GOP playbook with a hard hitting attack on Martinez's past. "It was the pounding I took for three months. It wasn't easy to overcome it," said Martinez, "and I sensed this."[37]

Martinez focused on maximizing his turnout among non-Cuban Hispanics and Anglos in Broward County. While he beat Diaz-Balart there, he did not even do as well as Frank Gonzalez in 2006. Even though Martinez is popular in Hialeah, it is a majority Republican area that he had hoped to win. He only won one precinct in Hialeah. At the end of the day, it seems that the DCCC abandoned Martinez in his time of need in order to throw the extra support behind Joe Garcia. On the other hand, when the polls tightened and Lincoln called for help from the RCCC, he received everything he needed. This may be because Martinez was a primary supporter of candidate Hillary Clinton and not of Barack Obama. It could also be because he was seen as adding to the culture of corruption in Washington and therefore not a worthy candidate after all to support in attempt of defeating a popular Republican incumbent.

Martinez allowed the Republicans to define him based on his prior involvement in scandals. "When you run for Congress against an entrenched incumbent, it is up to the challenger to dictate the terms of the race," said Fernand Amandi, executive vice president of Bendixen & Associates, a Coral Gables-based polling company. "Unfortunately Raul never did that. He allowed the caricature Diaz-Balart painted of him to become cemented in the minds of voters. That was a fatal mistake."[38] There were a significant number of undervotes especially in Democrat-heavy Broward County that voted for Obama. Some voters gave testimony to local media that they were unsettled by the negative ads and voted for president but left the congressional race empty.

Lincoln Diaz-Balart may invite another strong challenge in 2010 but at least initially, Martinez downplayed the chances of a rematch. Still, even as it looked at one point that Martinez may pull off the upset, the negative ad campaign, the general uncertainty over Martinez, and the popularity of Lincoln among Cuban Americans prevailed. "People underestimate how hard it is to unseat an incumbent," said Dario Moreno, a political science professor and director of the FIU Metropolitan Center.[39] The older Cubans came out for Lincoln and for John McCain, and the hard-line stance against Cuba continued to carry the day.

In District 25, Mario held on by a margin of 53 to 47 percent. On election night, the early results showed the race in a tie for several hours. It was the closest of the three races, but in the end voters returned Mario to Congress. Mario narrowly won Collier County by a 14,684 to 12,665 count. He beat Garcia in absentee ballots, but Garcia had a light edge in early voting. Mario's advantage in Miami-Dade was more decisive at 116,200 to 103,146.

Garcia had noted that for the first time a majority of Cuban American voters were born after 1980, causing them to hold different views on Cuba policy from the old guard. Many analysts saw these races as referenda on U.S. policy toward Cuba and expected to see a shift in voting resembling the shift in attitudes measured in recent years. The idea that the Cuban American community was becoming more liberal was defeated. "All this stuff about generational change is a myth," Lincoln said prophetically.[40]

NOTES

1. Berkeley Report, "RACE-BAIT '08: Lessons Learned from the Political Dirty Dozen, 12 Cases of Playing the Race Card, 1983–2007," a report by researchers at the University of California, Berkeley, December 2007, www.law.berkeley.edu/centers/ewi/RaceCardReportFinal.pdf.

2. Ian Swanson, "Sensing Cuba Shift, Democrats Target Trio of House Republicans in Florida." TheHill.com. Posted October 18, 2007.

3. Laura Figueroa and Alfonso Chardy. 2008. "It's Official: Martinez Takes on Diaz-Balart," *Miami Herald*, January 22, 2008.

4. Michael Barone and Richard E. Cohen, *The Almanac of American Politics: 2004* (Washington, DC: National Journal Group, 2003).

5. Barone and Cohen, *Almanac of American Politics*.

6. Barone and Cohen, *Almanac of American Politics*.

7. Swanson, "Sensing Cuba Shift."

8. Barone and Cohen, *Almanac of American Politics*.

9. Alfonso Chardy, "Ex-Mayor to Run for Congress," *Miami Herald*, January 22, 2008.

10. Barone and Cohen, *Almanac of American Politics*.

11. Television commercial run frequently in Miami during the campaign.

12. Lesley Clark, "House Race: Lincoln Diaz-Balart Noted for Stand on Cuba," *Miami Herald*, October 12, 2008.

13. Laura Figueroa and Alfonso Chardy. "It's Official: Martinez Takes on Diaz-Balart," *Miami Herald*, January 22, 2008.

14. Laura Wides-Munoz, "Miami's Diaz-Balarts Face First Real Test," *Miami Herald*, October 17, 2008.

15. Lesley Clark, "Congressional Challengers, Incumbents Fight to the End for Votes," *Miami Herald*, November 3, 2008.
16. Lesley Clark and Luisa Yanez, "Economy, Not Cuba, at Heart of 3 Congressional Races," *Miami Herald*, October 28, 2008.
17. Figeroa and Chardy, "It's Official."
18. Republican Party of Florida Press Release, January 22, 2008.
19. Beth Reinhard, "Raul Martinez Launches Tirade over Clinton Fundraising Flap," *Miami Herald*, September 11, 2007.
20. Glenn Milberg, "Truth Test: Attack Ad Targets Raul Martinez," Justnews.com, October 14, 2008.
21. Lesley Clark, "Attack Ads Knock Issues in Lincoln Diaz-Balart/Raul Martinez Race," *Miami Herald*, October 17, 2008.
22. Glasgow, "More 'Good Deeds' by Rep. Lincoln Diaz-Balart," *Miami New Times*, July 26, 2001.
23. Dan Christensen, "Diaz-Balart's Campaign Committee May Face More Queries," *Miami Daily Business Review*, 2001.
24. Dan Christensen, "Congressman Diaz-Balart's Earmarks Raise Eyebrows," *Miami Herald*, October 5, 2008.
25. Alfonso Chardy and Casey Woods, "Lincoln Diaz-Balart Denies Link to Puerto Rican Money Scandal," *Miami Herald*, October 9, 2008.
26. Lesley Clark, "Dade GOP Incumbents Pull Out of Debates," *Miami Herald*, May 22, 2008.
27. Lesley Clark and Patricia Mazzei, "2 Unions Deny Endorsing Diaz-Balart," *Miami Herald*, July 1, 2008.
28. Francisco Alvarado, "Kaboom: The Sound You Hear Is Raul Martinez's Popularity Hitting Bottom," *Miami New Times*, November 13–19, 2008.
29. Alvarado, "Kaboom."
30. *Miami Herald*, October 14, 2008.
31. *Miami Herald*, October 14, 2008.
32. Clark and Mazzei, "2 Unions Deny."
33. Clark, "Congressional Challengers."
34. Wides-Munoz, "Miami's Diaz-Balarts."
35. Fredreka Schouten, "Independent Groups Spend More Than Candidates in Some Contests," *USA Today*, October 10–12, 2008.
36. Alvarado, "Kaboom."
37. Alvarado, "Kaboom."
38. Alvarado, "Kaboom."
39. Myriam Marquez, "Cuba Issue vs. the Power of Incumbency," *Miami Herald*, November 7, 2008.
40. Jose de Cordoba, "Democrats Woo Cuban American Voters," *Wall Street Journal*, April 15, 2008, A4.

10

Florida District 13 Race (Jennings v. Buchanan)

Rematch—a Clash of Politics and Personalities

Peter Bergerson and Margaret E. Banyan

Christine Jennings
Age: 63
Sex: Female
Race: Caucasian
Religion: Jewish
Education: No college
Occupation: Banker
Political Experience: Democratic nominee for Congress (2006)

Vern Buchanan
Age: 57
Sex: Male
Race: Caucasian
Religion: Baptist
Education: MBA (University of Detroit, 1986); B.A. (Cleary University, 1975)
Occupation: Automobile dealer (1992–2006); founder, American Speedy Printing (1976–1992)
Political Experience: U.S. House of Representatives (2007–present)

In 2008, Florida's 13th Congressional District race was set in the context of a bitter, vitriolic, campaign and legally contested election in 2006 between Republican Vern Buchanan and Democrat Christine Jennings. This was an open congressional seat formerly held by Republican congresswoman, Katherine Harris (R-FL), the controversial former chief elections official who presided over the contested presidential election of 2000 in Florida. Harris resigned from her safe congressional seat to run unsuccessfully for the U.S. Senate. It is ironic that it was Harris's seat, given the vote count brouhaha that enveloped the 2006 and 2008 elections.

In 2006, a significant controversy arose over 18,000 ballots (cast in Sarasota County), which apparently did not register a vote for this race on Florida's new touch-screen voting system, installed after the failure of the punch-card voting system in 2000. This amount comprised roughly one in six ballots, far higher than the usual number of "undervotes" in any given election. In fact, more people voted in local races and obscure board elections than on the high-profile congressional race in 2006. Particularly disturbing for Jennings was that Sarasota County was one of her strongholds, voting for her by a six-point margin. Jennings alleged "pervasive malfunctioning" of the touch screens and carried her fight to Florida's secretary of state, the Florida courts, federal court, and the U.S. House of Representatives. The official tally was that Buchanan had defeated her by less than 350 votes and the touch-screen voting system did not produce paper ballots for a manual recount.

Ultimately, by the end of November of 2006, the certified results were upheld and businessman Vern Buchanan was declared the winner of the election, defeating Christine Jennings by 369 votes. A judge supported the ruling in January of 2007. However, the U.S. House of Representatives must seat new members of Congress, and a three-person task force was convened in spring of 2007 to examine the case. The task force recommended a speedy investigation by the Government Accountability Office, but the report affirming the results was not issued until the summer of 2008.[1]

The contentious 2006 campaign—one that saw Buchanan invest over $5 million of his own fortune, and prominent Republicans such as former governor Jeb Bush (R-FL), Senator Mel Martinez (R-FL), and former Massachusetts governor Mitt Romney (R-MA) campaign for Buchanan—carried over into and defined the 2008 race. For the past two years, Jennings devoted her energy to defeating Buchanan in the 2008 rematch.

CHARACTERISTICS OF THE DISTRICT

Congressional District 13 includes the counties of DeSoto, Hardee, Sarasota, as well as portions of Charlotte and Manatee. The district is on the lower-central Gulf coast of Florida and includes the cities of Sarasota, Venice, and Bradenton. Representative Vern Buchanan was first elected to the U.S. House of Representatives in 2006. Figure 10.1 outlines the district's boundaries.

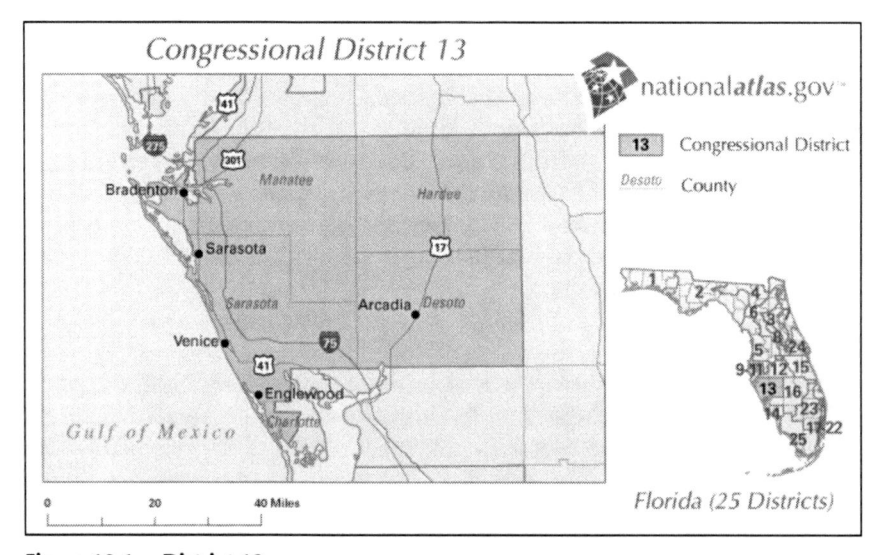

Figure 10.1. District 13.
Source: National Atlas of the United States, www.nationalatlas.gov

Demographics

The 13th Congressional District population was 746,046 as of the 2007 American Community Survey's one-year estimates. In 2007, more whites were represented than other races when compared to the national average. The district was 81 percent white, 10.7 percent Hispanic or Latino, 5.2 percent black, and 1.6 percent Asian. However, the birth origin of residents was not too far off the national average with 86.5 percent of the district's residents born in the United States, 1.4 percent in U.S. territories or to American parents, and 12.1 percent foreign born. The vast majority of those born abroad originated from Latin America (53.1 percent) and Europe (28.1 percent).[2]

Social, Economic, and Housing Characteristics

The 13th Congressional District earned nearly as much as the national average of $50,740. The median income of the district in 2007 was $49,105. However, there were fewer families living below the poverty level than the national average of 9.5 percent. The district had only 6.4 percent of families living below the poverty line. In terms of education, more residents had earned a high school diploma than national averages, with 87.3 percent of the population possessing a high school degree or higher (compared to 84.5 percent nationally). However, those earning a bachelor's degree (27.6

percent) was consistent with the national average (27.5 percent). Thirteen percent of the district's residents had dropped out of high school.

The district has a higher vacancy rate than the rest of the country, possibly due to the burst of the housing bubble in early 2007, which hit Florida harder than most states. Within the 419,000 housing units, 25 percent were vacant in 2007, compared to a 12 percent vacancy rate nationally. The area also shows considerable new growth, with 34 percent of housing units built since 1990, compared to 26 percent new housing nationally.[3]

Age

The median age of the district was 46.1, older than the national average of 36.1. This is further indicated by the higher population than the national average of those that are over sixty-five years old. In 2007, the district had 26 percent of its population over sixty-five years old, compared to the national average of 12.5 percent.[4]

History of the District

Manatee County originally encompassed most of today's 13th Congressional District. The area was settled about 1842 by Josiah Gates, Hector Braden, and Joseph Braden. The major industries were cattle ranching, citrus, and fishing. Further industrial growth was supported by the deep water port of Port Manatee. Due to the county's large size, Manatee County was later split into DeSoto, Hardee, Charlotte, Highlands, and Glades counties. The area enjoyed significant economic growth in the late 1800s when railroads opened access and phosphate was discovered. Today, the district has the reputation as a quiet, small-town, rural environment that welcomes winter "snow birds" from northern states and Canada, and over the last sixteen years has made the political transition from voting Democrat to Republican.[5]

Voting Patterns

In its current configuration, District 13 has been dominated by the Republicans. Voters chose the Republican Party candidate in every contest for the U.S. House of Representatives since 1992 (Florida Department of State Division of Elections, 2008). This district showed a Republican preference in the 2000 and 2004 presidential election in which George W. Bush won 54.13 percent and 59.47 percent, respectively, of the district's vote. Registrations also show Republican dominance. In the 2008 general election, 44 percent of the district registered Republican, 37 percent Democrat and 19 percent no party affiliation. This pattern is different from the state average of 36 percent Republican, 42 percent Democrat, and nearly 19 percent with no party affiliation.

Party affiliation in the district changed little from 2006 to 2008; despite Democrat gains of 2 percent and a corresponding Republican loss. Very little, it seems, would compel the 13th Congressional District to turn to the Democratic Party. It is not surprising, then, that Buchanan was the candidate of choice for this district. More surprising was Jennings's clear threat in a consistently Republican-leaning district. The very fact that a Democrat could mount such support in both 2006 and 2008 was perhaps indicative of the national anti-Republican mood and low approval rating of President George W. Bush in both elections.[6]

THE CANDIDATES

Neither Buchanan nor Jennings had opposition in the Florida primary election in August 2008, and so faced off again in the general election. In addition to Buchanan and Jennings, two No Party Affiliation (NPA) candidates were on the ballot: former 13th District Democratic nominee, Jan Schneider, and Don Baldauf. Baldauf, a disgruntled Republican born in Butler, Pennsylvania, sought the congressional seat as a NPA candidate. Baldauf had no formal education beyond high school, but considered himself in the self-taught tradition of Abraham Lincoln, specialization in behavioral science and business management. He was a Florida Licensed Alarm Contractor and had over twenty-five years of experience "solving other people's problems." Baldauf described his community activities as limited because he did not "want to participate in community projects with the intent to hold them up as trophies."[7]

Baldauf's motivation to run for office was due to his disappointment with the two major political parties. According to Baldauf, both parties deserted their supporters, and it was time to focus on the person and not the political party. He openly campaigned for the NASCAR vote. His website proudly advocated in large font "How government can learn from auto racing." Perhaps recognizing that winning the election was a long shot at best, he stated, "I'm up against well-known and well-funded political machines." Neither the other candidates nor the voters considered him a serious candidate.[8]

The second unaffiliated candidate was Jan Schneider, an attorney with twenty-five years of legal and legislative experience in Washington, DC. In addition to a law degree from Yale, she earned a master's degree in international politics from Columbia University and a Ph.D. in political science from Yale. An award-winning author, she has published articles on environmental protection. Her resume reflects her involvement with Democrat Party politics for a number of years, including the two presidential campaigns of

Bill Clinton. Her volunteering activities included service on the governing boards of the American Society of International Law, International Law Association, United Nations Association, the Council on Ocean Law, and the Lemon Bay Conservancy. She was a commissioner in the Sarasota County Commission on the Status of Women 2000 and served as a poll watcher with the New York and New Jersey Lawyers for Clinton-Gore 1996.

Schneider's detailed and specific positions on the issues clearly placed herself as a liberal. She took a strong stand on ending the war in Iraq as soon as possible, and took an activist position on the concerns of seniors, middle-class Americans, veterans, and women. Schneider had an abundance of academic training and legal experience and was a former three-time Democrat candidate for the congressional seat, who had defeated Christine Jennings in the 2004 Democratic primary. On balance, however, she was given little chance against the better-known and financed candidates of the two major parties. Yet, in a close race like 2006 it would be possible that Schneider might hurt Jennings among liberal voters.

Buchanan

Vern Buchanan grew up in Michigan, the son of a factory foreman in a family of six children. When he graduated from high school in 1969, he joined the Michigan Air National Guard and served for six years. Buchanan received a bachelor's degree in business administration from Cleary University in Michigan and an MBA from the University of Detroit. In 1992, Buchanan bought a Honda and Acura dealership in Ocala, Florida. He continued to acquire dealerships but in 2006 he sold five dealerships. A multimillionaire, Buchanan turned his attention to other interests including Caribbean-based automobile reinsurance companies and Bahamian real estate developments.

However, Buchanan's business interests have been the subject of federal investigations and scandal. Buchanan resigned from the helm of one of his companies just three days before bankruptcy was declared and did not repay a multimillion-dollar loan. Indeed, many lawsuits have been filed against him, including franchisees on grounds that Buchanan made false claims to them and creditors suing him for taking excessive compensation from failed businesses. He has also been the subject of an Internal Revenue Service dispute over his taxes and offshore holdings.

In his financial disclosure filing of June 2007, Buchanan reported having over $100 million in assets, making him among the five wealthiest members of Congress. He also reported ownership interests in about fifty other businesses from which he received at least $19.5 million in income for 2006.

Active in his community, Buchanan was chairman of the Greater Sarasota and Florida State Chambers of Commerce. He was also a member of the board and the executive committee of U.S. Chamber of Commerce. Buchanan has given both time and money to diverse community causes, including the Boys and Girls Club, the Community Foundation of Sarasota County, the Walk to Cure Juvenile Diabetes, the American Heart Walk, the *Mote* Marine Laboratory, and the Ringling Museum of Art.[9]

During his first term in congress, Buchanan demonstrated a strong fiscal conservative philosophy toward government. One contradiction, however, was the first piece of legislation he sponsored, which addressed Florida's insurance crisis. The legislation, the Homeowners Insurance Protection Act, was designed to establish a federal reinsurance catastrophic fund that would provide lower-cost insurance to states and ensure more affordable property insurance. Buchanan also introduced a balanced budget amendment to require a balanced federal budget and supported the Earmark Accountability and Reform Act, which attempts to reform the process through which federal funds are "earmarked" for pet projects. The congressman's other top legislative priorities were national security, maintaining tax relief, providing seniors and veterans with benefits, and protecting the environment. During his first term in office, Congressman Buchanan served on the House Committee on Transportation and Infrastructure, the House Committee on Veterans, and the House Committee on Small Business.[10]

Christine Jennings

Christine Jennings was born and raised in New Boston, Ohio, in a family where her father was a steel mill worker, a disabled WWII veteran, and a minister. Her mother ran a beauty parlor out of the family home. At age seventeen, Jennings began work as a bank teller and eventually worked her way up through the ranks to become the founder and president of Sarasota Bank. After moving to Sarasota in 1984, she served in numerous leadership positions with various banks before leading Sarasota Bank. Jennings retired from the banking industry in 2004, following a forty-year career in which she was described as a "community banker."[11]

Jennings has been actively involved in numerous community activities including serving as president for five community organizations: the John and Mable Ringling Museum of Art; the Sarasota Film Festival; the Mental Health Association of Sarasota County; the Sarasota Ballet; and the Downtown Association of Sarasota. Jennings served on the Executive Committee United Way of Manatee County and numerous others including the Community AIDS Network and Big Brothers/Big Sisters. She has been honored by many organizations, including the United Negro College Fund, the National Council of Jewish Women, and the National Association of Fundraising Executives. A long-time Democrat activist, Jennings was appointed by Governor Lawton Chiles to chair the Real Property-Lease Procurement Task Force.

Endorsements

As with most elections, endorsements by the media, interest groups, and politicians were important not so much in the election's outcome but in terms of providing information about the candidates and issues of the district. Buchanan picked up several endorsements from groups who had previously endorsed Jennings in the hotly contested 2006 election. These included the Florida Police Benevolent Association and all local newspapers. The most notable newspaper endorsement came from the *Sarasota Herald-Tribune*, which is the largest newspaper in the 13th District. Other Buchanan supporters included the Humane Society, Osteopathic Doctors, the Political Action Committee of the Veterans of Foreign Wars, and a variety of organizations wisely established by the campaign, such as Democrats for Vern, Mayors for Vern, Elected Officials for Vern, Law Enforcement for Vern, Business Owners for Vern, and so on.

Jennings's endorsements came primarily from those organizations that are considered traditionally Democrat or supportive of women. These included: EMILY's List, ActBlue, United Auto Workers, United Food & Commercial Workers Union, National Leadership PAC, International Brotherhood of Electrical Workers, PAC to the Future, New Democrat Coalition, American Federation of Teachers, Ironworkers Union, Plumbers/Pipefitters Union, Teamsters Union, and AmeriPAC. She also enjoyed support from the Fund for a Greater America, Operating Engineers Union, National Association of Letter Carriers, Carpenters & Joiners Union, American Associa-

2008 Campaign Financing

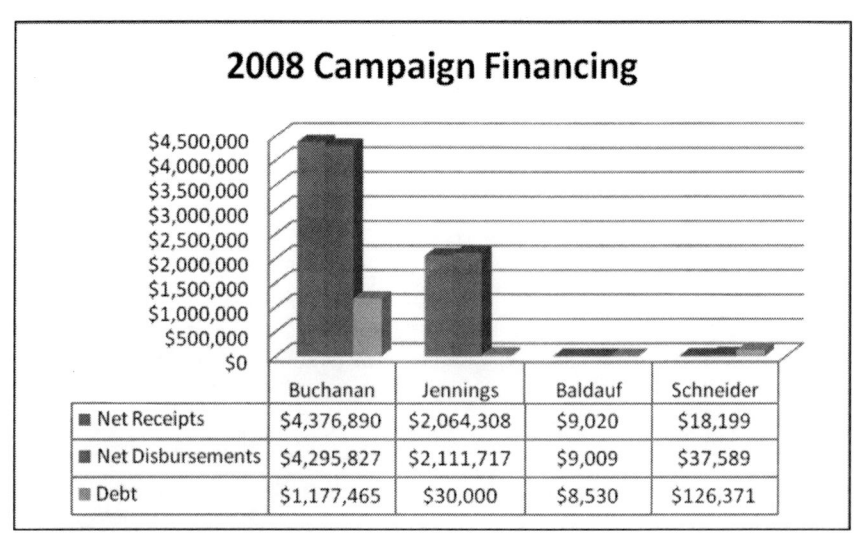

	Buchanan	Jennings	Baldauf	Schneider
Net Receipts	$4,376,890	$2,064,308	$9,020	$18,199
Net Disbursements	$4,295,827	$2,111,717	$9,009	$37,589
Debt	$1,177,465	$30,000	$8,530	$126,371

Figure 10.2. Campaign Financing.
Source: Federal Elections Commission

tion for Justice, American Postal Workers Union, Blue Dog Political Action Committee, Communications Workers of America, and the National Air Traffic Controllers Association.

Campaign Financing

In the campaign finance match-up, Buchanan was the clear winner. Buchanan outspent Jennings by more than two to one. Figure 10.2 shows the net receipts, disbursements, and debt for each of the candidates in the general election.

Further analysis into both campaigns' donations shows that Jennings's contributions from individuals and PACs comprised a greater percentage of funding than Buchanan. Jennings received over 67 percent of her total financing from individuals and 28 percent from PACS. Buchanan enjoyed support by individuals at 52 percent and PACS at 14 percent. But Buchanan received nearly one million dollars more than Jennings from individuals. Both candidates received negligible contributions from their parties.

CAMPAIGN STRATEGY

The campaign for District 13 featured all the traditional elements of a congressional campaign such as speaking engagements, press conferences, position papers, websites, and Internet communications. Four forums were also held in which the candidates addressed their positions and policy concerns. The non–major party candidates, Baldauf and Schneider, were relegated to front-row observer status, and neither impacted the campaign in any significant way.

At one of the campaign forums, Jennings tried to define the campaign by stating, "This election is not about issues. This election is about leadership."[12] However, the primary focus of the campaign from the standpoint of the media and most voters was the fact that the race featured a rematch of the close and controversial race between Buchanan and Jennings in 2006. Though it is not uncommon for political campaigns to become personal and emotional, this was a major feature of the Buchanan-Jennings rematch.

The campaign became personal and contentious from the opening salvo from Jennings. In an obvious reference to Buchanan, she attempted to contrast herself from her opponent while trying to rise above the negative tone set in the previous race by promising a campaign of "honesty, integrity, hard work and keeping my promises."[13] Yet, the campaign was defined by bitter feelings the candidates had toward one another. Throughout the campaign and at the side-by-side forums, Jennings questioned incumbent Buchanan's character, ethics, and business dealings. Trying to exploit her opponent's questionable investments, Jennings repeatedly hammered Buchanan about his legal troubles, including a recent rash of lawsuits against him and his car dealerships. She pointed to the more than 190 lawsuits Buchanan and his businesses have faced in his thirty-two-year career. She also never missed an opportunity to remind voters that Buchanan had the dubious distinction of being placed on a Washington watch-dog group as one of the "20 most-corrupt members of Congress" with a reputation as a shady "wheeler-dealer." In addition, Jennings cited IRS concerns that Buchanan used controversial strategies to shield his income from taxes. For example, in 2002, following eight years of court battles, Buchanan finally settled a tax claim with the IRS for $1.2 million plus an additional $1.3 million in penalties and interest.[14]

Jennings stayed on the attack throughout the campaign and Buchanan fired back. Buchanan labeled Jennings's support for expanding healthcare to the uninsured as "socialized medicine" and promised to oppose such. The tension escalated so high that, in one forum, the moderator called for security to avoid physical conflict. Not surprisingly, negative campaign advertisements by Buchanan and Jennings became a major campaign issue. Jennings defended her ads, saying in one heated exchange between the two contestants, "It is your job when you're running for office to draw a contrast between you and the person you're running against. . . . There's nothing wrong when you state facts." Buchanan responded that the Jennings attacks were "false and negative attacks . . . this is the type of politics and why people hate Washington, because of the nonsense that goes on like this."[15]

CAMPAIGN ISSUES

Toward the end of the campaign, with most internal and public polls showing Buchanan leading, the Republican largely declined to respond to Jennings's criticisms, instead repeatedly emphasizing his long list of endorsements from the district's newspapers and elected officials as well as his voting record in Congress. One example of his attempt to respond to his record was on the question of first opposing and then favoring the federal bailout of the financial industry in late summer. Of the bailout legislation, Buchanan defended his votes, saying the second package was a better deal for taxpayers.

Although the issues were overshadowed by the personalities and negativity of the campaign, there were some important policy issues impacting the race. One of them was energy and the high gasoline prices of 2008. On energy, Buchanan called for all options to be considered with the exception of drilling off Florida beaches in the Gulf of Mexico, a point where he differed from the position of his political party. Jennings favored conservation, alternative energy sources, and a comprehensive energy plan. On Iraq, Buchanan said, "I do believe we're going to reduce the troops. We're not going to telegraph that time table."[16] He also touted his role in securing $26 million of federal money for a veterans' cemetery in Sarasota County. Jennings opposed the conduct of the Iraq War and implicated Buchanan for his close support of what she deemed to be the failed policies of President George W. Bush both at home and abroad.

Buchanan tried to emphasize his independence from Bush and the national Republican Party, but Jennings countered that Buchanan was out of touch with the citizens of the district. While Buchanan touted his congressional record, Jennings was quick to attack Buchanan as a tool of big business interests. She pointed out that Buchanan voted against the Alternative Minimum Tax bill to provide tax relief to 21 million taxpayers nationwide, yet he supported eliminating specific tax breaks for private equity managers, hedge fund managers, and certain foreign corporations. The corporate CEOs would get better tax deals than their company's secretaries under Buchanan.

Candidates Jennings and Buchanan did find some common ground on two issues during their last of the four debates. Buchanan and Jennings said the bailout package was necessary to prevent an even greater economic meltdown. In addition, both were opposed to oil drilling off Florida's coastlines, arguing that clean beaches are essential to Florida's quality of life and the tourism industry. Though the candidates had different philosophies on tax and economic policies, both supported lowering the tax burden. Buchanan advocated more tax breaks for the middle class and small businesses, stating, "If you raise taxes, more jobs will be lost."[17] Jennings supported tax relief for the same groups, saying they have not received any help from the Bush administration, but argued for retaining capital-gains tax rates. Buchanan, on the other hand, argued for cutting or eliminating capital-gains taxes.

ELECTION RESULTS

Jennings's closing appeal to the voters emphasized her forty years' experience as a "community banker," intimate engagement and knowledge in the district, and a bipartisan commitment to national policy in Washington, DC. Furthermore, she continued her attack on Buchanan's legal, ethical, and character issues. Buchanan responded that Jennings negative campaign was nothing more than "sour grapes" over the 2006 election results. He touted his endorsements for reelection and his first-term accomplishments, while pledging not to raise any taxes and to vote for the continuation of President Bush's tax cuts. Buchanan portrayed himself as a maverick that occasionally broke with his party while Jennings did the same, touting her fiscal conservatism.

Jennings's challenge in a solidly Republican district was ultimately unsuccessful. The final vote was a solid win for the Republican incumbent, Vern

Table 10.1. Final Election Results

	Vern Buchanan (REP)	Christine Jennings (DEM)	Don Baldauf (NPA)	Jan Schneider (NPA)
Total	204,382	137,967	5,358	20,289
% Votes	55.5%	37.5%	1.5%	5.5%

Buchanan, and much closer than the nail-biter between the two candidates in 2006. Buchanan won 55.5 percent of the vote to Jennings's 37.5 percent. The two NPA candidates shared the remaining votes. Baldauf won 1.5 percent of the vote and Schneider won 5.5 percent, not enough votes to have helped Jennings.

The 2008 Buchanan-Jennings congressional rematch was a heavy fight by two competing community and political elites. The factors that shaped the outcome of the election were those that historically determine congressional elections: incumbency, money, campaign messages, and organizations. Initially, the race was seen as a toss-up and it was one of the exceptions to the trend in 2008 that favored Democrats because of the unpopularity of President Bush and the national Republican Party. One poll in early September concluded that the Jennings-Buchanan race was within the margin of error and "too close to call with the atmospherics that favor Jennings."

It also helped Buchanan that he was the incumbent and had a record to point to, which allowed him to be less negative than his opponent. It also permitted Buchanan to portray himself as a responsible and effective congressman and for the voters of southwest Florida and the "favorite son" of the district.

Meanwhile, Jennings was unable to take advantage of the national disapproval with Bush or her effort to frame the 2008 campaign as a referendum on the allegations of business and personal ethics of the incumbent. But the anti-incumbent mood and suspect business practices of Buchanan were upstaged by the ugly tone of the race. Jennings's campaign came off as a personal vendetta and grudge match over the razor-thin defeat in 2006. As a multimillionaire and incumbent, Buchanan was able to raise and spend more than twice the amount of money available to Jennings, including sums from his own fortune. This enabled him to hire a professional organization, spend more money on media advertisement, and promote his legislative record. Money still matters.

ACKNOWLEDGMENTS

The authors would like to thank Sean Gibbons and Michael Fiigon for their research assistance in the preparation of this case.

NOTES

1. U.S. House of Representatives, House Information Resources, 2006. See www.house.gov and House Information Resources. "Congressman Vern Buchanan: Representing the 13th District of Florida," buchanan.house.gov/index.shtml (accessed November 22, 2008).

2. United States 2007 Census, "Congressional District 13, Florida (110th Congress) Selected Social Characteristics in the United States: 2007," factfinder.census.gov (accessed November 22, 2008).

3. Census, "Congressional District 13."

4. Census, "Congressional District 13."

5. DeSoto County, "DeSoto County . . . Because We Care!" co.desoto.fl.us/ (accessed November 2, 2008); WebCoast, "Manatee County History," www.webcoast.com/manatee.htm (accessed November 23, 2008).

6. Florida Department of State Division of Elections, "General Election Results," https://doe.dos.state.fl.us/elections/resultsarchive/Index.asp?ElectionDate=11/7/200&DATAMODE= (accessed December 4, 2008).

7. Don Baldauf for Congress, www.donslineitemveto.com/ (accessed December 6, 2008).

8. "About Jan Schneider," www.votejan.com/bio.html (accessed December 4, 2008).

9. Vern Buchanan for U.S. Congress, vernbuchananforcongress.com/pages/?page_id=2 (accessed December 6, 2008).

10. Sourcewatch, "Vern Buchanan," www.sourcewatch.org/index.php?title=Vern_Buchanan (accessed December 6, 2008).

11. "Christine Jennings for Congress," www.christinejenningsforcongress.com (accessed December 6, 2008).

12. C. E. Lee, "Jennings' Long Campaign Nears Climactic Day," *Sarasota Herald-Tribune*, October 19, 2008, BN1.

13. "Christine Jennings for Congress."

14. J. Wallace, "The Taxman Cometh for Two Buchanan Firms," *Sarasota Herald-Tribune*, www.heraldtribune.com/article/20080614/NEWS/806140307 (accessed December 4, 2008).

15. Z. Anderson, "Fireworks at Jennings-Buchanan Debate," *Sarasota Herald-Tribune*, October 16, 2008, 1.

16. D. Marsteller, "Dist. 13 Candidates Find Common Ground," *Bradenton Herald*, www.christinejenningsforcongress.com/node/199 (accessed December 6, 2008).

17. Marsteller, "Dist. 13 Candidates."

III
SENATE ELECTIONS

11

Louisiana Senate Race (Landrieu v. Kennedy)

History and Incumbency
Benefit a Vulnerable Candidate

Joshua Stockley

> Mary L. Landrieu
> *Age*: 52
> *Sex*: Female
> *Race*: Caucasian
> *Religion*: Roman Catholic
> *Education*: B.A., sociology (Louisiana State University, 1977)
> *Occupation*: Senator
> *Political Experience*: United States senator (1996–present); Louisiana state treasurer (1988–1996); Louisiana House of Representatives (1980–1988)
>
> John N. Kennedy
> *Age*: 56
> *Sex*: Male
> *Race*: Caucasian
> *Religion*: Methodist
> *Education*: B.C.L. (Oxford University, 1979); J.D. (University of Virginia, 1977); B.A., political science (Vanderbilt University, 1973)
> *Occupation*: Attorney and law professor
> *Political Experience*: Louisiana state treasurer (1999–present); secretary of the Department of Revenue (1996–1999)

The 2008 Louisiana Senate race featured two-term U.S. senator Mary Landrieu (D-LA) and three-term state treasurer John Neely Kennedy (R). Heading into the 2008 election cycle, political observers and strategists unanimously agreed that more Republican incumbents than Democrat incumbents were vulnerable. The 28 percent of Americans identifying themselves as

Republicans amounted to the lowest level since 1999, substantially the result of an unpopular Republican president, an increasingly unpopular conflict in Iraq, and a sluggish economy.[1] Although Republicans were suffering setbacks across the nation, in Louisiana, Republican registration rates were growing, Republican candidates were winning, and President Bush was maintaining a favorability approval rating over 50 percent.[2]

Senator Landrieu's largest and most loyal constituency, African Americans in New Orleans, had been dislocated by Hurricane Katrina. This was troubling to the Landrieu campaign because she had won her previous two elections by only 5,000 and 40,000 votes, respectively. In the South, seventeen of the twenty-two senators were Republicans, with Landrieu being the only Democrat of the five to hail from the heavily conservative Deep South. Accordingly, Republicans had legitimate reasons to believe they could unseat Landrieu. Political pundits and insiders agreed that Landrieu might have been vulnerable. Going into the election, both *Congressional Quarterly* and the *Cook Political Report* tabbed the seat as one that "leans Democrat" and the *Rothenberg Political Report* called it a "toss-up." In the end, Landrieu's incumbency proved to be too much for her challenger and propelled her to a 52 to 46 percent victory in what turned out to be a disastrous election cycle for Republicans around the country.

CHARACTERISTICS OF THE STATE

To fully appreciate the Landrieu—Kennedy Senate race, it is imperative that one have an appreciation for the unique social and electoral dynamics shaping Louisiana politics. At first glance the state shares many similar characteristics of its Deep South neighbors Alabama, Mississippi, Georgia, and South Carolina. Republican registration is growing, President Bush remains popular, and Republicans hold a majority of statewide and federal offices. However, Republican consolidation was slow to take root in Louisiana because of the state's heterogeneity stemming from large African American and Catholic populations. While Republicans made major gains throughout the South in the 1990s, Democrats in Louisiana still managed to control the governorship, a majority of statewide offices, both houses of the state legislature, a majority of the congressional delegation, and both U.S. Senate seats.[3]

Party Balance, Voting, and Electoral History

Partisan identification lags behind electoral behavior in Louisiana. The partisan transformation has been a top-down phenomenon, beginning at the presidential level and problematically trickling down the ballot. Louisiana's Republican advance began in earnest only a decade ago in 1995 when Mike

Foster became the second Republican governor since Reconstruction and two Democrats defected, resulting in the first Republican congressional delegation majority since Reconstruction. At this time Democratic registration stood at 68.4 percent and Republican registration stood at 20.0 percent of Louisianans, over a three-to-one margin.[4] Republican success was overshadowed by the Democrats' ability to maintain control of a majority of statewide offices, both houses of the legislature, and both U.S. Senate seats. Additionally, Louisiana was one of only three southern states carried twice by Bill Clinton. In 1996, 1998, and 2002 Democrats won every U.S. Senate race in the state. In 2003, Democrats regained the governor's mansion, won all but one statewide office, and held a decisive sixty-seven to thirty-seven majority in the state House and a twenty-four to fifteen majority in the state Senate.

Since 2003, however, Democrats have had very little to cheer about and partisan balance has tilted in favor of Republicans. In 2004, Republicans broke the Democratic monopoly in the U.S. Senate when David Vitter became Louisiana's first Republican senator since Reconstruction. Representative Rodney Alexander switched his party affiliation, which expanded the Republican delegation majority to a five to two margin. To cap it all off, the state cast 57 percent of its votes for Bush, a steady improvement over the 53 percent he captured in 2000. Exit polls revealed that 41 percent of those who voted identified themselves as Republicans, which was particularly interesting given that 55 percent of the state was registered Democratic and only 22 percent Republican. From 2004 to 2008, Republican registration increased and Democratic registration decreased.

The 2006 and 2007 election cycles confirmed this pro-Republican shift. In 2006 Republicans retained their five to two congressional advantage in Louisiana despite losing thirty-three seats nationally. In 2007, led by Bobby Jindal's decisive gubernatorial victory, Republicans won five out of the seven statewide offices and nearly captured the Louisiana House of Representatives for the first time since Reconstruction. A sixty-seven to thirty-seven Democratic advantage was reduced to a razor-thin fifty-one to forty-nine Democratic advantage. Republican victories in the Pelican State had Democrats reeling as the 2008 election cycle approached. Today 52 percent of all Louisianans are registered Democrat; the lowest in state history and down 16 percent from a decade before. Republican registration is up to its highest point ever at 25.2 percent, up from only 0.9 percent in 1960. However, Landrieu had history on her side—no sitting Louisiana senator has been ousted since 1932.

Demographic Characteristics of the Electorate

Due to the devastating effects of Hurricanes Katrina in 2005, Louisiana has experienced a racial shift in the electorate. Prior to the hurricane, African

Americans comprised 32.6 percent of the state's population and 29.8 percent of the state's registered voters. This is the second highest percentage in the nation. Louisiana has lost 4 percent of its population since 2005, but 9 percent of the African American population—some 100,000 residents—and just 3 percent of the white population.[5] Most African Americans lived in Orleans Parish—ground zero for the storm. Estimates indicate that 13 percent of the parish's residents, mostly black, have not yet returned. Some relocated to other parts of Louisiana like Baton Rouge, but many left the state altogether.[6] Given that Landrieu won her two elections by only 5,000 votes and 40,000 votes, respectively, this racial shift put her at a disadvantage.

The second major characteristic of Louisiana is the fact that it is a poor, undereducated, blue-collar state. The state's poverty rate is 7 percent higher than the national average, and the state's median income is $9,000 less than the national average. Louisiana has a below average number of residents with college degrees—18.7 percent compared to the national average of 24.4 percent—and high school degrees—74.8 percent compared to the national average of 80.4 percent. Consequently, the workforce is 25 percent blue-collar, which is 5 percent above the national average and 56 percent of Louisiana's workforce is white-collar, 4 percent below the national average. In Louisiana, distinct voting patterns exist between poor, undereducated, blue-collar workers and wealthy, educated, white-collar workers. The poor, undereducated, blue-collar workers vote for Democrats in Louisiana, but it is often difficult to get them out to vote. This demographic shift threatened to work against Landrieu.

The third major characteristic of Louisiana is its conservatism. Polls indicate that at least 40 percent of Louisiana voters identify themselves as "conservative" and another 40 percent identify as "moderate." Democrats in Louisiana must distance themselves from the national party and take more moderate or conservative positions on various social, environmental, and economic issues. The typical southern Republican strategy is to portray Democrats as liberal and tie them to national, liberal Democrats.[7] While Barack Obama's candidacy promised to boost African American turnout, Landrieu's endorsement of him threatened to diminish her support from moderate and conservative white voters. Early poll results in Louisiana showed a 53 percent unfavorable view of Obama and a 41 percent "very unfavorable" view of Obama.[8] Landrieu was forced to defend this endorsement; Kennedy exploited it.

Key Voting Blocs

Louisiana does not have voting blocs in the traditional sense of the term. Wayne Parent sees the three major blocs—African Americans, Southern European Louisianans, and Northern European Louisianans—as "ethnic groups." He writes, "These are ethnic groups with strong group consciousness and a lack of trust in other groups for extended periods of time—thus, the volatility."[9] Most African Americans live in Baton Rouge and New Orleans, but significant concentrations can be found in southeastern, central, and northwestern Louisiana parishes. If a Democrat can carry 90 percent of the African American vote (given normal black turnout of 58 to 64 percent), then they need to capture only 30 percent of the white (given normal white turnout of 62 to 70 percent) to win.[10] The higher the African American turnout, the less support a Democrat needs from white voters. However, Democrats still need to attract white voters. If the Democrat panders too much to conservative whites, they risk losing African American support.

Louisiana's white voters are not a monolithic bloc. South Louisiana is primarily Catholic, the product of a French and Acadian heritage. North Louisiana is Protestant and culturally similar to Mississippi. Twenty-nine parishes in the northern part of the state are majority Baptist, while thirty-one parishes in the southern part of the state are majority Catholic. The two regions are congruent on the issue of economic conservatism and abortion, but have split over issues such as gambling, alcohol, and prayer in schools. Endorsements by the evangelical Family Research Council resonate powerfully in the north. Catholics are more tolerant and socially liberal, so politicians that are too socially conservative do not do as well. Unsuccessful Republicans can generally trace their losses to a lack of southern, Catholic support. The state's only nonblack Democratic Congressman, Charlie Melancon, represents a southern district. At times northern and southern Louisiana will unite against African Americans, other times southern Louisiana unites with African Americans against northern Louisiana.

Democrats cannot win the state of Louisiana without forging a biracial coalition of southern Catholics and African Americans. In her previous two elections, Landrieu was able to do this. Kennedy was faced with the task of trying to dampen African American turnout and unite economic conservatives in southern Louisiana with social conservatives in northern Louisiana.

Major Urban Areas and Employment/Occupational Characteristics

The Democratic base is concentrated in urban areas with high African American populations, like Monroe, in the northeast; Shreveport, in the northwest; and Alexandria, in the center of the state. Combined with New Orleans and Baton Rouge, Democrats have a strong urban base. These areas alone will not win a statewide election for Democrats. Republicans counter with rural areas in the central part of the state; suburban areas on the Northern shore of Lake Pontchartrain and surrounding Baton Rouge; and smaller urban areas like Bossier City, in the northwest, West Monroe, in the northeast, Houma, in the southeast, and Lafayette, in the south central part of the state. Rural voters take their voting cues from parish leaders like sheriffs and parish presidents, so their endorsement is critical. They are largely conservative, but can be persuaded to vote Democratic. Successful statewide candidates must forge rural and urban coalitions.

The heart of the Louisiana economy is oil and gas; the key to winning in Louisiana is securing the support of the oil and gas industry. The state has sixteen refineries, among the companies with Louisiana production facilities are Exxon, Shell, Citgo, Mobil, Marathon, Conoco, BP, and STAR. Related to the oil and gas industry are shipbuilding, fabrication, and transportation. Outside of Louisiana these industries are decidedly pro-Republican, but within Louisiana Democrats and Republicans are equally able to secure their endorsement through pro-energy platforms. The military is another significant economic force in Louisiana. Fort Polk and Barksdale Air Force Base are estimated to have a direct economic impact of at least $6 billion annually; military contractors such as Northrop Grumman and Textron have a significant presence in Louisiana. They are looking for politicians who can deliver contracts and protect bases from future closings. Louisiana has a sizable agricultural economy; its cash crops include rice, soybeans, cotton, sweet potatoes, and sugar. These industries demand protection from international markets and subsidies for domestic production.[11] Landrieu's seats on the Appropriations Committee and Energy Committee give her an advantage in supporting these industries. As a member of the minority party and lacking any guarantee of serving on these committees, Kennedy faced a difficult task of persuading these interests that he could deliver as effectively as Landrieu.

THE CANDIDATES

The Incumbent: Mary Landrieu

Mary Landrieu, fifty-two, is the scion of a prominent New Orleans political family. Her brother is lieutenant governor. Her father, Maurice Edwin "Moon" Landrieu, was councilman from 1966 to 1970, mayor of New Orleans from 1970 to 1978, and secretary of housing and urban development from 1978 to 1980. While a councilman and mayor, he led the fight to desegregate New Orleans by hiring African Americans and appointing them to top positions in city government where previously there had been none. As HUD secretary, Moon Landrieu acquired federal funds to rebuild black neighborhoods, establish minority-owned businesses, and revitalize the Central Business District and French Quarter. Moon Landrieu became incredibly popular with African Americans, and he escaped the corruption typically associated with New Orleans politics.[12] Mary Landrieu benefited from her father's stature and political connections to win a seat in the Louisiana House of Representatives in 1979 at the tender age of twenty-three. In 1987, she ran for state treasurer and won. In 1991, she faced no opposition and was reelected.

In 1995, Mary Landrieu ran unsuccessfully for governor, finishing third behind Republican Mike Foster and Democrat Cleo Fields. Cleo Fields, an African American, accused Mary Landrieu of making the argument that voters should support her because an African American could not win a statewide office in Louisiana (and had not won a statewide office since Reconstruction). She was forced to hold a press conference stating that her campaign had never made such statements, but the damage had been done. African American turnout was higher than normal, and Fields squeezed by Landrieu into the runoff. She subsequently refused to endorse Fields against Foster, who defeated Fields by a 63 to 36 percent margin.

In 1996 Senator J. Bennett Johnston (D) announced his retirement, and Landrieu ran for his seat. It turned out to be the most exciting race of the year. First, Cleo Fields withheld his endorsement in retaliation for the 1995 gubernatorial race. The Fields-Landrieu feud threatened to tear apart the Democratic Party. Vice President Al Gore came to Louisiana and forced the two to reconcile, culminating with a Fields endorsement. Second, New Orleans archbishop, Philip Hannan, sparked controversy when he publicly declared, "If a person believes in Catholic doctrine, I don't see how they can avoid [a vote for Landrieu] being a sin."[13] After the dust settled, Landrieu squeaked by with a 5,000-vote victory despite losing thirty-eight of Louisiana's sixty-four parishes. Her victory margin was courtesy a 100,000-vote advantage from predominately black Orleans Parish and an above average performance among white Catholics in the southern parishes. They felt her challenger, Woody Jenkins, was too conservative—according to exit polls, 66 percent of self-described moderates voted for Landrieu.

Landrieu became a natural Republican target in 2002. She barely won in 1996, and Bush carried Louisiana with 53 percent of the vote in 2000. However, her presumptive opponent, Representative John Cooksey, made the mistake of saying shortly after 9/11, "If I see someone's coming in and he's got a diaper on his head and a fan belt around that diaper on his head, that guy needs to be pulled over and checked." As a result, Cooksey lost all national support, but remained in the race because of his popularity with social conservatives in northern Louisiana. National Republicans scrambled to find another challenger and came up with Suzanne Haik-Terrell, who had defeated another darling of conservatives, Woody Jenkins, back in 1999. Cooksey and Terrell fractured the Republican Party during their fight to challenge Landrieu. Terrell emerged victorious over Cooksey, but failed to hold onto 43,000 of his conservative supporters. Landrieu won by 40,000 votes and carried thirty-nine parishes, a nine-parish increase over

1996. Her victory margin again came courtesy of a lopsided performance in Orleans Parish (won by 80,000 votes) and a stronger showing in southern and central parishes. Landrieu was twice able to forge biracial coalitions and urban-rural coalitions by convincing conservatives that she was conservative enough and African Americans that she was liberal enough.[14]

In 2002, Senator Landrieu landed a seat on the powerful Appropriations Committee to go along with her seats on the Energy and Natural Resources Committee and Homeland Security Committee. Her Homeland Security assignment included chairing the subcommittee responsible for monitoring the Federal Emergency Management Agency. Landrieu also joined the so-called Gang of 14, seven Democrats and seven Republicans who agreed to abandon party affiliation in order to end the Democratic judicial filibuster on ten Bush appointees and begin working together. This led to the creation of the Common Ground Coalition with Senator Olympia Snowe (R-ME) and the Gang of 20. *Congressional Quarterly* called Landrieu one of the party's "most prominent moderates," and the *National Journal* declared her the "ideological center" of the Senate. She has staked a position in the middle of the Senate and used her committee assignments to lure federal funds to the state.

The Challenger: John N. Kennedy

John Neely Kennedy, fifty-six, grew up in Zachary, Louisiana, in East Baton Rouge Parish, but calls Madisonville in St. Tammany Parish home. After receiving three college degrees, Kennedy went into private law practice and became a partner at the Baton Rouge law firm of Chafee McCall. He left private practice in 1988 when then-Democratic governor "Buddy" Roemer appointed him as his special counsel and, later, secretary of the governor's cabinet in 1990.[15]

Kennedy's first attempt at elected office came in 1991 when he ran as a Democrat for attorney general. He finished third in a six-candidate field eventually won by Calcasieu district attorney Richard Ieyoub. Kennedy again returned to his law career, but returned to state government in 1996 when Republican governor Mike Foster appointed him to be the secretary of the Department of Revenue and Taxation. Kennedy made another attempt at an elected office in 1999 by running as a Democrat for state treasurer, defeating the incumbent Democrat Ken Duncan. He won reelection without opposition in 2003. In 2004, John Breaux announced his retirement from the U.S. Senate. Kennedy was one of three Democrats to run, joining African American state senator Arthur Morrell and U.S. representative Chris John. The lone Republican in the field was U.S. representative David Vitter. Kennedy ended up finishing third in Louisiana's open primary with 15 percent of the vote, well behind Vitter (50 percent) and John (29 percent). In running against Vitter, Kennedy touted his endorsement of John Kerry, opposition to the Bush tax cuts, and support for a timetable in Iraq. Kennedy resumed his duties as state treasurer and won reelection without opposition in 2007.

On August 27, 2007, Kennedy announced via a letter posted on his website that he was switching his partisan affiliation from Democrat to Republican. The announcement came after weeks of speculation and meetings with prominent local and national Republicans, the most notable of these being Karl Rove.[16] The announcement was interpreted as an unofficial declaration of his impending entrance into the 2008 Senate race. Kennedy's attractiveness as a candidate is borne out of the lessons of the Jenkins-Cooksey senatorial challenges. Louisianans, particularly white, Catholics, had rejected previous Republican nominees for being too socially conservative. The Cooksey-Terrell dispute also taught the GOP that some conservatism was still necessary to rally the base. Kennedy was pro-life, but he also had a track record of constantly butting heads with notable Democrats like former Governor Kathleen Blanco and former agriculture secretary Bob Odom. The hope was that Landrieu's pro-choice position and Kennedy's history of Democratic obstruction would excite pro-life, social conservatives in the north and siphon moderate, white Catholics in the south. Kennedy became the de facto nominee after a long list of notable Louisiana Republicans announced their non-candidacies. Among them were Representative Richard Baker, Representative Charles Boustany, Representative Jim McCrery, and Secretary of State Jay Dardenne.[17] Dardenne's announcement followed the release of a poll showing him trailing Landrieu, 38 to 53 percent. Despite being a lifetime Democrat, having run recently for the Senate as a Democrat, and having endorsed John Kerry for president, Kennedy announced November 29, 2007, that he would challenge the two-term Democratic incumbent.[18]

CAMPAIGN ISSUES

Oil and Gas

One leading campaign issue was oil and gas. The Pelican State is the number one producer of petroleum, the number two producer of natural gas, and generates an estimated $70 billion from this industry.[19] Polls show 75 percent of Louisianans favor offshore drilling. Landrieu spent considerable time publicizing her pro-oil record and votes in the Senate. Among her highlights was the Gulf of Mexico Energy Security Act cosponsored with Senator Pete Domenici (R-NM), which opened 8.3 million acres for drilling in the Gulf of Mexico and generated $23.1 million. Most importantly, she increased Louisiana's share of oil and gas royalties. Landrieu publicized her breaks from her party to lift the ban on offshore drilling, support drilling in ANWR, and block additional tax increases on oil and gas companies. She voted for the 2005 Energy Bill that included an additional $14.5 billion for domestic production of oil, coal, natural gas, and nuclear energy.

The Kennedy campaign attempted to neutralize this issue by mentioning Landrieu's tie-breaking vote against a Republican amendment to lift a ban on mining and processing oil shale in Colorado. Kennedy repeated this fact in all four debates and created several campaign advertisements highlighting the vote. Landrieu defended her vote as repayment to Senator Ken Salazar (D-CO) for his support on the Gulf of Mexico Energy Security Act. Salazar wanted an environmental impact study to gauge the potential impact of oil shale drilling on Colorado's natural resources.[20] This issue gave Kennedy three attacks: (1) Landrieu's anti-oil shale vote was an anti-oil and gas vote; (2) her vote limited gas price relief for consumers; (3) her vote indicated that the Democratic Party's position on energy was contrary to what was best for the state. Landrieu's track record prevented this one vote from doing much damage, but the Kennedy campaign kept this issue at the fore of its campaign.

Earmarks

Both candidates spent considerable time talking about earmarks; however, they approached the subject in different ways. Kennedy's most damaging attack came from Landrieu making the "Top 20 Most Corrupt Members of Congress" report by the independent organization Citizens for Responsibility and Ethics in Washington (CREW). CREW discovered Landrieu inserted a $2 million earmark into an appropriations bill for the Voyager Expanded Literacy Program just days after securing a $30,000 donation from them.[21] Landrieu was forced to defend the timing of the contribution and the appropriation, persistently declaring that no investigation ever found evidence of wrongdoing. Kennedy repeatedly made use of this allegation in campaign appearances, debates, and advertisements.

The second part of Kennedy's earmark attack was copied from the McCain campaign; he, like McCain, had an image of standing up to powerful interests and opposing wasteful earmarks. He had developed a reputation as an obstructionist and fiscal hawk while state treasurer. Kennedy had opposed the controversial and unpopular Lacassine sugar syrup mill project run by de facto Democratic Party leader and agriculture secretary Bob Odom. The project went $11 million over budget and ultimately led to Odom's defeat in 2007. In 2007, Kennedy presented Governor Blanco with $3 million in recommended cuts, but Blanco ignored the recommendations. Both maneuvers drew the ire of Democrats. Kennedy also highlighted how his management of over 300 statutory funds in separate investment portfolios generated billions in revenue and saved taxpayers money.

Landrieu's strategy was to delineate earmarks from "dedicated federal spending." She openly touted how she was able to "dedicate spending"—$3 billion for the Road Home program; $1.8 billion for levee improvements in the New Orleans; $7 billion for hurricane protection, flood control, and navigation projects; $30 million to help New Orleans schools recruit teachers; $600 million for the state's historically black colleges; and billions in defense contracts for Barksdale Air Force Base and Fort Polk. Landrieu countered Kennedy by stressing how earmarks account for only 1 percent of the budget, and she voted for legislation to make earmark requests more open to public scrutiny.[22] Kennedy tried to paint Landrieu as fiscally reckless and corrupt; Landrieu spent her time publicizing her ability to bring federal funds to Louisiana. The corruption charge was overshadowed by Landrieu's appropriations.

The Name Game: Confused Politician versus Liberal

The final campaign issue was not an issue in the traditional sense, but more of a strategic attempt to define the other candidate in a negative light. The campaign between Kennedy and Landrieu was decidedly and consistently negative, featuring a lot of name calling. Landrieu fired the first salvo in early August. The ads discredited Kennedy by pointing out reversals in his tax positions, Social Security, War in Iraq, endorsements, and partisan affiliation. It finished with the slogan, "John Kennedy: One Confused Politician." Landrieu ran at least a dozen more television advertisements focusing upon the confused politician theme. The advertisements were shown on television, played on the radio, and sent by mail throughout the campaign. Landrieu ran only one television advertisement that failed to use the "one confused politician" slogan. It came in the wake of Hurricane Gustav. It complimented Louisiana for weathering another deadly storm and closed with her promise to continue to rebuild and strengthen Louisiana.

The persistent barrage caught the Kennedy campaign off guard, defined his campaign, and cast doubts in the minds of voters. It put the Kennedy campaign on the defensive, forcing them to produce advertisements rebutting the various claims. To his credit, Kennedy did a much better job trying to focus on issues, but to no avail. Landrieu enjoyed a huge financial advantage and received significant support from the Democratic Senatorial Campaign Committee (DSCC). She was able to inundate the airwaves day and night with the advertisements. The confused politician attack even spilled over into the debates, with Landrieu refusing to apologize for or remove the advertisements. The Kennedy campaign, with the help of the NRSC, attempted to fire back with the "corrupt liberal" charge. The name calling became a signature piece of the campaign and overshadowed issues. However, Kennedy was in a tough spot regarding issues because both opponents held very similar records on the most significant issues in Louisiana. Outside of abortion, the concrete policy differences were minimal.

CAMPAIGN STRATEGY

Media

The campaign featured four debates in sixteen days. The first debate was a nontelevised town hall forum held October 6 at the Baton Rouge Press Club. The second debate was televised from the campus of Louisiana State University in Baton Rouge on October 12. The third debate was held on October 15 on the campus of the University of New Orleans and carried by NBC affiliate WDSU-TV and C-SPAN. Few people watched the third debate because it was held the same night as the final presidential debate. The second and third debates featured Kennedy repeating many of the lines used by John McCain. Eventually an exasperated Landrieu uttered, "John, I know you're trying very hard, but Senator McCain's coattails are not long enough for you." It became the most memorable line of the campaign. The final debate was October 22 at a TV studio in New Orleans. It was broadcast by six state stations and C-SPAN2. The fourth debate was the most spirited, featuring frequent jabs and continual interruptions by the two candidates and panelists. The candidates even began to argue with the panelists.[23] The fourth debate featured a new strategy by Kennedy, whereby he failed to mention McCain once. It was also his strongest performance, and he had Landrieu on the defensive most of the evening. Although Kennedy more than held his own in all four debates, he was unable to produce a knockout punch or to deliver a memorable one-liner.

Image and Advertising

Landrieu's campaign benefited by hiring political heavyweights that operated with a more coherent and successful strategy. Her public opinion researcher and media strategist was Mark Mellman, a nationally known consultant who has never lost an incumbent election. Landrieu's campaign manager was Jay Howser, who engineered Representative Brad Ellsworth's (D-IN) upset victory over six-term incumbent John Hostettler (R-IN) in 2006. Her press secretary was Scott Schnieder, formerly a deputy communications director in the U.S. Senate.

Kennedy's media strategy was coordinated by OnMessage, Inc., a relatively new Republican-allied consortium run by Brad Todd, Curt Anderson, and

Wes Anderson. They had handled the polling and media for Bobby Jindal and the Republican National Committee. Kennedy hired Leonardo Alcivar to serve as campaign manager and communications director. Alcivar served previously as press secretary for Mayor Rudolph Giuliani, communications director for Lynn Swann's unsuccessful Senate campaign in Pennsylvania, and convention spokesman for the Republican National Committee.

The advertising war began in August with a folksy piece showing Kennedy walking to work with a sack lunch and a voiceover discussing how he saved the state money during his tenure as state treasurer. His advertisements promised to end wasteful earmarks and painted his opponent as a liberal. Kennedy was consistently more positive and more specific about his issue positions. He closed his commercials with, "If you want to change the U.S. Senate, at least in Louisiana, you've got to change the senator." On the other hand, Landrieu's ads were overwhelmingly negative. They aimed to undermine the honest reformer image that Kennedy was trying to portray and remove any enthusiasm conservatives might have by highlighting his Democratic past. They spent less time defining her and more time redefining Kennedy.

Both candidates benefited from media buys by the national committees. The DSCC made several ads pounding Kennedy unmercifully for his party switch. The NRSC also committed resources to the Kennedy campaign. Decidedly more negative than Kennedy's regular ads, they focused on two themes, presenting Landrieu as: (1) a typical corrupt Louisiana politician; (2) a liberal who supported Democratic nominee Barack Obama 81 percent of the time. Her picture was featured alongside other notable indicted Louisiana Democrats Edwin Edwards and Bill Jefferson. In addition to the media buy, the NRSC also created and supported a website called truelandrieustory.com to reinforce the corruption and liberal themes. The Landrieu campaign operated two websites—marylandrieu.com and oneconfusedpolitican.com. Oneconfusedpolitican.com featured all the attack advertisements, while marylandrieu.com focused on her issue positions.

The NRSC made the news when they decided to cancel future advertising for Kennedy three weeks before Election Day. They faced a financial shortfall and previously safe incumbents like Senator Mitch McConnell (R-KY) and Senator Saxby Chambliss (R-GA) found themselves clinging to narrow leads. The decision was interpreted to mean the NRSC had conceded victory. However, the NRSC abruptly changed course and announced a few days later it would continue to buy advertisements. Despite arguing that the decision had nothing to do with electoral prospects, the damage had been done and the perception remained.[24]

Kennedy benefited from an independent expenditure by the American Family Business Institute, which ran an ad criticizing Landrieu for voting against oil-shale exploration in Colorado and voting against the repeal of the estate tax.[25]

Finances

The Landrieu-Kennedy campaign was the most expensive Senate campaign in Louisiana history and the ninth most expensive campaign in the 2008 election cycle—$15 million was raised and $12 million was spent.[26] Landrieu's $10.6 million campaign was the eighth highest amount raised by an incumbent and doubled the $6.6 million national average. Twelve years in the Senate gave her time to develop national financial networks with political action committees (PACs), party committees, leadership PACs, and other wealthy individuals. Out-of-state sources accounted for 54 percent of her contributions and PACs accounted for 29 percent or $3 million. The DSCC gave the Landrieu campaign $39,000, but her congressional colleagues donated another $274,000. Landrieu's individual contributions revealed bipartisan support. Major Republican Party financier and friend of President Bush, Gary Chouest, owner of Edison Chouest Offshore and the state's largest oil rig operator, was her fourth most generous contributor. Her top industry contributors were lawyers, real estate, lobbyists, and oil and gas.

The oil and gas industry plays a large financial role in Louisiana. They are typically a pro-Republican industry and give 75 percent of their contributions to Republicans. Landrieu received the third highest amount of money, $300,000, from the oil and gas industry. She was the only Democrat in their top ten and one of only three Democrats among their top twenty biggest recipients. Despite putting up $300,000 for Landrieu, they still donated $117,900 to Kennedy's campaign. He was the twelfth largest recipient of oil and gas money.[27]

Kennedy did a remarkable job raising money in a tough financial cycle for Republicans. In a year where the average challenger raised $963,000 and the average Republican challenger raised $547,961, Kennedy managed to haul in $4.4 million dollars. His fund-raising was assisted by fund-raisers featuring President Bush, First Lady Laura Bush, Dick Cheney, and Mitch McConnell. Kennedy had to rely more on individual donations because only 10 percent ($448,000) of Kennedy's money came from PACs. National support was also hard to come by, as he received only $35,500 from national party committees. Landrieu demonstrated tremendous fund-raising prowess. She significantly outraised and outspent Kennedy, which allowed her to blanket the state with her advertising.

Grass Roots

Both campaigns organized coordinated campaigns to take advantage of state and federal resources and to mobilize voters. The Republican campaign, Victory 2008, was slower to develop. Headquarters in Republican regions like Ouachita Parish and St. Tammany Parish did not open until

October; Hurricane Gustav knocked southern headquarters out for over a month. Once established, the coordinated campaign identified likely voters through phone calls and then blanketed those precincts with door-to-door canvassing, mass mailers, and additional phone calls. In one weekend alone, dubbed "Super Saturday," the coordinated campaign knocked on 60,000 homes and made 14,000 phone calls in New Orleans, Baton Rouge, Alexandria, Houma, Lafayette, Monroe, and Shreveport. Overall, Victory 2008 claimed 139,000 phone calls and 534,000 doors knocked.[28] Victory 2008 attempted to take advantage of the Internet by creating LaGOP.net, a social networking site for activists to interact, create profiles, write blogs, and organize events. This strategy did not blossom, however, as the site registered only 248 members, displayed but a few pictures, and advertised only a couple of campaign events. In the end, Kennedy focused on urban areas like Baton Rouge, Lafayette, Shreveport, Alexandria, Lake Charles, Houma, and Morgan City. He appeared at gun and outfitter shops, local festivals, National Rifle Association events, and several livestock shows in an effort to rally the conservative base.

The Democratic coordinated campaign, Louisiana Victory, claimed over 819,951 phone calls, but only 27,906 doors knocked. As October rolled around, Louisiana Victory averaged 50,000 phone calls a week with the assistance of 2,500 campaign volunteers. Louisiana Victory dispersed fifty full-time staff members throughout the state to recruit volunteers and to coordinate canvassing efforts. Every major urban area in the state had a Landrieu or Democratic Party headquarters, most of which were up and running before September. Louisiana Victory used "robo-calls" to identify likely Democratic voters. With this information, the campaigned targeted these precincts with personal phone calls, door-to-door canvassing, and mailings.

Louisiana Victory also spent a concerted amount of time and energy registering voters and encouraging people to vote early. Louisiana Victory registered 60,000 new voters, and early voting among registered Democrats increased 129 percent. Louisiana Victory did not establish an Internet network like LaGOP.net, but Landrieu hosted a site on FaceBook and MySpace. Kennedy did not. These Internet efforts did not appear to generate a great deal of interest. In the last week of the campaign, Landrieu spent most of her time in Baton Rouge and New Orleans. Both campaigns featured bus tours and showed up to multiple LSU football games.

Bases of Support

During her twelve years in Congress, Landrieu gained an enviable reputation for her ability to forge coalitions, secure earmarks, and pass legislation beneficial to various constituencies. The result of which was a wide variety of endorsements from a range of Republicans and Democrats, among them the Legislative Black Caucus, Louisiana Sheriffs Association, Louisiana District Attorneys Association, Chamber of Commerce, and Veterans of Foreign Wars. Grabbing the biggest headlines were the twenty-seven Republican officeholders that endorsed Mary Landrieu, the most notable of these being St. Tammany Parish sheriff Jack Strain, Jefferson Parish sheriff Newell Normand, and St. Tammany Parish president Ken David.[29] Voters in more rural and suburban areas in Louisiana follow parish bosses. The importance of these particular endorsements cannot be understated because St. Tammany Parish and Jefferson Parish are strong Republican parishes. In 1996 and 2002, these parishes gave Republican candidates a 50,000 vote advantage. Landrieu secured the endorsement of former governor David Treen, the first Republican governor of Louisiana. She also received endorsements from the state's largest circulating newspapers—*Times-Picayune*, *Baton Rouge Advocate*, *Shreveport Times*, *Houma Courier*, and *Lafayette Daily Advertiser*.

Kennedy's endorsement list was conspicuously short. He was not endorsed by any major newspapers or by any of the state's congressional Republicans.[30] He did receive a favorable rating from the National Rifle Association and an endorsement from the Family Research Council, but this went largely unreported and unnoticed. The most significant endorsement, Republican governor Bobby Jindal, did not come until October 22. Jindal is the most popular officeholder in the state with a 64 percent favorability rating.[31] Most notable about this endorsement, other than the late timing, was that the twenty-two-second advertisement went fifteen seconds before even mentioning Kennedy's name.

ELECTION RESULTS

From the beginning to the end of the campaign, independent polls consistently showed Landrieu with double-digit leads and a level of support near 53 percent.[32] In the final week of the campaign John Kennedy abruptly changed his message. He had spent most of the campaign claiming to be Louisiana's version of John McCain. In his final speeches, rallies, and advertisements, Kennedy suddenly touted himself as a "firewall" against an Obama White House. He exhorted that an Obama-Landrieu alliance would result in higher taxes, higher gas prices, deficit spending, and the destruction of fetal life. The only way to protect traditional conservative values against the impending liberal supermajority was by sending him to the Senate.[33]

In the end it was too little too late and Landrieu won 52 to 46 percent. She won more votes (988,298) and more parishes (38) than in either of her two previous races. She increased her vote totals by 58,000 votes over 2002 and 115,000 votes over 1996. Landrieu was clearly able to separate herself from Obama, winning 200,000 more votes than him in the state. Like previous years, Orleans Parish delivered an overwhelming 99,000 vote advantage, but unlike previous years, and for the first time, she won the remaining 63 parishes by 21,000 votes. She increased her vote total by 1,000 or more votes in 29 parishes, by at least 5,000 votes in 10 parishes, and at least 10,000 votes in 4 parishes. Her biggest increase came from Republican stronghold St. Tammany Parish, where she increased her support by almost 15,000 votes. The Republican endorsements clearly played a huge role. Landrieu received fewer votes in only nine parishes, two of them—Orleans, St. Bernard—can be explained by lower populations from Hurricane Katrina. Her largest parish vote decrease between 2002 and 2008 was a mere 603 votes in Winn Parish.

The coattails from John McCain and Bobby Jindal were not long enough for Kennedy. He received 867,177 votes, 281,098 fewer votes than John McCain in Louisiana. Exit polls showed 24 percent of those that voted for McCain voted for Landrieu. Protestants gave 60 percent of their vote to McCain, but only 48 percent of their vote to Kennedy. Conservatives gave 80 percent of their vote to McCain, but only 69 percent of their vote to Kennedy. Moderates gave 54 percent of their vote to McCain, but only 35 percent of their vote to Kennedy.[34] Kennedy clearly failed to excite the base—moderate, conservative, Protestant, white voters. Kennedy's largest leads were in St. Tammany, Livingston, and Lafayette Parish. However, the support from his five strongest parishes gave him only a 70,000 vote advantage, but Landrieu's five most supportive parishes delivered a 170,000 vote advantage.

Not only did Kennedy fail to motivate the Republican base, but he was incapable of breaking Landrieu's Cajun-black alliance. He won only 51 percent of the northern vote, but Landrieu won 54 percent of Cajun country and 64 percent of New Orleans. Landrieu performed strongly across the entire state by carrying a majority of rural (53 percent) and urban voters (55 percent), and barely losing the suburban vote (48 percent). Other demographic trends held up as well—young, less-educated, low-income voters overwhelmingly gave their support to Landrieu and turned out in higher numbers.

Kennedy failed to provide voters with a sufficient cause to remove the incumbent and to convince moderate and conservative voters that he was truly conservative. Landrieu used her superior financial resources to inundate the state with a consistent barrage of attack advertisements framing her opponent as inconsistent and highlighting her ability to bring federal funds to the state. Kennedy was never able to grab the offensive, failed to tie his opponent to any national Democratic figures, and was not able to secure more Republican endorsements and support. He can point to several factors that did work: (1) Jindal's endorsement; (2) the fear of a filibuster-proof Senate; (3) staying more positive in advertisements. The electorate did not like Landrieu's negativity. Landrieu's unfavorable rating went from

36 to 42 percent and her favorability rating went from 61 to 56 percent.[35] Kennedy finished strong and reduced a double-digit deficit to 6 percent, but, again, it was too little too late. Given more time and funds, Kennedy might have been able to make further inroads.

Landrieu demonstrated what a Democrat must do and how a Democrat must operate to succeed in the South. First, she forged a biracial coalition. Although she won only 33 percent of the white vote, she won 96 percent of the African American vote. She was able to craft a message and position that attracted both groups without alienating both groups. Second, she cast herself as a moderate-to-conservative Democrat and separated herself from her liberal national colleagues. She broke with her party on critical issues important to Louisiana—drilling, late-term abortions, and tax cuts. Her 76 percent party unity score was the second lowest among all Democrats; her 64 percent presidential support score was the second lowest among all Democrats.

Third, incumbency has its advantages. Congress.org listed Senator Landrieu as the tenth "most effective legislator" in the Senate. She was able to deliver projects addressing the state's most pressing needs—levees for New Orleans, funds for coastal erosion, projects for defense industries and military bases, and leases for the oil companies. These projects did not go unnoticed by voters. Her ability to forge bipartisan support to create legislation and to secure funds beneficial to Louisiana industries helped her gain the respect, attention, money, and endorsements of pro-Republican and pro-Democratic industries and individuals. It is relatively safe to say that barring a scandal or major faux pas, Landrieu will probably be able to retain her seat for as long as she wants—though she will always have to work a little harder than the average incumbent. Although Republicans have made major gains in Louisiana, there is still a place for conservative Democrats.

NOTES

1. Jeffrey M. Jones, "Political Environment Continues to Favor Democrats," Gallup, April 13, 2007.

2. Ron Elving, "Democrats Losing Ground in Louisiana," Morning Edition, National Public Radio, August 18, 2008.

3. Wayne Parent and Huey Perry, "Louisiana: African Americans, Republicans, and Party Competition," in *The New Politics of the Old South*, 3rd ed. (Lanham, MD: Rowman & Littlefield, 2007).

4. Registration data and election results obtained from the Louisiana secretary of state.

5. Demographic data collected from U.S. Census Bureau.

6. Allison Plyer, "Population Growth Slows," Greater New Orleans Community Data Center.

7. For a broader discussion see James M. Glaser's *The Hand of the Past in Contemporary Southern Politics* (New Haven, CT: Yale University Press, 2005).

8. Melinda Deslatte, "Analysis: Obama Candidacy Tricky for Landrieu Re-election," *Times-Picayune*, August 2, 2008.

9. Wayne Parent, *Inside the Carnival*, 23.

10. For a broader discussion see Earle and Merle Black's *The Rise of Southern Republicans* (Cambridge, MA: Harvard University Press, 2002).

11. Alan Sayre, "Analysis: Louisiana's Economy Awaits Obama," *Forbes*, November 8, 2008.

12. Ken Rudin, "Moon over New Orleans," National Public Radio, April 27, 2006.

13. Parent, *Inside the Carnival*, 53.

14. Parent and Perry, "Louisiana."

15. Marsha Shuler, "Kennedy Began Career as Counsel to Roemer," *Baton Rouge Advocate*, October 26, 2008.

16. Eric Kleefeld, "Louisiana Treasurer Switches to GOP—May Potentially Run for Senate," Talking Points Memo, August 27, 2007.

17. Gerard Shields, "Boustany Won't Run for Senate," *Baton Rouge Advocate*, March 6, 2007; Bruce Alpert and Bill Walsh "On the Hill: News from the Louisiana Delegation in the Nation's Capital," *Times-Picayune*, March 11, 2007.

18. Ian Swanson, "Louisiana Treasurer Announces Landrieu Challenge," *The Hill*, November 29, 2007.

19. Loren C. Scott, "The Energy Sector," The Louisiana Mid-Continent Oil and Gas Association, September 2007.

20. Bruce Alpert, "Kennedy Attacks Landrieu on Shale Vote," *Times-Picayune*, July 25, 2008.

21. Report available online at www.crewsmostcorrupt.org/node/427.

22. Nathan Stubbs, "Pork Plate," *The Independent*, July 2, 2008.

23. Ed Anderson, "Candidates Defend Negative Advertising," *Times-Picayune*, October 23, 2008.

24. Chris Cizilla, "National Republican Pull Ads in Louisiana," *Washington Post*, October 15, 2008; John McArdle, "NRSC Rethinks Decision to Pull Louisiana Ads," *Roll Call*, October 17, 2008.

25. Bill Barrow, "Kennedy Ad Draws Landrieu Complaint," *Times-Picayune*, September 30, 2008.

26. All financial data compiled from Opensecrets.org.

27. Eliza Krigman, "Money to Watch IV: Money Flowing from Oil and Gas," Center for Responsive Politics, September 29, 2008.

28. Jeremy Alford, "Outreach O-Rama," *The Independent*, October 1, 2008; Ed Anderson and Bill Barrow, "Landrieu Backs Aid for First Responders," *Times-Picayune*, October 30, 2008.

29. Anderson and Barrow, "Landrieu Backs Aid for First Responders."

30. Ed Anderson, Bill Barrow, and Jan Moller, "Mary Landrieu, John Kennedy Square Off Tonight in Third Debate," *Times-Picayune*, October 15, 2008.

31. SurveyUSA Election Poll #13803 at www.surveyusa.com.

32. All polls taken during the course of the campaign can be found at pollster.com.

33. Bill Barrow, "Kennedy Tweaks Campaign Message," *Times-Picayune*, October 21, 2008.

34. All exit poll data can be found at www.cnn.com/ELECTION/2008/results/polls.

35. Jan Moller, "Landrieu Maintains Lead in New Poll," *Times-Picayune*, October 24, 2008.

12

Virginia Senate Race (Warner v. Gilmore)

A Presidential Campaign and a New Kind of Democrat Turn the Old Dominion Blue

Bob N. Roberts

Mark Warner
Age: 54
Sex: Male
Race: Caucasian
Religion: Presbyterian
Education: J.D. (Harvard Law School, 1980); B.A. (George Washington University, 1977)
Occupation: Investor, businessman
Political Experience: Governor of Virginia (2002–2006); chair, Democratic Party of Virginia (1993–1994); Commonwealth Transportation Board (1990–1994); Northern Virginia director, Douglas Wilder for Governor Campaign (1989)

Jim Gilmore
Age: 59
Sex: Male
Race: Caucasian
Religion: Methodist
Education: J.D. (University of Virginia Law School, 1977); B.A. (University of Virginia, 1971); course work at the Army Intelligence and Defense Language Institute
Occupation: Lawyer
Political Experience: Chair, Republican National Committee (2001–2002); governor of Virginia (1998–2002); Virginia attorney general (1994–1997); Henrico County attorney (1988–1993)

CHARACTERISTICS OF THE STATE

Party Balance

In 1949, V. O. Key Jr. aptly described Virginia as a political museum piece.[1] During the mid-1920s, Harry F. Byrd Sr. assumed the leadership of the Democratic political machine that had imposed an iron grip on all aspect of political life in the Old Dominion. Through the 1960s and 1970s, the passage of the Voting Rights Act of 1965 and the realignment of the national Republican Party that attracted disaffected Southern white voters led directly to the Commonwealth of Virginia becoming a competitive two-party state during the 1970s.[2] Equally important, the rapid growth of metropolitan regions in Northern Virginia, the Tidewater area of Virginia, and the Richmond regions forced both the Democratic Party and Republican Party to compete vigorously for the exploding number of suburban voters. The combination of the removal of legal barriers to voter registration and suburbanization led to a steady increase in the number of registered voters from the mid-1970s through the 2008 presidential election. The efforts of both Democrats and Republicans to adapt to the new electoral environment were complicated by the historical election cycle designed to reduce voter turnout in an effort to protect the Democratic political machine. As table 12.1 demonstrates, it has been difficult for either party to make significant gains either in state or federal elections in a single election because the fragmented election cycle limits the so-called coattail effect.

Elections for governor, lieutenant governor, and attorney general occur every four years in the year following the election for president of the United States. Elections for members of the Virginia Senate occur every four years but do not coincide with the election of the governor, lieutenant gov-

Table 12.1. Virginia Election Cycle: Federal and State Elections

Year	Offices
2004	Federal elections: U.S. president, U.S. vice president, U.S. Senate, U.S. House of Representatives
2005	State elections: Virginia governor, attorney general, lieutenant governor, House of Delegates
2006	Federal elections: U.S. Senate; U.S. House of Representatives
2007	State elections: Virginia Senate; Virginia House of Delegates
2008	Federal elections: U.S. president, U.S. vice president, U.S. Senate, U.S. House of Representatives
2009	Virginia elections: Virginia governor, attorney general, lieutenant governor, Virginia House of Delegates

ernor, or attorney general. These elections take place the year following congressional midterm elections.

Elections for the Virginia House of Delegates occur every two years but do not coincide with elections for federal offices. Elections for the U.S. Senate occur on six year cycles tied to either presidential election years or mid-term congressional elections. Elections for U.S. House of Representatives occurred every two even years and do not coincide with state elections for governor, attorney general, lieutenant governor, Virginia House of Delegates, or Virginia Senate. At the same time, unlike any other state, the Virginia Constitution limits governors to one consecutive four-year term, making it exceptionally difficult for Virginia governors to build coattails to help members of their party to win state legislative races.

The fragmented election cycle also leads to large differences in voter turnout from election to election. As table 12.2 demonstrates, voter turnout is significantly higher during presidential election years then for elections for statewide offices and elections for members of the Virginia Senate and House of Delegates.

Table 12.2. Virginia Registration and Turnout Statistics, 1992–2008

Year	Total	Registered	Total Voting Turnout (% of registered voters)
2008*	5,034,660	3,714,055	73.76%
2007	4,549,864	1,374,526	30.2%
2006	4,554,683	2,398,589	57.7%
2005	4,452,225	2,000,052	45.0%
2004*	4,517,980	3,223,156	71.4%
2003	4,217,227	1,296,955	30.8%
2002	4,219,957	1,331,915	39.4%
2001	4,109,127	1,905,511	46.4%
2000*	4,073,644	2,789,808	68.5%
1999	3,808,754	1,373,527	36.1%
1998	3,724,683	1,229,139	33.3%
1997	3,565,697	1,764,476	49.5%
1996*	3,322,740	2,468,229	74.3%
1995	3,038,394	1,585,783	52.2%
1994	3,000,560	2,078,106	69.3%
1993	2,975,121	1,817,777	61.1%
1992*	3,055,486	2,582,966	84.5%

Source: The table is based upon data provided by the Virginia State Board of Elections, www.sbe.virginia.gov/cms/Statistics_Polling_Places/Registration_Statistics/voting_statistics.html.
*Presidential election year

Voting and Electoral History

The passage of the Voting Rights Act of 1965 sealed the fate of the Byrd political machine which relied heavily upon rural whites to maintain political control. In the aftermath of Richard Nixon's 1968 presidential election victory, the Virginia Republican Party moved to assemble a new coalition of suburban voters and white voters who now viewed the Virginia Democratic Party as under the control of liberals instead of conservative Democrats. During the 1970s, the Republican Party took advantage of deep divisions within the Democratic Party over civil rights and other social issues to emerge as a force in Virginia politics. As table 12.3 demonstrates, for the first time since the end of Reconstruction, in 1969 Virginia voters elected a Republican governor.

The table also demonstrates that from 1969 through 2005, Virginia voters elected five Republican governors and five Democratic governors. Virginia went from being a one-party state dominated by conservative Democrats to a competitive two-party state. The 1970s saw the election of two Republican governors; the 1980s saw the election of three Democratic governors; the 1990s saw the election of two Republican governors; and the first half of the 2000s saw the election of two Democratic governors. Interestingly, beginning with the 1976 election of Democratic presidential nominee Jimmy Carter, the party that won the presidency lost the governorship of Virginia the following year.[3]

The period from the late 1960s through the early 1980s saw the transition of Virginia politics from a one-party system to a competitive two-party system with both Democrats and Republicans forced to compete for the growing suburban communities that held the balance of power in statewide races. Many of these new suburban voters moved into the Northern Virginia, Richmond, and Tidewater regions from out of state and did not have a history of partisan loyalties. Consequently, both Democratic and Republican candidates for statewide office found it necessary to tailor their message to this increasingly important bloc of voters.

Beginning in the late 1960s, all candidates for statewide offices, particularly candidates for governor, ran on pro-business and economic develop-

Table 12.3. Virginia Elections for Governor, 1969–2005

Year	Name	Party	Year	Name	Party
1969	Linwood Holton	Republican	1989	L. Douglas Wilder	Democrat
1973	Mills Godwin	Republican	1993	George Allen	Republican
1977	John N. Dalton	Republican	1997	James Gilmore	Republican
1981	Charles Robb	Democrat	2001	Mark Warner	Democrat
1985	Gerald Baliles	Democrat	2005	Tim Kaine	Democrat

ment platforms which sought to pay for new government investments in education, transportation, and infrastructure primarily with revenue generated by economic growth rather than higher taxes. Only one Republican governor, Linwood Holton (1969–1973), supported a significant tax increase.[4] Only after winning election, did Democratic governors Gerald Baliles (1985–1989)[5] and Mark Warner (2001–2005),[6] seek and obtain substantial tax increases from the Virginia General Assembly to expand state support for basic government services such as transportation and education. Warner, only after facing a multibillion shortfall in state government revenue, went back on a campaign pledge not to seek an increase in statewide taxes after winning the governorship in 2001.

Although Democratic and Republican candidates for statewide offices generally agreed on economic development and taxation issues, sharp differences emerged in the past four decades over social issues such as abortion and gay marriage. The fact that the Republican Party became increasingly reliant on evangelical Christians for support further shaped their candidates' opposition to abortion and gay rights and the party's support for so-called cultural issues.[7]

Besides the strong two-party competition for the governorship, since the 1970s, the Virginia Republican party embarked on a steady but slow effort to capture control of the Virginia General Assembly. For instance, in the 1993 General Assembly elections Democrats won twenty-two Senate seats to the Republicans' eighteen seats, while the Democrats held fifty-two and the Republicans forty-seven seats in the House. In the 1999 election, Republicans won control of both houses of Virginia's legislature for the first time since the end of Reconstruction in 1877. With James Gilmore (R) as governor, and Republicans in control of both chambers, in early 2001 the Virginia General Assembly redrew the boundaries for congressional districts and state Assembly districts which helped Republicans gain even greater majorities.[8] Not until 2007 did Democrats regain control of the Virginia Senate by a narrow margin of twenty-one to nineteen and reduce the Republican majority in the House of Delegates to fifty-four to forty-four with two independents.

The resurgence of the Republican Party was evident in presidential elections, which resulted in victories in Virginia in every year since 1952 except for 1964 and 2008 (see table 12.4). In 1976, Virginia was the only southern state Jimmy Carter failed to carry.

Beginning in the 1970s, races for the U.S. Congress also became competitive. As table 12.5 demonstrates, with the exception of the 1980 Reagan landslide and the aftermath of reapportionment in 2000, the Democratic and Republican parties have vigorously contested seats in the House of Representatives. Of particular significance, the 2008 congressional races saw Democrats win one open seat previously held by a Republican.[9] More

Table 12.4. Virginia Votes: Presidential Elections

Election Year	Victor	Party	Percentage Vote
1952	Eisenhower	Republican	56.3
1956	Eisenhower	Republican	55.4
1960	Nixon	Republican	52.4
1964	Johnson	Democrat	53.5
1968	Nixon	Republican	43.4
1972	Nixon	Republican	67.8
1976	Ford	Republican	49.3
1980	Reagan	Republican	53.0
1984	Reagan	Republican	62.3
1988	Bush, H. W.	Republican	59.7
1992	Bush, H.W.	Republican	45.0
1996	Dole	Republican	47.7
2000	Bush, W.	Republican	52.5
2004	Bush, W.	Republican	53.7
2008	Obama	Democrat	52.6

significantly, Democrats took seats away from Republican incumbents in the Senate and 5th Congressional District.[10]

Unlike the contested races for House of Representatives, the period from the early 1970s through the late 1980s, saw the Republican Party dominate races for the U.S. Senate. From the end of Reconstruction through the early 1970s, conservative Democrats held both of Virginia's Senate seats. In 1970, Harry F. Byrd Jr. ran for reelection as an independent rather than a Democrat because of his dissatisfaction with the positions of the national Democratic Party. In 1972, Republican William L. Scott became the first Republican elected to the U.S. Senate since Reconstruction when he upset Democratic incumbent William B. Spong Jr. In 1976, Virginia voters again reelected Byrd to the Senate as an independent. When Republican Senator William B. Sprong Jr. declined to run for reelection in 1978, former Navy secretary John Warner succeeded in holding the seat for Republicans by narrowly defeating former Virginia attorney general Andrew P. Miller. When Byrd declined to run for reelection in 1982, Paul Trible defeated Virginia lieutenant governor Richard J. Davis for Byrd's seat. For the first time since the end of Reconstruction, Republicans held both U.S. Senate seats. When Warner ran for reelection in 1984 he defeated Democrat Edythe C. Harrison, a former state legislator, with 70 percent of the vote.

In 1988, to the surprise of the Republican Party, Trible declined to run for reelection. Trible's unexpected decision set the stage for former Virginia governor Charles Robb to easily defeat Republican Maurice A. Dawkins, giving the Democrats a rare victory in that chamber. When John Warner ran for election in 1990, the Democrats proved unsuccessful in finding a candidate to challenge Warner.

By 1994, the political fortunes of Senator Robb had suffered a number of major setbacks, including an extramarital affair and a federal criminal investigation over whether he had come into possession of illegal recordings of phone calls by former governor Douglas Wilder. The bitter feud between Wilder and Robb led Wilder in 1994 to launch an independent bid for the U.S. Senate.[11] Democrats feared that an independent run by Wilder might deprive Robb of badly needed African American votes. Iran-Contra scandal figure Oliver North won the Republican nomination to take on the Robb.

North had become a national name during the late 1980s Iran-Contra investigation. During congressional testimony, the Marine Lt. Colonel admitted to a congressional committee that he had lied in previous testimony to Congress regarding White House efforts to get around a law prohibiting U.S. funds being spent to support the Contras' efforts to overthrow the Communist Sandinista government in Nicaragua. North detailed to the staff of the National Security Council (NSC) directed efforts to raise foreign funds to support the Contras and to divert funds from the secret sale of military parts to Iran to the Contras. A U.S. Court of Appeals subsequently overturned North's convictions on lying to Congress and accepting illegal gratuities on the grounds that Independent Counsel Lawrence Walsh had used immunized testimony of North before Congress to obtain his convictions.

Despite winning the Republican nomination to go against Robb, the incumbent, and Wilder, the independent, a number of influential Republicans refused to support North because of his admission that he lied to Congress while under oath. Of particular significance, Republican Virginia senator John Warner made clear in no uncertain terms he could not support North. Reflecting this split within Republican ranks, Republican Marshall Coleman, whom Robb had defeated for the governorship of Virginia in 1981, entered the race as an independent. On September 15, 1994, under intense pressure from state and national Democratic leaders and with little chance of winning, Wilder withdrew from the race.[12] In the most hotly contested Senate race since the passage of the Voting Rights Act of 1965, Robb prevailed with 938,376 to North's 882,213 votes. To the surprise of many political observers, Marshall Coleman drew 235,324 votes primarily from moderate Republican unwilling to back North.

In 1996, Senator John Warner faced a serious challenge within the Republican Party. A number of conservative Republicans sought to strip Warner of the Republican nomination because of his refusal to back North in 1994. Warner fully understood that he stood a good chance of losing the Republican nomination if the Republican Party made use of a caucus convention selection process. To significantly increase his chances of winning the nomination, Warner invoked a provision of Virginia law which allowed incumbent officials to select either a caucus/convention or primary to decide the party's nominee. Virginia election law permitted Democrats, independents, and Republicans to vote in the 1994 Republican primary. Early in June of 1996, John Warner received 66 percent of the vote in defeating former Reagan budget director James C. Miller.[13]

Interestingly, in contrast to 1990, the Virginia Democratic Party searched for a well-known Democratic figure to challenge Warner. When this effort failed, the Democratic Party turned to telecom multimillionaire Mark Warner to take on John Warner. To the surprise of many political observers, Mark Warner ran a much stronger race than anticipated and only lost by a margin of 119,762 votes. Mark Warner ran as a socially progressive Democratic who advocated applying business principles to government. As a result of his run for senator, Mark Warner became the rising star of the Virginia Democratic Party.

In 2000, Senator Robb again found himself facing a strong challenge from former Virginia governor George Allen. Elected governor in 1993, Allen was popular and had laid the foundation for the 1999 Republican takeover of the Virginia General Assembly. Equally significant, Democratic presidential nominee Al Gore all but conceded Virginia to the Republican nominee George W. Bush, which left Senator Robb without the aid of his party's presidential campaign. Allen went on to defeat Robb by a margin of 52.7 to 47.7 percent—approximately the same margin of victory by Bush in the state. In 2002, the Democratic Party proved unable to find anyone willing to take on the popular incumbent senator, John Warner.

Senator Allen was up for election in the 2006 midterm races. Few political observers believed that Democrats could field a candidate with any opportunity to unseat Allen, who was being considered as a possible presidential candidate in 2008. In a June 2006 primary, Jim Webb, former Marine and Reagan administration secretary of the navy defeated Harris Miller, a long time Democratic activist and close friend of Mark Warner, by roughly 7 percentage points. Political observers initially believed that Webb would face a great deal of difficulty convincing Democratic voters to support a former Reagan official. But, a number of well-known national Democratic officials threw their support behind Webb largely because of their belief Webb would be able to run a more competitive campaign in conservative and pro-military Virginia.

During a rally on August 11, 2006, Allen pointed to a Webb volunteer, S. R. Sidarth, who had been following Allen to campaign events around Virginia.[14] Allen then stated that "[t]his fellow here, over here with the yellow shirt, macaca, or whatever his name is. He's with my opponent. He's following us around everywhere. And it's just great."[15] Allen went on to urge the crowd to welcome "macaca." Within days, Allen's comments appeared on YouTube and caught the attention of the media. A debate erupted because Sidarth was Indian American and the term macaca referred to "a monkey that inhabits the Eastern Hemisphere or a town in South Africa" or "a racial slur against African immigrants."[16] Despite the fact that Allen later apologized for possibly offending Sidarth and subsequently apologized to Sidarth in person, the macaca comment helped to focus on prior conduct by Allen which had raised questions about his cultural sensitivity to different groups. Before Allen ran for governor in 1993, for instance, civil rights groups criticized Allen "for keeping a Confederate flag in a cabin near his Charlottesville home."[17] And in 1997 Allen angered civil rights groups when he proclaimed April Confederate History month.[18] By mid-September of 2006, Allen found himself in an increasingly close race with Jim Webb.

Much like other Republicans across the country during the 2006 midterm congressional elections, Allen was hurt by President Bush's unpopularity. In September of 2006, reports surfaced that Allen might have used a racial slur to refer to African Americans while he attended the University of Virginia in the early 1970s.[19] Although Allen vigorously denied the allegation, the new allegations further damaged the campaign. Webb upset Allen 49.59 to 49.20 percent.

Demographic Character of the Electorate

In 2007, the U.S. Census Bureau provided a snapshot of the demographic characteristics of Virginia's 7,642,884 residents (see table 12.5).

Key Voting Blocs

In the 2006 U.S. Senate contest, Webb beat Allen by only a few thousand votes.[20] Allen received the votes of 62 percent of white men and 53 percent of white women. Webb received the votes of 75 percent of nonwhite males and 82 percent of nonwhite females. Allen carried 65 percent of born again

Table 12.5. Virginia in Focus

Selected Characteristics	Virginia	U.S.
Median age	36.9%	36.4%
Women	50.8%	50.7%
White alone, not Hispanic or Latino	67.7%	66.4%
Black alone	19.9%	12.8%
Hispanic or Latino	6.3%	14.8%
Median household income	$56,277	$48,451

Source: Virginia in Focus: Census Bureau Pre-Primary Snapshot.

or evangelical Christians. Webb won 61 percent of individuals from urban areas, whereas Allen received the votes of 52 percent of voters from rural areas and 55 percent of suburbanites. Most important, Webb carried Northern Virginia with 60 percent, although Allen won 57 percent of the vote in the conservative western region of the state.[21] Democrats in statewide races had become dependent on nonwhite voters and Northern Virginia, while the Republican base remained white male, rural, and evangelical.

Major Urban Areas and Employment

In recent decades, a larger percentage of Virginia's population lived in metropolitan regions (see table 12.6).

The Virginia Employment Commission reported in 2006 that the private sector employed 3,051,700 individuals, state government employed 152,600, local governments employed 367,700, and the federal government employed 154,500 civilian employees in Virginia.[22]

Table 12.6. Virginia's Largest Population Centers (2006)

County	Population	Region
Fairfax	1,010,443	Northern Virginia
Prince William	357,503	Northern Virginia
Henrico	284,399	Richmond
Chesterfield	269,718	Richmond
Loudoun	268,817	Northern Virginia
Arlington	199,776	Northern Virginia
Spotsylvania	119,529	Northern Virginia
Albemarle	92,035	Central Virginia
Roanoke	90,482	Southwestern Virginia
Rockingham	72,564	Western Virginia
Frederick	71,187	Western Virginia
Augusta	70,910	Western Virginia
Virginia Beach	435,619	Tidewater
Norfolk	229,112	Tidewater
Chesapeake	220,560	Tidewater
Richmond	192,913	Richmond
Newport News	17,281	Tidewater
Alexandria	136,619	Northern Virginia
Hampton	145,017	Tidewater
Portsmouth	101,377	Tidewater
Roanoke	91,552	Southwest
Suffolk	81,071	Tidewater

THE CANDIDATES

Late in August of 2007, Republican senator John Warner, aged eighty, announced his decision not to seek reelection.[23] Warner chose to make the announcement on the north steps of the Rotunda at the University of Virginia. With Warner's decision not to seek reelection, speculation immediately focused on whether former Virginia governor, Mark Warner, would be the Democratic contender. Speculation also focused on a number of possible Republican candidates including Representative Thomas M. Davis III and former governor James Gilmore. Early in October of 2006, Mark Warner announced his decision not to seek the Democratic presidential nomination largely because of family reasons. To much fanfare in the Democratic Party, Warner announced his Senate campaign in mid-September of 2007.

On the Republican side, political pundits expected Davis to fight it out with Gilmore for the nomination. However, in October of 2007, the Republican State Central Committee voted to hold a nominating convention rather than a primary to select the nominee.[24] Most political experts believed the use of a convention favored Gilmore, with ties to the conservative base, over Davis, who was a moderate. Later that month, Davis announced that he would not run for Senate. Three weeks later, Gilmore announced his campaign.[25] In January of 2008, Robert G. Marshall, a member of the Virginia House of Delegates from Prince William County, announced his intention to challenge Gilmore for the Republican Senate nomination. Elected to the House of Delegates in 1991, Marshall had established himself as the most outspoken critic of abortion and as a social conservative on a range of issues.[26] Not surprisingly, few political observers gave Marshall much hope of winning. Yet, over the next six months Marshall ran a particularly effective grassroots campaign. Marshall argued that in order to have any hope of possibly defeating Mark Warner, the Republican candidate for Senate would have to motivate social conservatives to come out to vote.[27] From January through June of 2008, Gilmore assured the media and his supporters he would have little difficulty obtaining the Republican nomination. Yet, when the Republican convention met in June, Gilmore prevailed by only 70 votes out of 10,378 votes cast.[28] Gilmore's narrow Republican convention victory provided strong indication of deep divisions within the Republican Party over who should take on Mark Warner.

Mark Warner: The New Age Democrat

Mark Warner was born in Indianapolis, Indiana, on December 15, 1954. He grew up in Illinois and later moved to Vernon, Connecticut, where he graduated from Rockville High School. Warner enrolled at George Washington University and graduated with a degree in political science in 1977. He graduated in 1980 from Harvard Law School and returned to Washington, DC, "to work as an $18,000-a-year fundraiser for the Democratic National Committee."[29] Warner then decided to enter the business world. During the mid-1980s, Warner saw tremendous opportunities in the cellular phone industry and a new federal program which saw the Federal Communications Commission (FCC) award some "1,468 licenses for cellular phones markets across the nation."[30] Warner proved skilled at assembling investors who had the financial resources to meet the requirements to qualify for one of these licenses, then brokered a number of deals where these investors sold licenses for enormous profits with Warner receiving a fee for each transaction. Warner subsequently became a cofounder of Nextel, the telecommunications giant.[31]

After amassing a large fortune, Warner took time out to enter the political arena not as a candidate but as the Northern Virginia campaign coordinator for Douglas Wilder's 1989 campaign for governor.[32] After Wilder won a narrow victory over Marshall Coleman, Warner served as Wilder's transition director but declined a position in the administration. Through the first half of the 1990s, Warner remained active in Democratic politics while pursuing various business opportunities. Then in 1996, he agreed to run against incumbent Republican senator John Warner, who had fought off a tough primary challenge. Although Mark Warner lost by a margin of 52.48 to 47.39 percent, he did much better than pundits had expected and emerged as the Democrat with the best chance to turn back the 1990s Republican surge in Virginia.

In 2001, the Virginia Democratic Party turned to Mark Warner to attempt to reverse a tide of defeats which had led to the election of two successive Republican governors and the 1999 Republican Party takeover of the Virginia General Assembly. Throughout the 2001 campaign for governor, Warner defined himself as a new type of Democrat who had the ability to apply business methods to government while recognizing the important role of government in stimulating economic growth and helping the less fortunate. Warner also pledged not to raise taxes. Warner defeated Virginia attorney general Mark Earley by 5 percent of the vote. As expected, Warner did particularly well in Northern Virginia. For instance, Warner carried Fairfax County by a margin of 54.47 to 44.9 percent. The significance of Fairfax was that, of the total 1,886,721 votes cast statewide, Fairfax County voters cast 269,014. Warner also carried most of the state's large independent cities.[33] But he also campaigned heavily in rural areas of the state and did surprisingly well there for a Democrat.

The new governor did not have time to celebrate. From 2001 through 2003, the Warner administration and the General Assembly found itself forced to close a $6 billion revenue shortfall. The situation forced Warner to make billions of dollars in cuts in government programs. Facing additional cuts, in January of 2004, Warner took the controversial step of asking the General Assembly to raise a billion dollars in new taxes.[34] Even though Republicans controlled both chambers, a majority of the Senate supported increasing state revenue in order to prevent further cuts to essential state services. Warner faced more difficulty in the House, where Republicans were dead set against tax increases. Through the spring of 2008, a stalemate ensued until seventeen Republicans broke from their party in late April and "approved a package of tax increases and cuts that would generate $1.36 billion in new revenue over the next two years."[35] The tax plan increased the state sales tax from 4.5 to 5 cents a dollar and raised the excise tax on cigarettes from 2.5 cents a pack to 30 cents a pack.[36] Despite the tax increase, Warner left office early in 2006 with high approval numbers.

Jim Gilmore: A New Republican for the Old Dominion

James Gilmore was born in Richmond and grew up in Henrico County, just outside of Richmond. His father worked as a grocery store meat cutter. His mother was a church secretary. In high school, Gilmore played the clarinet in the all-county band.[37] After graduating from John Randolph Tucker High School, Gilmore became the first member of his family to attend college when he enrolled at the University of Virginia. Upon graduation in 1971, he joined the U.S. Army and served as an intelligence specialist in West Germany from 1971 to 1974. Gilmore then graduated from the University of Virginia Law School. From 1977 to 1987, Gilmore practiced law in the Richmond area. In 1987, the voters of Henrico County elected him as commonwealth attorney, a position he occupied until running for and being elected as attorney general of the state in 1993. In 1997, he won the governorship by a big margin.

Gilmore's tenure benefited from the national and "dot.com" booms, which allowed him to provide funds "for 4,000 new teachers to reduce class sizes" and to freeze college tuition increases by providing public universities additional funds to cover increased costs.[38] However, Gilmore had a stormy relationship with the Virginia General Assembly and, by 2000 it became clear that economic growth and low taxes could not sustain the growing demands of education and other issues. Throughout the 2000 legislative session, the Senate sought to make adjustments in taxes to balance the budget, but Gilmore and his allies in the House refused to back off their tax cuts. For the first time in modern Virginia history, the governor and legislature failed to pass a revised budget, and Gilmore had to cut more than $400 million from agencies to make up the shortfall while still paying for tax cuts.[39] Critics accused Gilmore of refusing to make compromises in the best interests of Virginia. Supporters of Gilmore argued that he had promised Virginians tax relief.

Surprisingly, in late 2000 President Bush asked the Republican National Committee (RNC) to appoint Gilmore as chair of the RNC.[40] Not surprisingly, Virginia Democrats sharply criticized Gilmore for neglecting the state.[41] Although Gilmore initially received good reviews as RNC chair, the November 2001 victory of Democrat Mark Warner over Republican Mark Earley and other problems hurt Gilmore's leadership. On November 30, 2001, Gilmore resigned as RNC chair to devote full-time to his practice of law and various business ventures. From 2002 to 2007 Gilmore practiced law in Washington, DC, and in 2006 served as chair of a Bears Stearns subsidiary marketing mortgage securities.[42]

CAMPAIGN ISSUES

Gilmore and Warner adopted markedly different strategies in their quest for the Senate. Much like his 2001 campaign for governor, Warner defined himself as someone able to compromise and solve problems in a bipartisan manner. On April 16, 2008, both candidates appeared at the annual Shad Planking event in Sussex County.[43] At the event, Warner pledged to become a "radical centrist" if elected to the Senate.[44] At the same event, Gilmore "ripped into Warner, describing him as an untrustworthy and tax-happy opportunist who abandoned campaign pledges."[45]

Oil, Oil, Oil

Late in April 2008, following the lead of Republican presidential candidate John McCain, Gilmore sought to exploit rising public anger over the dramatic increase in the price of gasoline. Gilmore threw his full support for expanding offshore drilling, including off Virginia's coast.[46] Through early June, Gilmore hammered on the oil drilling issue and attempted to blame Warner and the Democrats for the $4 dollar a gallon gas price because of their opposition to new off-shore oil drilling and increased drilling in Alaska. The Gilmore campaign hoped voters would blame Democrats for the gas prices and thus vote against them.

In June, Warner used his large advantage in campaign contributions to launch a counteroffense on the oil issue. By the end of May, Warner had raised $7.8 million and still had $5.3 million in hand. In contrast, Gilmore had raised only $1 million since entering the race and had $208,000 on hand.[47] To counter Gilmore's attack, Warner, in a series of campaign speeches and ads, stressed the need to clamp down on speculators who had driven up the price of oil. Warner also expressed his support to "allow exploratory drilling off the Atlantic and Pacific coasts for natural gas and oil reserves" but wanted to leave it up to the states.[48] Finally, Warner stressed the need for a long-term plan to increase the production of fuel-efficient hybrids and greater use of alternative energy sources such as wind power. This campaign negated Gilmore's charges and the growing public anger over rising gasoline prices during the summer of 2008.

The lack of campaign funds forced Gilmore to rely heavily on free media to get his message on oil drilling to the electorate. In a drive-time interview with Jimmy Barrett of WRVA, a Richmond radio station, Barrett asked Gilmore whether his "drill-now, drill-here" stance included drilling on his Henrico County property. Gilmore replied, "I'd do it if it would help people get their gas prices down."[49] However, Gilmore's use of free media could not substitute for paid campaign ads as a way to get his "drill-now" position to voters.

On July 19, 2008, Warner and Gilmore participated in their first debate hosted by the Virginia Bar Association in Hot Springs. Even though the debate provided Gilmore the opportunity to pound away on the drilling issue and Warner's support for raising taxes, the debate was untelevised and received little media coverage.[50] Through the summer of 2008, the drilling issue had little impact on public opinion polls. Gilmore continued to trail Warner by more than 20 points in polls and had a rough time raising money. At the end of June, Warner had a $5 million to $116,000 advantage over Gilmore.[51]

To Debate or Not to Debate

Late in August of 2008, with a large lead in the polls, Warner shocked political observers by informing the Virginia Chapter of the League of Women Voters that he would not participate in their scheduled statewide televised debate. The Warner campaign argued that it did not have time to fit the debate in the sixty-eight days remaining until the November 4 election.[52] The Gilmore campaign sharply criticized Warner for refusing to debate. More important, the Gilmore campaign used the controversy over the debate to release its first campaign ad.[53] Paid for by the Virginia Republican Party, the ad highlighted footage from Warner's 2001 governor's race debate where Warner declared, "I will not raise your taxes."[54] The ad went on to claim that Warner was committed to "even higher taxes, bigger spending and limiting domestic oil production-costing you more at the pump."[55] The Warner campaign immediately responded by releasing its own add arguing that he had no choice but to seek a tax increase because Gilmore, as governor, "used irresponsible, dishonest gimmicks to cover up the biggest budget shortfall in Virginia history."[56] The *Washington Post* ran an editorial sharply criticizing Warner for backing out of the televised debate, and Warner agreed to participate in a televised debate with Gilmore.[57] Interestingly, the flap over Warner's refusal to debate had no measurable impact on Warner's standing in the polls.

It's the Economy, Stupid

By mid-September, the price of gasoline began to decline but the nation faced a growing financial crisis. On September 19, 2008, Warner and Gilmore squared off in their second debate. Both Warner and Gilmore agreed that the nation's financial institutions needed much tighter regulation to prevent the reoccurrence of future financial meltdowns. Yet, Warner and Gilmore sharply disagreed over how well each had managed the state's finances during their respective terms as governor and how to solve the nation's energy crisis.[58]

On October 3, 2008, Gilmore and Warner met in their only statewide televised debate. By this time Congress had voted to approve a $700 billion emergency relief passage for the financial industry. Unlike Warner who reluctantly supported the bailout, Gilmore denounced the bailout and Warner for supporting it.[59] "You don't go and vote in the Senate, as Mark Warner said he would have done, to have 700 billion of the taxpayers' dollars and put it into these high rollers on Wall Street," argued Gilmore.[60] Gilmore's decision to break from his party's presidential nominee on the bailout package represented another attempt by Gilmore to reverse the direction of the campaign. A September 24, 2008, *Washington Post* poll indicated that Gilmore had "not gained any traction for his U.S. Senate campaign" during the prior month.[61] According to the poll, Warner now led Gilmore by thirty points.

CAMPAIGN STRATEGY

From the outset of the campaign, Gilmore sought to define Warner as untrustworthy largely because of his 2004 support of a large tax increase while serving as governor. Instead of focusing his campaign on attacking Gilmore, Warner sought to define himself as a leader who had shown an ability to get beyond divisive ideologically driven politics to find solutions to pressing problems.

Media Strategy

The vast disparity in campaign funds available to Warner and Gilmore led to sharply different media strategies by the respective candidates. With a large campaign war chest, Warner focused on persuading voters that he had the ability to go to Washington to solve problems by building a consensus between opposing groups. The Warner campaign relied on largely positive campaign ads to define Warner as a nonpartisan problem solver. In sharp contrast, Gilmore relied on free media to attempt to get his message to the voters. Specifically, Gilmore made extensive use of radio and television interviews to argue that voters could not trust Warner to represent their interests if he won a Senate seat.

Image and Advertising

During the campaign, Warner received $25,782,162 in contributions. In sharp contrast, Gilmore received $2,025,788 in contributions. The vast advantage in contributions permitted Warner to run numerous campaign ads in every market across the state, including the expensive Northern Virginia market. Late in May of 2008, even before Warner had officially received the Democratic nomination, his campaign began to run an ad named "Budget Mess." The thirty-second spot detailed the fact that when Warner took office in January 2001, Virginia faced a huge budget shortfall. The ad went on to stress that Warner made large cuts in the budget to deal with the shortfall and then worked with Republicans and Democrats to reform the tax code to put Virginia on sound financial footing. During the ad, former Republican senator from Virginia John Chichester praised the Democrat Warner for his efforts to deal with Virginia's financial crisis.

On July 15, 2008, the Warner campaign issued its second major ad, titled "Energy Plan." The Warner campaign released the ad in an effort to rebut Gilmore's attack that Warner and his fellow Democrats were to blame for higher gas prices. The ad stressed that Warner would seek greater investments in alternative energy sources, expand domestic oil production, and crack down on oil speculators. The ad also stated that Warner wanted "to expand oil and gas production at home" and emphasized this point by showing footage of an offshore oil platform.[62] Despite the generally positive tone of Warner's campaign, on September 9, 2008, Warner launched a negative ad titled "Preposterous." The ad accused Gilmore of using "irresponsible," "dishonest" "gimmicks" to cover up the largest budget shortfall in Virginia history while Gilmore served as governor. On October 14, the Warner campaign released an ad titled "A Fresh Approach," where Warner presented a number of solutions to the financial crisis that had rocked Wall Street. In the ad, Warner discussed the serious economic problems facing Americans and stated that the country could not allow CEOs to walk away with millions of dollars while their companies went into the ditch. Warner concluded the ad by stating that the country needed leaders who put their country's interest, and not partisanship, first.

The lack of campaign funds made it impossible for Gilmore to conduct an effective media campaign. On September 8, 2008, Gilmore released an ad titled "Principled," which did not air in Northern Virginia. The ad opened with a tape of Mark Warner pledging not to raise taxes during a 2001 debate. The ad then blamed Warner for raising taxes and showed Warner campaigning with Barack Obama. It claimed the election of Warner and Obama would bring much higher taxes and increased government spending.

In a final effort to reverse the direction of the campaign, in October the Gilmore campaign posted a Web ad. The ad included comments made in 1994 by Warner to fellow Democrats and was titled "Freedom un-American (Really)." Listeners could barely hear Warner making the following comments regarding ongoing changes in the Republican Party:

> One thing you are going to see is a coalition that has just about completely taken over the Republican Party in this State and if they have their way; it's going to take over state government. It's made up of the Christian Coalition. Its made up of the right to lifers. It's made up of the NRA. It's made up of the home schoolers. It's made up of a whole coalition of people that have all sorts of different views that I think most of us in this room would find threatening to what it means to be an American.[63]

After posting the audiotape, Gilmore "took Warner to task for denying that he had made the statements."[64] In responsive, Warner stated his regret for the statements. Interestingly, the allegation was not new. Late in October of 2001, the Republican Party released the transcript of Warner's talk to the National Jewish Democratic Council in Northern Virginia on May 25, 1994.[65] At the time, Warner denied that he ever had intended to put down people of faith. The Web ad drew only limited media attention and failed to persuade the media to highlight Warner's 1994 comments.

Finance

On October 15, Warner announced he had raised $12.3 million for his campaign and still had $3.6 million to spend the last three weeks of the campaign. Over 11,000 donors had contributed to the Warner campaign. On October 15, the Federal Election Commission (FEC) revealed that the Warner campaign had received $25,782,162 in contributions. Gilmore had received only $2,025,788 in contributions.

THE ELECTION

Mark Warner easily defeated James Gilmore by a margin of 64.74 to 34.0 percent. For obvious reasons, the presidential contest between Democratic presidential nominee Barack Obama and John McCain overshadowed the Warner-Gilmore race. Early in the presidential campaign, the Obama campaign decided to fight for Virginia's thirteen electoral votes despite the fact Virginia had not voted for a Democratic presidential candidate since 1964. Obama prevailed by a margin of 52.31 to 46.64 percent in Virginia. Warner's margin of victory was not limited to the Democratic strongholds of Northern Virginia and major cities such as Richmond and Norfolk. Warner lost only five of ninety-four counties.[66] Of thirty-nine cities, Warner only lost one.[67] In contrast, Republican presidential candidate John McCain carried the majority of Virginia's ninety-five counties and twelve of thirty-nine cities.[68]

The fact that a significant number of Virginia voters cast ballots for both John McCain and Mark Warner demonstrated the ability of Warner to attract Democrats, Republicans, and Independents.

NOTES

1. V. O. Key Jr., *Southern Politics* (New York: Alfred A. Knopf, 1949), 19.
2. Frank B. Atkinson, *The Dynamic Dominion* (Fairfax, VA: George Mason University Press, 1992), 285–393.
3. Jimmy Carter (president, 1976, D); John Dalton (Virginia governor, 1997, R); Ronald Reagan (president, 1980, R); Charles Robb (Virginia governor, 1981, D); Ronald Reagan (president, 1984, R); Gerald Baliles (Virginia governor, 1985, D); George W. H. Bush (president, 1988, R); L. Douglas Wilder (Virginia governor, 1989, D); Bill Clinton (president 1992, D); George Allen (Virginia governor, 1993, R); Bill Clinton (president, 1996, D); James Gilmore (Virginia governor, 1997, R); George W. Bush (president, 2000, R); Mark Warner (Virginia governor, 2001, D); George W. Bush (president, 2004, R); Tim Kaine (Virginia governor, 2005, D).
4. Helen Dewer, "Holton Seeks $300 Million in New Va. Taxes," *Washington Post*, January 13, 1972, A1.
5. Donald P. Baker and R. H. Melton, "Baliles Tax Plan Gets No Major Challenge: Proposals Seek to Ease Impact on Poor," *Washington Post*, September 17, 1986, C1.
6. James Dao, "A Governor's Hard Sell: Higher Taxes in Virginia," *New York Times*, January 20, 2004, A12.
7. Mark J. Rozell and Clyde Wilcox, *Second Coming: The New Christian Right in Virginia Politics* (Baltimore: John Hopkins University Press, 1996).
8. At the beginning of the 2002 General Assembly session, Republicans held sixty-four seats in the House of Delegates while the number of Democratic seats had declined to thirty-four. The House of Delegates also included two independents.
9. The 11th Congressional District located in Northern Virginia was won by Gerry Connolly.
10. In the 2nd Congressional District located in the Tidewater area of Virginia Democratic challenger Glen C. Nye III defeated incumbent Republican Thelma D. Drake. In Virginia's 5th Congressional District, Tom S. P. Perriello (D) held a narrow lead over Republican incumbent Virgil H. Goode Jr. at the time of the completion of this chapter.
11. Richard L. Berke, "In Wilder's Senate Bid, Winning Is Only One Goal," *New York Times*, August 10, 1994, A1.
12. Special to the *New York Times*, "Facing Loss, Wilder Ends Bid for Senate," *New York Times*, September 16, 1994, A1.

13. "Warner Stills Conservative Opposition in Primary," *New York Times*, June 12, 1996, A19.

14. Tim Craig and Michael D. Shear, "Allen Quip Provokes Outrage, Apology; Name Insults Webb Volunteer," *Washington Post*, August 15, 2006, A01.

15. Craig and Shear, "Allen Quip."

16. Craig and Shear, "Allen Quip."

17. Craig and Shear, "Allen Quip."

18. Michael Hardy, "NAACP Denounces Allen; Governor Proclaimed Confederate History Month," *Richmond Times Dispatch*, April 11, 1997, A1.

19. Pamela Stallsmith, "Allen Denies Racial Epithet; Senator Disputes Claims of 3 Ex-U.Va. Teammates Reported in Online Story," *Richmond Times Dispatch*, September 26, 2006, A-1.

20. U.S. Senate, Virginia, exit poll.

21. U.S. Senate, Virginia, exit poll.

22. Virginia Auditor of Public Accounts-Commonwealth Data Point: Private Employment.

23. Bill Turque, "Sen. Warner to 'Quietly Step Aside'; Va. Republican, 80, Cites Demand of Service in Declining to Seek 6th Term," *Washington Post*, September 1, 2007, A01.

24. David Cook, "After Much Anticipation, Rep. Tom Davis Won't Seek U.S. Senate Seat in Virginia," *Christian Science Monitor*, October 26, 2007, p. 25.

25. Bob Lewis, "Gilmore Announces 2008 U.S. Senate Bid," Washingtonpost.com, November 19, 2007.

26. Bob Lewis, "Marshall Announces GOP Bid; Faces Nomination Battle with Ex-governor, Gilmore," *The Associated Press State & Local Wire*, January 7, 2008.

27. Lewis, "Marshall Announces GOP Bid."

28. Tim Craig and Anita Kumar, "Gilmore Beats Marshall in Nomination Nail-Biter; about 70 Votes Decide Virginia GOP's Choice for U.S. Senate," *Washington Post*, June 1, 2008, C01.

29. Warren Fiske, "Mark Warner—a Hard-Driver Pushing for His Goals," Pilotonline.com, hamptonroad.com/print/483859.

30. Fiske, "Mark Warner."

31. Fiske, "Mark Warner."

32. Donald P. Baker, "Wilder Retains Edge; Coleman Gains," *Washington Post*, August 16, 1989, B3.

33. Bristol, Chesapeake, Colonial Heights, Harrisonburg, Manassas Park, Manassas City, Poquoson, Staunton, Virginia Beach, and Waynesboro.

34. Dao, "A Governor's Hard Sell," A12.

35. Michael Sluss, "Virginia General Assembly Agrees on Tax Increase," Roanoke.com, April 28, 2004, roanoke.com/roatimes/news/story166209.html (accessed October 16, 2008).

36. Sluss, "Virginia General Assembly."

37. Dale Eisman, "Jim Gilmore—a Candidate Driven by a Pugnacious Personality," Pilotonline.com, hamptonroads.com/print/483860 (accessed October 17, 2008).

38. Anita Kumar, "Budget Flap Is Gilmore's Legacy in Va.," *Washington Post*, October 29, 2008, B1.

39. Kumar, "Budget Flap."

40. Ron Fournier, "Virginia Gov. Gilmore to Head RNC for Bush," *The Associated Press State & Local Wire*, December 21, 2000. Available at Lexis Nexis Academic Universe (accessed October 16, 2008).

41. Craig Timberg, "Divided Democrats Can Find Agreement in Attack on Gilmore, Governor Accused of Neglecting State," *Washington Post*, January 26, 2001, B4.

42. "Gilmore Led Bear Stearns-Subsidiary, Former Governor Challenges Assertion by Money Manager That He Was Naïve in Finance," *Richmond Times Dispatch*, March 19, 2008, B-9.

43. "Gilmore Led Bear Stearns-Subsidiary," B-9.

44. Bob Lewis, "Warner Talks Unity; Gilmore Rips Warner," *The Associated Press State & Local Wire*, April 16, 2008. Available at Lexus Nexus Academic Universe (accessed October 16, 2008).

45. Lewis, "Warner Talks Unity."

46. Seth McLauthlin, "Gilmore Pledges to Fight Oil Prices; Tries to Woo Voters to GOP," *Washington Times*, April 29, 2008, B01. Available Lexus Nexus Academic (accessed October 17, 2008).

47. Tyler Whitley, "Warner Handily Outraising Gilmore; Democrat Has More than $5 million on Hand for Senate Race," *Richmond Times Dispatch*, May 23, 2008, B-10. Available at Lexus Nexus Academic Universe (accessed October 17, 2008).

48. Olympia Meola, "Warner, Gilmore Talk Energy; Senate Candidates Agree on Lifting Offshore-Drilling Ban, but Differ Otherwise," *Richmond Times Dispatch*, June 19, 2008, B-3. Available at Lexus Nexus Academic (accessed October 18, 2008).

49. Jeff E. Schapiro, "Gilmore Jokes about Drilling for Oil in His Own Backyard," *Richmond Times Dispatch*, June 21, 2008, B-3. Available Lexus Nexus Academic Universe (accessed October 18, 2008).

50. Bob Lewis, "Debate Focuses on Trust, Energy Policy," *The Associated Press State & Local Wire*, July 19, 2008. Available at Lexus Nexus Academic Universe (accessed October 18, 2008).

51. Tyler Whitley, "Gilmore Stumps for Support in Henrico, He's Trailing Warner in Polls, Money, but Says Republicans Back Him," *Richmond Times Dispatch*, August 21, 2008, B-1. Available at Lexus Nexus Academic Universe (accessed October 18, 2008).

52. Bob Lewis, "Group Says Warner Spurned TV Senate Debate Invite," *The Associated Press State & Local Wire*, August 28, 2008. Available at Lexus Nexus Academic Universe (accessed October 18, 2008).

53. Tim Craig, "Gilmore Campaign Takes Its Fight to TV; Commercial Doesn't Air in N.Va.," *Washington Post*, September 8, 2008, B05.

54. Craig, "Gilmore Campaign."

55. Jeff E. Schapiro, "Senate Campaign Picks Up; Gilmore Begins TV Ad, Warner Garners Two Endorsements," *Richmond Times Dispatch*, September 9, 2008, B-6.

56. Warren Fiske, "Senate Candidates Launch Attack Ads on TV," *Virginian-Pilot*, September 10, 2008, B4.

57. Editorial, "Dodging Debate; Why Won't Mark Warner Agree to a Statewide Televised Debate with Jim Gilmore?" *Washington Post*, September 10, 2008, A14.

58. Dale Eisman and Warren Fiske, "Candidates Level Personal Attacks in Second Debate," *Virginian-Pilot*, September 19, 2008, A1.

59. Bob Lewis, "Gilmore Pummels Warner on Bailout; Last Senate Campaign Debate," *Washington Times*, October 4, 2008, A05. Available at Lexus Nexus Academic Universe (accessed October 18, 2008).

60. Lewis, "Gilmore Pummels Warner."

61. Tim Craig and Jennifer Agiesta, "Warner Leads Gilmore by 30 Points, Poll Finds; GOP-Held U.S. Senate Seat from Va. Is at Stake," *Washington Post*, September 24, 2008, B01. Available at Lexus Nexus Academic Universe (accessed October 18, 2008).

62. Bob Lewis, "Warner Airs New Ad with Fat Cash Edge over Gilmore," *The Associated Press State & Local Wire*, July 15, 2008. Available at Lexus Academic Universe (accessed October 18, 2008).

63. Youtube.com, hk.youtube.com/watch?v=vdXfwaf2ncs (accessed October 19, 2008.

64. Jeff Mellott, "Promise Keeper: Gilmore: Senatorial Vote about Trust," *Daily News Record*, October 16, 2008, A1-A3.

65. Nuckols, "Warner Condemns, 'Disrespectful' Ad Republican-Funded Radio Spot Accusing Him of Intolerance Is Inaccurate, He Says," *Virginian-Pilot*, October 31, 2001, B6. Available in Lexus Nexus Academic Universe (accessed October 19, 2008).

66. Virginia Election Results: United States Senate. Gilmore won Amelia County, Augusta County, Hanover County, Powhatan County, and Rockingham County.

67. Virginia Election Results: United States Senate. Poquoson.

68. Virginia Election Results: United States Senate. McCain won the following counties: Accomack, Alleghany, Amelia, Appomattox, Augusta, Bath, Bedford, Bland, Botetourt, Buchanan, Campbell, Carroll, Charlotte, Chesterfield, Craig, Culpeper, Cumberland, Dickenson, Dinwiddle, Fauquier, Floyd, Fluvanna, Franklin, Frederick, Giles, Gloucester, Goochland, Grayson, Greene, Halifax, Hanover, Henry, Highland, Isle of Wright, James City, King George, King William, Lancaster, Lee, Louisa, Luneburg, Madison, Mathews, Mecklenburg, Middlesex, New Kent, Northumberland, Nottoway, Orange, Page, Patrick, Pittsylvania, Prince George, Pulaski, Rappahannock, Richmond, Roanoke, Rockbridge, Rockingham, Russell, Scott, Shenandoah, Smyth, Southampton, Spotsylvania, Stafford, Tazewell, Warren, Washington, Wise, Wythe, and York. McCain also won the following cities: Bedford, Bristol, Buena Vista, Chesapeake, Colonial Heights, Galax, Lynchburg, Norton, Poquoson, Salem, Virginia Beach, Waynesboro.

13

Alaska Senate Race (Begich v. Stevens)

Scandal, Upset, and the End of an Era

Gerald McBeath and Amy Lauren Lovecraft

Mark Begich
Age: 46
Sex: Male
Race: Caucasian
Religion: Catholic
Education: No college degree
Occupation: Mayor of Anchorage (2003–2009)
Political Experience: Mayor of Anchorage (2003–2009); Anchorage Municipal Assembly (1989–1999)

Ted Stevens
Age: 85
Sex: Male
Race: Caucasian
Religion: Episcopalian
Education: L.L.B. (Harvard University, 1950); B.A. (University of California, Los Angeles, 1947)
Occupation: United States senator (1968–2009)
Political Experience: United States Senate (1968–2009); Alaska State House of Representatives (1965–1968)

In November 2008, Anchorage mayor Mark Begich narrowly defeated Ted Stevens, the longest serving Republican U.S. senator in American history. In this chapter we treat four topics—characteristics of the state, the candidates, campaign issues, and campaign strategy—which explain this unusual election result, considered to be one of the biggest upsets of the 2008 election.

CHARACTERISTICS OF THE STATE

Party Balance

Alaska is a nominally Republican state, and has voted Republican in every presidential election since 1968. However, in state politics Democrats have been competitive. For the 26th Alaska Legislature (elected in 2008), this is reflected in a state senate which is evenly divided between the parties and managed by a bipartisan coalition with a Democratic majority. The State House, on the other hand, has been under Republican control since the 1994 election, although the size of the majority has declined since then.

Voter registration rules in Alaska do not require identification with a political party; in fact, providing any information about political affiliation is optional. As noted in table 13.1, Republicans have a sizable edge over Democrats in the state, but nonpartisan and undeclared voters are a majority of registrants, some 53 percent.

Voting and Electoral History

Alaska entered the union in 1959 as a Democratic state. Its first governor, Bill Egan, and federal representatives were Democrats, and this party also controlled the State Senate (control of the State House alternated between parties). In 1966, Wally Hickel defeated Egan for the governorship. This election marked the decline of Democratic Party dominance in the state. As mentioned, from the 1968 presidential election to the present, Alaska has voted Republican (McCain/Palin won 59.5 percent of the presidential vote in 2008). Republican presidential

Table 13.1 Alaska Statewide Voter Registration

Affiliation	Number	Percentage
Alaska Independence Party	13,828	2.8
Democratic	77,036	15.5
Libertarian	6,926	1.3
Republican	127,446	25.7
Nonpartisan	77,582	15.6
Undeclared	185,320	37.3
Green	2.926	0.6
Republican Moderates	3,841	0.8
Veterans	1,922	0.4
Total	496,828	100.0

Source: Alaska Division of Elections, November 26, 2008.

tickets—with stronger emphases on economic development, less concern for environmental issues, and greater protection of gun ownership—have been more attractive to Alaskans than Democratic ones. So too, when oil began flowing through the pipeline in 1977, the population of the state became wealthier. The modernization of the state attracted professionals who were likely to vote Republican, and Alaska's large military population supported Republicans too.

The state's congressional delegation mirrored party competition from 1966 to 1980. The Senate seat originally held by Ernest Gruening remained under Democratic control until 1980, when Frank Murkowski defeated Democrat Mike Gravel. The seat held by Democrat Bob Bartlett until his death in 1968 fell to the Republicans when Governor Hickel appointed Ted Stevens to fill the vacancy in 1968. The House seat was held by both Democrats and Republicans until Don Young won a special election in 1973 to replace Democrat Nick Begich (declared missing, later presumed dead, after a plane crash), and he has held this seat since then. From the 1980 election to 2008, the state's delegation had only Republicans, reflecting the increased power of incumbency in congressional seats nationally.

In Alaska's fifty years of statehood, it has had Democratic governors for twenty-eight years and Republican governors for twenty-two (including Wally Hickel's second term from 1990 to 1994, even though formally he ran for the office under the Alaska Independence Party label). The state constitution limits governors to two four-year terms, and the main reason Bill Egan lost the 1966 race to Hickel was the perception that he had served two terms already and was ineligible. In fact, Egan had been ill at the start of his first term, and the secretary of state substituted for him; technically he remained eligible. Only two governors have served eight years since then—moderate Republican Jay Hammond (1974-1982) and moderate Democrat Tony Knowles (1994-2002). Two governors lost primary elections while pursuing reelection (Democrat Bill Sheffield and Republican Frank Murkowski). Two governors—Democrat Steve Cowper and Republican Wally Hickel—declined to seek reelection to a further term. Overall, there is a Republican bias to recent gubernatorial elections, but parties are weak in Alaska and attractive candidates and campaigns on issues and personality keep the office competitive.

In just one period of Alaskan statehood did a single party exercise relatively long-term dominance in the State Legislature. The 1994 election brought Republican control to both house and senate. Enabled by "bush (rural) Democrats" who supported Republican legislative leadership, the party held nearly veto-proof majorities until after the 2006 election. However, for most of the earlier period, bipartisan coalitions ran one or both houses, a pattern reappearing in 2007. In short, both parties are competitive at the state level, which is helped because, more than partisan loyalty, these elections emphasize what legislators can do to help constituents. Facilitating party competition is a relatively high turnover rate in the State Legislature. For most politicians, attending the legislative sessions in Juneau (the only state capital not accessible by road) is inconvenient, and the perks of legislative service (the part-time salary was just $24,000 until it doubled in 2009) are an insufficient incentive for long service.

Demographic Character of the Electorate

Alaska's population in 2008 stood at about 683,000. The average annual growth rate was 1.1 percent in 2000–2007, slightly above the average U.S. growth rate. Natural increase is responsible for most of this population change. While Alaska has the highest population turnover of the American states, the rate of transiency has declined significantly since statehood.

The oil industry is the single-most important facet of the Alaska economy, and taxes on oil/gas production and royalties supply 85 percent of revenue for the state's operating budget. About 10 percent of Alaskans work for the oil producers and support contractors. Indirect effects of spending by oil employees create an additional 29,000 jobs. Both state and local governments distribute oil revenues to communities in the form of services and government positions (e.g., school teachers), and they comprise another 20 percent of the workforce. Alaska also is highly dependent on federal expenditures for the four large military installations in the state, for the management of federal lands covering more than 60 percent of Alaska, for off-shore fisheries management, and for distribution of federal payments and services to Alaska Natives, seniors, and disabled residents. Civilian and military federal employees make up nearly 20 percent of the state's population.

The per capita income of Alaskans in 2006 was $37,271, up 5 percent from the previous year, and the twenty-eighth highest growth rate among states. Yet the state has large pockets of rural poverty. One in ten Alaskans is below the poverty line. Notwithstanding directed efforts to develop rural areas where one-third of Alaskans live, in 2006 some 34 percent of Alaska villages still lacked running water and waste disposal.

Alaska Natives, at 16 percent of the population, remain the state's largest minority. Although most continue to live near areas settled thousands of years ago, rural migration to the cities, especially of young women, has increased in recent years. Numbers of other ethnic/racial minorities—blacks, Latinos, Asians—collectively approach those of Alaska Natives. Caucasians, however, comprise 70 percent of the state's population. Education levels resemble those of other states, with 60 percent having graduated from high school and taken some post-baccalaureate work, graduated from college, or gained a graduate degree. Finally, the median age of the state is rising (6.6 percent are sixty-five or older) and the sex disparity (52 percent male) is narrowing. In these two respects, the Alaska population increasingly resembles that of other states.[1]

Key Voting Blocs

Alaska is America's largest state in area, and it has distinct biogeographical regions—rural areas of the north and west, whose population is mostly Alaska Native; the Interior centering on Fairbanks, but with many road system towns and Native villages; South-central with the state's largest city, Anchorage, and extending north to the expanding bedroom areas of Matanuska-Susitna Borough (Mat-Su) and south to the Kenai Peninsula; and the Southeast, the panhandle, most closely resembling the terrain and climate of the Pacific Northwest.

Regional differences explain most conflict in the State Legislature and, because they are overlaid with differences of ethnicity and income, they figure in elections to state and federal office. One distinct voting bloc is Southeast Alaska. Juneau, the capital city, is the Southeast's largest city and historically it has voted Democratic. Rural Alaska, populated by Alaska Natives and small numbers of school teachers, health, social and government administrators, also historically has voted Democratic.

Anchorage has the state's most diversified economy and has been competitive politically. Fairbanks, although home to the state's flagship university campus, is a blue-collar town, and typically leans Republican. The state's fastest growing region, Mat-Su, also is the most conservative. (It is the home and political base of Governor Sarah Palin.) Other Republican strongholds are the Kenai Peninsula and North Pole (south of Fairbanks).

Alaska is a strong union state; unions represent construction trades and most public sector jobs. About one quarter of the state's population is union-affiliated; spread throughout the state, union members and their families usually vote Democratic.

Major Urban Areas and Employment/Occupational Characteristics

Anchorage has about 40 percent of the state's population. It is the state's commercial center, and offers a larger profile of job opportunities than elsewhere. The state's second largest city is Fairbanks. Its commercial occupations are numerous but less diverse than those in Anchorage. Dominating its economy are the university, the nonprofit sector (including the hospital), and military installations at Fort Wainwright and Eielson Air Force Base. Juneau is the state's third largest city and, as mentioned, a government town. In contrast, rural/bush Alaska has few full-time jobs. A majority of the Native Alaska population is reliant on subsistence hunting/fishing/gathering for sustenance.

THE CANDIDATES

Ted Stevens

Senator Stevens was born in Indianapolis but after his parents divorced, he moved to California where he completed high school. In World War II, he served in the Army Air Corps for three years, and flew missions over China for the Flying Tigers. He received two Distinguished Flying Crosses and air medals for his bravery. After the war, Stevens finished his baccalaureate degree at UCLA and a law degree at Harvard. Then, in 1953, he moved to Alaska where he entered private practice in Fairbanks and then worked as a U.S. attorney (and later, in Juneau, as legislative counsel). During the later years of the Eisenhower Administration, Stevens was assistant to the secretary of the Interior and solicitor of the Department of the Interior. Returning to Alaska in 1960, he established a private practice in Anchorage. He ran unsuccessfully against Ernest Gruening for the U.S. Senate seat in 1962, gaining 42 percent of the vote. In the 1964 state elections, he won a seat in the State House. In his second term, he became majority leader of the house.

Governor Wally Hickel appointed Stevens to the U.S. Senate in 1968 after the death of Bob Bartlett, and he faced voters to retain this seat in a 1970 special election. At his second election—for a full six-year senate term in 1972—he won 77 percent of the vote. In succeeding elections he won by landslide figures—an average of 74 percent. In his most recent race, the 2002 election, he defeated a virtually unknown Democrat by 78 percent of the ballots.

Stevens's success at the polls had its roots in his singular legislative accomplishments for Alaska and his budgetary prowess. Early in his Senate career, Stevens angled for committees of greatest relevance to Alaska, gaining positions and, over time, seniority, on both Senate Appropriations and Commerce, Science, and Transportation committees. He figured in each of the major battles of Alaska's developing statehood: the fight in Congress for statehood and the Statehood Act (1958), the Alaska Native Claims Settlement Act (ANCSA, 1971), the Trans-Alaska Pipeline Authorization Act (1973), the Alaska National Interest Lands Conservation Act (ANILCA, 1980), and their amendments; and he led the state's efforts to open the Arctic National Wildlife Refugee (ANWR) for oil/gas exploration and development. Only in the latter case was he unsuccessful. Stevens' accomplishments extended to several areas of national policy, for example, protecting the American offshore fisheries through the Magnuson-Stevens Fisheries Conservation Act (1976; most recently revised in 2007).

Stevens's national reputation, perhaps unfairly, is based on his sophisticated use of the earmark process to "bring home the bacon" to Alaskans. Just in the last decade alone, he was responsible for more than $10 billion in special appropriations, bringing health clinics, sanitation systems, libraries, schools, research dollars, roads, harbors, airports—to nearly every community in the state. Alaskans call him "Uncle Ted" for his unsurpassed ability to shower federal dollars on the state of Alaska, and during this period, in most years, special federal appropriations (on a per capita basis) to Alaska outdistanced those of the closest other states by a factor of two to one. Groups such as Taxpayers for Common Sense and Citizens against Government Waste, and critics in the Senate such as John McCain, call Stevens the "King of Pork." The *Almanac of American Politics* refers to Stevens as "a philanthropist operating in the Senate Appropriations Committee."[2]

Stevens has the quick temper of a trial lawyer. In the Senate, he has been a combative advocate for Alaska's needs, who threatens retaliation when others cross his path, even wearing an "Incredible Hulk" tie to let opponents known he means business. Often appearing like a crusty old curmudgeon, for more than a year he declined to give interviews to the state's largest newspaper, the *Anchorage Daily News*, when it printed unflattering remarks (including verbatim transcripts of what he'd said on the Senate floor). Yet few can doubt Stevens's deep love for Alaska, and the care and affection he directs to Alaskans treated unjustly by government agencies and the disadvantaged.

Mark Begich

Begich was born in Anchorage and has spent nearly all his life in Alaska. His father, Nick Begich, was Alaska's Congressman in 1972 when his small airplane disappeared in the Gulf of Alaska during the reelection campaign. After graduation from high school, Begich did maintenance work and managed the family's forty-unit apartment complex, and his career has been in independent small businesses. At twenty-six (in 1988), he won a seat on the Anchorage municipal assembly, serving on it for ten years. He ran twice unsuccessfully for mayor, but in 2003 was elected to the position, and won reelection in 2006.

As mayor, Begich expanded growth of city services, especially in police, firefighters, and education. Under his watch, the city erased a $33 million budget deficit, and the economy grew 9,000 jobs. Begich also diversified the city's tax base, yet critics complain that tax rates and fees increased greatly.

Personally, Begich is low-keyed, respectful, and an experienced listener. He took a pragmatic approach to governing the state's largest city, emphasized inclusiveness, and earned good marks by the media for effectiveness.

CAMPAIGN ISSUES

Had the Department of Justice's Office of Public Integrity and the FBI not investigated oil field services company VECO in 2006–2007, no credible challenger would have opposed Ted Stevens for reelection in 2008, and he likely would have won the race with a vote count near 80 percent. However, the 2007 investigation of his Girdwood home, followed a year later by an indictment on seven felony charges, made his reelection bid competitive. This was the main issue of the campaign, but it is closely related to a second issue, the length of the Stevens's incumbency.

Felony Indictment and Conviction

VECO was a multibillion-dollar oil field services corporation, headquartered in Anchorage, but doing most of its business on the Alaskan North Slope. VECO's president Bill Allen was a long-time insider in Alaska politics. He used VECO dollars to influence the state's political officials to support continued corporate investment in oil exploration/development and construction of a natural gas pipeline from Prudhoe Bay to the Midwest. Allen's objective throughout was to ensure continued prosperity for his firm through oil industry investments and jobs for Alaskans. His primary methods were influencing elections and lobbying (and bribing) public officials. For the former purpose, Allen funneled $400,000 into Alaska elections, accomplished through giving bonuses to VECO executives who then made coordinated contributions to candidates favoring VECO and Big Oil interests. His firm also organized productive fund-raisers for favored candidates, and he formed very close personal relationships with legislators and officials to suborn them to the interests of VECO.

In 2006, the FBI targeted VECO because of Allen's connections with the self-styled "corrupt bastards club," composed of legislators who were suspected of unethical conduct. When Allen and his vice president, Mike Smith, were confronted with evidence of guilt, they cooperated with investigators and agreed to wiretaps of their phones and video surveillance of the VECO suite where deals were made. This led to investigations of six current or former legislators and the former governor's chief of staff. By the end of 2007, the chief of staff and three legislators had pled guilty or been tried and convicted on charges of bribery and corruption. In July 2007, the ongoing investigation reached Senator Stevens, a long-time friend of Allen, concerning extensive renovations VECO employees performed on his home from 1999 to 2006. In late July 2007, Stevens's Girdwood home was raided by FBI agents, which was the first occasion when the residence of a sitting U.S. senator was searched.

During the year after the investigation, Stevens said little about it, prompting Governor Palin (who had come to office in an insurgent campaign in 2006 emphasizing the need for ethics reform) to ask that he explain himself. Stevens declined to do so because he was the subject of an ongoing criminal investigation and did not want any remarks he made about the case to be used against him. He filed for reelection in February 2008, but the investigation had already reduced his approval ratings to the forties, and opponents saw him as vulnerable. Mark Begich had garnered support in Alaska and from the Democratic Senatorial Campaign Committee in Washington, DC, for a race against Stevens. In March, he filed for the Democratic nomination.

In late July 2008, less than a month before the August 26 primary, Stevens was indicted on seven counts of failing to disclose gifts from 1999 to 2006, totaling over $250,000. Most of the charges pointed to the difference between what Stevens paid and what his Girdwood home renovations cost, but they also included the value of a new car for his daughter for whom he traded an old model, and other smaller items. The accounts were based on information collected by the FBI and IRS, and it included testimony from Bill Allen and taped conversations between Allen and Stevens. Legally, Stevens's law team headed by experienced Washington, DC-based counsel Brendan Sullivan, sought a speedy trial, and one held in Anchorage, so that Stevens would be able to campaign. Politically, Stevens prepared for the primary election where he faced two opponents—Dave Cuddy and Vic Vickers. Cuddy, a former Anchorage bank president, had run against Stevens in the 1996 primary, gaining less than a quarter of the votes while spending more than $1 million. Vickers was a Florida lawyer and college professor who registered in Alaska only in January 2008. His media campaign blasted Stevens as corrupt and arrogant, but observers regarded Vickers as a carpetbagger (and some called him a Democratic plant). Stevens won 64 percent of the vote and spent less than the $2 million used in his opponents' campaigns.

District Court judge Emmet Sullivan granted Stevens's request for a speedy trial, but declined to change the venue from DC to Anchorage. Thus, from September 22 when the trial began until the verdict was rendered on October 27, Stevens remained in Washington, DC, and this forced a change in campaign strategy (discussed below). The jury was composed mostly of black women, and the defense suspected they believed all politicians were crooks. So too, at the outset of the trial, the prosecution had not shared evidence with the defense, which caused the defense to call for a mistrial, a call it repeated when the prosecution allowed a witness to return to Alaska without testifying. Judge Sullivan considered the defense objections, and castigated the prosecution for the sloppiness of its preparation, but allowed the trial to continue.

Little standard campaigning occurred during the three weeks of presentation and cross-examination of witnesses, yet Alaskans paid close attention to media accounts, which added substance to discussion of the senator's integrity. The prosecution's case was based on physical evidence of the extensive renovation of Stevens's Girdwood residence, direct testimony of workmen who had participated, Bill Allen's statements of his relationship with Stevens, e-mail and written evidence to the effect that Stevens knew that work more expensive than he had paid for had been done and gifts received that he knew were not recorded as such. Particularly damning was a taped conversation in which Stevens told Allen he believed they had done nothing wrong but raised the possibility they could go to jail if they were not careful: "They're not going to shoot us. It's not Iraq. . . . [At worst] we might have to pay a fine and serve a little time in jail."[3]

The defense produced evidence that Stevens wanted to pay for every renovation to his property but had not been billed, and that the "gifts" were items he did not want and had asked to be removed. His wife, Catherine, said she paid the bills for the Girdwood home and Stevens said he had been in the residence only twenty times or so in the seven-year period under review. The defense also called character witnesses—Senator Daniel Inouye (D-HI), Stevens's closest friend in the Senate and chair of Senate Appropriations, who vouched for Stevens's integrity, as did Senator Orrin Hatch (R-UT). An even more compelling character witness was former general and Secretary of State Colin Powell, who visibly impressed the jury. Stevens took the stand in his own defense, but observers believed his combative responses "verged on the contemptuous," and did not aid his case.[4]

Jury deliberations were irregular as well. The foreman sent the judge a note requesting a recess because one juror had become obstreperous. Then, a juror left the panel because of a death in the family. When she could not be located (she had lied about the death and had traveled to California to bet in a horse race), the judge replaced her with an alternate. This rearrangement quickened the process, and on October 27, the jury found Stevens guilty on all seven counts. Stevens told the press: "I will fight this unjust verdict with every ounce of energy I have. I am innocent. . . . I ask that Alaskans and my Senate colleagues stand with me as I pursue my rights. I remain a candidate for the United States Senate."[5]

Challenger Begich did not comment much on the Stevens indictment, and at the conviction, he simply said it was a sad day for Alaska. Initially, Governor Palin stated she was sure the senator would do "what's right for the people of Alaska." But now she was the Republican Party's vice presidential candidate, and the next day she followed John McCain in calling on Stevens to resign. Chair of the Republican Senatorial Campaign Committee, John Ensign (R-NV), and Senate minority leader Mitch McConnell (R-KY) also urged Stevens to drop out of the race, fearing adverse effects of the felony conviction on other close races nationwide. In Alaska, polls showed that Begich led Stevens eight points (52 percent to 44 percent) after the verdict was announced.

Incumbency versus Change

A second and not unrelated campaign issue was the length of Stevens's service, and whether it was time for a change. While the indictment and conviction of Stevens were the subtext of the opposition, Stevens's long and highly effective career in the Senate were the main text of his campaign and support. This led supporters to trivialize the charges against him, so as to make them appear inconsequential to voters. The related tactic was to accuse the prosecution of bias and incompetence, which denied justice to the senator. The day after his conviction, Stevens's legal team requested the attorney general to investigate misconduct of federal prosecutors, and set in motion an appeal of the conviction. The Stevens campaign organization said: "Alaskans should decide who our senator is. It should not be up to 12 people who have never been to Alaska to decide who represents us in Washington, D.C."[6]

Other Issues

A comparison of the issue positions of Stevens and Begich shows few significant differences. They agreed on the need for continued earmarks, on government intervention in the markets to protect families, to continued spending on the National Missile Defense System in Alaska, on more effective drug control policies, on improvement of federal emergency management capabilities, and on support of federal contracting preferences for Native Alaskans. They both sought federal assistance for the natural gas pipeline development, and for opening ANWR for oil and gas development. Like most Alaska Democrats, Begich is a supporter of gun owners' rights. Begich and Stevens disagreed, along partisan lines, on terms for the extension of the Bush tax cuts, on U.S. strategy in Iraq, on issues of Native sovereignty in Alaska, and on reauthorization of the No Child Left Behind (NCLB) Act.[7] Begich did attempt to differentiate himself from Stevens by discussing issues including climate change, health care, and renewable energy resources that had received little attention from the state's congressional delegation to date.

CAMPAIGN STRATEGY

Media, Image, and Advertising

Both campaigns spent most resources on TV spots, followed by some use of radio, and then advertising in newspapers and direct mail. Of course, the Internet played a role as well. TV spots took the lion's share of the media budgets of both campaign organizations. The Stevens ads emphasized testimonials on his established effectiveness and what it has meant to Alaska's development. Media images pictured the senator at work, and often in hearings and other congressional settings, as well as in conversations with constituents. Well-known Alaska Republicans, such as former state senator John Binkley, also did several TV ads. Begich's spots emphasized his record of success as Anchorage's mayor, and also pictured him in issue contexts (for example, near a gas handling facility). Wearing outdoor gear, the spots featured his relative youth and vigor.

Both candidates ran positive media campaigns and expressed forward-looking messages. Other groups stirred negative vibrations. The Democratic Senatorial Campaign Committee produced many ads on the Stevens indictment and trial, and compared his "wrong" ethical choices with "wrong" votes on issues of concern to labors, minorities, and families. The TV ads ended with the tag line "It's not about Alaska anymore," and accused Stevens of helping himself and family members.[8] Stevens received no media support from the National Republican Senatorial Campaign Committee, and his campaign staff often railed against the "outside special interests seeking to buy Senator Stevens' seat."[9] Both candidates took advantage of free coverage by TV and radio, but the indictment and conviction set the terms of these exchanges.

Originally, the candidates had agreed to meet at seven TV debates. The trial in DC reduced this to one debate on public TV in Anchorage, on October 30. The debate was polite and restrained. Begich asked Stevens whether he regretted his relationship with Bill Allen and VECO, and the senator allowed that he had trusted this relationship more than he ought to have. However, he conveyed far greater knowledge of Alaska policy needs from the Congress, and greater experience in their representation, than the mayor. Begich complimented the senator on his contributions to the state. He did not confront him directly on the jury's verdict (partly because Stevens outlined the steps he would take to prove his innocence). No panel of speech experts evaluated the debate, but to the authors, Stevens was the clear winner.

The day before the election, the Stevens campaign aired a two-minute "informercial" on TV statewide. It began with a former federal prosecutor who debunked the trial and verdict, and then Stevens said:

> I know that I'm innocent. In America, everyone has the right to a fair trial and an appeal because some times innocent men are found guilty. This is one of those times. . . . I have been and will continue to be effective for Alaska. . . . When you vote on Tuesday, ask yourself: who will fight for Alaskans to provide affordable access to health care, lower energy costs, and work hard to ensure a bright future during these uncertain economic times? Experience counts and empty promises just don't cut it.[10]

This expensive spot aimed to garner support on each of the issues identified above: (1) to minimize Stevens's felony conviction; (2) to register the importance of Stevens's experience; and (3) to implicitly criticize Begich's ability to deliver on any of the campaign promises he made.

Newspapers perhaps play a greater role in Alaska elections than in the other states, because there are only three TV markets—Anchorage, Fairbanks, and Juneau—and other parts of the state receive relays from these or public TV which does not carry political messages. Both candidates advertised in the state's three largest papers—the *Anchorage Daily News (ADN)*, *Fairbanks Daily News-Miner (FDNM)*, and the *Juneau Empire (JE)*. Toward the end of the campaign, campaign organizations ran full-page testimonial ads. Both the *ADN* and *JE* endorsed Begich, which was not unexpected. The *FDNM* claims that it does not endorse candidates for office; however, in the days leading up to the election, this journal, whose former publisher was a close friend of Stevens in the battles for statehood, urged voters to consider the senator's experience and contributions to Alaska before being swayed by the indictment.

A great deal of advertising appeared in residents' postal boxes during the campaign. The campaigns were responsible for part of this, but affiliated groups did most of the work. For Republicans, the Alaska Republican Party sent several flyers. Notices from Democratic affiliates were far more numerous in this election race: the AFL-CIO, Alaska Democratic Party, and the Public Employees Association (APEA). At this level, the advertisements tended to be more negative than positive.

Finally, both campaigns took ample advantage of the Internet by developing attractive websites (Begich.com and TedStevens2008.com). These introduced the candidates and described their issue positions. The Stevens website had relatively detailed policy statements on a range of issues in which the senator had been engaged. Begich's positions were general and lacked detail. A fair number of bloggers for a sparsely populated state followed the campaign, offered opinions, and solicited commentary. These, too, focused on the indictment and conviction and also evoked images of stability and change. They produced little issue discussion.

Overall, both candidates projected positive images and avoided attack ads and negative campaigning. However, because the Democratic Senatorial Campaign Committee targeted Stevens and handsomely funded its independent attack ads, and because the Alaska Democratic Party and labor unions saw a rare chance to crack the Republican congressional delegation, Begich was able to present himself as a positive agent of change without getting his hands dirty by attacking Stevens directly. Stevens's problem was partly that his reelection campaign occurred in a year when more Republican than Democratic senators were up for reelection and partly because the indictment and then the conviction made him a political leper whom national Republicans wanted to avoid. No more telling of this pattern was Governor Palin's silence on the Begich-Stevens race throughout the general election campaign, after Stevens had lavishly congratulated her performance in Ohio when she joined the Republican presidential ticket in late July.

In the view of an experienced observer of Alaska politics, the decision of the Stevens campaign organization to avoid what might be perceived as negative campaigning cost him the election. At no point did the Stevens campaign compare the background and political experience of the two candidates, which would have found Begich (absent even a college degree or any experience above the municipal level) lacking. Nor did the Stevens campaign examine rises in costs of Anchorage government to taxpayers, when the national economy had slumped.[11] Perhaps this decision to go soft on Begich denotes a lack of aggressiveness, an aging of Stevens himself, and his political organization. Surely, the campaign gave no reason to voters as to why they should *not* vote for Begich. But perhaps this decision—or nondecision—was a reflection of Stevens's personal distaste for going negative in campaigns.

Finance

The 2008 senate race between Begich and Stevens was one of the most expensive in state history. By late October, the Stevens campaign had reported raising $4.98 million and the Begich campaign $3.5 million, an apparent gap of $1.5 million favoring Stevens. However, Stevens had leftover dollars from previous campaigns. Begich did not file for the office until March 2008 and began with a zero balance.

The Democratic Party nationally made $2.3 million in independent expenditures in support of the Begich candidacy, and party coordinated spending and contributions added an additional $191,372 to the campaign. The combined total of $6 million exceeded Stevens's funding by one million. The total funding outpaced the $11 million raised by Tony Knowles and Lisa Murkowski in their 2004 senate race.

Because the Stevens campaign received a waiver from federal reporting rules, the amount of campaign funds diverted to legal expenses was not known until January 2009. The Stevens campaign received relatively more contributions from both in-state and out-of-state contributors than Begich. Although corporate PACs (for Stevens) and labor PACs (for Begich) donated heavily to the campaigns, individual contributions comprised nearly two-thirds of the total amounts raised by the candidates.

Grass Roots

Alaska campaigns for U.S. House and Senate seats invariably feature a strong grassroots element, because in this sparsely populated state, people believe they should be able to meet and greet candidates personally during the election season. Begich began at a disadvantage in this respect, because his campaign did not launch until eight months before the election. Also, he had much lower name recognition in other parts of the state than in his home base, Anchorage. For these reasons, he campaigned throughout Alaska with a focus on the Interior and rural areas. He was helped by the rising visibility of Democrats as the Obama campaign established five field offices in Alaska after winning the Democratic presidential caucuses in February.

For Stevens, the trial in Washington, DC, forced a change in grassroots strategy. His campaign workers plastered urban neighborhoods with yard signs and cars with bumper stickers to show visible support for the senator. The campaign set up 200 central sites to coordinate and disseminate messages. Then, the senator's campaign placed automatic calls to supporters, which they patched through to "town halls" conducted by the senator after the close of daily sessions during the month-long trial process. Finally, the campaign used the conviction and Stevens's return to Alaska to stage large rallies in Fairbanks, Anchorage, Kenai, and Mat-Su, where hundreds of supporters gave him a hero's welcome.

Bases of Support

The highly competitive nature of the 2008 federal election mobilized the partisan base in Alaska. Stevens enjoyed support from most of the 25 percent of those identifying themselves as Republicans; Begich drew more than the 15 percent of Democratic identifiers. Statewide labor, the public employees especially, and the umbrella AFL-CIO took unequivocal positions supporting Begich over Stevens. (The AFL-CIO endorsed both Republican Don Young and Democrat Ethan Berkowitz in the U.S. House race.) Labor is unable to commit members to endorsed candidates in Alaska, because of the myriad personal connections local unions and their members have with legislators and federal candidates of both parties. Yet organizational support is critical to canvassing neighborhoods and last-minute get-out-the-vote work, such as holding candidate signs at busy intersections during the frigid temperatures of Election Day. In 2008, labor came through for Begich.

ELECTION RESULTS

On the night of the election, Stevens led Begich by 3,700 votes in a very close race. It seemed possible that for the first time in American history, a convicted felon would be returned to office. However, nearly one quarter of the votes had not yet been counted—upwards of 80,000 ballots. These included a very large number of early votes cast in the three week window up to November 4, before Stevens had returned to Alaska and reenergized campaign workers. The Democratic Party and candidates had urged voters to go to election offices early, both to avoid a predicted rush of Election Day voting and to ensure that less committed voters got to the polls. Because twenty-six early voters in the August primary election voted again on Election Day, the state Division of Elections determined to avoid fraud by verifying the authenticity of each ballot, which delayed ballot counting. Questioned ballots were numerous as well, and because they were from voters casting ballots out of their precincts, election officials needed to verify them too. Questioned ballots also tend to favor Democratic candidates.

Finally, more absentee ballots than normal made the final outcome hard to predict. Usually, absentee ballots in Alaska favor Republicans, because they are cast by those out-of-town on business trips or by seniors unable to get to the polls. In 2008 many military voters were on deployment, and votes from military installations counted on November 4 suggested that these votes would not necessarily favor Republican candidates. Like early votes, the absentee ballots were cast before movement toward Stevens developed in the final days of the campaign.

It took two weeks to count the remaining ballots, during which time the presidency and majorities in the House and Senate had been confirmed to be under Democratic control. The Senate Republican Steering Committee chair, Jim DeMint (R-SC), said that if Stevens were reelected, he would lose his seniority in the committees he sat on. Some senators discussed holding an Ethics Committee meeting preparatory to expelling Stevens from the senate, but his supporters said this would not transpire before the appeal had run its course.

The remaining ballots were counted in batches, and Stevens's lead soon disappeared. Begich pulled ahead and by November 18, when nearly all remaining ballots had been counted, Begich emerged the clear winner. With a turnout rate of 65 percent of registered voters for this race, Begich had 47.76 percent of the vote and Stevens 46.58 percent. (Three minor party candidates divided the remaining 5.66 percent of the vote.) Begich won with slightly more than 1 percent of the ballots, or 3,724 votes.

Begich's support came from Alaska's largest cities and smallest villages. He led in ten of the fifteen House districts representing Anchorage, four of the five House districts in Fairbanks, and four of the five districts in Southeast Alaska centering on Juneau. Begich also led in five of the six rural Alaska districts. Stevens took all four districts in Mat-Su, and four of six districts on the Kenai Peninsula. However, some of the leads for both candidates expressed fewer than 100 votes, and as the final count reveals, this election was very close in most parts of the state.

In a victory speech on November 19, Mark Begich said, "I am humbled and honored to serve Alaska in the United States Senate. It's been an incredible journey getting to this point. . . . Alaska has been in the midst of a generational shift—you could see it."[12] A day later, Stevens gave a gracious valedictory speech in the Senate chamber. He promised to pursue his appeal to prove his innocence, reflected on his service as America's longest-serving Republican senator, and said, "My mission in life is not completed." The audience in the galleries and on the floor erupted with applause, giving him a standing ovation.[13] Most Alaskans had bittersweet feelings about this changing of the guard and turn of fate.

POSTSCRIPT

Stevens's defense challenged the justice of the trial and outcome, and his appeal prevailed. In February 2009, the judge held Brenda Morris and another prosecutor in contempt of court. Then U.S. Attorney General Eric Holder announced that the Department of Justice found new evidence of prosecutorial misconduct and that the conviction should be voided. The following week Judge Sullivan dismissed all convictions and asked for a criminal investigation of the lead prosecutors. For some analysts and jurors, doubt remains about Stevens's innocence.

NOTES

1. Jerry McBeath, "Alaska," *Annual Western States Budget Review* (Center for Public Policy and Administration, University of Utah, May 2008), 4–5; Jerry McBeath, Matthew Berman, Jonathan Rosenberg, and Mary F. Ehrlander, *The Political Economy of Oil in Alaska* (Boulder, CO: Lynne Rienner, 2009), 6–7.
2. Michael Barone with Richard E. Cohen, *The Almanac of American Politics* (Washington, DC: National Journal Group, 2007), 78.
3. Neil A. Lewis, "Senator Warned a Friend That Jail Was a Risk," *New York Times*, October 7, 2008.
4. Neil A. Lewis, "Showdown Is Expected in Ethics Trial of Senator," *New York Times*, October 20, 2008.
5. *Fairbanks Daily News Miner*, October 28, 2008.
6. See www.TedStevens2008.com, October 27, 2008.
7. "Ballot Summary," *Fairbanks Daily News-Miner*, October 26, 2008.
8. *Fairbanks Daily News-Miner*, October 9, 2008.
9. See www.TedStevens2008.com, November 3, 2008.
10. Personal communication with David Dittman, November 28, 2008.
11. Paul Kane, "Ted Stevens Loses Battle for Alaska Senate Seat," *Washington Post*, November 19, 2008, A01.
12. Laurie Kellman, "Stevens Gives Last Senate Speech as Staffers Weep," *Washington Post*, November 20, 2008.
13. Kellman, "Stevens Gives Last Senate Speech."

14

Colorado Senate Race (Udall v. Schaffer)

A Campaign of Ideological Differences and a Changed Political Landscape

Robert J. Duffy, Kyle L. Saunders, and Andrew Kear

Mark Udall
Age: 58
Sex: Male
Race: Caucasian
Religion: Presbyterian
Education: B.A. (Williams College, 1972)
Occupation: Teacher
Political Experience: U.S. House of Representatives (1999–2008); Colorado General Assembly (1997–1998)

Bob Schaffer
Age: 46
Sex: Male
Race: Caucasian
Religion: Catholic
Education: B.A. (University of Dayton, 1984)
Occupation: Businessman
Political Experience: U.S. House of Representatives (1997–2002); Colorado State Senate (1987–1995)

CHARACTERISTICS OF THE STATE

Party Balance

Voter interest in Colorado was high in 2008, with the prospects of a competitive Senate race, several tight House races and, of course, a contested presidential election. Voter registration in 2008 exceeded 2004 figures by 100,000, or 3.2 percent. Going into the 2008 election, unaffiliated voters (1,069,294, up 4.3 percent from 2004) barely outnumbered registered Republicans (1,063,347, down 5 percent from 2004) and registered Democrats (1,051,643, up 12 percent from 2004).[1] As table 14.1 illustrates, voter registration figures have changed dramatically in recent years, as Republicans have lost what was once a commanding advantage in party registration and unaffiliated voters have become the largest bloc of the electorate in 2008.

Voting and Electoral History

Colorado has a mixed political history in recent decades, although it has typically favored Republicans over Democrats at the presidential level. For example, Colorado voted Republican in nine of the previous eleven elections, with the exceptions of Johnson in 1964 and Clinton in 1992 (see table 14.2). In elections for other statewide offices, though, Colorado voters have been more unpredictable, electing seventeen Democrats and twelve Republicans to the governorship in the last 100 years.[2]

As table 14.3 illustrates, Colorado's U.S. Senate elections have been competitive and rather cyclical. Until 1998, when Ben Nighthorse Campbell switched parties and became a Republican, there was a forty-year period when one of the state's Senate seats was held by a Democrat and the other by a Republican. Both seats were then held by Republicans until 2004, when Democrat Ken Salazar won the seat vacated by Campbell's retirement.[3]

By the late 1990s Colorado seemed solidly Republican. George W. Bush won the state fifty-one to fort-two in 2000 and in 2002 Governor Bill Owens, who won a close contest in 1998, was reelected by almost two-thirds of the electorate. That same year Senator Wayne Allard, after trailing in many polls, was reelected by a five-point margin. Republicans also retained control of the General Assembly, regained a majority in the state Senate,

Table 14.1. Colorado Voter Registration Trends, 2004–2008

	Democrats	Δ2008–2004	Republicans	Δ2008–2004	Unaffiliated	Δ2008–2004	Total	Δ2008–2004
2008	1,051,643	12%	1,063,347	-5%	1,069,294	4%	3,184,284	3%
2006	904,767		1,070,190		1,013,177		2,988,134	
2004	942,025		1,118,597		1,024,973		3,085,595	
2008 Proportion	33.0%		33.4%		33.6%			

Source: Colorado Secretary of State
NB: Increase in registration statewide of 200k from 2006 to 2008, 110k of that is Democratic

Table 14.2. Colorado Presidential Elections, 1964–2008

2008	Obama (D) 54	McCain (R) 45	
2004	Bush (R) 52	Kerry (D) 47	
2000	Bush (R) 51	Gore (D) 42	
1996	Dole (R) 46	Clinton (D) 44	
1992	Clinton (D) 40	Bush (R) 36	Perot (I) 23
1988	Bush (R) 53	Dukakis (D) 45	
1984	Reagan (R) 63	Mondale (D) 35	
1980	Reagan (R) 55	Carter (D) 31	Anderson (I) 11
1976	Ford (R) 54	Carter (D) 43	
1972	Nixon (R) 63	McGovern (D) 35	
1968	Nixon (R) 50	Humphrey (D) 41	
1964	Johnson (D) 61	Goldwater (R) 38	

Table 14.3. Colorado Senatorial Elections, 1968–2008

Year	Winner	Loser
2008	Udall (D) 53	Schaffer (R) 42
2004	Salazar (D) 51	Coors (R) 47
2002	Allard (R) 51	Strickland (D) 46
1998	Campbell (R) 62	Lamm (D) 35
1996	Allard (R) 51	Strickland (D) 46
1992	Campbell (D) 52	Considine (R) 43
1990	Brown (R) 56	Heath (D) 42
1986	Wirth (D) 50	Kramer (R) 48
1984	Armstrong (R) 64	Dick (D) 35
1980	Hart (D) 50	Buchanan (R) 49
1978	Armstrong (R) 59	Haskell (D) 40
1974	Hart (D) 57	Dominick (R) 40
1972	Haskell (D) 49	Allott (R) 48
1968	Dominick (R) 59	McNichols (D) 41

Source: Colorado Secretary of State
Note: Totals may not add up to 100 percent, as minor party candidates are not included; percentages rounded to nearest integer.

and picked up Colorado's newly created 7th Congressional District, designed to be competitive for both parties, by 121 votes.[4]

Beginning with the 2004 election, however, Democrats began to make dramatic gains at every level of government in the state. Although Bush did defeat John Kerry in the presidential race, Ken Salazar won a hotly contested race for the Senate, and his brother John captured the 3rd Congressional District seat.

Perhaps most surprisingly, the Democrats regained control of both chambers of the state legislature for the first time in forty years. The election results were a harbinger of a new and interesting time in Colorado politics.

The Democratic resurgence continued in 2006, when Democrats won almost every major contest. Bill Ritter won the race for governor handily, and Ed Perlmutter won an easy victory in an open seat race in the very competitive 7th District in the Denver suburbs. These results were, of course, partially due to a national political context caustic for Republicans, notably an increasingly unpopular president and an unpopular war. But Democrats also won because they chose socially moderate candidates who pledged to govern from the middle, while many of the defeated Republican candidates ran as staunch, ideological conservatives, emphasizing social issues like abortion and gay marriage. This was a formula that proved successful in 2008 as well.

Demographic Character of the Electorate

Although Colorado is a large state, 80 percent of its estimated 5 million residents live in the rapidly growing urban corridor along the Front Range of the Rocky Mountains, most within a two-hour drive of Denver. Colorado's population increased 50 percent from 1990 to the present; only 41.1 percent of current residents were born in-state. Colorado is relatively wealthy and educated, ranking seventh nationally in per capita income and second in percentage of college graduates. Like most states in the Mountain West, Colorado is disproportionately white (just under three-fourths of the population), but Hispanics constitute 17.1 percent of the voting-age population. In fact, Colorado has one of the highest proportions of Hispanic citizens of any U.S. state; only five states have a higher percentage. The state is also home to a large proportion of military veterans, which constitutes 14 percent of the population.[5]

Colorado's overall population, like many other western states, is predominantly Christian (65 percent). Of this group, a plurality (44 percent) are Protestants, 23 percent are evangelicals, 19 percent are Catholic, and nearly one third express no religious affiliation.[6] The Catholic population has increased in recent years as the Hispanic share of population has grown. The more conservative regions of Colorado, especially Colorado Springs, serve as the headquarters of numerous Christian groups, including Dr. James Dobson's Focus on the Family.

Major Urban Areas and Employment/Occupational Characteristics

Colorado's population is primarily an urban and suburban one; as mentioned above, around 80 percent of the state's population lives within a comfortable driving distance from Denver (see figure 14.1), a Democrat stronghold. Other areas of Democratic strength include the college towns

Figure 14.1. Population by Census Tract.
Source: U.S. Census Bureau, Census 2000 Summary File 1

of Fort Collins and Boulder, southern Colorado, and a few western ski resort counties. The Republicans are strongest in Colorado Springs, Greeley, some Denver suburbs, the rural eastern third of the state, and the more sparsely populated western slope.

Colorado's economy is diverse, but is focused primarily on white-collar technology and energy jobs. White-collar jobs comprise 64.5 percent of the Colorado workforce, while 21 percent are employed in blue-collar and 14.5 percent in gray-collar jobs. The public sector in Colorado is relatively small, constituting just 14 percent of the population. The most prevalent industrial sectors of Colorado's economy include professional (29 percent), trade (15 percent), and manufacturing (14 percent). Construction, finance, and agriculture also play important roles in Colorado's economy.[7]

THE CANDIDATES

Mark Udall

In many ways, Mark Udall seemed destined for a life in politics. His father, Morris "Mo" Udall, served in the U.S. Congress for thirty years, and his uncle Stewart Udall served in the House and as a secretary of Interior under Presidents John Kennedy and Lyndon Johnson. But as a young adult, Udall chose a different type of public service, working for twenty years as an educator and then as executive director of the Colorado Outward Bound School. He made his first run for public office in 1997, winning a seat in the Colorado State House. After serving just two years, Udall then ran for the U.S. House, and represented Colorado's 2nd Congressional District for five terms. While in the House, Udall was a member of the House Armed Services and Natural Resources Committees, served as chair of the Science, Space, and Aeronautics Subcommittee, and served as cochair of the House Renewable Energy and Energy Efficiency Caucus. As his committee work suggests, Udall has been a longtime advocate for veterans, the environment, and alternative energy.

Udall had a liberal voting record in the House, including votes against the Patriot Act and against the war in Iraq. The Second District includes what Republicans like to call "the people's Republic of Boulder," the city that is home to the University of Colorado, and a frequent target of conservative ridicule. Throughout his time in the House, though, Udall exhibited a willingness to reach across the aisle to solve difficult political problems. Udall, for example, worked with conservative Republicans like Rep. Jeff Flake (R-AZ) and Rep. Tim Ryan (R-WI) to curtail the abuse of federal earmarks in an attempt to restrain unnecessary federal spending. Similarly, Udall worked with Colorado Republican senator Wayne Allard to facilitate cleanup of the Rocky Flats Superfund Site.

Given Udall's pedigree, experience, and popularity, he was a logical choice by the Democrats to run for the open Senate seat. Udall had considered a Senate bid in 2004, but stepped aside when Ken Salazar entered the race. At the time, many thought Udall was too liberal to win a statewide race. Udall's decision to bow out in 2004 earned him points within the Democratic Party, and so when Allard announced his retirement, it was widely seen as Udall's turn. Accordingly, he ran unopposed in the primary election and won his party's nomination.

Bob Schaffer

Bob Schaffer has an extended history of public service in addition to a successful business career. Schaffer first entered public service in 1987, when he was elected to the State Senate from the 14th District. During his nine years in the state legislature, he served as the chairman of the Senate Finance Committee, chairman of the State Veterans and Military Affairs Committee, and as vice chairman of the Senate Education Committee. From the outset, Schaffer was an unabashed movement conservative, critical of many government programs, and strongly opposed to regulation, taxes, abortion, and gay rights. He was also keenly interested in education, and was a strong advocate for market-based reforms.

In 1996, Schaffer won the open 4th District Congressional seat, replacing Allard, who gave up his seat in a successful bid for the U.S. Senate. Schaffer's pledge to term limit himself after six years was a central part of his campaign, which he won easily. During his three terms in the House, Schaffer served on several committees, most notably Agriculture, Education and

Workforce, and Natural Resources. Schaffer's committee and subcommittee work reflected his interest in public education reform, tax reform, and natural resource development. Despite many pleas from fellow Republicans to reconsider his term limit pledge, Schaffer honored his promise and stepped down from the House in 2002. After leaving Congress, Schaffer served as vice president for CHx Capital, the investment arm of Aspect Energy, a fossil fuel development firm.

His political aspirations were not satisfied, however, and just two years later, Schaffer sought the Republican nomination for the U.S. Senate seat being vacated by retiring Republican incumbent Ben Nighthorse Campbell. Initially, Schaffer's prospects looked promising—he had the support of popular Republican governor, Bill Owens, and his only primary opponent was ReMax founder David Liniger, a political newcomer. The late entrance of brewing tycoon, Pete Coors, however, sparked an exceptionally bitter and divisive primary battle, marked by Owens's last minute decision to shift his support to Coors. During the primary, Schaffer attacked Coors for his firm's policies on same sex partners and abortion, arguing that Coors was insufficiently conservative. Coors eventually won the nomination with 61 percent of the vote, but lost the general election to Democrat Ken Salazar. Many of Schaffer's backers failed to support Coors, who they believed was too moderate on key social issues such as abortion and gay rights.

Undaunted by his loss to Coors, Schaffer won a seat on the Board of Education and bided his time; he then jumped into the race to succeed incumbent senator, Wayne Allard. This time, however, Schaffer ran unopposed and thus avoided another damaging primary.

CAMPAIGN ISSUES

Energy

Energy issues played a prominent role throughout the 2008 Colorado Senate race, and were the central topic in many of the candidates' debates. Soaring energy and gasoline prices in the spring and summer meant that neither candidate could ignore the issue, and both sought to use it as an electoral wedge, with each blaming the other for rising gas prices. Energy issues have great resonance in Colorado, where energy exploration increased dramatically in the Bush years. The politics of energy are tricky, however, because although energy production creates jobs and revenue, it also causes environmental damage. As a result, both candidates were sensitive to the local implications of energy debates. For example, both agreed that oil and gas leasing on Colorado's Roan Plateau should be prohibited, but disagreed on whether and how Colorado's oil shale should be developed. Schaffer urged quicker development while Udall cautioned against turning the area into a "national sacrifice zone."[8]

Initially, Udall and his allies touted his long history of support for renewable energy at the state and federal levels as a solution to problems ranging from oil dependency to job creation. He frequently touted his role in passing a renewable energy amendment requiring major Colorado utilities to get at least 10 percent of their energy from renewable sources. Early in the year, Schaffer also touted his support for renewable energy, but as gas prices continued to climb, Schaffer and his supporters sensed an opening and began to argue that Udall's consistent opposition to domestic energy production cost American jobs, raised energy prices, eroded national security, and increased dependence on foreign oil. For a while, Udall continued to call for increased fuel efficiency and other forms of conservation and clean energy, but the relentless attacks from Schaffer and outside groups forced Udall to change course and announce that he now supported offshore drilling. Schaffer then accused Udall of flip-flopping on the issue.

Energy issues were also central to many of the attacks launched by interest groups on both sides. In January, the League of Conservation Voters named Schaffer to its Dirty Dozen list, citing his poor record on environmental and energy issues. Later that spring, the LCV joined with the Sierra Club, Clean Water Action, and Defenders of Wildlife Action Fund to criticize Schaffer's ties to the oil and gas industry as well as his support of billions in oil and gas subsidies. ProgressNowAction, a progressive advocacy group, created a "Big Oil Bob" website and aired television ads criticizing Schaffer on the same issues, claiming that he earned $400,000 from an energy company (Aspect Management Corp.), and received nearly $150,000 in campaign contributions from the oil and gas industry.[9]

Social Issues

Part of what intrigued many pundits about this senate race was the stark contrast between Udall's relatively liberal record on many social and fiscal issues and Schaffer's well-known advocacy of conservative viewpoints, especially on social issues—and how that contrast was going to play itself out in a statewide race. Schaffer's long record of social conservatism, formed over time in an era when social conservatism led to Republican electoral success, included strong stances against abortion, stem cell research, and other issues that, in retrospect, had little chance of playing well in a time of economic turmoil. On the other hand, Udall's reassuring message and stances seemed to match the Colorado electorate in 2008.

Schaffer did try to reinvent himself to adapt to the changing electoral environment, most notably by opposing the so-called personhood amendment, which defined life as beginning at conception.[10] Schaffer also did all that he could to avoid talking about other charged social issues, such as gay rights or abortion, and instead trumpeted a "family values" message which, as noted below, his own campaign undercut.

Had the election been closer, Udall would have had many cards to play showing the dissonance between the old, staunchly conservative Bob Schaffer and the new moderate model Schaffer was offering in 2008. In the end, however, Udall did not need to make that case as voters, especially unaffiliated and moderate Republicans, just did not find Schaffer's reinvention credible enough to vote for him.

Campaign Tactics and Tone

Schaffer premised much of his campaign on his personal integrity and a rather undefined family values platform. Throughout 2008, however, a series of events helped undercut both claims. In April, the *Denver Post* broke a story about a trip Schaffer took in 1999 to the Northern Mariana Islands (a U.S. protectorate). The trip was paid for by the Traditional Values Coalition, and its ostensible purpose was to check on the well-documented human rights abuses of factory workers and women. But according to the *Post*, "this trip was partly arranged by the firm of now-jailed lobbyist Jack Abramoff, who represented textile factory owners fighting congressional efforts to reform labor and immigration laws on the islands and who was being handsomely paid to keep the islands' cherished exemptions."[11] The campaign's initial reaction was weak, and Schaffer's claim that he did not witness any forced abortions during his trip was ridiculed. Schaffer's earlier comments that he viewed the factories there as "model operations" were also an embarrassment. Campaign Money Watch criticized Schaffer for his link to Abramoff, for denying the well-publicized human rights abuses, and for supporting the island's tax breaks when in Congress. Even some anti-abortion groups joined in denouncing Schaffer.

One month later Bill Orr, a former Schaffer business associate, was convicted on twenty-two counts of defrauding the federal government. According to the *Colorado Independent*, "Orr's scheme involved defrauding the federal government with a $3.6 million congressional earmark he landed to test a fuel additive that he promised was a proven success." In 2004, Schaffer served on the board of the organization which had received the earmark.[12] Although Schaffer denied any knowledge of Orr's wrongdoing, their association attracted media attention and did little to bolster the campaign's integrity theme.

In July the *Grand Junction Daily Sentinel* reported that Schaffer visited Iraq when he worked for Aspect Energy, and helped negotiate an oil deal with the Kurdistan regional government. The problem, according to the paper, was that the U.S. State Department had concluded that the deal contradicted official U.S. policy and undercut our democracy-building efforts in

Iraq. Schaffer said that he "was unaware the State Department had warned energy firms not to strike oil deals with the Kurdistan regional government at the time of his visit."[13]

In early August, Schaffer's campaign manager and head of the state's Republican Party, Dick Wadhams, became the focus of several stories about negative campaigning. Wadhams was no political neophyte, having managed Wayne Allard's reelection campaign in 2002, John Thune's (R-SD) upset of Senate majority leader, Tom Daschle (D-SD), in 2004, and George Allen's (R-VA) unsuccessful Senate campaign in 2006. Wadhams was well known for running aggressive, take-no-prisoners campaigns. Because Wadhams spoke far more frequently with the press than did the candidate himself, he became the campaign's public face. His combative personality made life easy for reporters, as he was eminently quotable, but it is not clear that his prominence helped Schaffer.[14] In one memorable instance, Wadhams vowed to remind voters that Udall missed a vote that would have kept Congress in session to consider an energy bill favored by Republicans. Wadhams said, "He's not going to get away with it. We're going to shove a bunch of 30-second ads up his ass on this issue over the course of the campaign."[15] When asked if he regretted his comments, Wadhams laughed and said, "I embrace what I said Friday. I have no apologies. I won't back down at all. If Democrats want to embrace Boulder liberal Udall who missed votes in Washington so he could fund raise in Colorado, let's have that debate."[16] Wadhams's remarks were certainly entertaining, but aside from being red meat for rabid Republicans, it is unlikely that they were helpful to his candidate in a year when Colorado voters seemed to reject Karl Rove-style campaign tactics.

A few days later the campaign had to battle an embarrassing story about Schaffer's son Justin, a college student at the University of Dayton. According to published reports, Justin Schaffer had posted a number of offensive images on his Facebook page. One depicted an image of pyramids with the words, "Slavery gets shit done." Another showed an image of Jesus holding a machine gun in front of a Confederate flag, with a caption reading "What would a Republican Jesus Do?" He also claimed to be a member of a group called "Pole Dancers for Jesus."[17] By themselves, none of these stories was especially harmful, but the cumulative effect was to seriously undermine Schaffer's campaign message of personal integrity and family values.

CAMPAIGN STRATEGY

Media

With the exception of numerous stories in the summer about the candidate's sparring on energy issues, the bulk of media coverage of the race by local papers and television stations was of the horse-race variety, with Udall's lead in the polls and in fund-raising driving many stories. There were numerous accounts, for example, detailing the heavy spending by outside organizations, primarily on negative television ads,[18] and by the decisions of the party's senatorial campaign committees to initiate or curtail their ad spending.[19]

Overall, the tone of much of the coverage suggested that the Schaffer campaign was, at a minimum, beleaguered. Starting in the spring, for example, there were numerous newspaper accounts detailing Schaffer's ties with disgraced lobbyist Jack Abramoff and his involvement in a controversial oil deal in Iraq. The Schaffer campaign was also embarrassed by media accounts of its first television ad, a biographical spot intended to highlight the candidate's family life and his Colorado roots. In the ad, Schaffer states that he proposed to his wife on Pike's Peak, but the mountain featured in the ad was actually Alaska's Mount McKinley. To be sure, this was a minor misstep, but one result of the lighthearted controversy was to cast doubt on Schaffer's ties to the state.[20]

The campaign's nasty tone was another common media theme. This was illustrated most humorously by stories calling attention to Wadhams's relentless repetition of the phrase "Boulder liberal Mark Udall." The state's most popular political blog featured several stories on the topic, including one noting that a Wadhams's press release on second quarter fund-raising used the phrase "Boulder liberal" eight times in five paragraphs.[21] A *Denver Post* story at about the same time noted that Wadhams used the term six times in less than a minute in an interview with a reporter from Politico, the online political website.[22] In fact, Wadhams used the phrase so often that there was even media coverage on the decision by a reporter to "edit" Wadhams's comments in one story by replacing "Boulder liberal" with the more neutral term "Democratic congressman."[23]

For his part, Schaffer did not help himself with an aggressive and argumentative appearance with Udall on *Meet the Press*. Schaffer often raised his voice and interrupted Udall an average of once every forty-five seconds, and came across as rude and obnoxious.[24] In another instance Schaffer held up another televised debate for nearly thirty minutes by insisting that he have access to notes, even though both campaigns had previously agreed that notes were prohibited.[25] During the exchange, which was reported in several media outlets, Schaffer remarked "You know, this is a campaign for the United States Senate, it's not a talent contest."[26] The cumulative effect of such stories probably did not do much to enhance unaffiliated voter's perceptions of the Schaffer campaign.

Most of the state's newspapers endorsed Udall, including the *Denver Post*, the state's largest daily. In its endorsement, the *Post* noted Udall's "proven track record of bipartisan accomplishments" and said that he would be the more likely of the two candidates to act as a moderate if elected.[27] Udall also received endorsements from the *Boulder Daily Camera, Colorado Springs Independent, Durango Herald, Fort Collins Coloradoan, Greeley Tribune,* and *Longmont Daily Times.* The *Grand Junction Sentinel* and the *Pueblo Chieftain* were the only major dailies to endorse Schaffer. In its editorial, the *Sentinel* said that "we believe Schaffer's staunchly conservative ideas are more in line with what Colorado and this country need right now than Udall's liberal views."[28] The usually conservative *Rocky Mountain News*, which many expected to back Schaffer, declined to issue endorsements in 2008.

Advertising

In an unusual move, the Udall campaign launched its first television ads in mid-May. Schaffer campaign manager Dick Wadhams and other pundits criticized the million dollar ad buy as a waste of money at a time when voters are typically not paying attention. But according to Mike Melanson, Udall's campaign manager, "It was important to define Mark early before the attacks we knew were coming came."[29] The first ads were designed to introduce Udall to the many voters who did not know him; the ads were positive in tone, stressing Udall's work on renewable energy, veteran's issues, and his record of bipartisanship.

With more money to spend, Udall ran fifteen television ads with nearly half emphasizing his commitment to renewable energy, green jobs, and to Colorado's "new energy economy." As gas prices soared during the summer, Udall's ads shifted to signal his support for "responsible" domestic oil and gas drilling and for eliminating the billions in energy company tax breaks that "Big Oil Bob" Schaffer supported. Udall's television spots also emphasized his work on the House Armed Services Committee and his support of veterans and the military. Overall, two-thirds of Udall's television ads offered a positive message about his willingness to reach across the aisle, his support for renewable energy, tax cuts for the middle class, veteran benefits, and education funding. Five of Udall's ads were critical in tone, attacking Schaffer for his oil company ties, his inability to work in a bipartisan manner, and for supporting tax breaks for corporations who exported American jobs.

Schaffer made a $300,000 ad buy in May for a positive spot emphasizing the economy, and his support of a balanced budget and limited government spending. Schaffer's advertising strategy differed from Udall's in several respects. With less money to spend, Schaffer ran only seven different ads, a mix of positive spots and attack ads. Lower taxes and reduced government spending were a central theme in all Schaffer commercials. The attack ads criticized Udall for supporting higher taxes and invariably referred to his opponent as "Boulder liberal Mark Udall." The positive messages emphasized Schaffer's ties to Colorado, his support for family values, and his commitment to energy independence, lower taxes, and smaller government.

The Democratic Senatorial Campaign Committee (DSCC) spent just under $4.3 million in the race, primarily on television ads attacking Schaffer. The DSCC began its assault in August, and continued without letup through Election Day. According to figures compiled by the Center for Responsive Politics, the DSCC spent more in only four other Senate contests.[30] The DSCC ran five critical ads attacking "Big Oil Bob" for giving oil companies billions in tax breaks, shipping jobs overseas, and making a healthy salary as an oil executive while Coloradoans paid record gas prices. The DSCC also criticized Schaffer for supporting privatization of Social Security and for his record of supporting President George Bush and his failed economic policies.

The National Republican Senatorial Committee (NRSC), on the other hand, spent almost $3 million in its efforts to defeat Udall, with the vast majority going to anti-Udall television ads.[31] In September, for example, the NRSC ran a series of ads slamming Udall for saying "no to offshore drilling, no to more domestic exploration and no on expanding energy production."[32] These commercials blamed Udall for the soaring gas prices, our dependence on foreign oil, and for blocking domestic energy exploration. NRSC ads also criticized Udall for failing to support both active duty military and veterans, for being a liberal, and for having a voting record similar to House Speaker Nancy Pelosi (D-CA).

Like its Democratic counterpart, the NRSC went on the air in August, but it was not long before the committee seemed to reconsider. Newspaper reports later that month noted that the organization's independent expenditure arm had canceled about a quarter of its ad buy, from $4.8 million to $3.6 million. The reports noted that the action was a result of NRSC's lackluster fund-raising during the cycle and that John Ensign, the committee's chair, may have been trying to cajole reluctant donors into contributing.[33] Later, in mid-October, rumors began circulating on political blogs that the committee was going to cancel its television ad buys and shift its resources elsewhere. An NRSC spokesperson initially denied these reports, but the Committee did in fact pull its ad buys shortly thereafter.[34] On the heels of the NRSC's withdrawal, the steady drumbeat of polls showing Udall ahead, and a growing sense that the presidential race was slipping away from John McCain, the news conveyed the impression that the party was cutting its losses and abandoning Schaffer. Although his campaign manager insisted that the NRSC's withdrawal was actually a sign of Schaffer's strength, the final results suggest that he was putting the best face on a bad situation. Although the committee's $3 million in spending was not insignificant, it was a far cry from its initial $4.8 million budget.

For much of the summer and fall, the Colorado airwaves were full of attack ads by a wide array of interest groups. In fact, as of late September, groups had spent more in Colorado than in any other Senate contest, with Republican-leaning groups outspending Democratic ones by almost three to one.[35] The spending slacked off when polls continued to show Udall leading, and as some of the groups shifted their resources to other contests. Republican-affiliated groups spent $10.4 million, compared to just $3.4 million by Democratic groups. Freedom's Watch spent $1.71 million on ads criticizing Udall for "skipping" a key energy policy vote in August, for supporting a "Department of Peace," and for being weak on national security. Similarly, the U.S. Chamber of Commerce, the Associated Builders and Contractors for Free Enterprise, and the American Future Fund paid for TV spots and direct mail blasting Udall for blocking domestic oil exploration and blaming him for high gas prices. Udall supporters including the LCV, Campaign Money Watch, the AFL-CIO, and the Colorado First Project spent considerably less on TV advertising but worked the ground war more vigorously. Their negative message hammered Schaffer for his record on energy policy, the environment, labor issues, health care, and Social Security.

Finance

Because it was widely presumed to be among the nation's most competitive Senate races, the expectation was that the Udall-Schaffer contest would spur record fundraising and spending by the candidates, parties, and interest groups. When the dust cleared, the candidates had spent a combined $19.8 million, fifth most in the nation, easily surpassing the previous state record set in the 2004 Senate contest between Democrat Ken Salazar and Republican Pete Coors.[36] The two candidates were not the only ones spending in 2008—the parties and outside groups spent an additional $27 million, primarily on a barrage of television ads that began in 2007.[37]

According to figures compiled by the Center for Responsive Politics, Mark Udall raised and spent nearly 50 percent more than his opponent.[38] Udall raised $12.6 million, including $1.26 million transferred from his House campaign account,[39] and spent just over $12.75 million,[40] the most by any candidate in Colorado history. According to Mike Melanson, Udall's campaign manager, the campaign spent approximately $6.3 million on television and radio advertising, and also spent heavily on research and polling.[41] In fact, Udall ended the race more than $230,000 in debt. PAC contributions accounted for $2.1 million, or 19 percent of his receipts. Of that total, business PACs contributed approximately 45 percent, ideological PACS 22 percent, and labor PAC's 17 percent.[42]

Bob Schaffer raised nearly $7.4 million and spent just under $7.1 million, an impressive amount but not nearly enough to compete with Udall. Trailing in the polls throughout the race, Schaffer undoubtedly had a harder time convincing potential donors that he could win. PACs contributed 14 percent of Schaffer's funds, with 74 percent coming from individual donors.[43] Schaffer ranked ninth among Senate candidates in candidate-to-candidate giving, pulling in more than $340,000 from Republican members of Congress.[44]

Grass Roots

Because the race was expected to be close, both sides devoted significant energy and money to mobilizing and turning out their supporters. With unaffiliated voters accounting for approximately one-third of the electorate, both campaigns knew they would have to win over this critical bloc of voters. Both campaigns also made special efforts to encourage their supporters to vote either absentee or early. In Colorado, absentee ballots were mailed out in the first week of October, and early voting began on October 20, meaning that Election Day lasted for nearly one month.

In addition to turning out their base vote, the Udall campaign was especially interested in winning over unaffiliated voters, suburban voters outside Udall's own congressional district, and Republican women. According to Mike Melanson, all of their campaign mail was targeted to unaffiliated voters. The campaign also set a goal of matching or beating the 13 percent of Republican voters won by Ken Salazar in 2004. The aim was to compete statewide, to expand Udall's margins in places where Democrats typically did well, and to limit his losses in places they did not.[45]

The Udall campaign also placed a high priority on the Latino vote. In fact, Melanson described the Latino vote as key, noting that the campaign had set out to increase the Latino vote to about 9 percent of the total electorate.[46] To facilitate that, the campaign conducted a "massive outreach effort" that included Latino staffers, campaign events, and a postcard campaign urging Latino supporters to contact their friends on Udall's behalf. Speaking to reporters about the outreach effort, Udall's press secretary Tara Trujillo said, "Mark is reaching out to Latino voters because he believes it is important that they have a seat at the table—something they haven't always had under the Republican administration—when it comes to the issues that matter most to them."[47]

Despite the growing importance of Latino voters, the Schaffer campaign made no special effort to mobilize them. In April, Schaffer met with a group of Republican Latinos who advised him to hire Latino staffers and to attend political events in the Latino community. According to Gil Cisneros, who worked on Latino outreach for the McCain campaign, Schaffer said, "Well,

I've never campaigned like that. I consider myself an American first." Cisneros interpreted those remarks to mean that Schaffer did not like to think about voters in racial or ethnic categories. Dick Wadhams, Schaffer's campaign manager, said Schaffer had no specific Latino outreach effort but expressed hope that his policy stances on education and lower taxes would appeal to Latino voters.[48]

On the Republican side, the coordinated campaign known as the Victory Program exceeded most of its voter contact goals and was later recognized by the RNC as one of the top performing programs nationally. According to Michael Britt, the executive director of the Colorado Republican Committee (CRC), the campaign recorded more than 2.4 million voter contacts between June 1 and Election Day, nearly doubling the total from 2004. The CRC Victory Program knocked on more than 600,000 doors, the most in the nation, and made nearly 1.85 million phone calls, which ranked fifth. To put those numbers in context, the Republican coordinated campaigns in Ohio and Virginia, which are larger and more valuable in the Electoral College, reported knocking on just 245,000 and 221,000 doors, respectively.[49]

Bases of Support

Labor unions, environmental organizations, women's groups, and other progressive organizations provided Udall with support in the form of contributions, enthusiastic volunteers, and independent expenditure campaigns, some of them significant. Among the labor groups supporting Udall with direct mail, volunteers, or television advertising were the Colorado AFL-CIO, Working America, an AFL-CIO community affiliate, SEIU-COPE, the Colorado Education Association (CEA), the National Education Association (NEA), and America's Agenda Kid's Health.org. Labor unions contributed to the Democratic coordinated campaign and helped pay for much of the direct mail in the race. Unions also devoted considerable resources to voter registration and GOTV efforts. Udall's long record on behalf of the environment and renewable energy ensured that environmental organizations would be enthusiastic boosters. As a case in point, the League of Conservation Voters named Bob Schaffer to its Dirty Dozen list and spent nearly $1 million dollars to defeat him. Although its primary focus in the state was defeating incumbent Republican Marilyn Musgrave in the 4th District, Defenders of Wildlife Action Fund was also active on Udall's behalf, sending several pieces of direct mail as well as canvassing to identify and persuade unaffiliated voters. Other environmental groups, like the Sierra Club and Clean Water Action, also provided support in the form of volunteers and mail.

Schaffer's bases of support consisted of religious conservatives, anti-abortion groups, business organizations, anti-tax activists, and a variety of other conservative groups. Although Schaffer took some steps to portray himself as a moderate, it seems that most culturally conservative organizations understood that was mere political posturing and enthusiastically supported him. Focus on the Family Action, the National Right to Life PAC, Catholic Citizens, and the Susan B. Anthony List provided financial support and helped mobilize supporters for Schaffer. As noted above, a wide array of conservative and business organizations aired television ads attacking Udall, including the Chamber of Commerce, Freedom's Watch, Patriot Majority, American Future Fund, and the Associated Builders and Contractor's Free Enterprise Alliance, who were all major players. Energy companies, along with the Chamber and other business groups, contacted employees and encouraged support for pro-business candidates such as Schaffer and John McCain. The National Rifle Association Political Victory Fund (NRAPVF) supported Schaffer and urged its members to do so as well.

ELECTION RESULTS

Despite expectations of a close race and assertions that he was too liberal to win a statewide race, Udall defeated Schaffer by more than 10 percentage points, 52.8 percent to 42.5 percent (see table 14.4). Although polls had shown Udall ahead throughout the year, most observers were surprised by the size and scope of his victory. Udall prevailed by more than 240,000 votes, a margin larger than Barack Obama's win over John McCain, and considerably larger than Ken Salazar's 2004 win over Pete Coors in Colorado. In fact, Udall's share of the vote was the largest by a Democratic Senatorial candidate in the state since Gary Hart's 57 percent in 1974, in the midst of Watergate.[50] Perhaps most importantly, Udall also did much better than Schaffer among independents, winning that group by a margin of three to two. With independents accounting for approximately one-third of the state's voters, Udall's success was decisive.

Table 14.5 provides further evidence of the extent of Schaffer's defeat by comparing the electoral margins in the ten most populous counties in Colorado, which contain around 77 percent of Colorado's 2008 vote. Peter Coors,

Table 14.4. Colorado Senatorial Election Results, 2008

Bob Schaffer	Republican	990,755	42.49%
Mark Udall	Democrat	1,230,994	52.80%
Bob Kinsey	Green	50,004	2.14%
Douglas "Dayhorse" Campbell	ACP	59,733	2.56%
Write-Ins		135	0.00%
Total Votes		2,331,621	100.00%

Source: Colorado Secretary of State

Table 14.5. Colorado Senatorial Election Results in Colorado's Ten Largest Counties, 2004 and 2008, by County

	Schaffer		Udall		Coors		Salazar	
Adams	56,194	38.6%	89,541	61.4%	55,438	42.1%	76,101	57.9%
Arapahoe	106,553	43.4%	139,108	56.6%	105,921	46.8%	120,225	53.2%
Boulder	43,375	27.0%	117,042	73.0%	47,899	31.0%	106,481	69.0%
Denver	60,199	23.5%	196,252	76.5%	60,387	26.3%	169,580	73.7%
Douglas	84,552	59.5%	57,587	40.5%	72,911	61.6%	45,425	38.4%
El Paso	148,716	59.6%	100,876	40.4%	151,414	65.0%	81,403	35.0%
Jefferson	121,888	44.6%	151,612	55.4%	127,048	48.0%	137,554	52.0%
Larimer	70,268	45.9%	82,727	54.1%	67,597	48.0%	73,204	52.0%
Pueblo	26,566	39.2%	41,290	60.8%	26,160	39.7%	39,687	60.3%
Weld	51,253	53.0%	45,522	47.0%	47,986	56.3%	37,320	43.7%
Population	1,791,121							
	769,564		1,021,557		762,761		886,980	
Percent of State	76.8%	43.0%		57.0%		46.2%		53.8%
					1,649,741			

Source: Colorado Secretary of State
Notes: Criteria for inclusion of county in this list is 70,000 votes cast in 2008, which results in the ten most populated counties. Third party candidates and write-ins excluded from percentages.

the 2004 Republican Senate candidate, ran stronger in every one of these counties than Schaffer did. In short, Udall improved upon the game plan of Ken Salazar, whose ability to attract votes in the rural, largely Republican areas was said to be a model for Democrats seeking to compete in Colorado.

Exit polls show that Udall's win was both broad and deep. He won large margins among the voting blocs one would expect, but he also carried some groups that have traditionally voted Republican. For example, Udall ran up big margins among women (56 to 41 percent), but he also won among men (50 to 46 percent). Udall carried Latino voters by more than a two-to-one ratio (63 to 30 percent), but he also carried white voters (50 to 47 percent). Udall also won every age group except those age sixty-five and older, which Schaffer captured narrowly (50 to 48 percent). In addition, many more self-identified Republicans (10 percent) voted for Udall than did Democrats defecting to Schaffer (4 percent).[51] Perhaps most importantly, though, Udall captured unaffiliated voters by a wide fifty-five to forty margin, and carried self-described moderates by an even larger sixty-three to thirty-two margin. With independents accounting for approximately one-third of the state's voters, Udall's success among this group was decisive.

In addition, Udall won among urban voters, suburban voters, and claimed a 1 percent point edge among rural voters. By region, Udall won the populous regions around Denver and Boulder, captured 52 percent of the western part of the state, while Schaffer ran up big margins in the sparsely populated eastern plains.

Latino voters were also critical to Udall's winning margin. According to a report by Project Vote, Latinos cast approximately 123,000 more votes in Colorado than in 2004, an increase of more than 70 percent. Whereas Latinos made up just 8 percent of the state's electorate in 2004, in 2008 the share increased to 13 percent. While the Latino vote seems to have increased dramatically, white voters actually cast fewer ballots than in 2004, while turnout among black voters increased 6 percent, or about 5,000 votes.[52] Udall's decision to target the Latino vote, discussed above, seems to have been a wise decision that contributed substantially to his vote totals.

The exit polls indicate, not surprisingly, that Schaffer won fewer voting blocs. He won a narrow victory among those who did not attend college, and split the votes of those making $30,000 to $50,000 per year. Not surprisingly, Schaffer also carried the 21 percent of voters who described themselves as white evangelical, born again Christians, by a decisive three to one ratio. But this was more than offset by Udall's edge among the 79 percent of Colorado voters who were not white evangelical, born-again Christians.

The exit polls also shed some light on the reasons for Udall's impressive victory. Most notably, just under 70 percent of Colorado voters disapproved of how President Bush was handling his job, and Udall won 73 percent of their votes. Clearly, Bush was a significant drag on Schaffer, as he was on many Republican candidates in 2008. The exit polls also showed that the most important issues for Colorado voters were the economy (54 percent), Iraq (12 percent), and terrorism and health care (10 percent each). Udall won 56 percent of the votes of those who said the economy was the most important issue, and 63 percent of those who said Iraq was the key issue. He also won 75 percent of those who cited health care as the top issue, while Schaffer won nearly 80 percent of those who said terrorism was the most important issue. In other words, on three of the top four issues for voters, Udall was the preferred candidate.

To be sure, 2008 was a bad year to run as a Republican. Schaffer's half-hearted efforts to distance himself from his long record of social conservatism were unsuccessful, and Schaffer was simply on the wrong side of the issues that were most important to voters. Schaffer's campaign was out of sync with the mood of Colorado voters in this election cycle. His television ads (as well as those by the NRSC and the veritable army of outside groups) and the party's direct mail gave voters plenty of reasons to not vote for Mark Udall, but they also provided little reason for them to vote for Bob Schaffer. In fact, a Mason-Dixon poll released just before the election showed that voters viewed Udall more positively than Schaffer, and had done so throughout the race.[53] Schaffer's failure to offer voters—especially unaffiliated voters—a positive agenda that addressed their core concerns was a critical mistake. In 2008, it was not enough to tell people that you were "a good family man"; voters expected some substantive, positive message.

Contrary to early reports attributing Udall's win to a combination of a demoralized Republican rank and file and a wave of new Democratic voters brought into the electorate by Obama, reports issued by the Secretary of State's office in December revealed that not only did Republican voters outnumber Democrats in November, but they also turned out at a slightly higher rate. All told, about 15,600 more Republicans voted in the election, and 80 percent of registered Republicans cast a ballot, compared to 79 percent of Democrats. In contrast, turnout among unaffiliated voters was just 67 percent. The key to Udall's win was that he captured the lion's share of unaffiliated voters who, as noted above, are now the largest group in Colorado.[54]

Republicans used to be able to win in the state by turning out their base, but that is no longer the case. By all accounts, Colorado Republicans succeeded in turning out their base vote in 2008, but Schaffer and McCain both lost by wide margins. Unaffiliated voters now hold the keys to the kingdom in Colorado, and since 2004 they have been expressing a decided preference for Democratic candidates. If Republican candidates are to succeed in future races, they will need to find new ways of appealing to unaffiliated voters, who have seemingly grown tired of the relentless attack politics and the emphasis on divisive social issues like abortion and gay marriage that have characterized many Republican campaigns in recent years.

NOTES

1. Colorado Secretary of State, "November 2008 Voter Registration Numbers: Voter Recap by Party," www.elections.colorado.gov/WWW/default/2008%20Voter%20 Registration%20Numbers/October_22_2008/vr_stats_by_party_10.22.2008.pdf (accessed November 25, 2008) and "December 2004 Voter Registration Numbers by Party," www.elections.colorado.gov/DDefault.aspx?tid=480&vmid=134 (accessed November 25, 2008).

2. Almanac of American Politics, "Colorado," 0-www.nationaljournal.com/almanac/2008/states/co (accessed December 2, 2008) and "Colorado Presidential Voting History," www.cnn.com/ELECTION/2004/pages/pre/CO/history.html (accessed December 2, 2008).

3. US Elections Atlas, "Colorado Election Results," www.uselectionatlas.org/RESULTS/state.php?fips=8&f=0&off=99 (accessed December 2, 2008) and "Colorado Presidential Voting History," www.cnn.com/ELECTION/2004/pages/pre/CO/history.html (accessed December 2, 2008).

4. Almanac of American Politics, "Colorado," 0-www.nationaljournal.com/almanac/2008/states/co (accessed December 3, 2008).

5. Almanac of American Politics, "Colorado."

6. The Pew Forum on Religious and Public Life, "US Religious Landscape Survey" religions.pewforum.org/reports (accessed December 12, 2008). The Association of Religion Data Archives, "State Membership Report, Colorado (2000)," www.thearda.com/mapsReports/reports/state/08_2000.asp (accessed December 12, 2008).

7. Almanac of American Politics, "Colorado."

8. Ed Sealover, "Schaffer, Udall Spar over Energy," *Rocky Mountain News*, July 15, 2008, www.rockymountainnews.com/news/2008/jul/15/schaffer-udall-spar-over-energy-before-loud/ (accessed December 28, 2008); Stephen K. Paulson, "Senate Candidates Clash in Debate—Udall, Schaffer Spar on Energy Policy," *Boulder Daily Camera*, August 14, 2008, www.dailycamera.com/news/2008/aug/14/senate-candidates-clash-debate/ (accessed August 15, 2008).

9. Steven K. Paulson, "Schaffer, Udall Spar over Gas Prices," *Aspen Times*, June 16, 2008, www.aspentimes.com/article/20080616/NEWS/879314769&parentprofile=search (accessed December 23, 2008).

10. For example, "Personhood Colorado," www.coloradoforequalrights.com/.

11. Michael Riley, "Abramoff Ties Cloud Schaffer's '99 Fact-Finding Trip," *Denver Post*, April 10, 2008.

12. Cara Degette, "Slip-ups Mar Bob Schaffer," *Colorado Independent*, July 14, 2008, coloradoindependent.com/3918/slip-ups-mar-bob-schafferaos-shaky-entrance-into-us-senate-race (accessed on December 28, 2008).

13. Mike Saccone, "Schaffer Role in Iraq Oil Deal Revived with Group's Impending Endorsement," *Grand Junction Daily Sentinel*, October 14, 2008, www.gjsentinel.com/search/content/news/stories/2008/10/14/101408_3A_Schaffer_endorsement.html (accessed on December 28, 2008).

14. Michael Riley, "Love or Loathe Him, Wadhams Plays for Keeps," *Denver Post*, August 5, 2008, www.denverpost.com/newsheadlines/ci_10097864 (accessed August 6, 2008).

15. Lynn Bartels, "GOP Bashes Udall over Missing Recess Vote," *Rocky Mountain News*, August 1, 2008, www.rockymountainnews.com/news/2008/aug/01/udall-votes-oppose-ending-congressional-session/.

16. Lynn Bartels, "Dems Rip Schaffer Campaign Manager's Language," *Rocky Mountain News*, August 5, 2008, www.rockymountainnews.com/news/2008/aug/04/dems-rip-schaffer-campaign-managers-language (accessed August 6, 2008).

17. Michael Riley, "Schaffer's Son Sorry for Facebook Slavery, Jesus Jokes," *Denver Post*, August 5, 2008, www.denverpost.com/newsheadlines/ci_10099292 (accessed August 6, 2008).

18. See, for example, Michael Riley, "Attack Ads Inundate State Race for Senate," *Denver Post*, September 25, 2008, www.denverpost.com/senate08/ci_10550738 (accessed September 25, 2008).

19. Lynn Bartels, "GOP Committee Pulls Schaffer TV Ads," *Rocky Mountain News*, October 24, 2008, www.rockymountainnews.com/news/2008/oct/24/gop-committee-pulls-schaffer-tv-ads/ (accessed October 24, 2008).

20. John C. Ensslin, "Schaffer's Ad Moved Mountains," *Rocky Mountain News*, May 14, 2008, www.rockymountainnews.com/news/2008/may/14/schaffers-ad-moved-mountains/ (accessed May 16, 2008).

21. Coloradopols, "Boulder Liberal Udall (Outraises Schaffer by $600,000)," Coloradopols.com, July 15, 2008, coloradopols.com/showDiary.do?diaryId=6681.

22. Michael Riley, "Candidates Rely on Name-Calling," *Denver Post*, May 13, 2008, www.denverpost.com/newsheadlines/ci_9238394.

23. Jason Salzman, "What Boulder Liberal?" Big Media Blog, June 2, 2008, bigmedia.org/?p=75 (accessed June 3, 2008).

24. Leslie Jorgensen, "*Meet the Press* Airs Debate Interruptus," *Colorado Statesman*, October 3, 2008, www.coloradostatesman.com/content/%3Fmeet-press%3F-airs-debate-interruptus (accessed December 18, 2008).

25. Michael Riley, "Schaffer Note Flap Delays Debate," *Politics West*, October 14, 2008, www.politicswest.com/31543/schaffer_note_flap_delays_debate, (accessed October 15, 2008).

26. Cara Degette, "Dick Wadhams and the Politics of Mouthwash," *Colorado Independent*, November 5, 2008, coloradoindependent.com/14384/dick-wadhams-and-the-politics-of-mouthwash (accessed November 5, 2008).

27. *Denver Post*, "Udall Is Best for Colorado," *Denver Post*, October 11, 2008, www.denverpost.com/endorsements/ci_10682435 (accessed December 18, 2008).

28. Editorial, "Schaffer for Senate," *Grand Junction Daily Sentinel*, October 9, 2008, www.gjsentinel.com/search/content/news/opinion/stories/2008/10/09/101008_6A_Schaffer_edit.html (accessed December 18, 2008).

29. Mike Melanson, campaign manager, Udall for Colorado, interview with Robert Duffy, Denver, CO, December 1, 2008.

30. Center for Responsive Politics, "Democratic Senatorial Campaign Committee: Independent Expenditures," www.opensecrets.org/parties/indexp.php?cycle=2008&cmte=DSCC&cycle=2008 (accessed December 17, 2008).

31. Center for Responsive Politics, "National Republican Senatorial Committee: Independent Expenditures," www.opensecrets.org/parties/indexp.php?cmte=NRSC&cycle=2008 (accessed December 17, 2008).

32. For National Republican Senatorial Committee TV advertisements see www.boulderliberalmarkudall.com/videos/ and www.youtube.com/watch?v=IM796rtk3E8 (assessed December 28, 2008).
33. Michael Riley, "GOP Cuts Funding for Races," *Denver Post*, August 24, 2008, www.denverpost.com/senate08/ci_10286474 (accessed August 24, 2008).
34. Lynn Bartels, "GOP Committee Pulls Schaffer TV Ads," *Rocky Mountain News*, October 24, 2008, www.rockymountainnews.com/news/2008/oct/24/gop-committee-pulls-schaffer-tv-ads/ (accessed October 24, 2008).
35. Michael Riley, "Attack Ads Inundate State Race for Senate," *Denver Post*, September 25, 2008, www.denverpost.com/senate08/ci_10550738 (accessed September 25, 2008).
36. Center for Responsive Politics, "2008 Overview: Most Expensive Races," www.opensecrets.org/overview/topraces.php (accessed December 17, 2008).
37. Lynn Bartels, "Udall, Schaffer Set Senate Fundraising Record," *Rocky Mountain News*, December 9, 2008, www.rockymountainnews.com/news/2008/dec/09/udall-schaffer-set-senate-fundraising-record (accessed December 11, 2008).
38. Center for Responsive Politics, "Total Raised and Spent, 2004: Colorado District 7," www.opensecrets.org/politicians/summary.asp?cid=n0002544&cycle=2004 (accessed December 12, 2004).
39. Bartels, "Udall, Schaffer."
40. Center for Responsive Politics, "Congressional Elections: Colorado Senate Race: 2008 Cycle," www.opensecrets.org/races/summary.php?cycle=2008&id=COS2 (accessed December 17, 2008).
41. Mike Melanson, campaign manager, Udall for Colorado, interview by Robert Duffy, Denver, CO, December 1, 2008.
42. Center for Responsive Politics, "Congressional Elections: Colorado Senate Race: 2008 Cycle," www.opensecrets.org/races/pacs.php?cycle=2008&id=COS2 (accessed December 17, 2008).
43. Center for Responsive Politics, "Congressional Elections: Colorado Senate Race: 2008 Cycle."
44. Center for Responsive Politics, "2008 Overview: Candidate to Candidate Giving," www.opensecrets.org/overview/cand2cand.php.
45. Melanson interview.
46. Melanson interview.
47. Michael Riley, "Latino Voters a Force in Senate Race," *Denver Post*, September 29, 2008, www.denverpost.com/breakingnews/ci_10585405 (accessed December 17, 2008).
48. Riley, "Latino Voters a Force."
49. Michael Britt, "Post Election Update," www.cologop.org/NewsBack.aspx?guid=22af34f5-2743-46c8-b8a4-105d33e4aa25 (accessed December).
50. Lynn Bartels, "Udall Beat Schaffer in Senate Race by 10.31 Percentage Points," *Rocky Mountain News*, December 6, 2008, www.rockymountainnews.com/news/20008/dec/06/udall-beatschaffer-in-senate-race.html (accessed December 19, 2008).
51. CNN, "U.S. Senate/Colorado/Exit Polls," www.cnn.com/ELECTION/2004/pages/results/states/CO/S/01/epolls.0.html (accessed November 19, 2004).
52. Project Vote, Research Memo, December 18, 2008, www.projectvote.org (accessed December 17, 2008).

53. Michael Riley, "Independent Voters Side Big with Udall," *Denver Post*, November 1, 2008, www.denverpost.com/senate08/ci_10876317 (accessed November 1, 2008).

54. John Ingold, "Colorado Election Turned Out Surprises," *Denver Post*, December 17, 2008, www.denverpost.com/breakingnews/ci_11248097 (accessed December 17, 2008).

IV
CONCLUSION

15

The Legacy of Election 2008

Robert Dewhirst

The outcome of the 2008 congressional elections was driven by four powerful political forces: (1) a major nationwide economic downturn; (2) widespread public dissatisfaction with President George W. Bush; (3) an unpopular war in Iraq; and (4) the brilliant and near-flawlessly executed presidential campaign by an exciting candidate, Barack Obama. These factors, coupled with an array of other increasingly serious domestic problems, combined to torment congressional Republican candidates and energize their Democratic rivals throughout the course of the campaign season.

Events in 2008 helped to "nationalize" congressional elections insofar as they provided an array of concerns which were deemed to be important by voters in virtually every state. For instance, voters became increasingly wary of the wars in Iraq and Afghanistan and support built for bringing the troops home from the long conflicts. Nightly news reports of the casualties, suffering, and continued problems with suicide and roadside bombings kept the issue in the public eye and framed the issue beyond the Bush administration's ineffective efforts to make a case for the wars.

One of the few issues capable of displacing the war as the main issue was the economy, and a growing array of economic crises proved to be even bigger concern to voters than terrorism. High-profile failures in the banking and insurance industries, problems in the housing market, growing unemployment numbers, rampant business closures, and rising national deficits and debt dominated the news during the final weeks of the 2008 campaign. The growing unemployment rates meant that a record number of Americans were without health care protection, which brought the issue back to the forefront of public concern.

Many commentators and reports indicated that the economy was in worse shape than any time since the Great Depression. Indeed, unemployment rates and business failures were growing to levels not seen since the 1930s. Voters increasingly complained that the only things growing rapidly during the fall campaign were health care costs, personal indebtedness, the price of gasoline, and the prevalence of "going out of business" signs. The facts that Republicans controlled the Congress for much of previous fourteen years and an unpopular Republican president was finishing his second term in the White House meant the public blamed the GOP for the problems.

The crises were compounded shortly before the election when leading Wall Street banks and investment firms went "belly up." The ramifications of the financial crisis sent shock waves through other sectors of the American economy, such as housing, insurance, and manufacturing. These firms and their surviving competitors, along with the country's automobile industry, were forced to plead for financial relief from Washington, DC.

News media coverage of these latter developments assuredly contributed to the "nationalization" of many congressional elections, contests normally dominated by local concerns. Loss of jobs, health care concerns, and high gasoline prices became leading local concerns. The combination of these forces made 2008 a good year for Democratic candidates and an equally bad one for Republicans. After the election, House Democrats picked up 22 seats to increase their party caucus to 257. Senate Democrats gained eight seats, giving them a majority at fifty-seven, three members short of a sixty-vote majority which, with party unity, could overcome filibusters. However, the Senate's two independents, Joseph Lieberman of Connecticut and Bernard Sanders of Vermont, again chose to caucus with the Democrats, extending the Democratic advantage to fifty-nine seats. The consensus among politicians and journalists alike was that the 2008 elections were a referendum on the failed policies and presidency of George W. Bush. His continued low ratings in public opinion polls energized Democrats and his corresponding reverse "coattails" helped to defeat Republicans.

PRESIDENTIAL "COATTAILS" AND THE 2008 CONGRESSIONAL ELECTIONS

The notion that a popular president who wins an election by a large margin can carry into office "on his coattails" many congressional candidates of his party has been around since the presidency of Abraham Lincoln. Another possible example of this phenomenon was when the popular Franklin D. Roosevelt—along with an economic crisis blamed on a Republican administration—helped to carry much less popular congressional Democratic candidates to victory in 1932 and afterward. Of course, this definition of presidential coattails is based on an electorate preferring straight-ticket voting. However, the likelihood of presidential coattails helping congressional candidates win close contests waned in the second half of the twentieth century because many voters preferred splitting their tickets between the political parties and partisan loyalties diminished. Hence, elections often produced a divided national government, where a new president of one party confronted one or both houses of Congress dominated by the rival party.

On the other hand, elections sometimes were thought to produce a "reverse coattail effect" where an unpopular president, such as Gerald Ford in 1976, Jimmy Carter in 1980, or George H. W. Bush in 1992, would anger just enough voters to cause the defeat of fellow party congressional candidates. In the 1994 midterm elections, for instance, then–House Speaker New Gingrich led an effort for Republicans to nationalize the congressional races as a referendum on President Bill Clinton's scandals. As a result, Republicans enjoyed an historic victory and gained control of both chambers of Congress. Similar angry winds were blowing in 2008. However, with President Bush ineligible to run again, congressional Republican candidates were left to face the political firestorm individually.

George W. Bush

With this backdrop then, the name of the most important person influencing the outcome of the 2008 congressional elections did not appear on any ballot. President Bush, whose public opinion support scores hovered in the low 20 percent range throughout the summer and fall, was widely accepted as a major factor affecting the outcome of the congressional elections.

Widespread public dissatisfaction with President Bush influenced congressional elections in a number of ways. First, intense anger with the president among traditional Democratic voters and their allied interest groups stimulated increased campaign donations to party candidates. Bush's widespread unpopularity also helped attract donations from disillusioned independent voters not normally giving to political campaigns. Bush proved to be the best tool for Democratic fund-raisers. In addition, this dissatisfaction, coupled with the president's low public support, ignited a growing belief that "this was a Democratic year" among partisans considering running for Congress. Such conditions enhanced both the number and quality of Democrats seeking election. Democratic officials found it comparatively easy to recruit their best candidates to run for open House or Senate seats or to challenge an incumbent Republican, while many would-be Republican candidates declined to run.

On the other hand, those factors often exerted a nearly equal but reverse pressure on Republican faithful. In virtually every region of the country, Republican House and Senate candidates were seen running for Congress by running away from President Bush. Campaign fund-raising was down and frequently was surpassed by the success of Democratic campaigns, an outcome that ran contrary to many trends. Likewise, ambitious and talented Republican politicians declined invitations to run for Congress. Finally, a wave of incumbent Republicans decided to retire rather than face either an intense uphill reelection campaign or, for the most vulnerable members among them, certain bitter electoral defeat.

Congressional candidates tended to be caught between two powerful forces outside their campaign efforts—the widespread unpopularity of President Bush and the deft trend-setting campaign of the Democrat's presidential nominee, Barack Obama.

Barack Obama

The Obama campaign expanded the number of potential Democratic voters in all regions of the nation and mobilized them to show up and vote on Election Day. This proved to be the difference-maker in many close congressional races.

Obama's campaign was a model of efficient and creative use of modern technology, particularly the Internet and new communication technologies. The campaign employed text messaging and cell phones, which proved to be effective in reaching young voters in particular. Moreover, this helped to establish the tone of a nationwide yet personal conversation with supporters and was valuable in mobilizing both quickly and cheaply grassroots volunteers. More importantly, through the skillful use of the Internet, particularly e-mails, websites, YouTube, MySpace, and Facebook, the Obama campaign was able to raise a financially staggering record amount of money. By the end of the campaign, they had raised nearly $750 million of which more than $656 million coming from individual donors. Moreover, most of those contributions were classified in the "small" range of $25 to $200.[1]

This was important for congressional campaigns because everything the Obama campaign did, from voter registration, party building, media buys, and get-out-the-vote efforts, also energized and expanded the party's electoral "base" of supporters, while helping other Democrats. This also meant that the party could afford to wage a "fifty-state campaign" sought by Howard Dean which, among other things, forced Republicans to spend funds on campaigns they otherwise would have ignored as electorally "safe." In campaigns past, Democratic presidential candidates were not competitive in many southern or Rocky Mountain states, which made congressional races in those states even more difficult to win for Democrats.

A POLITICAL REALIGNMENT?

A realigning election is one in which a political party becomes the majority party among both the American electorate and elected offices held.[2] To be sure, a political realignment is widely considered to be a major watershed in American political history. The nation's last definitive realigning election occurred in 1932 when the Democratic ticket, headed by Franklin Roosevelt, won the presidency and a solid majority of seats in both the House and Senate. The Republicans, which had held all of those centers of power, became the minority party for a generation after the 1936 election confirmed that the 1932 outcome was indeed a realigning election. Democrats controlled both houses of Congress for much of the middle and latter half of the twentieth century.

Since that time, scholars and observers had speculated on the arrival of the next realigning election. However, realigning elections are based upon straight-ticket voting. Instead the American electorate evolved into ticket splitting, which tended to stimulate conflict in institutional governing while also successfully blocking opportunities for a realigning election.

However, the 2008 election results soon led some observers to speculation about it being a realigning election. Although the strength and scope of commitment exhibited by the major elements of the Democrats' electoral coalition will not become apparent until the 2010 midterm and 2012 presidential elections. While it is too early to tell and some scholars suggest that the election result was more a product of the success of Obama and failure of Bush, some indicators suggest at least the possibility of a pending political realignment.

Finally, reapportionment and redistricting issues can influence the legacy of the 2008 congressional elections. Allegations of Republican gerrymandering in Texas and several other states was thought to have created a political "fire wall" protecting party incumbents who otherwise might have been vulnerable in 2008. On the other hand, Democratic gains in several state-level campaigns in 2008 could help that party in upcoming reapportionment and redistricting battles following the 2010 census. Barring court challenges, the 2012 congressional campaigns should be the first employing the new House political map.

Red, White, and Purple: The Colors of American Politics

Throughout the past two decades, American states were divided into two political camps. As noted earlier in this book, "red" states were those dominated by Republicans and "blue" states were those normally won by Democrats. Republicans traditionally dominated governments in states in the southeast and Rocky Mountain regions while Democrats were increasingly successful in Atlantic Coast/New England and West Coast states. This left several Midwest states as the primary battleground between the two major political parties.

However, the 2008 elections produced another color—purple—in the nation's political color palate. Purple states were those thought to be capable of being won by candidates from either party. Purple states often were the scene of the nation's most intense electoral struggles. In 2008, traditional red states such as Virginia, North Carolina, and Colorado were recalibrated from political red to purple. While Democrats did not gain dominance in such states, they did become much more competitive and won key races in those states.

In 2008, Democrats picked up eight Senate seats previously held by Republicans in the states of Oregon, Colorado, New Mexico, New Hampshire, Alaska, Virginia, North Carolina, and Minnesota. Al Franken (D-MN) apparently won the Minnesota seat by a slim 225 votes out of more than 2.9 million cast statewide in Minnesota. He later had to win repeated court challenges to his victory made by the incumbent Republican, Norm Coleman, thus delaying the final outcome of the contest until the following January. Republicans failed to win a single Senate seat previously held by a Democrat. Elsewhere, the Democratic victory in such a thoroughly red state as Virginia also made national headlines. In Virginia, the race pitted two previous governors—Republican James. Gilmore and Democrat Mark Warner—and ended with a 31 percent landslide by the Democrat.

On the other end of Capitol Hill, election returns among House candidates largely were similar to those of their Senate counterparts. The Democrats gained twenty-two House seats. Their victories included taking all twenty-two House seats from the New England states plus winning decisive majorities in delegations from New York, Pennsylvania, New Jersey, and the three Pacific Coast states. Democrats also picked up one House seat in each of three states that were generally red sates in the Mountain West: Arizona, Colorado, and Idaho. In addition, Democrats gained seats in two of the region's more competitive states, adding one seat in Nevada and two in New Mexico.

The best news for House Republicans came from Southeastern states where three of the party's pickups from the Democrats were attained. The party's other take away came in red state Kansas's 2nd District.

Turn On and Turn Out

Turnout is the percent of eligible voters casting their ballots on Election Day. The nation's turnout rate in 2008 was 61.6 percent, the highest recorded rate in four decades. Turnout increased in thirty-three states plus the District of Columbia. Minnesota had the highest turnout in the country at

77.8 percent, while West Virginia and Hawaii tied for the lowest rate at 50.6 percent, which is still an amount similar to national figures in recent presidential elections. These totals were based on the percentage of eligible voters among adult American citizens and it must be noted that states vary when determining who is eligible to vote. For example, most states disqualify not only noncitizens but convicted felons as well from voting.

Several factors likely contributed to the high voter turnout. The list is headed by several forces mentioned here—enthusiasm surrounding the Obama candidacy, dissatisfaction with the Bush presidency, growing fear stemming from the massive nationwide economic crisis, and the widespread voter registration and get-out-the-vote effort of the Obama campaign. In addition, early voting, allowed in many states, attracted a record turnout of 41 million people. Representing more than 31 percent of the electorate, these early voters possibly were motivated by many of the aforementioned factors combined with a desire to avoid waiting in anticipated long lines at polls on Election Day. As a result, for example, several states such as Florida recorded such high early voting numbers that the waits were often much longer for early voting than voting on Election Day. This increased high turnout rate was particularly noticeable among African American and young voters. Both voting blocs were motivated by the Obama campaign and were likely key in helping Democratic candidates win close congressional elections, such as the Senate races in Minnesota and North Carolina.

Overall, more Americans—131 million—voted on November 4, 2008, than any time in the nation's history. The Obama strategy of courting and activating young voters clearly paid off, as 53 percent of the eighteen to twenty-nine age group voted in 2008. This was the highest turnout of young voters since eighteen- to twenty-year-olds received the right to vote in 1972. While they were mobilized to support Obama, they likely wanted to further support him by voting for his party's candidates for Congress.

On the other hand, many Republican voters, discouraged by the Bush presidency, John McCain's lackluster candidacy and campaign, and the parade of bad economic news, decided to stay at home on Election Day and wait for more attractive events and candidates in later elections.

The Power of Incumbency Remained Strong

Despite the turmoil in 2008 and many upsets at the polls, incumbent candidates in both chambers tended to be successful in their reelection efforts, although clearly more so for Democrats than Republicans. Throughout the past six decades, incumbent congressional candidates traditionally have won reelection with ease. The success rate among incumbent representatives has tended to be higher, often in excess of 90 percent, than the success rate of senators up for reelection, which has often been around 65 percent or higher. In 2008, a noteworthy 100 percent of incumbent Democrat senators won reelection while 73 percent of Republican senators retained their seats. All twelve incumbent Democrats were reelected while eleven of fifteen incumbent Republicans won a new six-year term. The four defeated incumbent Republicans were Norman Coleman of Minnesota, Elizabeth Dole of North Carolina, Gordon Smith of Oregon, and John Sununu of New Hampshire, reflecting the different regions of the country. In addition to defeating incumbent Republicans, the Democrats picked up four open seats previously held by Republicans.

In the House, twenty incumbents, four Democrats, and sixteen Republicans were defeated for reelection. Three of the sixteen Republicans lost primary contests. The reelection rate was more than 98 percent for House Democrats and 94 percent for House Republicans seeking reelection.

Finally, some members retired from Congress. Among the many reasons members retire is to avoid either a tough reelection fight or a sure electoral defeat. In 2008, five senators—all Republicans—retired while twenty-six representatives—all but three of them Republicans—chose to leave Capitol Hill.

CONCLUSIONS AND LESSONS: ENDURING DILEMMAS, NEW CHALLENGES

The 2008 campaign might have been a realigning election. The thought will either be rejected or affirmed after the passage of time and outcomes from policy decisions made by Democratic congressional majorities and Barack Obama in the next few years. The difficulty of meeting the many challenges posed by crises in foreign relations and the economy, plus other domestic affairs was daunting, to say the least. And it will remain so. Obama and the Democrats come to power at a time when America is facing a bewildering array of serious challenges perhaps unseen in history. As a result, public perception of policy failures in the next few years could very well turn the anti-Republican and anti-incumbent mood found among voters in 2008 into an anti-Democrat and anti-incumbent mood.

As important and historic as the 2008 congressional elections were, some things did not change. That included the unsavory side of politics, in that the election had more than its share of scandals, several of which are profiled in this book. Senator Ted Stevens (R-AL) narrowly lost his reelection bid after being found guilty one week before Election Day of seven felony counts for failing to report gifts from businesses. Illinois produced even more political turmoil in the process of replacing the victorious Barack Obama in the U.S. Senate. Federal officials investigating allegations of corruption by Governor Rod R. Blagojevich announced (D-IL) they had recordings of telephone conversations where the governor was attempting to sell the Senate nomination to the highest bidder. Amid widespread calls for his resignation, indictment, and/or impeachment, the governor proceeded to nominate a former Illinois Attorney General, Roland W. Burris (D-IL), to fill Obama's vacant seat, thus initiating more scandal among state politicians attempting to impeach Blagojevich and members of Congress who vowed not to seat anyone the governor appointed.

Membership of the 111th Congress

The new 111th Congress produced by the 2008 elections was distinctive in many ways. For instance, its members were older than its predecessors. In the House, the average age of members was fifty-seven while in the Senate it was sixty-three. The election also saw the defeat of the last House Republican to represent a New England state—Chris Shays of Connecticut.

The new House freshman class of fifty-four was below the average of seventy-eight new members commonly found in elections in the post–World War II period. In addition, the new House of Representatives had forty-one African Americans (all Democrats), twenty-five Hispanics (twenty-two of them Democrats), seven of Asian heritage (five Democrats, one Republican, one Independent), and seventy-seven women (sixty Democrats and seventeen Republicans).

In the Senate, there were no African Americans (pending the approval of the nomination of Roland Burris of Illinois), three Hispanics (two Democrats and one Republican), two Asians (both Democrats), and seventeen women (thirteen Democrats and four Republicans). In addition, entering the new Senate was a pair of cousins, Tom Udall (D-NM) and Mark Udall (D-CO).

However, many of the party's new House members won close elections to represent districts composed of a majority of conservative voters. The prevailing pressure on many of these new Democrats likely would be to be independent of the liberal Democrats which dominate the party in both the House and Senate. This will be a challenge for the majority party, but Democrats helped their cause during the campaign by running and nominating candidates who were generally more moderate, better fund-raisers, and electable.

It was a notable election, potentially as important for the immediate future of the American body politic as the presidential election. It was also an election with as much intrigue and controversy as the presidential race and, with the stakes potentially higher than any time in modern American history, the new Congress will play a role in making or breaking America.

NOTES

1. A great source for monitoring campaign fund-raising at an array of campaigns is OpenSecrets.org, a website of the Center for Responsible Politics.

2. The concept of realigning elections was initially formulated by V. O. Key in "A Theory of Critical Elections," *Journal of Politics*, February 1955, 3–18, and expanded on by Angus Campbell in "A Classification of Presidential Elections," in *Elections in the Political Order*, by Angus Campbell, Philip Converse, Warren Miller, and Donald Stokes (New York: Wiley, 1966).

Appendix A: Constitutional Requirements for Congress

	Age	Citizenship	Residency
House	25	U.S. citizen for 7 years	Resident of state representing
Senate	30	U.S. citizen for 9 years	Resident of state representing

Source: Article I of the U.S. Constitution specifies three requirements.

Appendix B: Party Control of Congress

		HOUSE			**SENATE**			**MAJORITY**	
Congr	Years	Dem	Rep	Other	Dem	Rep	Other	House	Senate
57th	1901–1903	151	200	6	32	56	2	Rep	Rep
58th	1903–1905	176	203	3	33	57	0	Rep	Rep
59th	1905–1907	135	251	0	32	58	0	Rep	Rep
60th	1907–1909	167	223	1	31	61	0	Rep	Rep
61st	1909–1911	172	219	0	32	60	0	Rep	Rep
62nd	1911–1913	230	162	2	44	52	0	Dem	Rep
63rd	1913–1915	291	134	10	51	44	1	Dem	Dem
64th	1915–1917	230	196	9	56	40	0	Dem	Dem
65th	1917–1919	214	215	6	54	42	0	Rep	Dem
66th	1919–1921	192	240	2	47	49	0	Rep	Rep
67th	1921–1923	131	302	2	37	59	0	Rep	Rep
68th	1923–1925	207	225	2	42	53	1	Rep	Rep
69th	1925–1927	183	247	5	41	54	1	Rep	Rep
70th	1927–1929	194	238	3	46	48	1	Rep	Rep
71st	1929–1931	164	270	1	39	56	1	Rep	Rep
72nd	1931–1933	216	218	1	47	48	1	Rep	Rep
73rd	1933–1935	313	117	5	59	36	1	Dem	Dem
74th	1935–1937	322	103	10	69	25	2	Dem	Dem
75th	1937–1939	334	88	13	76	16	4	Dem	Dem
76th	1939–1941	262	169	4	69	23	4	Dem	Dem
77th	1941–1943	267	162	6	66	28	2	Dem	Dem
78th	1943–1945	222	209	4	57	38	1	Dem	Dem
79th	1945–1947	242	191	2	57	38	1	Dem	Dem
80th	1947–1949	188	246	1	45	51	0	Rep	Rep
81st	1949–1951	263	171	1	54	42	0	Dem	Dem
82nd	1951–1953	235	199	1	49	47	0	Dem	Dem
83rd	1953–1955	213	221	1	47	48	1	Rep	Rep
84th	1955–1957	232	203	0	48	47	1	Dem	Dem
85th	1957–1959	234	201	0	49	47	0	Dem	Dem
86th	1959–1961	283	153	1	65	35	0	Dem	Dem
87th	1961–1963	263	174	0	64	36	0	Dem	Dem
88th	1963–1965	259	176	0	66	34	0	Dem	Dem
89th	1965–1967	295	140	0	68	32	0	Dem	Dem

Congr	Years	HOUSE Dem	HOUSE Rep	HOUSE Other	SENATE Dem	SENATE Rep	SENATE Other	MAJORITY House	MAJORITY Senate
90th	1967–1969	247	187	0	64	36	0	Dem	Dem
91st	1969–1971	243	192	0	57	43	0	Dem	Dem
92nd	1971–1973	255	180	0	54	44	2	Dem	Dem
93rd	1973–1975	242	192	1	56	42	2	Dem	Dem
94th	1975–1977	291	144	0	60	38	2	Dem	Dem
95th	1977–1979	292	143	0	61	38	1	Dem	Dem
96th	1979–1981	277	158	0	58	41	1	Dem	Dem
97th	1981–1983	242	192	1	46	53	1	Dem	Rep
98th	1983–1985	269	166	0	46	54	0	Dem	Rep
99th	1985–1987	253	182	0	47	53	0	Dem	Rep
100th	1987–1989	258	177	0	55	45	0	Dem	Dem
101st	1989–1991	260	175	0	55	45	0	Dem	Dem
102nd	1991–1993	267	167	1	56	44	0	Dem	Dem
103rd	1993–1995	258	176	1	57	43	0	Dem	Dem
104th	1995–1997	204	230	1	48	52	0	Rep	Rep
105th	1997–1999	206	228	1	45	55	0	Rep	Rep
106th	1999–2001	211	223	1	45	55	0	Rep	Rep
107th	2001–2003	212	221	2	50	50	0	Rep	Rep
108th	2003–2005	204	229	1	48	49	1	Rep	Rep
109th	2005–2007	202	232	1	45	55	0	Rep	Rep
110th	2007–2009	233	202	0	49	49	2	Dem	Dem
111th	2009–2011	256	178	1	58	40	2	Dem	Dem

Source: Office of the Clerk, U.S. House of Representatives

Appendix C:
Length of Service in Congress

	CONGRESS			
CHAMBER/TERMS	1st–56th (1789–1901)	57th–103rd (1901–1995)	104th–109th (1995–2007)	110th (2007–2009)
HOUSE				
One (up to 2 years)	44.0%	23.3%	13.6%	12.4%
Two to six (3–12 years)	53.4%	49.7%	56.4%	45.3%
Seven or more (12+ years)	2.6%	27.0%	30.1%	42.3%
Mean number of terms	2.1	4.8	5.3	6.1
SENATE				
One (up to 6 years)	65.6%	45.6%	33.8%	30.0%
Two (7–12 years)	23.4%	22.4%	27.4%	25.0%
Three or more (12+ years)	11.0%	32.0%	38.8%	45.0%
Mean number of terms	1.5	2.2	2.6	2.8

Source: Adapted from Mildred Amer, "Average Years of Service for Members of the Senate and House of Representatives," Congressional Research Service Report, RL32648, November 9, 2005.

Appendix D: Reelection Rates in Congress

HOUSE

Decade	Sought Reelection	Faced No Opponent	Lost Primary	Lost General	Percent Reelected
1950s	402	85	6	25	93.2
1960s	404	52	8	26	91.5
1970s	389	57	2	23	92.3
1980s	403	67	13	15	95.7
1990s	385	36	8	18	93.6
2000s (aver.)	394	59	4	13	95.9
2006	401	36	2	22	94.0

SENATE

Decade	Sought Reelection	Faced No Opponent	Lost Primary	Lost General	Percent Reelected
1950s	30	4	1	6	77.3
1960s	32	1	2	4	80.8
1970s	27	1	2	6	67.7
1980s	29	1	0	3	88.0
1990s	26	0	0	3	87.4
2000s (aver.)	27	2	1	3	96.7
2006	28	0	0	6	78.6

Source: CQ Weekly Report, April 5, 1980, 908; November 8, 1980, 3302; July 31, 1982, 2281; November 10, 1984, 2897, 2901; November 12, 1988, 3264, 3270; November 10, 1990, 3796–3805; November 7, 1992, 3557–64; November 12, 1994, 3291; February 15, 1997, 447–55; November 7, 1998, 3027–35; November 11, 2000, 2694–2706; December 14, 2002, 3289–97; November 6, 2004, 2653–60; November 13, 2006, 3068–75.

Appendix E: Margins of Victory in Congressional Elections

HOUSE

Year	Under 55	55–59.9	60+	Unopposed
1974	24	16	46	14
1976	17	14	56	12
1978	17	14	53	16
1980	18	14	60	8
1982	16	16	63	6
1984	12	13	61	14
1986	9	10	64	17
1988	6	9	67	18
1990	11	16	58	15
1992	20	18	58	3
1994	22	17	52	9
1996	22	18	57	3
1998	10	17	63	10
2000	23	12	59	15
2002	10	10	80	18
2004	7	14	64	15
2006	15	14	62	9

PERCENTAGE OF VOTE

SENATE

PERCENTAGE OF VOTE

Year	Under 55	55–59.9	60+	Unopposed
1974	41	18	35	6
1976	30	33	30	6
1978	24	33	36	6
1980	58	18	21	3
1982	30	27	43	0
1984	18	21	58	3
1986	38	15	47	0
1988	33	15	52	0
1990	26	11	49	14
1992	34	34	32	0
1994	32	34	34	0
1996	59	18	24	0
1998	29	9	62	0
2000	29	15	55	0
2002	38	18	44	4
2004	32	15	50	3
2006	24	21	55	0

Source: Roger H. Davidson, Walter J. Oleszek, and Frances E. Lee, *Congress and It's Members* (Washington, DC: CQ Press, 2008), 138.

Appendix F: Voting Turnout in Congressional Elections

PERCENT TURNOUT IN ELECTIONS

Year	Congress	President
1946	37	—
1948	49	51
1950	42	—
1952	58	62
1954	43	—
1956	56	60
1958	44	—
1960	59	63
1962	49	—
1964	58	62
1966	50	—
1968	55	61
1970	47	—
1972	50	55
1974	40	—
1976	49	55
1978	38	—
1980	48	53
1982	41	—

PERCENT TURNOUT IN ELECTIONS

Year	Congress	President
1984	48	53
1986	37	—
1988	46	51
1990	38	—
1992	52	55
1994	39	—
1996	48	48
1998	37	—
2000	47	50
2002	41	—
2004	50	56
2006	44	—
2008	56	56

Source: Michael McDonald, U.S. Elections Project, George Mason University, Fairfax, Virginia http://elections.gmu.edu/voter_turnout.

Note: Numbers are rounded to nearest percent

Index

AARP. *See* American Association of Retired Persons
abortion, 20, 22, 26, 35–36, 39, 140, 196
Abramoff, Jack, 253, 255
affirmative action, 20, 150
Afghanistan, 22, 23–24, 130
AFL-CIO. *See* American Federation of Labor—Congress of Industrial Organizations
Alabama, 186
Alaska, 227–43, 276, 278
Alexander, Rodney, 187
Alexandria, Virginia, 73–74, 90
Alger, Horatio, 26
Allard, Wayne, 12, 250–51, 254
Allen, George, 138, 213, 217, 254
Alliance, Ohio, 134
American Association of Retired Persons, 84, 141
American Federation of Labor—Congress of Industrial Organizations, 87, 140, 160, 163, 239, 241, 258, 260
Amtrak, 105
Anchorage, Alaska, 231, 233, 235, 241
Anthony, Susan B., 261
ANWR. *See* Arctic National Wildlife Refuge
Arctic National Wildlife Refuge, 135–36, 194, 232, 237
Arizona, 4, 96, 276
Ashland, Ohio, 130, 135, 138
Atanasio, Paul, 79, 84
Atwater, Lee, 148, 166
Aurora, Illinois, 55, 57

Baghdad, 102
Baker, Richard, 193
balanced budget, 6, 23, 25, 175
Baldauf, Dan, 173, 176, 180
Baliles, Gerald, 209
Barbour, Haley, 17, 28
Barnes, Kay Waldo, 33–52, 46
Bartlett, Bob, 229, 232
Baton Rouge, Louisiana, 189, 196, 199
Bay of Pigs, 155
Begich, Mark, 227–43
Begich, Nick, 233
Bennett, Bob, 130, 131
Berkowitz, Ethan, 241
Betancourt, Annie, 155
bicameral, 5
Biden, Joseph, 24, 164
Blagojevich, Rod, 278–79
Blanco, Kathleen, 193, 194
blogging, 7
Bloomberg, Michael, 81, 83, 88

"Blue Dog," 18
Blue Springs, Missouri, 35, 37
Boccieri, John, 127–46, *144*
Boehner, John, 114
Bond, Kit, 38
Bonilla, Henry, 96, 97, 99
Booneville, Mississippi, 21
Bossier City, Louisiana, 189
Boulder, Colorado, 248, 254, 255, 263
Boustany, Charles, 193
Boxer, Barbara, 114
Bow, Frank, 127
Bradenton, Florida, 170
Breaux, John, 163
Brooklyn, New York, 75–79, 82
Broomfield, Charles, *46*
Brown, Sherrod, 129
Brown, Ted, 123
Browning, Dave, *46*, 50
Buchanan, Vern, 169–81, *180*
Buck, Erik, *46*
Bureau of the Census. *See* Census
Burke, Lynda Billa, 108
Burns, Kevin, 57
Burris, Roland, 279
Bush, George H. W., *210*
Bush, George W., 4, 6–13, 20–24, 27, 30, 35–36, 37, 39, 41, 45, 46, 54, 59, 61, 76, 83, 103, 115, 116, 121, 122, 127–28, 131, 133, 136, 149, 150, 152, 153, 156, 162, 172, 179, 180, 186, 198, *210*, 212, 218, 251, 263, 271–74
Bush, Jeb, 170
Bush, Laura, 198
Bustamante, Albert, 97
Byrd, Harry, Sr., 206

Calderon, Michael, 155
California, 10, 11, 13, 96, 111–25, 236
Calvert, Ken, 124
Campbell, Ben Knighthorse, 251
Canseco, Francisco, 100, 105
Canton, Ohio, 128, 131, 138
Canusa, Jorge Mas, 150
capital punishment, 20
capitol, 3
Capitol Weekly, 123

Carson, Julia, 10
Carter, Jimmy, 208, 209, 273
Case Western Reserve University, 152
Castro, Fidel, 148, 149, 152, 155, 157
CBS, 75
Census, 11, 35, 77, 150, 155, 213, 275
Center for Responsive Politics, 107
Chambliss, Saxby, 197
Cheney, Dick, 13, 28, 45, 198
Chicago, Illinois, 54, 55, 63, 64
Chichester, John, 221
Childers, Travis, 17–32
Chiles, Lawton, 175
China, 23, 61, 232
Cirelli, Mary, 130
Citizens Against Government Waste, 37
civil rights policy, 7, 213
Clai, Rudy, 57
Claremont McKenna University, 113
Clark, Wesley, 115
Cleveland, Ohio, 142–43
Clinton, Bill, 6–7, 28, 35, 54, 174, 187, 246, 273
Clinton, Hillary Rodham, 62, 85, 87–88, 105, 158, 166
coattails, 6–7, 49, 206, 272
Cochran, Thad, 26, 28
Cochrane, Timothy, 84, *89*
Cole, Tom, 142–43
Coleman, Marshall, 22, 211, 216
Coleman, Norm, 13, 278
Colorado, 8, 12, 276
Colorado Springs, Colorado, 249, 256
Columbia University, 173
Columbus, Mississippi, 20, 29
Confederacy, 213, 254
Congress: apportionment, 11; approval, 4, 9–10; and campaign finance, 7–9, 11, 27, 31, 43–44, 57, 63, 100, 107, 117–18, *118*, 163–64, 177, 198, 218, 221, 240, 258–59, 274; committee system, 5, 9, 37; constituencies, 5; corruption, 3–4, 10, 12–13, 152, 159, 170; filibuster, 9, 13; legislative process, 5–6; and pork barrel politics, 4, 233; seniority system in, 13; and special interests, 4, 7, 28, 139–40

Congressional Quarterly, 13, 77, 186, 192
Connecticut, 9, 215, 272
Connolly, Lani, 101
Constitution, U.S., 3, 5
Contract with America, 153
Cook Political Report, 13, 54, 76, 128, 186
Cooksey, John, 191, 193
Coors, Pete, 251, 258, 261
Coral Gables, Florida, 161
Corinth, Mississippi, 20
Cornyn, John, 96
Cowpen, Steve, 229
Craig, Larry, 12
Creighton, Janet, 131
Cronkite, Walter, 38
Cuba, 148–56, 163
Cuban American National Foundation, 149, 153, 155
Cuddy, Dave, 235
Cuellar, Henry, 97, 99
Cunningham, Randall, 3–4
Cusack, Patrick, 153
Cusick, Michael, 78

Dann, Mark, 134
Danner, Steve, 35
Dardenne, Jay, 193
Daschle, Tom, 254
Davis, Charles, 17–32
Davis, Gray, 113
Davis, Richard J., 210
Davis, Thomas, III, 215
Dawkins, Maurice, A., 210
Dean, Howard, 274
Dekalb, Illinois, 55
DeLay, Tom, 3, 12–13, 114
Demint, Jim, 242
Denver, Colorado, 248, 263
Denver Post, 255
Diaz-Balart, Lincoln, 147–68
Diaz-Balart, Mario, 147–68
Dilger, Mike, 57
Dobson, James, 248
Dole, Bob, *210*
Dole, Elizabeth, 278
Dominican Republic, 150
Dominici, Pete, 12, 193

Dreier, David, 111–25, *118*, *119*
Duncan, Ken, 192
Duke University, 4

Eagle Pass, Texas, 98, 108
economic policy, 6–10, 18, 20, 22–23, 25–26, 30, 41, 65, 83, 116, 151, 156, 220, 264, 271
education policy, 98–99
Egan, Bill, 228–29
Eisenhower, Dwight, *210*, 232
Electoral College, 9
Elgin, Illinois, 55
Ellsworth, Brad, 196
El Paso, Texas, 105
EMILY's List, 38–39, 176
Emmanuel, Rahm, 130, 142
energy policy, 6, 9–10, 22–23, 39–42, 60, 135–36, 156, 178, 190, 193, 219, 221, 230, 234, 250–52, 254, 256–58, 272
Ensign, John, 236
environmental policy, 7, 39, 258
Everglades, 151–52, 162–63

Facebook, 26, 199, 254
Fairbanks, Alaska, 231, 241
family values, 22, 26, 36, 40–41, 48, 253–54
Fannie Mae, 43
Faye, Leslie, 73
FBI, 234–35
FEC. *See* Federal Elections Commission
Federal Elections Commission, 78, 86, 106, 114, 117, 130, 142, 159, 222
Feeney, Tom, 150
Fermi National Laboratory, 58, 66
Ferraro, Arnoldo, 80
Fields, Cleo, 191
fiscal policy, 18, 21
Flake, Jeff, 250
Fleischer, Ari, 136
Flickr, 26
Florida, 7, 11–13, 96, 147–81, *171*
Florida International University, 153, 162, 167
Florida Keys, 151

Flowers, Gennifer, 6
Focus on the Family, 248
Foley, Mark, 4, 12
Font, Jorge de Castro, 160
Ford, Gerald, 10, *210*, 273
foreign policy, 20, 37
Fort Collins, Colorado, 248, 256
Fort Lauderdale, Florida, 149
Fossella, Vito, 73–75, 84–90, *86*, 87
Foster, Bill, 53–71
Foster, Mike, 191
Founding, 3
Franken, Al, 13
Freedom Watch, 136
Friscia, John, 79, 82

Garcia, Joe, 147–68
gay rights, 12, 20, 22, 35–36, 40, 48, 122–23
George Washington University, 215
gerrymandering, 11, 96–97, 111, 150
GI Bill, 65
Gilmore, Jim, 205–26, 276
Gingrich, Newt, 61, 113, 273
Giuliani, Rudolf, 76, *118*
Gladstone, Missouri, 35
Goepfert, Alex, 138
Golden, Martin, 88
Gonzalez, Frank, 153, 166
Gore, Al, 150, 174, 191, 215
Gravel, Mike, 229
Graves, Samuel, 33–52, *46*
Great Depression, 272
Great Plains, 8
Greeley, Colorado, 249, 256
Green Party, 25, 228
Greer, Jim, 158
Grenada, Mississippi, 20
Guardian Angels, 79
Gulf of Alaska, 233
Gulf of Mexico, 178, 193–94
gun control, 7, 20, 22, 26, 29–30, 129, 134–35

Hagel, Chuck, 12
Haik-Terrell, Suzanne, 191
Haiti, 151
Hammond, Jay, 229
Harlem, New York, 83
Harvard University, 216, 232
Harris, Katherine, 169
Harrison, Edythe C., 210
Harrison, Stephen, 76, 78, 81–82, *82*, 86, 86–87
Hart, Gary, 261
Hastert, Dennis, 10, 54–56, 64, 68
Hatch, Orrin, 236
Havana, 152
Hawaii, 5, 276
health care policy, 6, 22, 30, 59, 98–99, 156, 178, 258
Hialeah, Florida, 151–54
Hickel, Wally, 228–29, 232
Holland, Steve, 22, 29–30
Holocaust, 10
Holton, Linwood, 209
homeland security, 22–24
Homestead, Florida, 152
Hood, Jim, 19
Huffington Post, 162
Hurricane Gustav, 199
Hurricane Katrina, 27, 186–87, 195, 201

Idaho, 12, 276
Illinois, 10–11, 30, 53–71
immigration, 24, 25, 36, 37, 40, 58, 61–62, 102–3, 112, 115, 120, 153, 157
Indiana, 10
Inouye, Daniel, 236
Internal Revenue Service, 122, 178, 235
Internet, 7–8, 26, 138
Iowa, 157
Iraq War, 20, 22, 23–24, 48, 58–59, 81, 84, 102, 115, 121, 123, 130, 156, 178, 250, 271
IRS. *See* Internal Revenue Service
Israel, 162

Jackson, Ohio, 131
Jacobs, Rick, 122–23
Jefferson, William, 4
Jenkins, Woody, 191
Jennings, Christine, 169–81, *180*
Jetton, Ron, 38

Index

Jindal, Bobby, 197, 201
John, Chris, 192
Johnson, Lyndon B., *210*, 246, 249
Jones, Paula, 6
Juneau, Alaska, 230-31, 242

Kansas, 276
Kansas City, Missouri, 34-39, 43, 45, 48
Kenai, Alaska, 241
Kendall, Florida, 151, 161, 165
Kennedy, John F., 247
Kennedy, John N., 185-204
Kent State University, 131
Kerry, John, 27, 76, 150, 193, 247
Kim, Jay, 112
King, Peter, 88
Knowles, Tony, 229, 240
Kurdistan, 254

Laesch, John, 56
Lafayette, Louisiana, 189
LaGuardia, Fiorello, 80
Lake Charles, Louisiana, 199
Landrieu, Mary, 185-204
Landrieu, Moon, 190
Lantos, Tom, 10
Lanza, Andrew, 76
Laredo, Texas, 99
Larson, Lyle, 95-110
Latin America, 171
Lauzen, Chris, 57, 62, 63, 65, 68
Lay, Kenneth, 160
League of Conservation Voters, 252
League of United Latin American Citizens, 97
League of Women Voters, 258
Lehtinen, Dexter, 154
Libertarian Party, 25, 79, 101, 112, 228
Liberty, Missouri, 35, 46
Lieberman, Joseph, 9, 272
Lincoln, Abraham, 173, 272
Lloyd, James, 111
lobbyists, 3
Long, Michael, 84
Lopez, Vito, 78
Los Angeles, California, 112
Los Angeles Times, 120, 122

Lott, Trent, 17, 28
Louisiana, 10, 30, 185-204
Louisiana State University 196, 199

Madrid, 152
"majority minority" districts, 5, 11
Manhattan, New York, 78, 79-80, 84
Marchi, John, 76
Marshall, Robert, 215
Martinez, Mel, 170
Martinez, Raul, 147-68
Maryville, Missouri, 44
Massachusetts, 11
Matthews, Cynthia, 114-15
McCain, John, 31, 36, 37, 50, 85, 86, 89, 114, 116, 117, *118*, 138, 144, 158, 163, 164, 194, 200-201, 222-23, 228, 259, 264, 276
McCaskill, Claire, 36
McConnell, Mitch, 197, 198, 236
McCrery, Jim, 193
McCullough, Glen, 21, 25, 30
McKinley, William, 128, 133
McMahon, Michael, 73-93, *82*, *86*, *89*
McNerney, Jerry, 122
Medicare, 22, 24-25, 104
Meek, Kendrick, 165
Meet the Press, 255
Melancon, Charlie, 189
Memphis, Tennessee, 19, 29
Mexico, 98, 102-3
Miami, 147-68
Miami Beach, Florida, 155
Miami Herald, 159, 162
Michigan, 10
Middle East, 6, 60
Midwest, 8
Miller, Andrew, 210
Miller, Harris, 212
Miller, James C., 212
Miller, Matt, 129, 130, 132
Minnesota, 8, 13, 163, 276, 278
Miramar, Florida, 151
Mississippi, 10, 17-32, 186
Mississippi River, 55
Mississippi State University, 17, 21
Missouri, 8, 33-52, *50*, 113

Molinari, Guy, 75, 81, 84, 88
Molinari, Susan, 75
Monroe, Louisiana, 199
Morano, Carmine, 80, *82*, *86*, *87*, *89*
Morrell, Arthur, 192
Mount McKinley, 255
MoveOn.org, 8
Murkowski, Frank, 229
Murkowski, Lisa, 240
Murphy, Patrick, 58
MySpace, 26, 199

Naples, Florida, 151
NASCAR, 173
National Association of Manufacturers, 139
National Education Association, 140
National Guard, 24
National Journal, 100, 192
National Organization for Women, 81
National Rifle Association, 22, 28, 135, 139, 199, 261
national security, 12, 18, 20, 22, 23
Native Alaskans, 230
NCLB. *See* No Child Left Behind
NEA. *See* National Education Association
Nebraska, 12
Nevada, 8, 117
New College/University of South Florida, 152
New Deal, 60
New England, 8, 276
New Hampshire, 8, 278
New Jersey, 11, 96, 174
New Middletown, Ohio, 133
New Mexico, 8, 12, 276
New Orleans, Louisiana, 188–90, 195, 196, 199
New York, 11, 13, 73–93, 95, 124
New York Giants, 74, 83
New York Times, 82, 149, 162
Nicaragua, 150
Nixon, Richard, 10, *210*
No Child Left Behind, 37, 237
Noriega, Rick, 97, 109
North, Oliver, 211

North Carolina, 11, 276, 278
Northeast, 8, 95
Northern Illinois University, 55
Northern Marianas Islands, 253
Northwest Missouri State University, 44
NOW. *See* National Organization for Women
NRA. *See* National Rifle Association

Obama, Barack, 7, 9–10, 22, 23, 26–27, 31, 36, 49, *50*, 62–63, 64, 68, 85, 96, 106, 109, 112, 116, 117, 121, 137, 164, 166, 188, 200, *210*, 222, 271, 274, 277
Oberweis, Jim, 53, 71
Odom, Bob, 194
Oelslager, Scott, 132
Ohio, 7, 8, 11, 127–46, 175, 240
Oklahoma, 143
Oliva Branch, Mississippi, 20
Oregon, 276, 278
Our Lady of the Lake University, 99
Overeem, Susan, 79
Owens, Bill, 246, 251
Owens, Major, 81

PAC, 27, 85–87, 106–7, 117, 123, 140, 160, 163, 177, 198, 240, 258
Palin, Sarah, 85, 86, 89, 143, 228, 231, 234, 239
Pang, Wally, 25, 29, 31
Park University, 38
Pasadena, California, 122
Pataki, George, 88
Pelosi, Nancy, 40, 42, 61, 257
Pembroke Pines, Florida, 151
Pennsylvania, 7, 11, 12, 58, 96, 173, 197, 276
Pepper, Claude, 148
Perry, Rick, 96, 97
Petraeus, David, 5
Pike's Peak, 255
Politico, 255
Pombo, Richard, 122
Powell, Colin, 236
Powers, Frank, 79
Price, David, 4

Progressive Democrats for America, 81
Project Exodus, 155
Puerto Rico, 150, 160

Rancho Cucamonga, California, 113, 122
Rangel, Charlie, 83
Reagan, Ronald, 6, 111, *210*, 212
Recchia, Dominic, 78, *86*, 87
Regula, Ralph, 127, 129–32
Regula, Richard, 129
religion, 26, 35
Richman, Gerald, 148
Richmond, Virginia, 208, 217, 219
Rinehart, Cathy, *46*
Rio Grande, 98, 102
Robb, Charles, 211, 212
"robo-calls," 61–62, 136, 199
Rockford, Illinois, 55
Rodriguez, Ciro, 95–110
Rodriguez, Sergio, 108
Roe, Jeff, 37, 48
Roll Call, 143, 161
Romney, Mitt, 170
Roosevelt, Franklin D., 272, 275
Ros-Lehtinen, Ileana, 148, 154, 160
Rothenberg, Stuart, 31
Rothenberg Report, 143, 186
Rove, Karl, 7, 254
Russell, Randy, 21, 25
Russia, 23
Ryan, Tim, 250

Salazar, Ken, 194, 246–47, *247*, 250, 251, 258, 259, 261
San Antonio, Texas, 96, 98–100, 105, 107
Sanders, Bernie, 9, 272
Sarasota, Florida, 170, 174–75
Savino, Diane, 78
Schaffer, Bob, 245–68
Schiffer, Paul, 132
SCHIP, 27, 30, 149
Schneider, Jan, 173, 176, 180
Schumer, Chuck, 85, 88
Schuring, Kirk, 127–46, *132*, *144*
Schwarzenegger, Arnold, 114
Second Amendment, 29, 134–35
SEIU, 87, 260

Serra, Joe, 56
Shays, Christopher, 279
Shettles, Sara Jo, 38, *46*
Shreveport, Louisiana, 199
Sierra Club, 260
Simon, Paul, 157
Sliwa, Curtis, 79
Smith, Gordon, 278
Social Security, 22, 24–25, 84, 104, 142, 258
Soldier Field, 58
Soto, Javier, 150
the South, 8, 10, 18, 20, 23, 26, 186, 202, 275–76
South Africa, 213
Southaven, Mississippi, 20, 21, 25, 30
South Carolina, 186
South Dakota, 119
Spain, 152
Specter, Arlen, 12–13
Sprong, William, Jr., 210
Staten Island, 74, 78, 80, 88–89
St. Boneventure University, 129
Stevens, Ted, 227–43, 278
Stien, Jotham, 56
St. Joseph, Missouri, 34, 38–39
St. Mary's University, 98
Straniere, Robert, 73–93, *82*, *86*, *89*
Strategic Petroleum Reserve, 136
Strickland, Ted, 129
Suarez, Xavier, 154
Sugar Grove, Illinois, 57
Sullivan, Emmet, 235
Sununu, John, 278
Swann, Lynn, 197
Swiftboat Veterans for Truth, 8

Taft, Robert, 133, 134
Talent, Jim, 36
Tamiami, Florida, 152
Tarkio, Missouri, 36–37
tax policy, 22–23, 25, 26, 37, 39, 41, 42, 62, 83, 103, 120, 121, 134, 139, 179, 197, 209, 216–17, 219, 221, 233, 256, 260
Tejada, Frank, 99, 108
Tennessee Valley Authority, 21, 29

terrorism, 23-24, 36, 61, 191
Texas, 12, 13, 95-110, *109*, 275
Texas A&M University, 100
Thune, John, 254
Toyota, 20, 98
trade policy, 23, 26, 162
Treen, David, 200
Trejada, Robert, 108
Trible, Paul, 210
Tupelo, Mississippi, 20, 21, 28, 29
TVA. *See* Tennessee Valley Authority

Udall, Mark, 245-68, 279
Udall, Tom, 279
unions, 87-88, 136, 239, 241, 260
University of Ashland, 128
University of California at Los Angeles, 232
University of Dayton, 254
University of Kansas, 38
University of Miami, 155
University of Mississippi, 17, 21
University of Missouri, 37
University of Missouri at Kansas City, 38
University of Richmond, 78
University of South Florida, 154
University of Texas at San Antonio, 104
University of Virginia, 215, 217
U.S. Air Force, 98, 108, 130, 195
U.S. Army, 217
U.S. Chamber of Commerce, 140, 175, 258
U.S. Coast Guard, 158
U.S. Department of Justice, 12
U.S. Department of State, 253
U.S. News and World Report, 114

Venezuela, 150
Venice, Florida, 120
Vermont, 9, 272
veterans, 116, 121, 175
veto, 5, 9, 27
VFW, 136, 176, 200
Vickers, Vic, 235
Vietnam, 10
Virginia, 7, 8, 12, 73-74, 205-26, *214*, 276

Vitter, David, 187, 192-93
voters: African American, 5, 19-20, 27-28, 31, 35, 77, 97, 151, 171, 186-89, 190-91, 195, 202, 213, 248, 279; Arab American, 77; Asian American, 5, 35, 77, 112, 171, 279; Catholic, 77; Christian evangelical, 7, 9, 189, 214, 248, 263; Hispanic, 5, 19, 35, 55, 64, 77, 96, 102, 108, 112, 147-68, 171, *213*, 248, 259-60, 279; Pacific Islanders, 5
voter turnout, 5-10, 28-29
Voting Rights Act, 96, 99, 206-7, 211

Wages, John, Jr., 25, 29, 31
Wagner College, 88
Wall Street, 66, 79, 105, 137, 272
Walsh, Lawrence, 211
war, 6, 9, 10, 101
Warner, John, 12, 211-12
Warner, Mark, 205-26, 276
Warner, Russ, 111-25, *118*, *119*
Washington, DC, 4, 29, 47, 74, 85, 119, 135, 173, 235, 242, 254
Washington Post, 128, 219, 220
Wasserman-Schultz, Debbie, 165
Watergate, 10
Webb, James, 212, 214
welfare policy, 153
Western states, 8
West Virginia, 276
Wicker, Roger, 10, 17-18, 21
Wilder, Douglas, 211, 216
Wilson, Charlie, 134
World War II, 232
Wright, Jeremiah, 26-27
Wyne, Jamshad, 79, 81-82, *82*, 86, 87

Yale University, 173
Young, Dan, 241
Youngstown, Ohio, 133, 134, 138
YouTube, 26, 138, 213
Yurkonis, Shirley, 46

Zefferetti, Leo, 79

Contributors

EDITORS

Robert P. Watson (Ph.D., Florida Atlantic University, 1991) is the coordinator of American studies at Lynn University in Florida, the founder and former editor of the journal *White House Studies*, and a board member of several scholarly journals, academic associations, and presidential foundations. As a commentator, Watson has been interviewed by CNN, MSNBC, the BBC, *USA Today*, the *New York Times*, *Time*, and hundreds of other media outlets. He serves as the political analyst for WPTV 5 (NBC), WIOD 610 (AM), and WFTL 850 (AM) in Florida, and writes a regular column for the *Sun-Sentinel* newspaper. Watson has published over 30 books and roughly 150 scholarly articles, book chapters, and reference essays. His books include *The Presidents' Wives: Reassessing the Office of First Lady*; *Campaigns and Elections: Issues, Concepts, Cases*; *Public Administration: Cases in Managerial Role-Playing*; and *Anticipating Madam President*. He also edited the encyclopedias *American First Ladies* (1st and 2nd editions) and *American Presidents* (3rd edition).

Robert Dewhirst (Ph.D., University of Nebraska, 1983) is professor of political science at Northwest Missouri State University and serves on the Executive Board of the National Social Science Association. Before his academic career, Dewhirst served as a public affairs officer for the U.S. Army in Vietnam, a public affairs director for the Illinois state government, and a reporter for the *Kansas City Star* and several other newspapers in the Midwest. Dewhirst's teaching and research cover American government/politics, state politics, Congress, the American presidency, campaigns and elections, media and politics, political parties, and public policy. He has published several books and numerous book chapters, articles, and essays. His books include *Rites of Passage: Congress Makes Laws, Government at Work* and *Congress Responds to the Twentieth Century*. He also directed such reference projects as *The Almanac of Missouri Politics* and *The Encyclopedia of the United States Congress* and coedited several earlier editions of *The Roads to Congress* series.

CONTRIBUTORS

Sunil Ahuja (Ph.D., University of Nebraska, 1995) is associate professor of political science at Youngstown State University. His academic specialization is in American politics and legislative institutions. He is coeditor of *Government at Work, Congress Responds to the Twentieth Century*, and previous editions of *The Roads to Congress* series. He is the author, most recently, of *Congress Behaving Badly: The Rise of Partisanship and Incivility and the Death of Public Trust*.

Jeffrey Ashley (Ph.D., Northern Arizona University, 1998) is associate professor of political science at Eastern Illinois University. He has written or coauthored three books and a number of articles on topics ranging from first ladies and environmental protection to congressional races and indigenous rights.

Margaret E. Banyan (Ph.D., Portland State University, 2003) is an adjunct professor at Florida Gulf Coast University. Her research specialties are in the areas of civic engagement, land use planning, and livable communities. She has been a contributor to previous editions of *The Roads to Congress* series.

Peter Bergerson (Ph.D., Saint Louis University, 1982) is professor of public affairs at Florida Gulf Coast University. The focus of his research has been American political institutions, ethics and public policy, and the diffusion of policy innovations. He has published three books and has been a frequent contributor for *The Roads to Congress* series.

William Binning (Ph.D., University of Notre Dame, 1970) is professor emeritus of political science at Youngstown State University.

Robert J. Duffy (Ph.D., Brandeis University, 1991) is chair of the Department of Political Science at Colorado State University. Duffy won the American Political Science Association's Lynton K. Caldwell Award for the best book on environmental politics and policy for his book *Nuclear Politics in America: A History and Theory of Government Regulation*. He teaches courses on American government, environmental and energy policy, public policy, congressional politics, and race and ethnicity.

Sean Foreman (Ph.D., Florida International University, 2003) is assistant professor of political science at Barry University. His dissertation was on the politics of public subsidies for professional sports stadiums and arenas. He is a frequent media contributor on local and national elections to several South Florida television and radio stations.

Richard Gelm (Ph.D., University of California, Davis, 1991) is professor of political science and chair of the Department of History and Political Science at the University of LaVerne in Southern California. Gelm completed his Ph.D. and M.A. in political science from the University of California, Davis and his B.A. in political science from the University of California, San Diego. He is the author of *Politics and Religious Authority: American Catholics Since the Second Vatican Council* and *How American Politics Works: Philosophy, Pragmatism, Personality and Profit*. He has teaching and research interests in American government, political behavior, voting and elections, Congress, and the American presidency. He has traveled across all fifty American states.

Marcia Godwin (Ph.D., Claremont Graduate University, 2000) is assistant professor of public administration at the University of La Verne. Godwin primarily teaches graduate public administration courses and has extensive experience in local government administration in Southern California. She has contributed chapters on the election of Senator Maria Cantwell, the defeat of Representative Gary Condit, and the reelection of Senator Barbara Boxer in previous editions of *The Roads to Congress*. She has coauthored an analysis on the future of women officeholders in *Women in Elective Office: Past, Present, and Future* (2nd edition). Her research interests include electoral politics, innovation in government, and the development of the next generation of public managers.

Andrew Kear (Ph.D. student, Colorado State University) is a doctoral student studying U.S. environmental politics and policy at Colorado State University. His dissertation research examines the contentious politics surrounding the present natural gas boom in the Rocky Mountain West. Kear combines past experience as an environmental consultant with present interests in public lands, regulatory, environmental justice, and electoral politics. He has written several energy policy papers exploring state and federal agenda setting.

Jeffrey Kraus (Ph.D., City University of New York, 1988) is associate provost and professor of government and politics and at Wagner College, where he has been on the faculty since 1988. Before coming to Wagner, Kraus taught at Kingsborough Community College (1980–1987) and Baruch College (1987–1988). Kraus has written about elections and campaign finance.

Tom Lansford (Ph.D., Old Dominion University, 1996) is professor of political science and academic dean of the Gulf Coast compus at the University of Southern Mississippi. Lansford serves on the boards of several scholarly journals and the National Social Science Association, and has published over twenty books and many dozens of scholarly articles on such topics as NATO, U.S. foreign policy, national security and terrorism, the presidency, and American politics.

Amy Lauren Lovecraft (Ph.D., University of Texas, 2001) is assistant professor of political science at the University of Alaska at Fairbanks and a research fellow with the Institutional Dimensions of Global Environmental Change Program. She was previously a Fulbright Scholar in Austria and currently serves as a member of the U.S. National Academics Polar Research Board. Her research and teaching interests are in natural resources, American political developments, the American presidency, political economy, and circumpolar governance. Dr. Lovecraft is principal investigator on NSF grants for "Understanding Northern Sustainability Debates" and "Fire-Mediated Changes in the Arctic System," and published broadly on policy subjects, including sea ice, wildland fire, marine mammals, and freshwater systems.

Gerald McBeath (Ph.D., University of California at Berkeley, 1970) is professor of political science and department chair at the University of Alaska at Fairbanks. He earned his B.A. and M.A. from the University of Chicago and, after teaching at Rutgers University and the City University of New York, joined the faculty of UAF in 1976. He has published fifty articles and fourteen books, including *Alaska Politics and Government, The Alaska State Constitution,* and *Wealth and Freedom: Taiwan's New Political Economy*. Dr. McBeath's research and teaching interests are in state and local government, Native politics, Taiwan and mainland China, comparative politics of East Asian states, and international political economy.

John David Rausch Jr. (Ph.D., University of Oklahoma, 1995) is associate professor of political science at West Texas A&M University, where his primary teaching and research interests include legislative politics, religion and politics, public policy, state and local politics, and European politics. He has been the editor or author of four books on American politics and has written numerous book chapters and scholarly papers.

Bob N. Roberts (Ph.D. and J.D., Syracuse University, 1981) is professor of political science at James Madison University, where he teaches courses on public administration, the legal environment of public administration, and state and local government. Roberts has published numerous articles in such journals as *Public Administration Review*, the *International Journal of Public Administration*, and *Public Integrity*, and he is the author or coauthor of *White House Ethics; From Watergate to Whitewater: The Public Integrity Wars; Public Journalism and Political Knowledge*; as well as the encyclopedias *Ethics in U.S. Government: An Encyclopedia of Investigations, Scandals, Reforms, and Legislation* and the *Encyclopedia of Presidential Campaigns, Slogans, Issues, and Platforms*. Professor Roberts is also a frequent media commentator on politics.

Kyle L. Saunders (Ph.D., Emory University, 2001) is associate professor of political science at Colorado State University. Dr. Saunders studies and interests include American politics, public opinion, political behavior, elections, political parties, and public policy. He has published numerous book chapters and journal articles in such publications as the *Journal of Politics*, *Political Research Quarterly*, and *American Review of Politics*. He is also frequently quoted in local and national media outlets.

Justin Sinner (M.A., Eastern Illinois University, 2008) works for the city of Arcola, Illinois. Winner of the EIU Department of Political Science's "Outstanding Graduate Student Award," Sinner has presented research on elections and public policy at conferences at both the regional and national levels.

Daniel E. Smith (J.D., University of Virginia, 1988) is assistant professor of political science at Northwest Missouri State University. A former practicing telecommunications attorney, his primary teaching and research interests include judicial politics, jurisprudence, and constitutional law, with an emphasis on personal rights-privacy, equal protection, and the First Amendment. He also has an interest in political theory and has published in *History of Political Thought*.

Joshua Stockley (Ph.D., University of Oklahoma, 2005) is assistant professor of political science at the University of Louisiana at Monroe. Stockley's teaching and research cover American government, campaigns and elections, political parties, culture and politics, media and politics, state politics, public policy, and public administration. He has written an article for *Race, Class, and Gender*, contributed to an earlier edition of *The Roads to Congress*, published several book reviews, and delivered papers at professional conferences around the country. Stockley writes a regular column for the *News-Star* and provides political commentary for a weekly radio show in Louisiana.